Art of the Golden Ratio

Stefan Hollos and J. Richard Hollos

Art of the Golden Ratio
by Stefan Hollos and J. Richard Hollos
Paper ISBN 978-1-887187-30-5
Ebook ISBN 978-1-887187-20-6

Abrazol Publishing

an imprint of Exstrom Laboratories LLC
662 Nelson Park Drive, Longmont, CO 80503-7674 U.S.A.

About the Cover

The cover incorporates art from this book.

Contents

iv

PREFACE

Mathematics is full of mystery and beauty. Few mathematicians would disagree with that. Most people would agree with the mystery part but not the beauty. There is however one mathematical object that has often been associated with beauty and aesthetics, at least by artists. That object is an irrational number called the golden ratio. It is believed by some that a piece of art that exhibits this ratio in some way is more aesthetically pleasing.

In a painting this could be as simple as making the ratio of the width to height equal to the golden ratio. In architecture it could mean making the dimensions of a room agree with the golden ratio. Whether these beliefs are true or not is not for us to say. Anyone wanting to explore these aesthetic ideas further can look at some of the references at the end of this book.

What we have found, and what this book is about, is the fact that the golden ratio does indeed encode many intricate patterns that can be turned into interesting drawings. We have collected 360 of these drawings together in this book. The book is an art book meant to stimulate your creativity and imagination. There is no mathematics required. We have included two appendices that contain a very short explanation of some of the mathematics behind the golden ratio and how the images are created, indexed by name. More detailed information on how to create the images can be found in our book:

Pattern Generation for Computational Art

May you find these images stimulating and inspirational, as we have found them.

Stefan Hollos and Richard Hollos
Exstrom Laboratories LLC
Longmont, Colorado

GALLERY

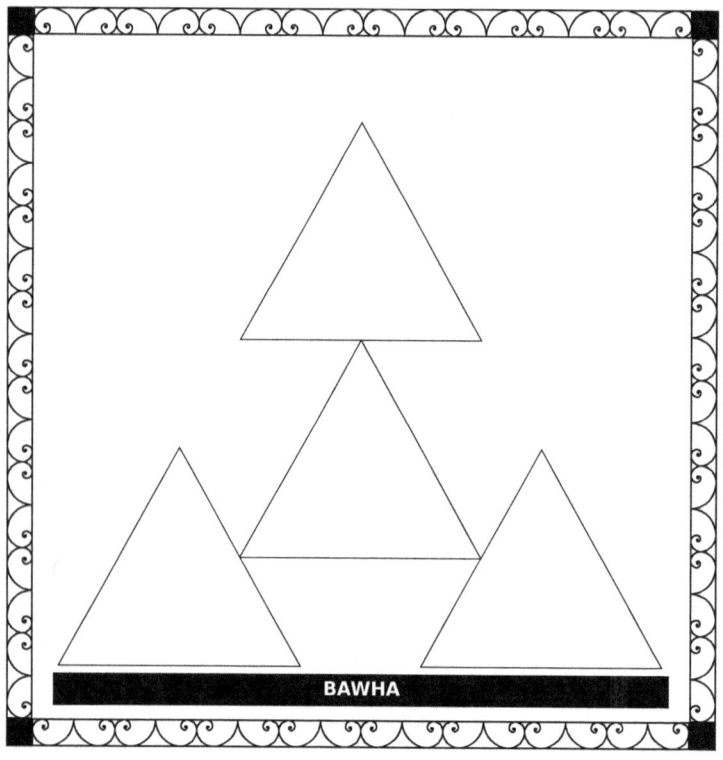

BAWHA

The new art must be based upon science — in particular, upon mathematics, as the most exact, logical, and graphically constructive of the sciences.
Albrecht Durer

4

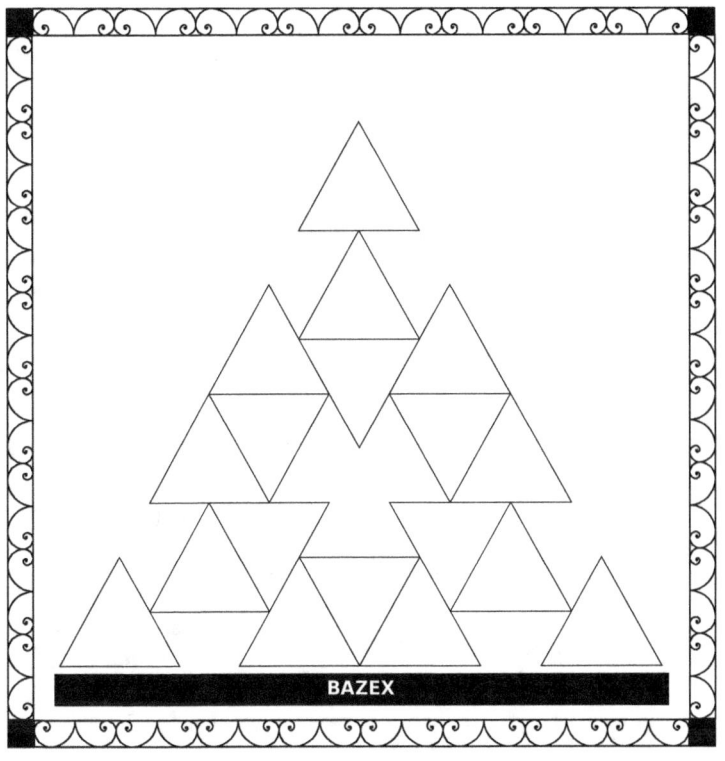

BAZEX

Study and in general the pursuit of truth and beauty is a sphere of activity in which we are permitted to remain children all our lives.
Albert Einstein

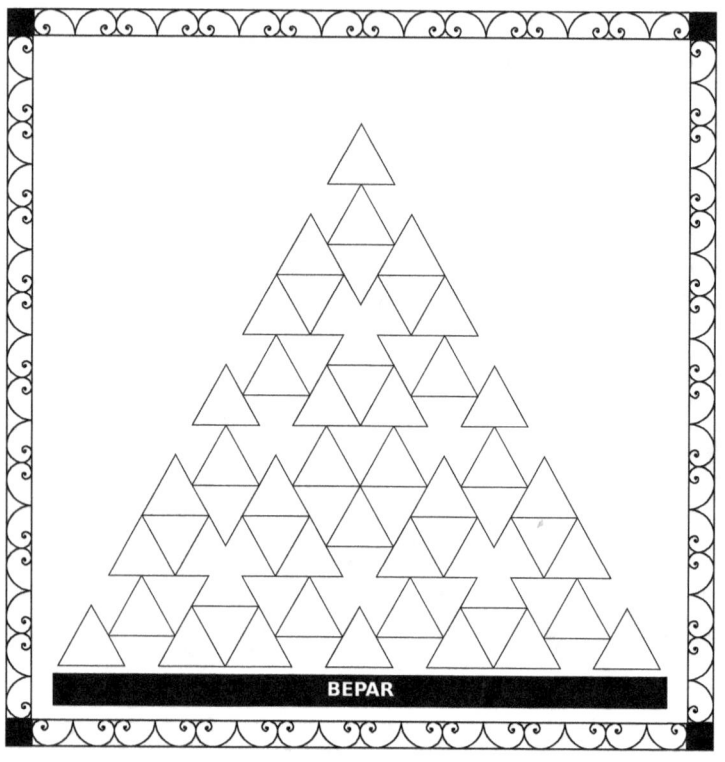

BEPAR

To be an artist you have to give up everything, including the desire to be a good artist.
Jasper Johns

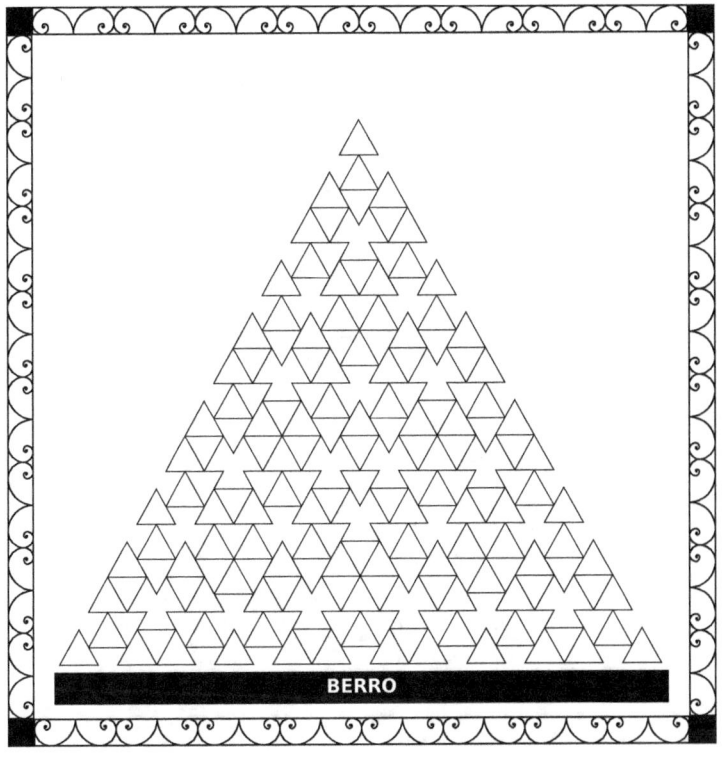

BERRO

The man with insight enough to admit his limitations comes nearest to perfection.
Johann Wolfgang von Goethe

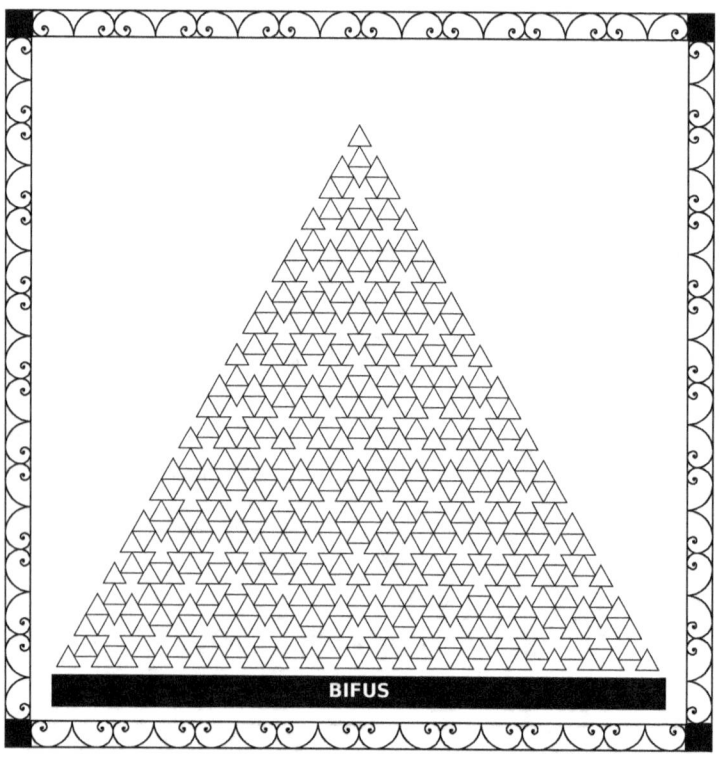

BIFUS

Great artists are people who find the way to be themselves in their art. Any sort of pretension induces mediocrity in art and life alike.

Margot Fonteyn

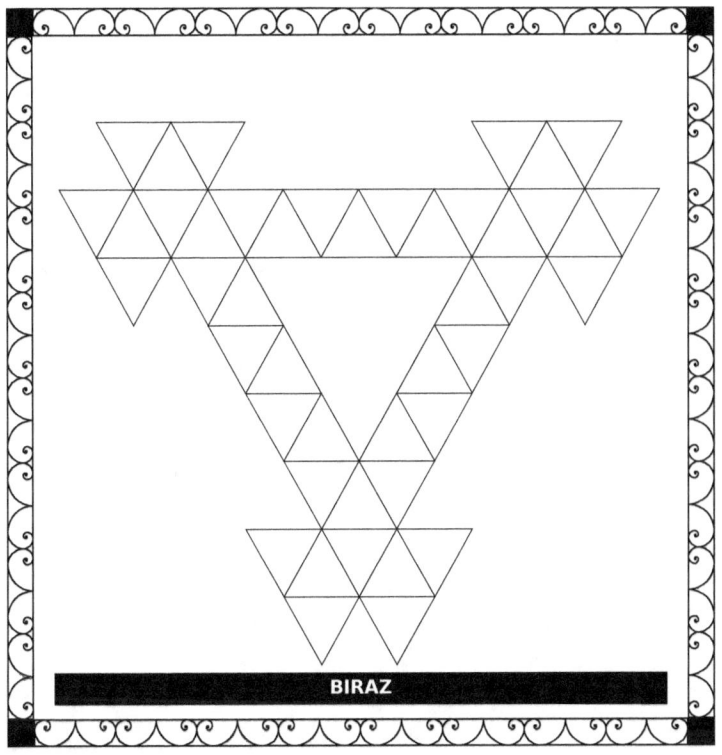

BIRAZ

The hardest battle you're ever going to fight is the battle to be just you.

Leo Buscaglia

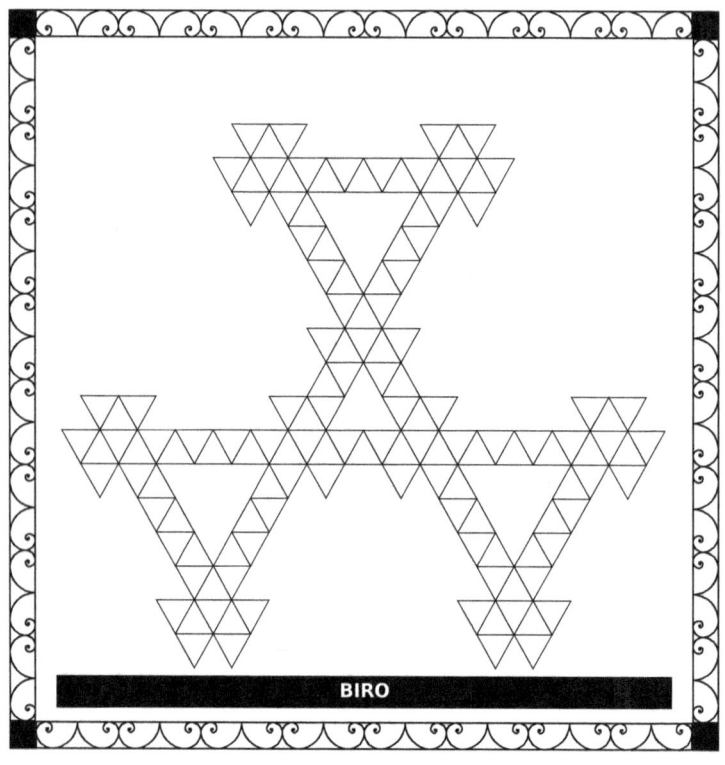

BIRO

When I think of art, I think of beauty. Beauty is the mystery of life. It is not in the eye, it is in my mind. In our minds there is awareness of perfection.
Agnes Martin, Beauty Is the Mystery of Life

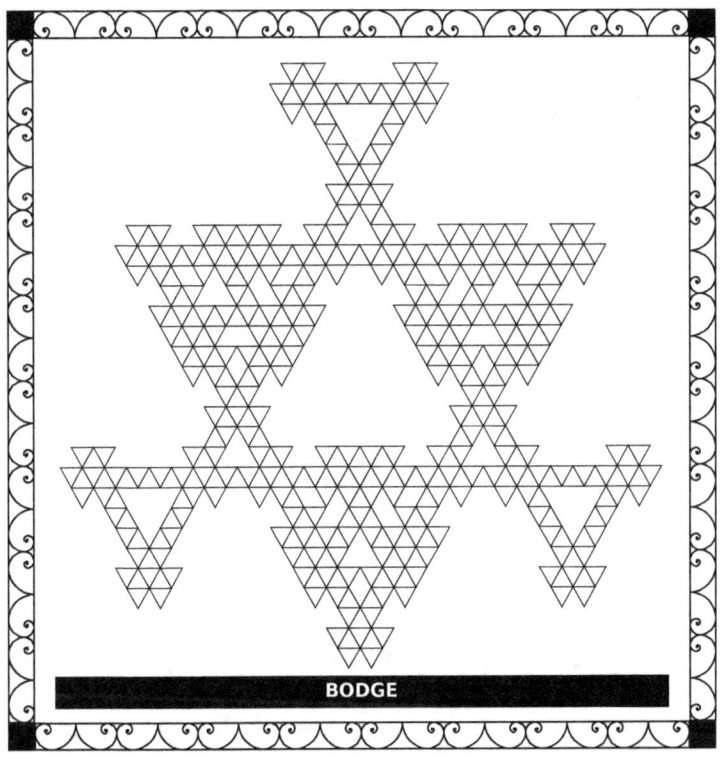

BODGE

Perhaps we cannot raise the winds. But each of us can put up the sail, so that when the wind comes we can catch it.
E. F. Schumacher

11

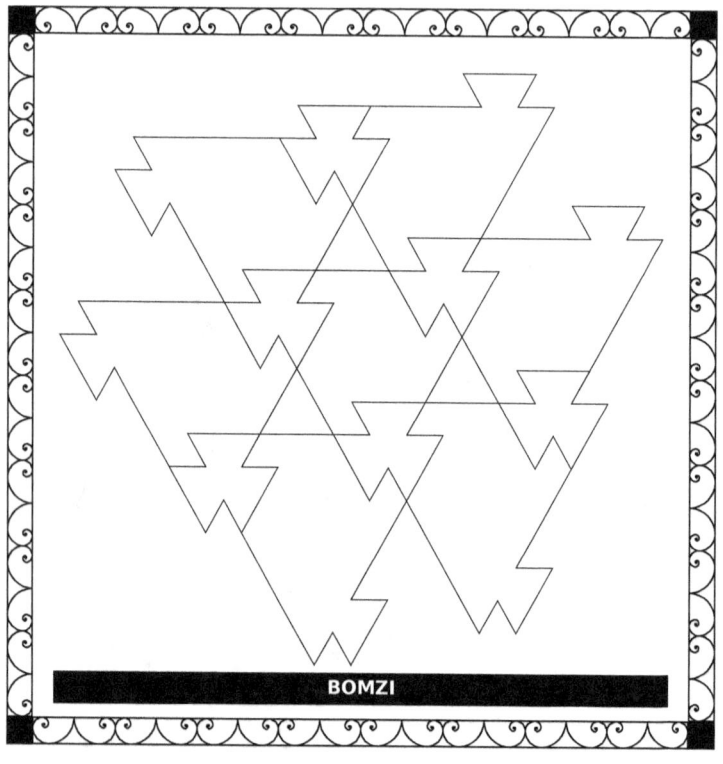

BOMZI

No great artist ever sees things as they really are. If he
did, he would cease to be an artist.
Oscar Wilde

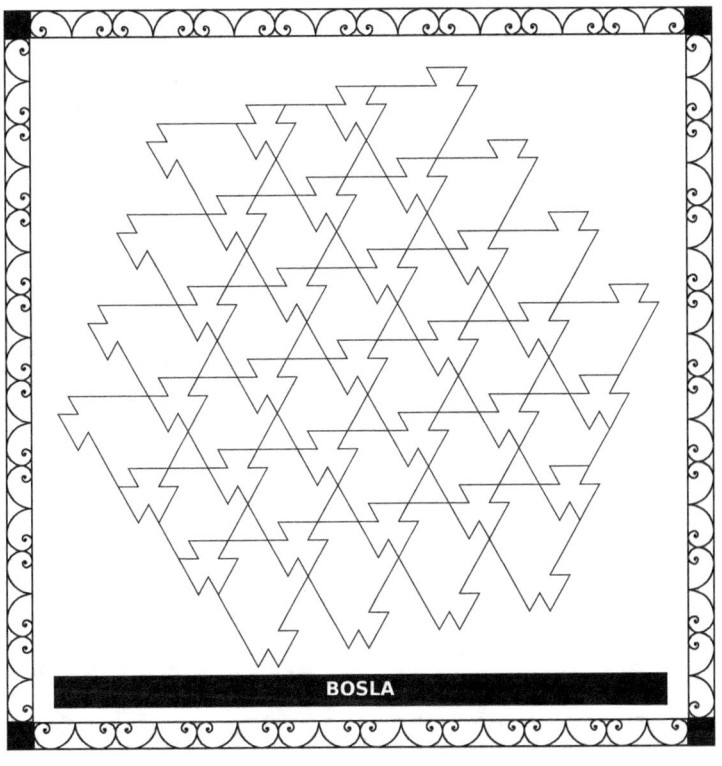

BOSLA

He that seeks popularity in art closes the door on his own genius: as he must needs paint for other minds, and not for his own.

Anna Jameson

13

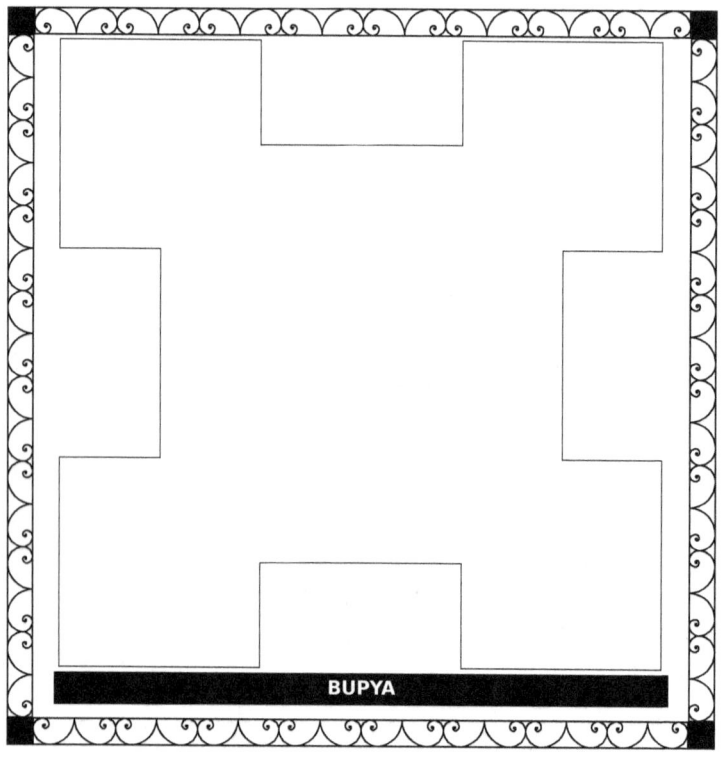

BUPYA

An artist must find his expression closely linked to his individual experience or else follow in the old grooves resulting in lifeless forms.
Mark Tobey

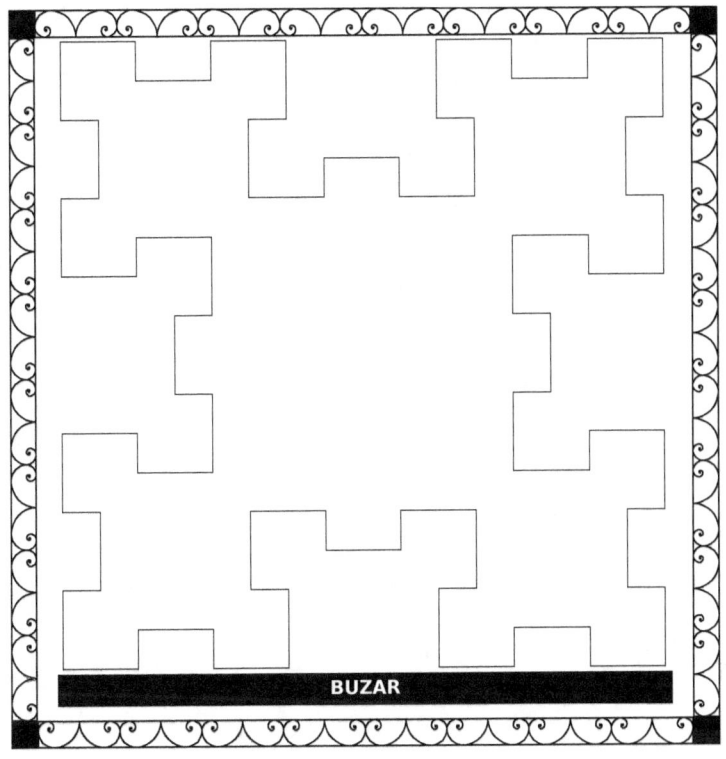

BUZAR

At very best, a person wrapped up in himself makes a small package.
Harry Emerson Fosdick

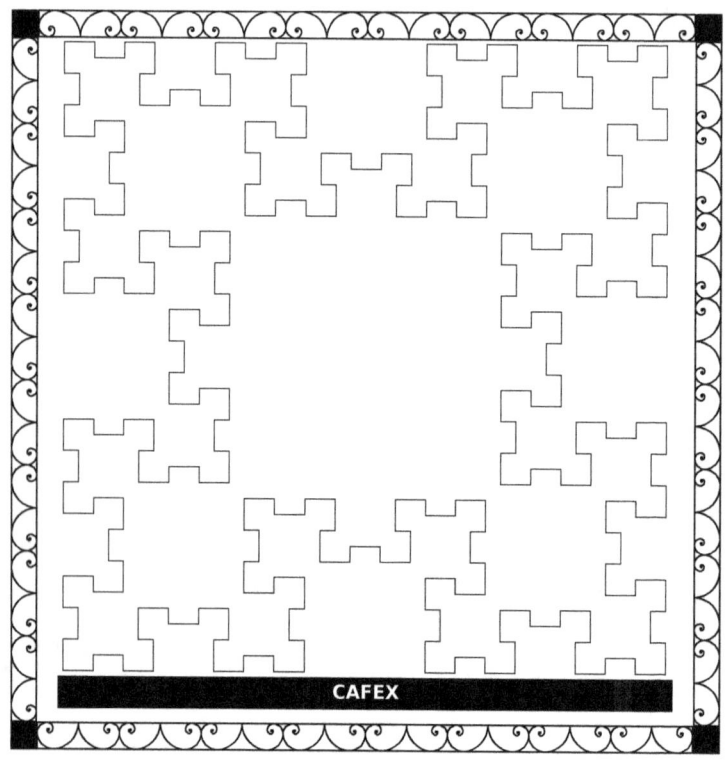

CAFEX

All we have, it seems to me, is the beauty of art and nature and life, and the love which that beauty inspires.
Edward Abbey

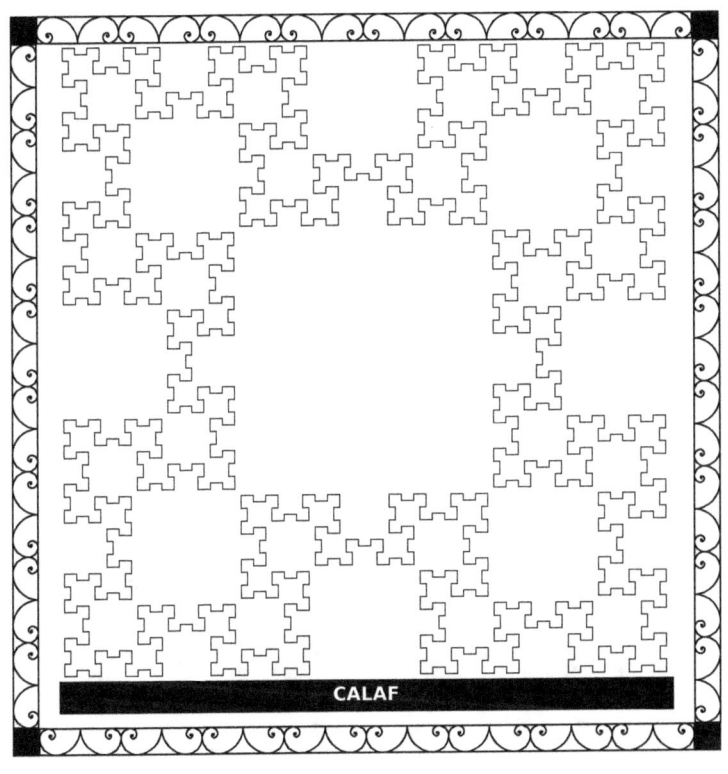

CALAF

There is no cosmetic for beauty like happiness.
Marguerite Gardiner, Countess of Blessington

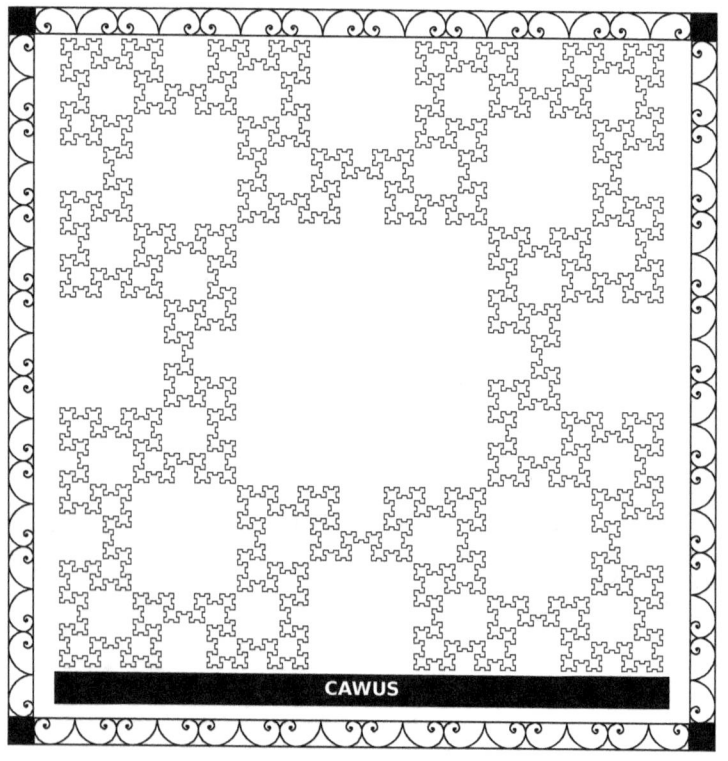

CAWUS

Modern aesthetics is crippled by its dependence upon the concept of beauty. As if art were about beauty as science is about truth!
Susan Sontag

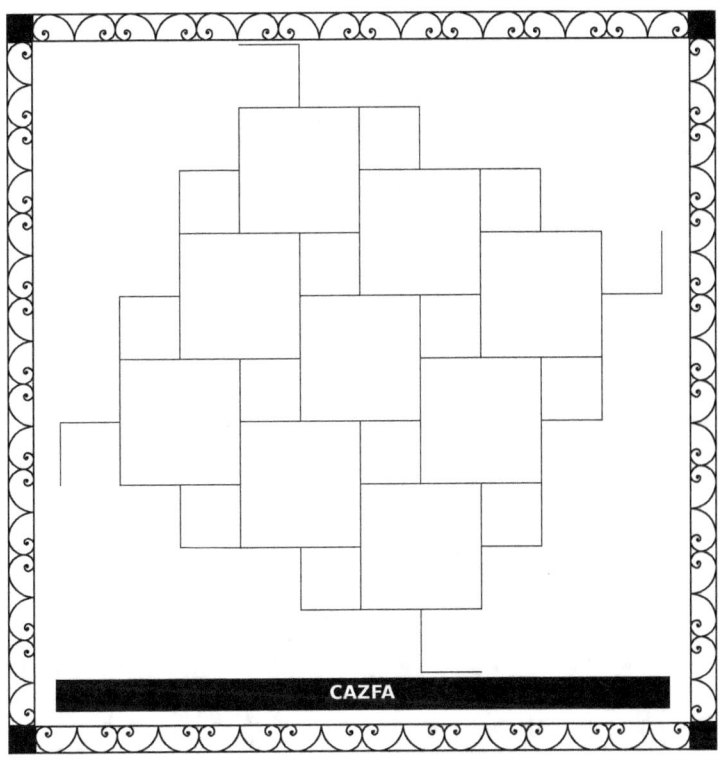

CAZFA

Religion and art spring from the same root and are close kin. Economics and art are strangers.
Willa Cather

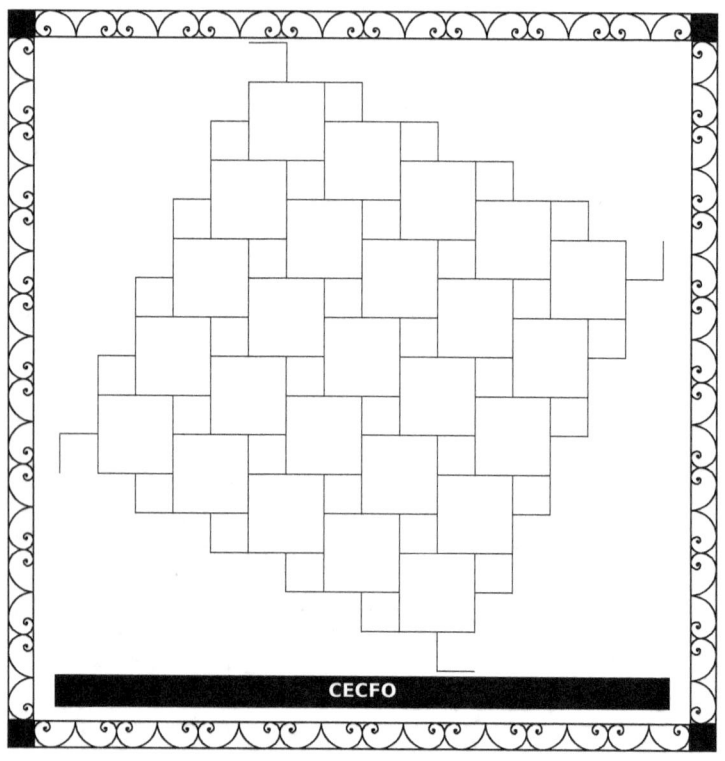

CECFO

There is only one pleasure - that of being alive. All the rest is misery.

Cesare Pavese

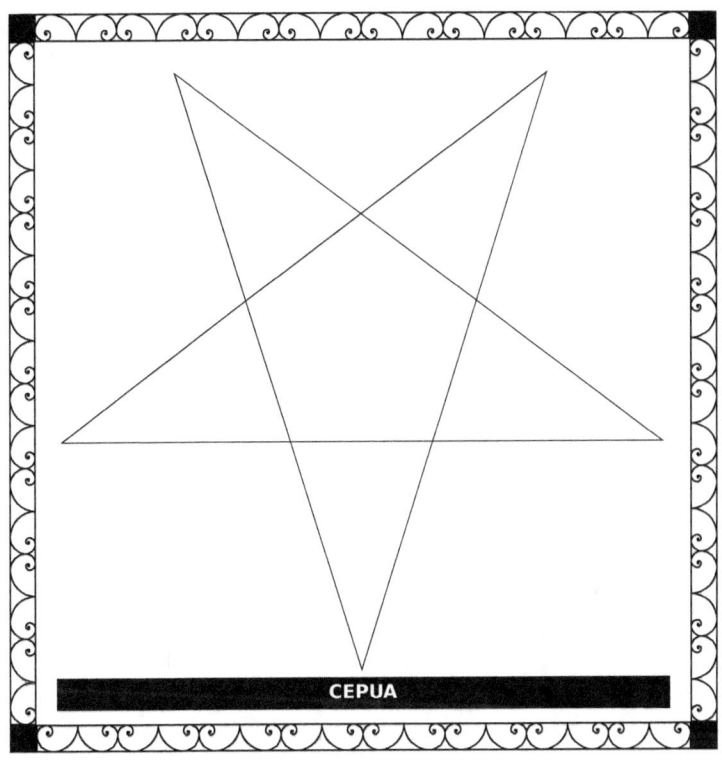

CEPUA

Every man is his own doctor of divinity, in the last resort.
Robert Louis Stevenson

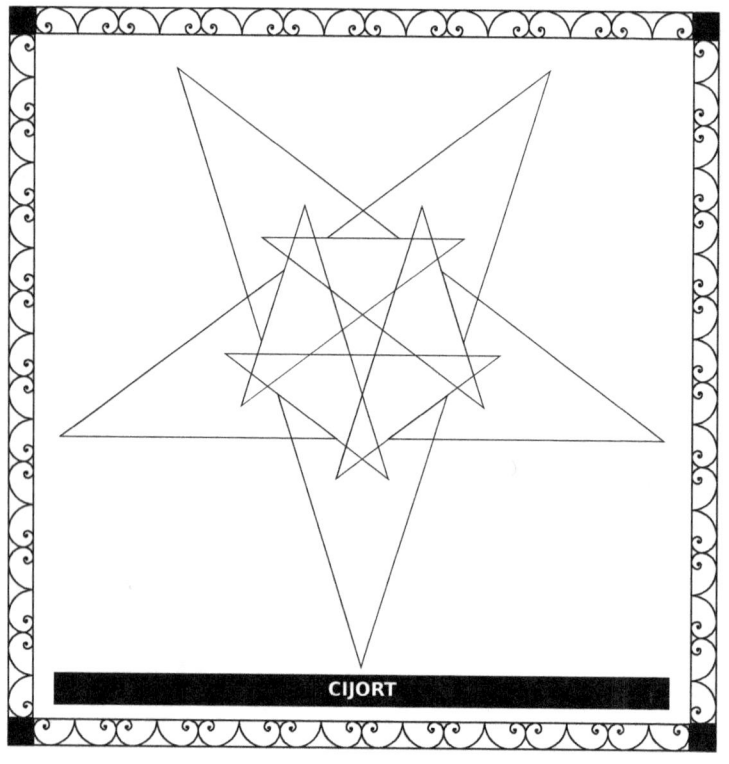

CIJORT

You have to grow all the time, I said. Not necessarily get bigger. But inside your head you have to grow, kid-boy. For us human-type people, that's what's important. And that kind of growing never stops. At least, it shouldn't. You can grow, kid-boy, or you can die. That's the choice you've got, and it goes on all of your life.
Samuel R. Delany

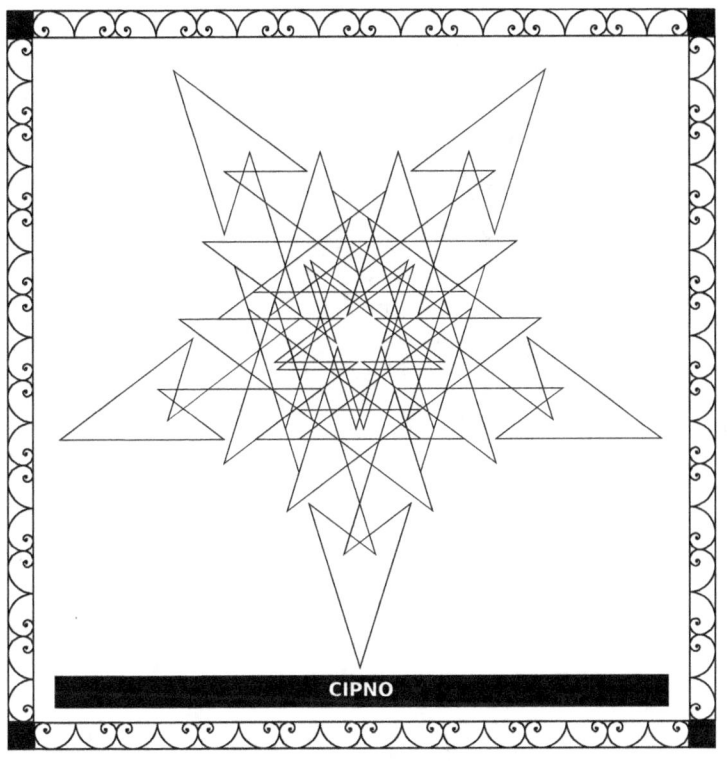

CIPNO

Mastering an art is like reaching the top of the passion mountain...at the top the passion dies out! So keep learning.
Siddharth Katragadda

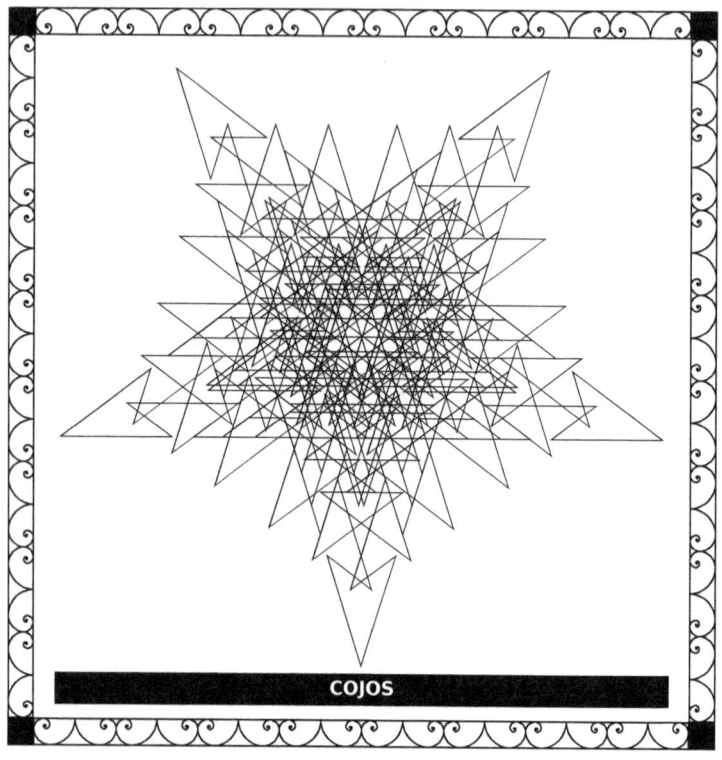

COJOS

Children wear their natures like brightly-colored clothes; that's why they lie so transparently. Adulthood is the art of deceit.
Robert Charles Wilson

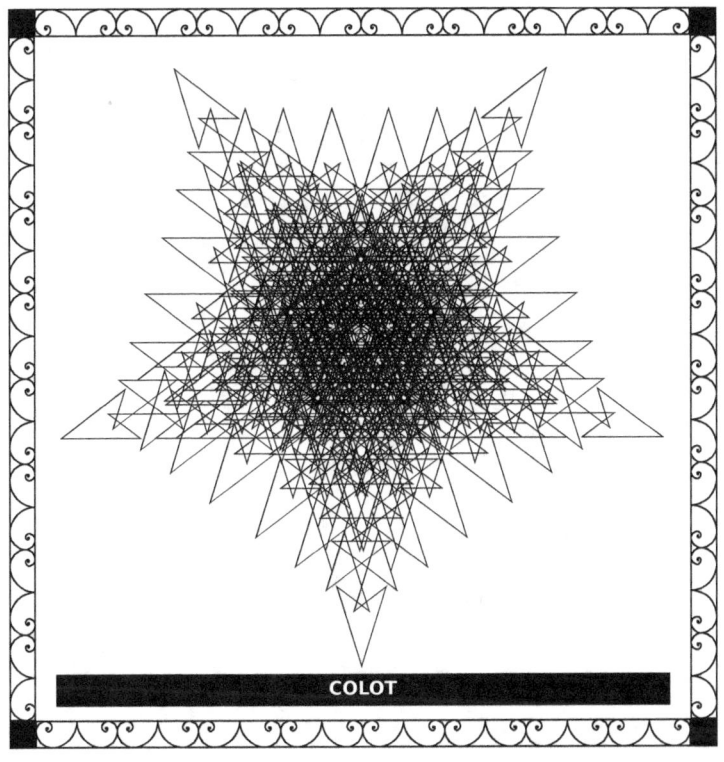

COLOT

All animals, except man, know that the principal business
of life is to enjoy it.
Samuel Butler

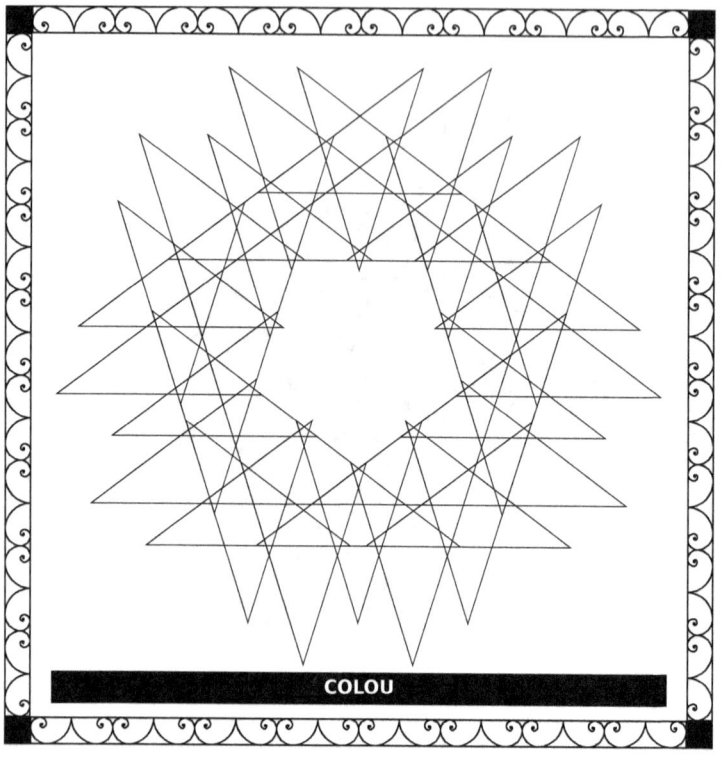

COLOU

How rare that an artist should make something which forces us to think, and encourages us to stop and think, to question why we behave the way we do.
Martin Firrell

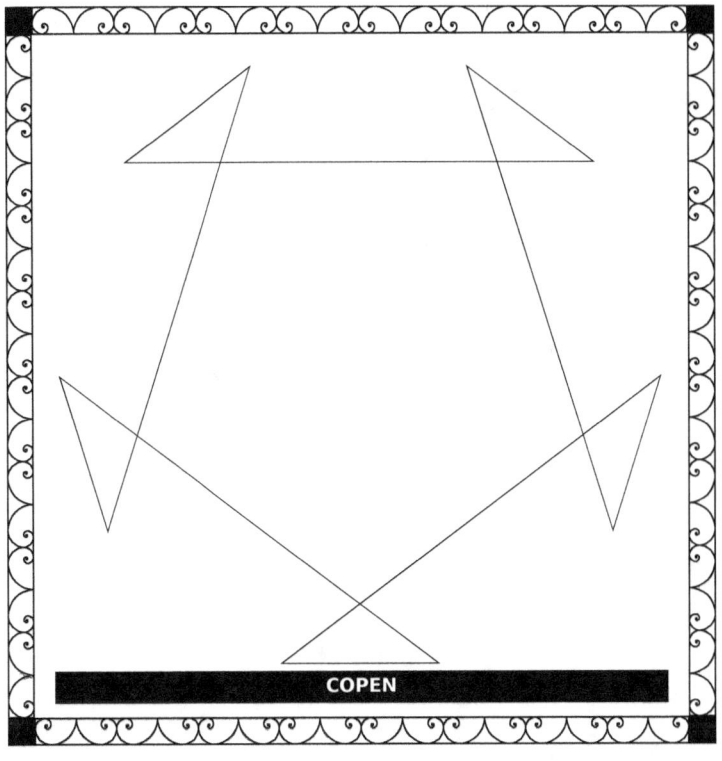

COPEN

Man, being essentially active, must find in activity his joy, as well as his beauty and glory; and labor, like every thing else that is good, is its own reward.

Henry Benjamin Whipple

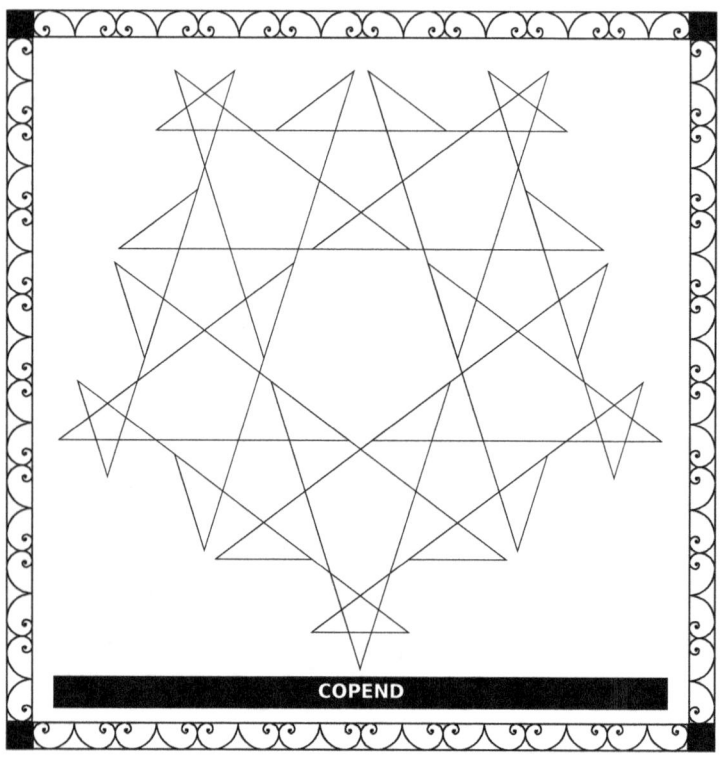

COPEND

The solution to all the problems of daily life is to cherish others.
Kelsang Gyatso

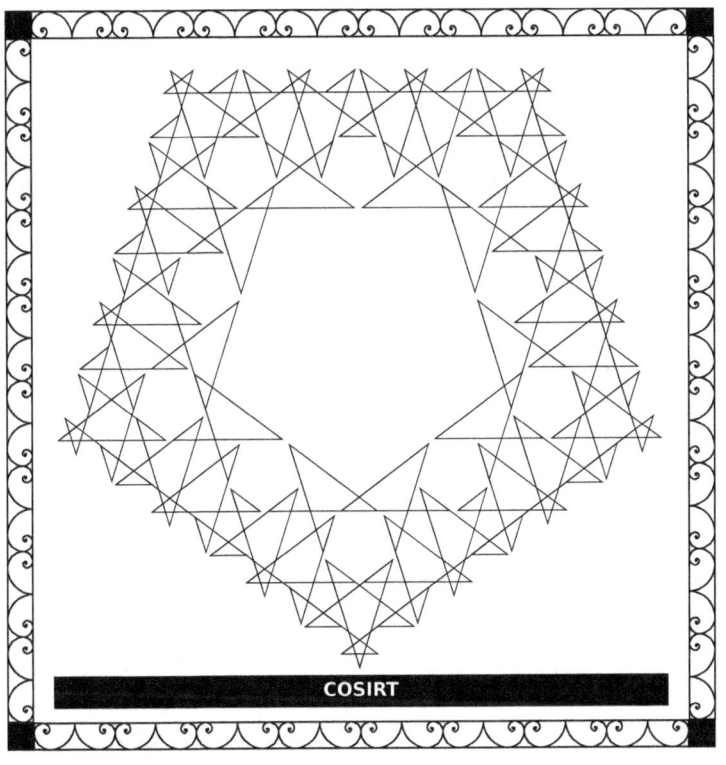

COSIRT

The truth comes as conqueror only because we have lost the art of receiving it as guest.
Rabindranath Tagore

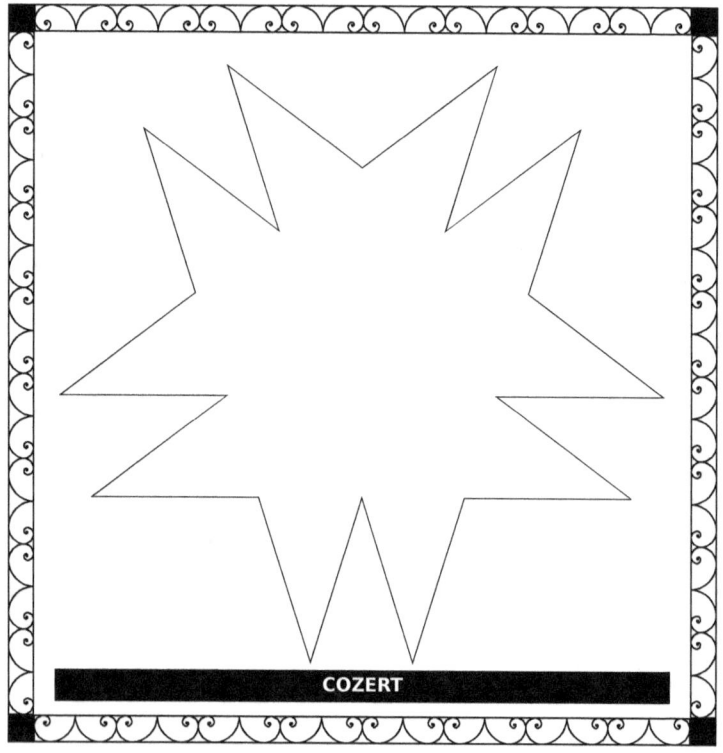

COZERT

The goal of life is happiness and to respond to life as though it were perfect is the way to happiness. It is also the way to positive artwork.
Agnes Martin, Beauty Is the Mystery of Life

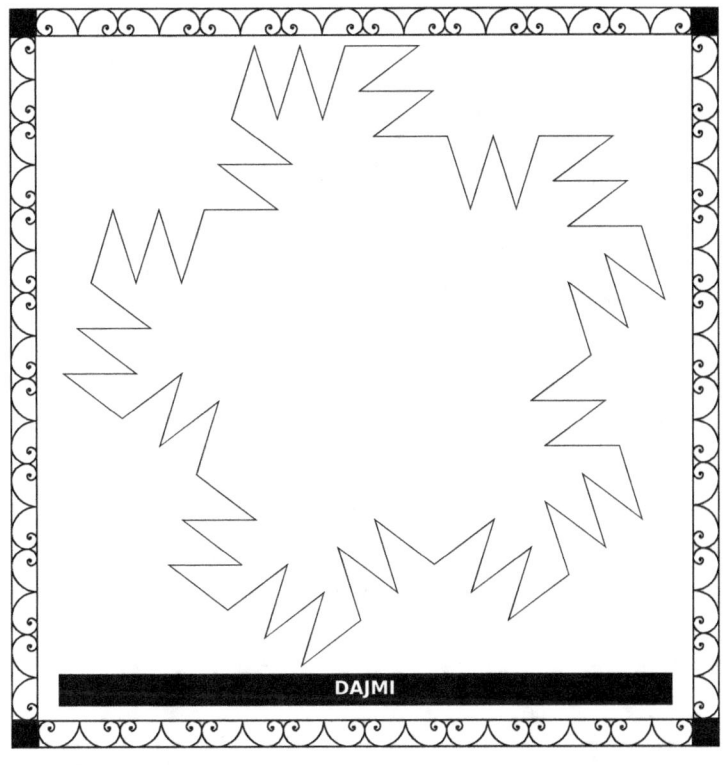

DAJMI

The activity of art is...as important as the activity of language itself, and as universal.
Leo Tolstoy

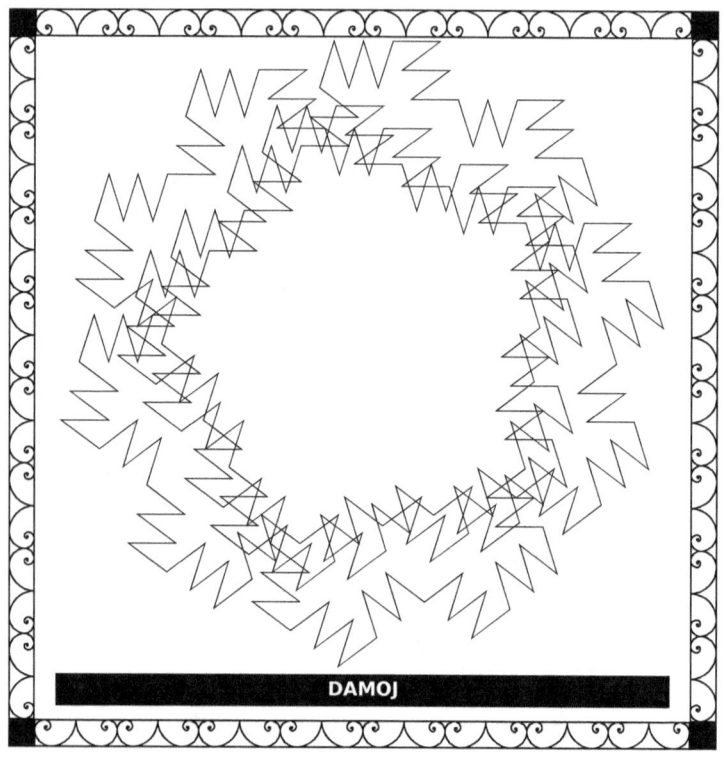

DAMOJ

The sole means of ridding man of crime is to rid him of freedom.

Yevgeny Zamyatin

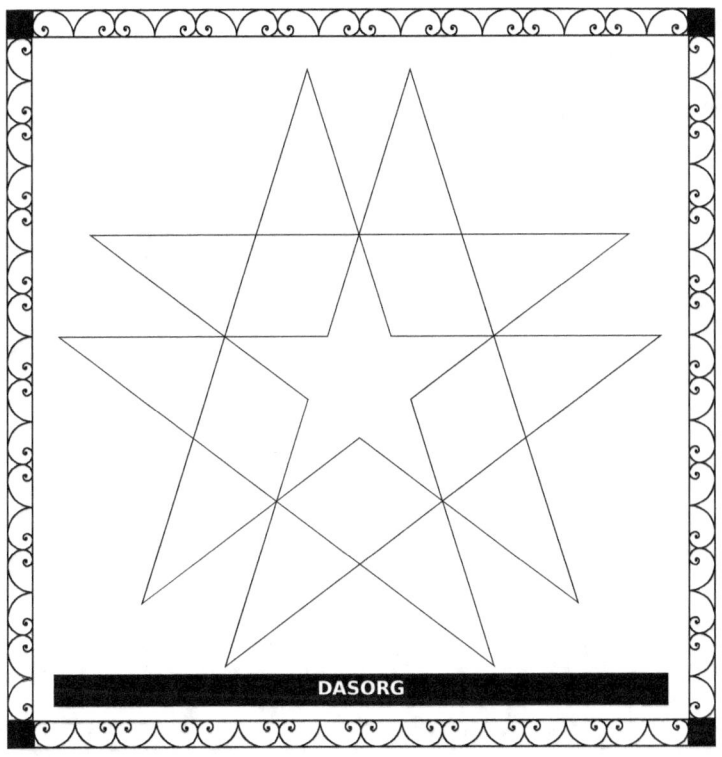

DASORG

The unicorn, through its intemperance and not knowing how to control itself, for the love it bears to fair maidens forgets its ferocity and wildness; and laying aside all fear it will go up to a seated damsel and go to sleep in her lap, and thus the hunters take it.

Leonardo da Vinci

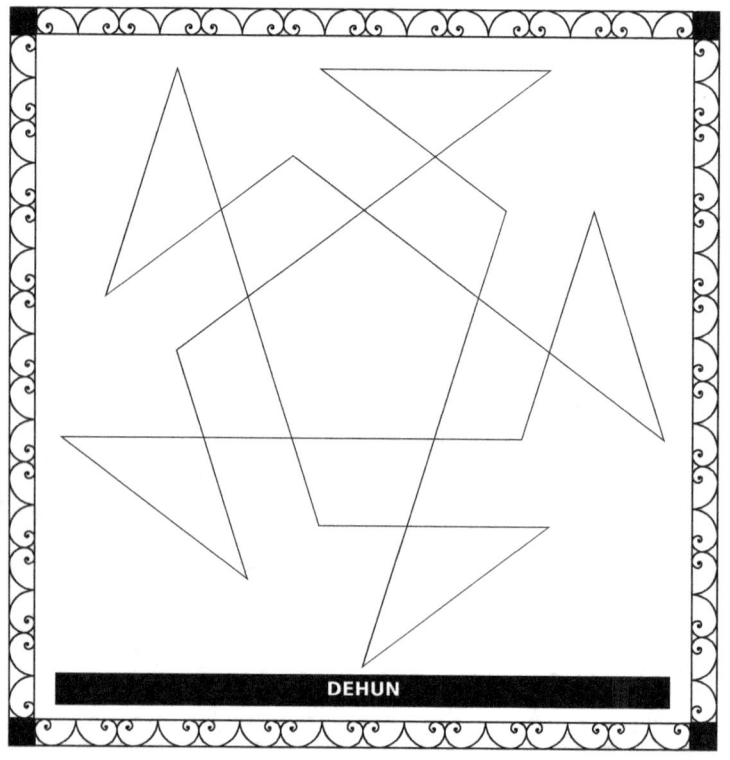

DEHUN

The art of acceptance is the art of making someone who has just done you a small favor wish that he might have done you a greater one.
Russell Lynes

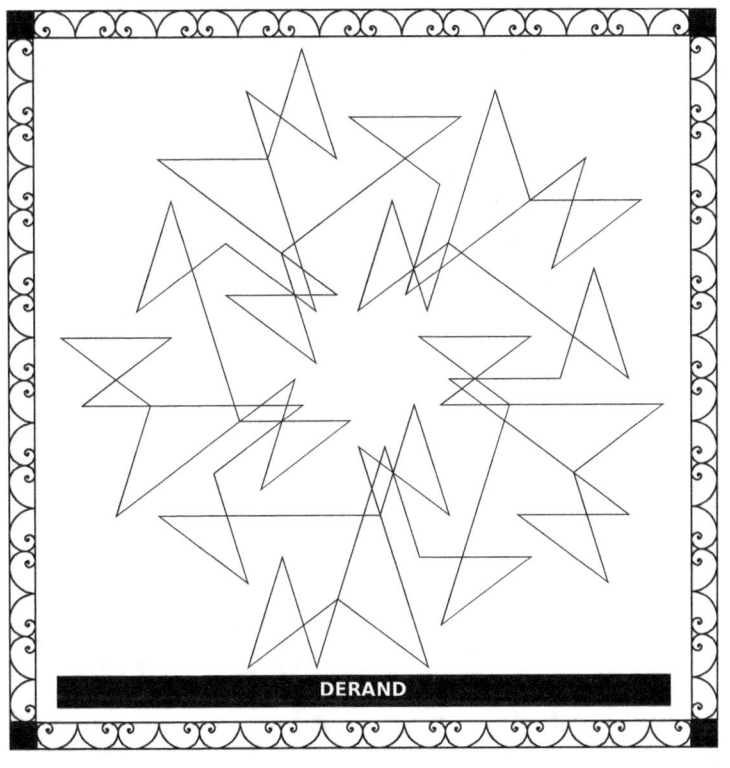

DERAND

The final purpose of art is to intensify, even, if necessary, to exacerbate, the moral consciousness of people.
Norman Mailer

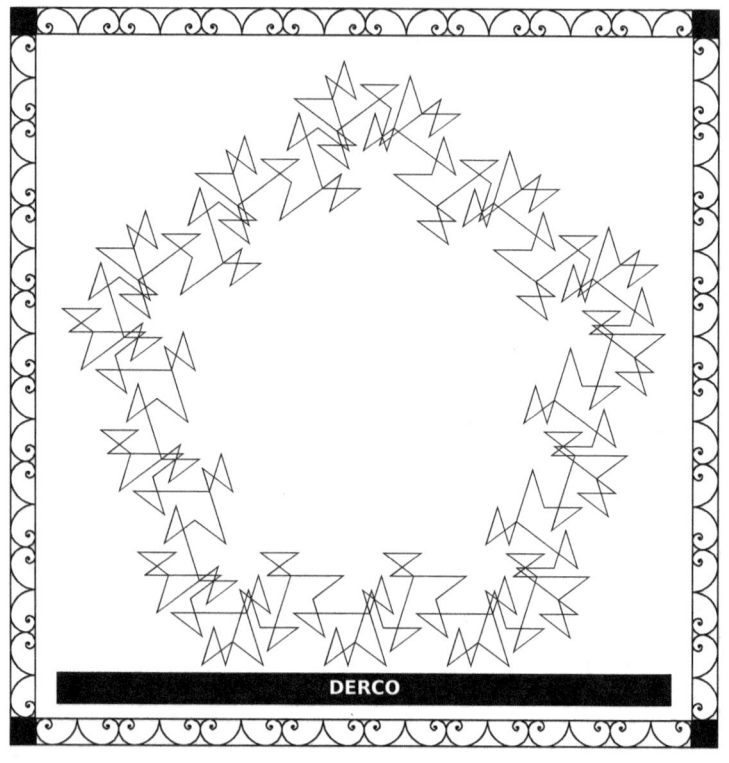

DERCO

When we are collecting books, we are collecting happiness.
Vincent Starrett

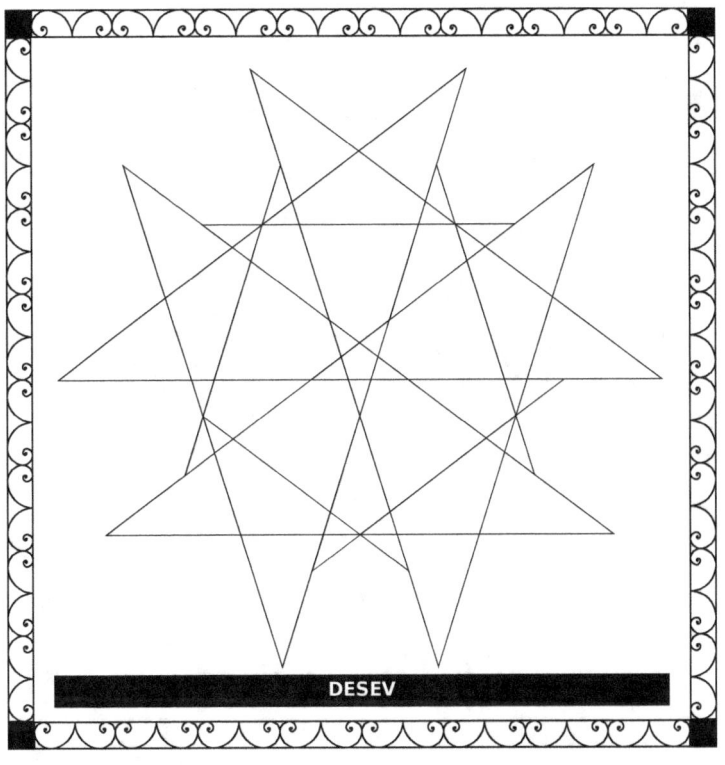

DESEV

My work has always been political, because the choice of being an artist is political in China.
Ai Weiwei

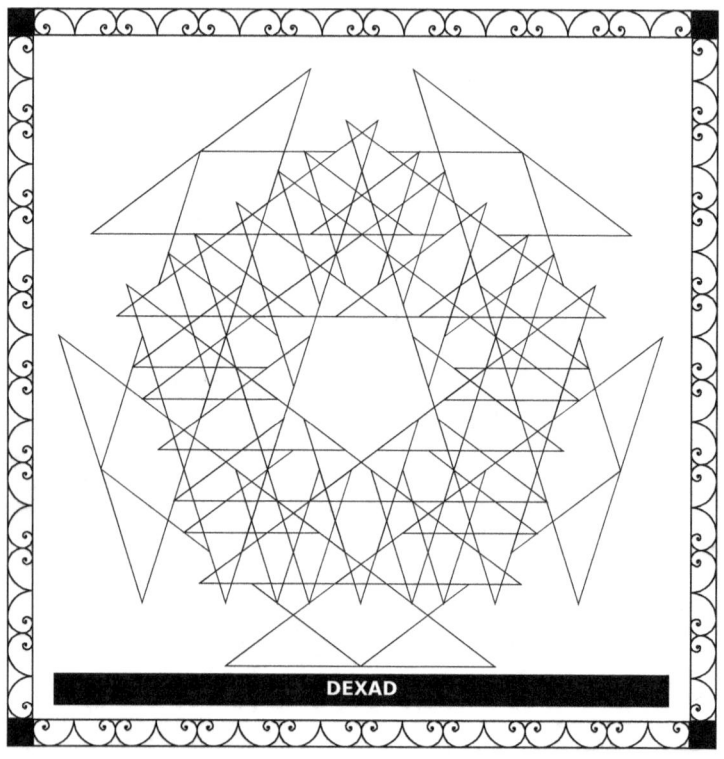

DEXAD

Every artist is crazy with respect to ordinary life.
Elsa von Freytag-Loringhoven

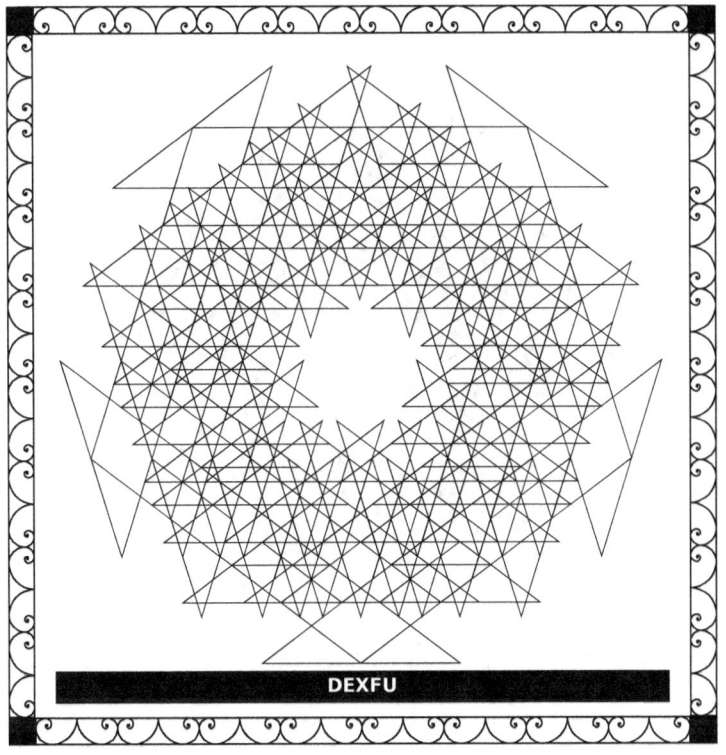

DEXFU

My principle is, the artist shall put forth, humbly & lovingly, without bitterness, the very best & highest that is within him, utterly regardless of contemporary criticism.
Sidney Lanier

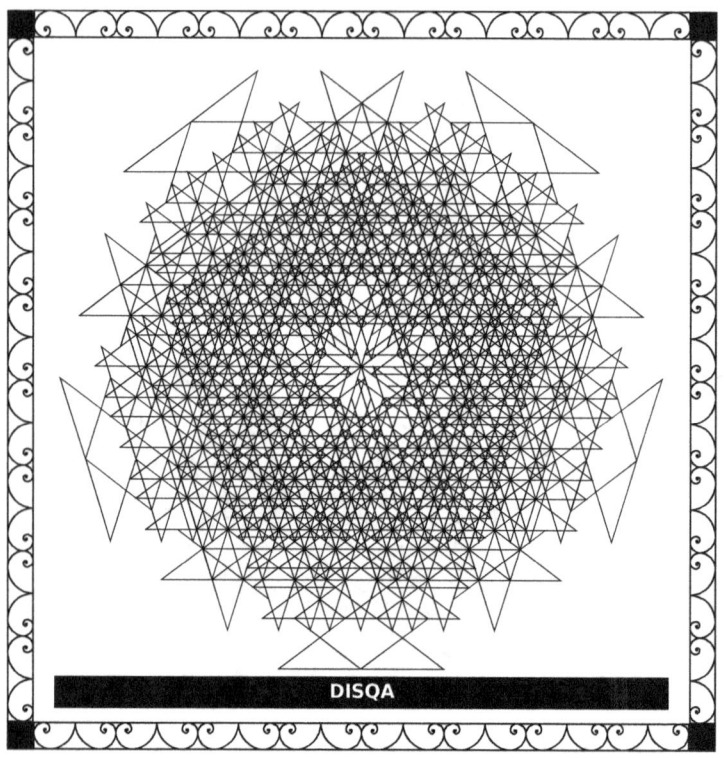

DISQA

All art is a form of artifice. For in art there can be no prejudices.
Arthur Symons

40

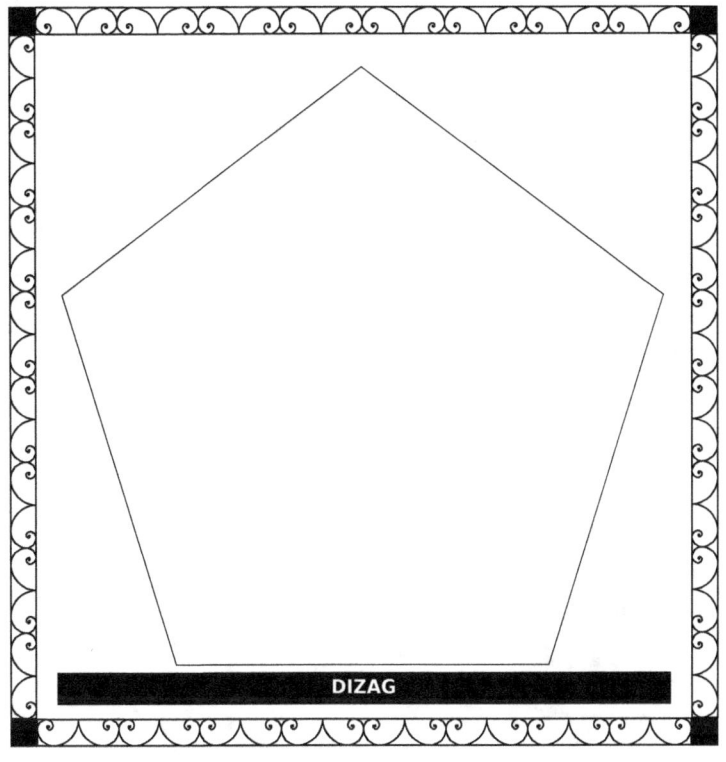

DIZAG

The advent of truth, like the dawn of day, agitates the elements, while it disperses the gloom.

Elias Lyman Magoon

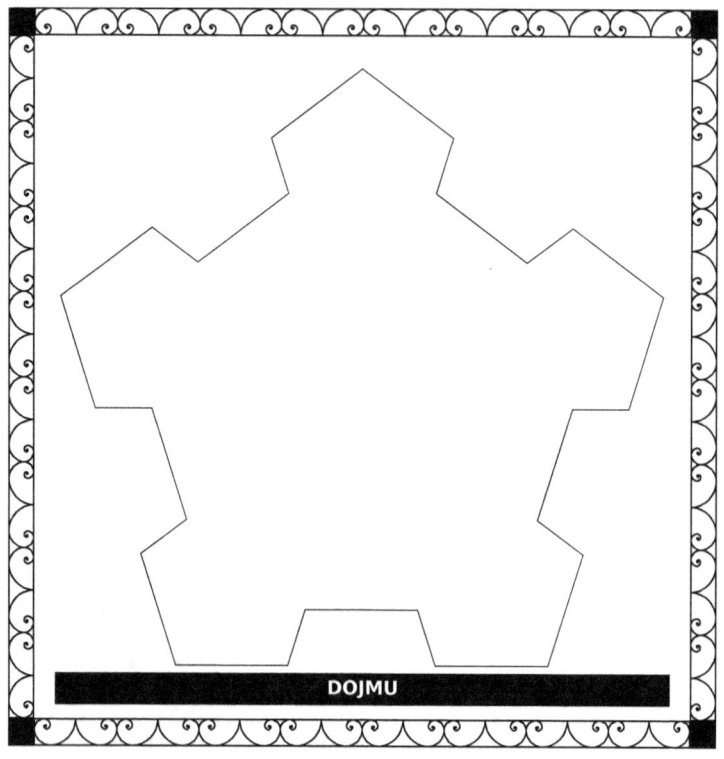

DOJMU

The artist who becomes thoroughly aware consequently ceases to be one.
Henry Miller

42

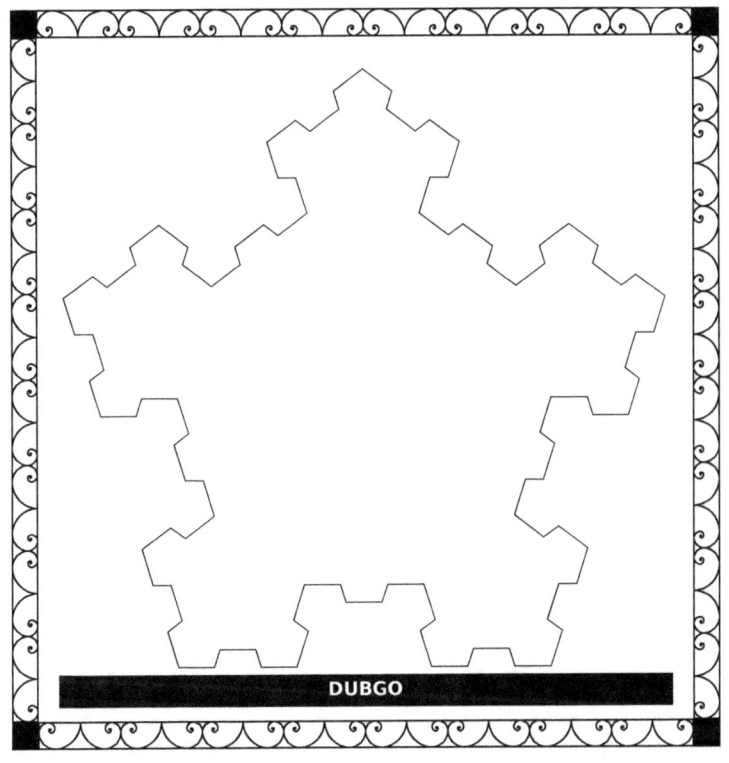

DUBGO

If the language of art is not accessible to ordinary language and ordinary experience, how can it be accessible to ordinary people?
Daniel Bell

43

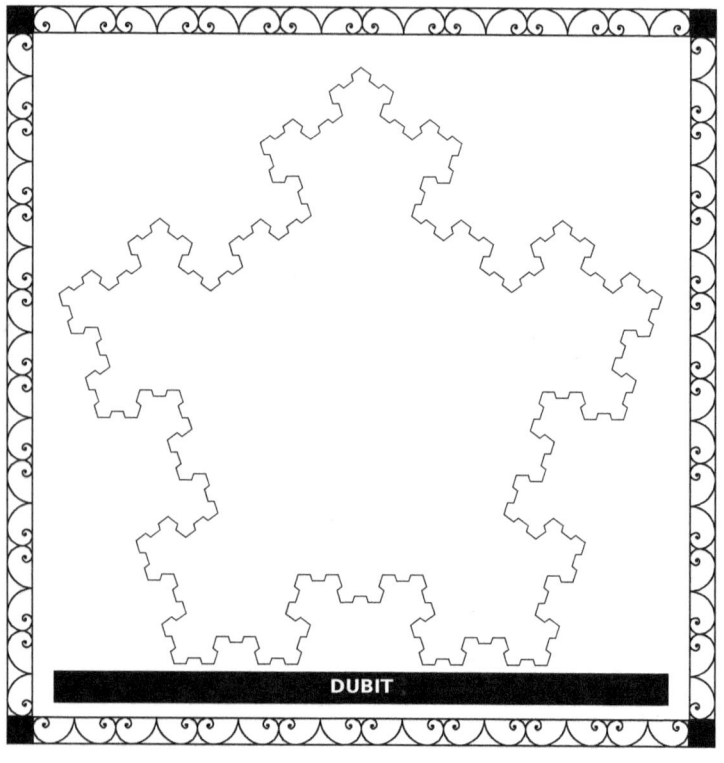

DUBIT

You must do over the same subject ten times, a hundred times. In art nothing must appear accidental, even a movement.
Edgar Degas

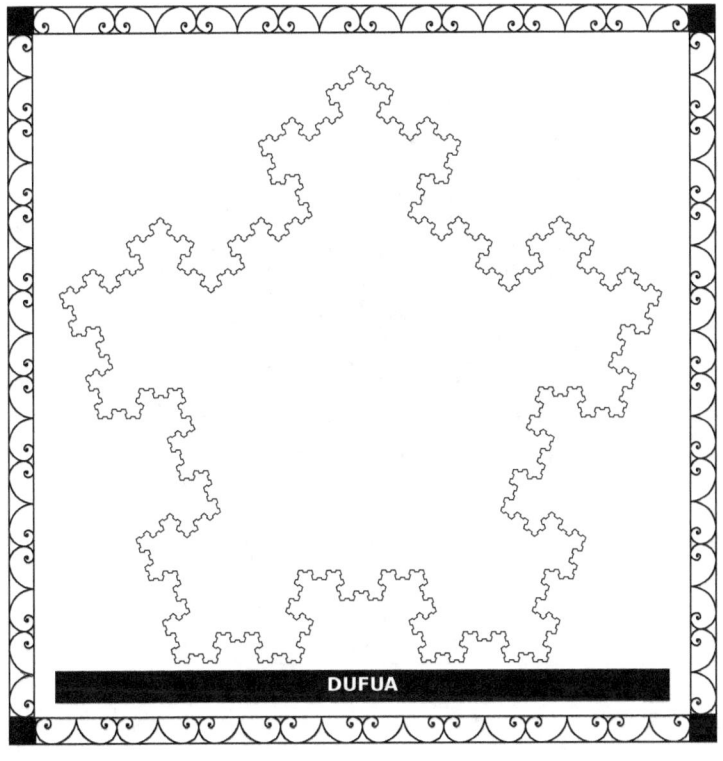

DUFUA

An artist needs not so much an audience, as to feel a need to answer, a promise to respond...a good feeling about his art.
Robert Pinsky

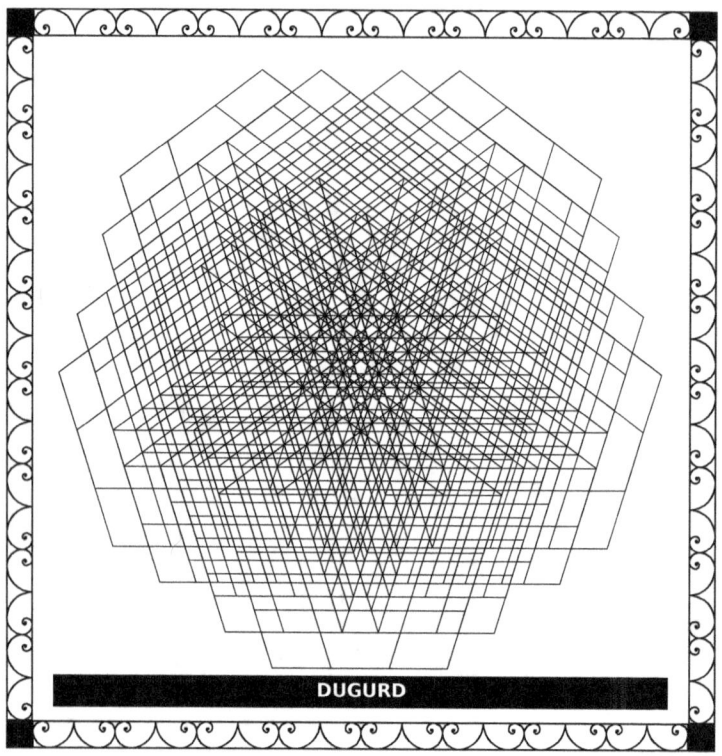

DUGURD

Film is not analysis, it is the agitation of mind; cinema comes from the country fair and the circus, not from art and academicism.
Werner Herzog

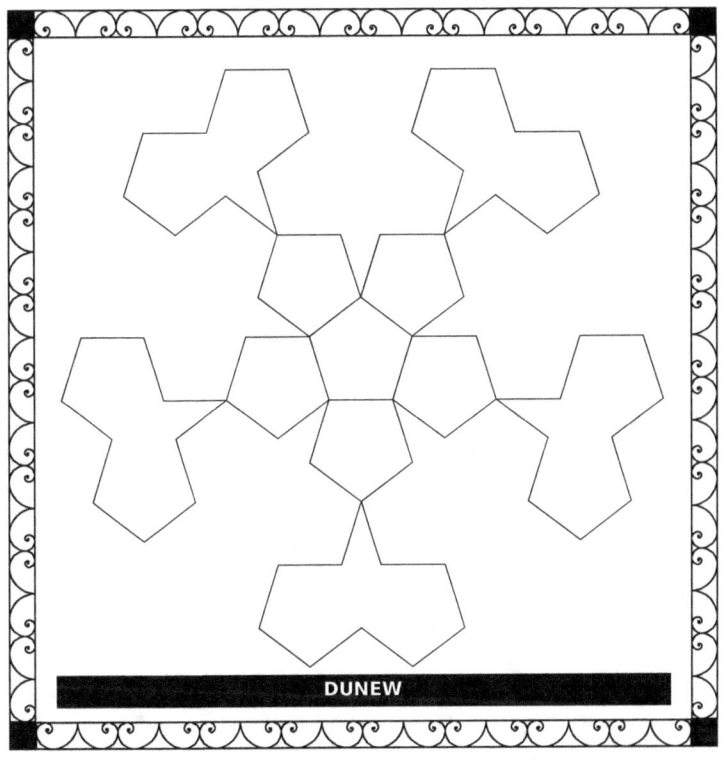

DUNEW

Art has two constant, two unending concerns: It always meditates on death and thus always creates life. All great, genuine art resembles and continues the Revelation of St. John.

Boris Pasternak

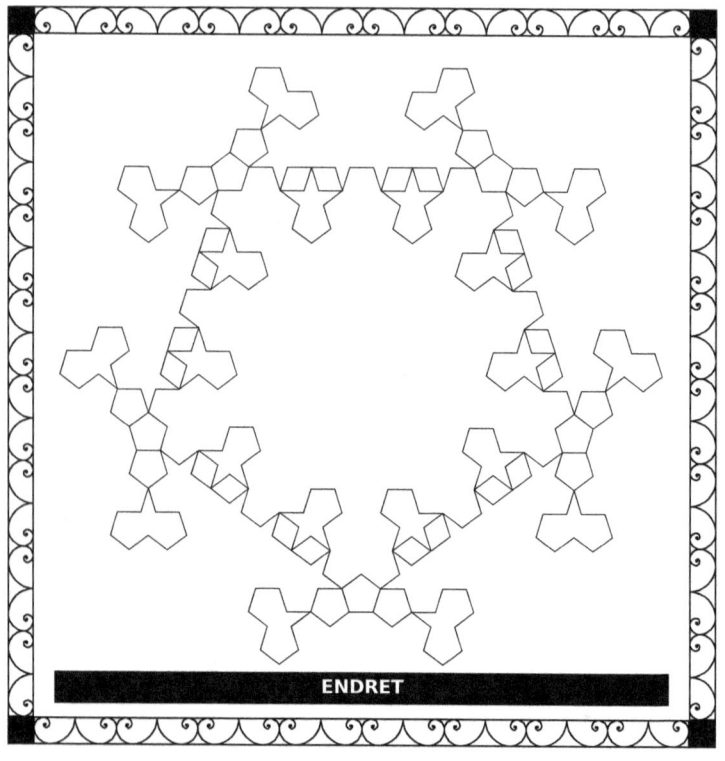

ENDRET

The artist is not the transcriber of the world, he is its rival.
Andre Malraux

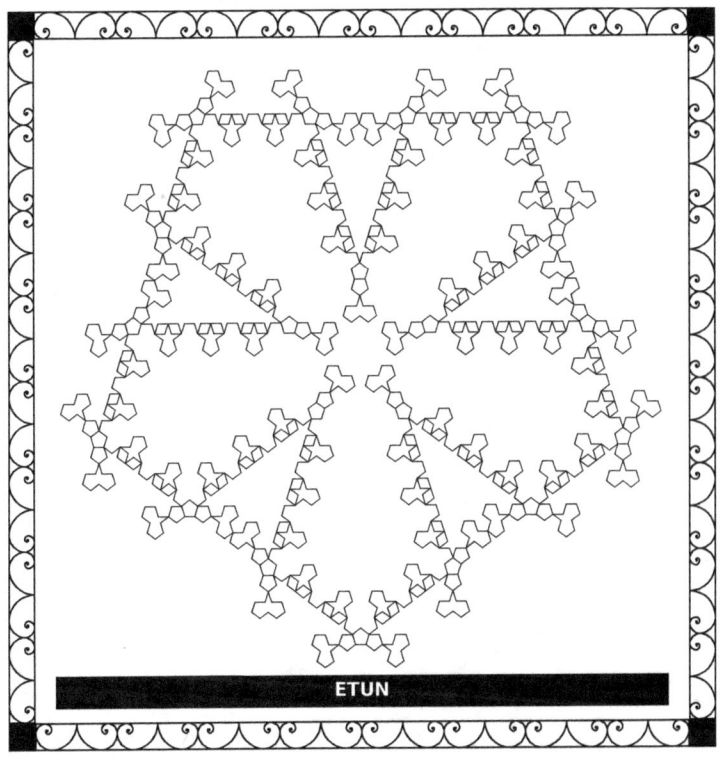

ETUN

Leonardo Da Vinci combined art and science and aesthetics and engineering. That kind of unity is needed once again.
Ben Shneiderman

49

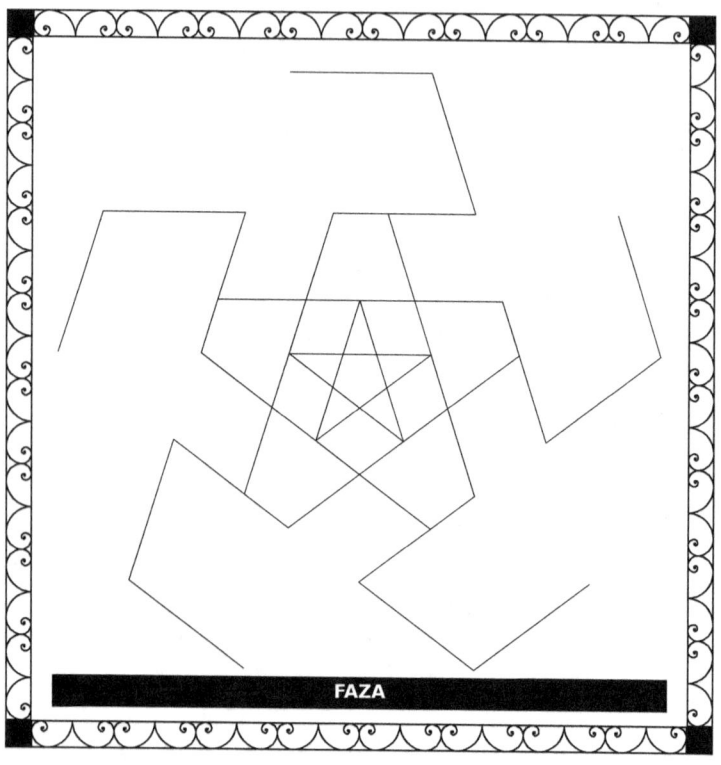

FAZA

If art is to survive it must describe and express people, their lives and times.

Raphael Soyer

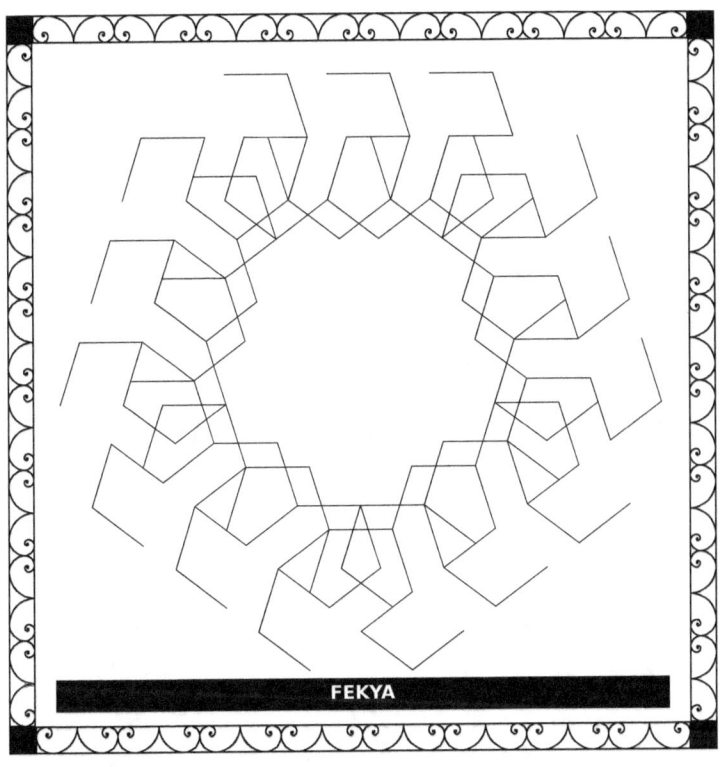

FEKYA

Art always opts for the individual, the concrete; art is not Platonic.
Jorge Luis Borges

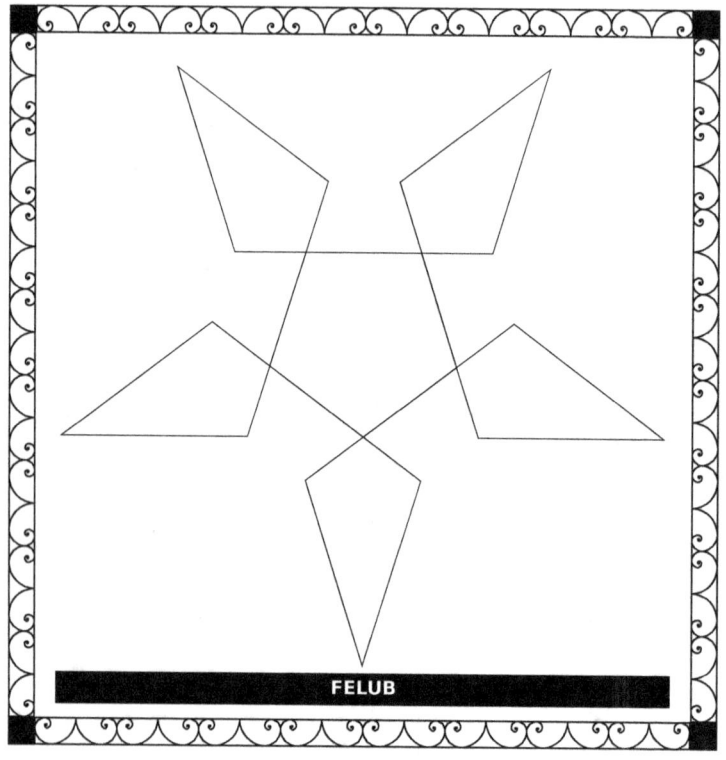

FELUB

The most valiant thing you can do as an artist is inspire someone else to be creative.
Joseph Gordon-Levitt

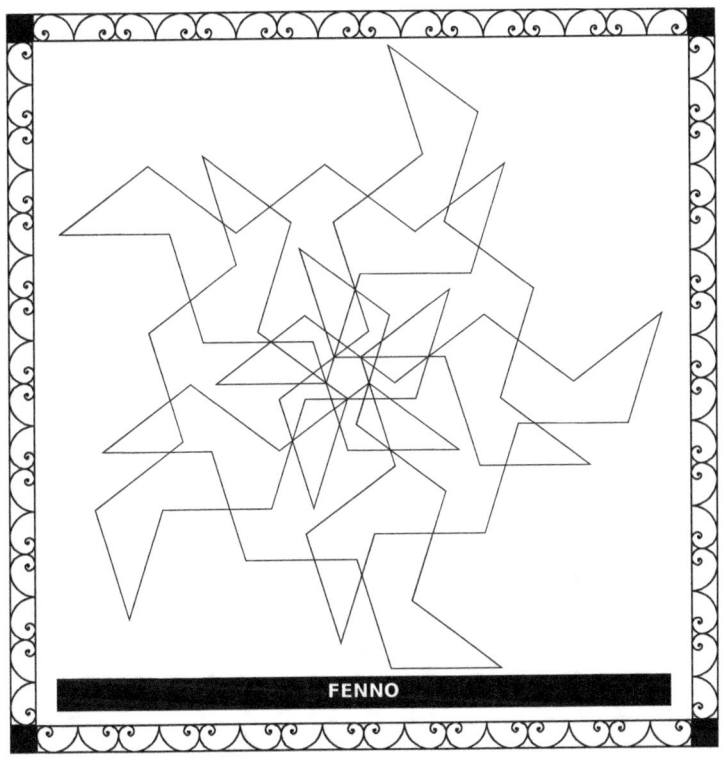

FENNO

To the man who loves art for its own sake...it is frequently in its least important and lowliest manifestations that the keenest pleasure is to be derived.
Arthur Conan Doyle

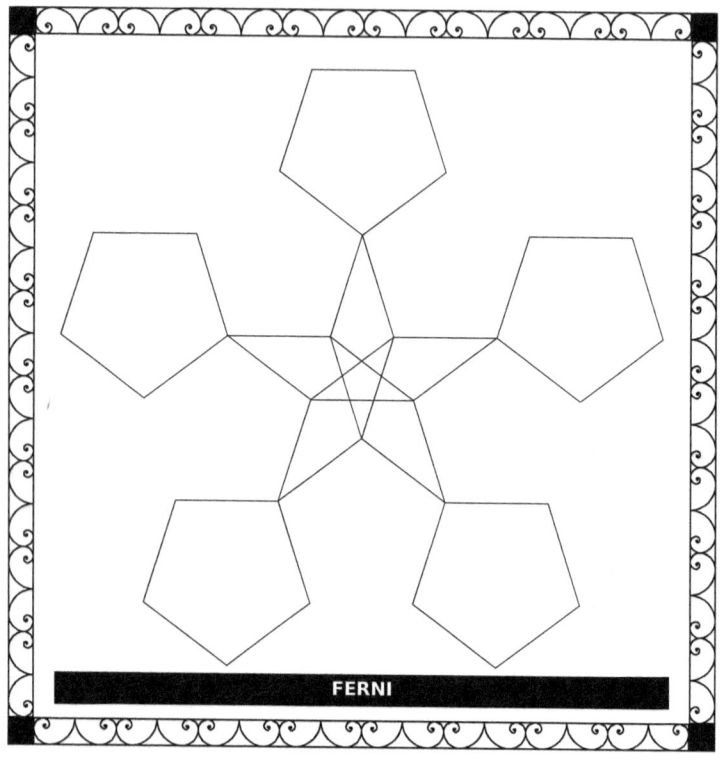

FERNI

No man should be hurried in his work, and an artist least of all.
Lewis Carroll

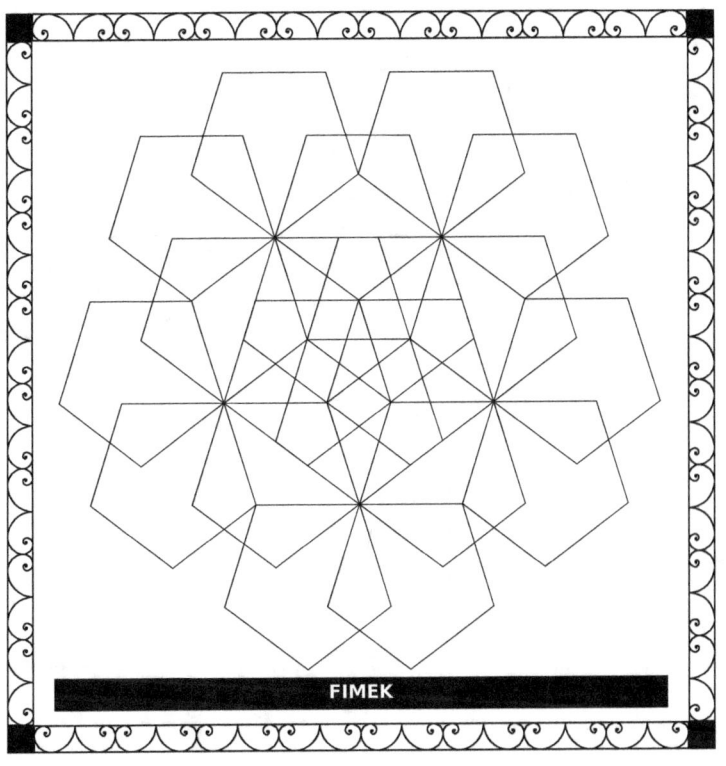

FIMEK

If you get simple beauty and naught else, you get about the best thing God invents.

Robert Browning

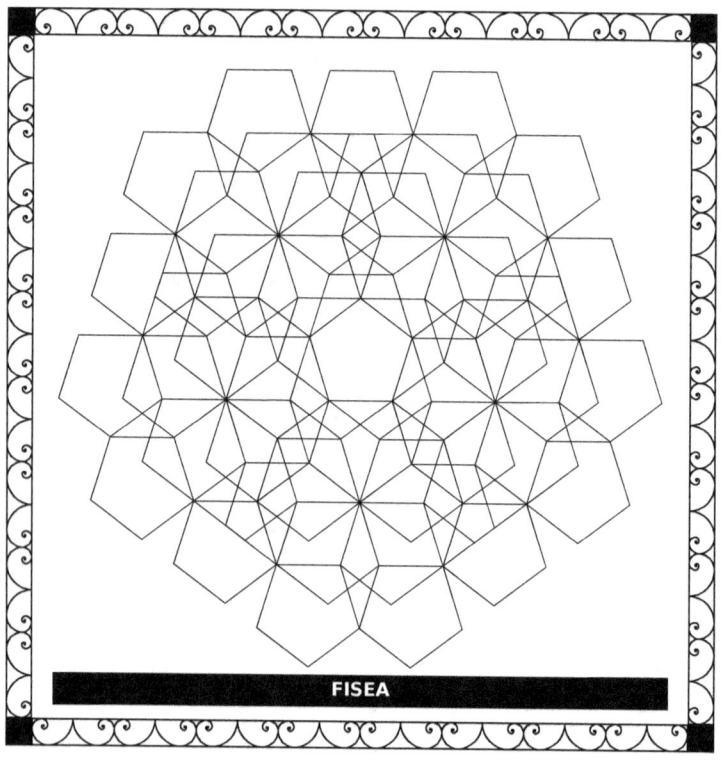

FISEA

For me, a landscape does not exist in its own right, since its appearance changes at every moment; but the surrounding atmosphere brings it to life — the air and the light which vary continually. For me, it is only the, surrounding atmosphere which gives subjects their true value.
Claude Monet

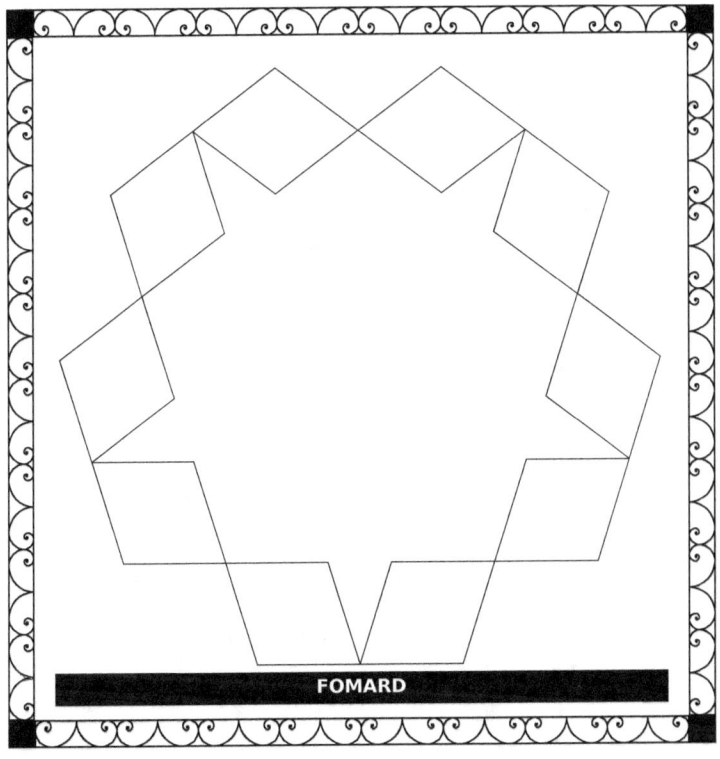

FOMARD

In an empirical sense, extremist art is a unified confirmation of one's resistance to and transcendence of status quo thinking.
Nick Zedd

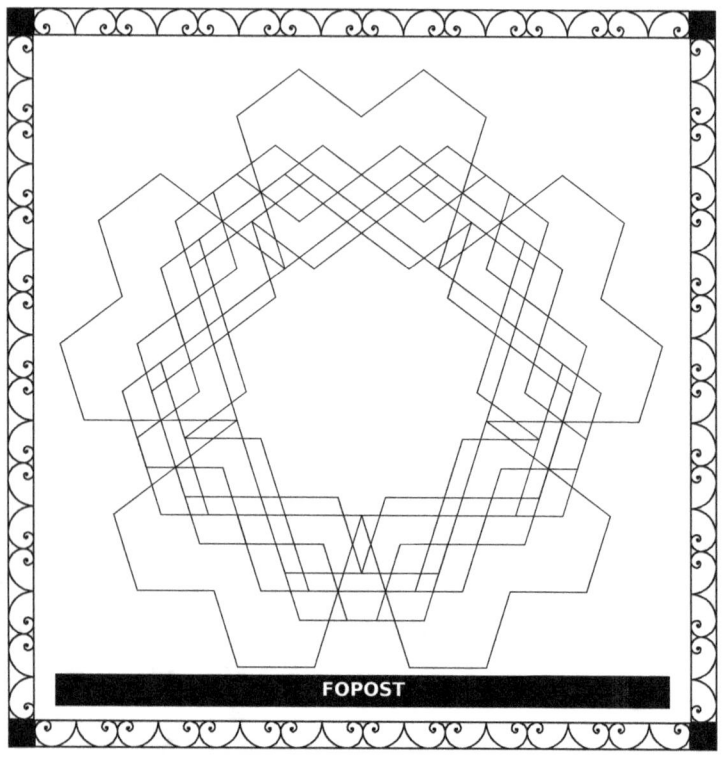

FOPOST

Nothing can be accomplished without love.
Henri Matisse

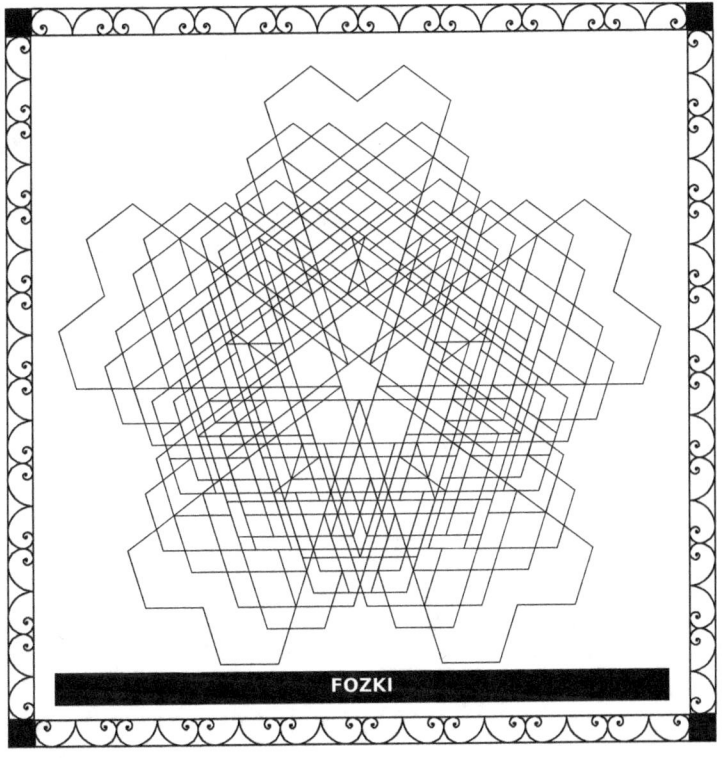

FOZKI

Anywhere I found wood I took it home and started working with it...to show the world that art is everywhere, except it has to pass through a creative mind.
Louise Nevelson

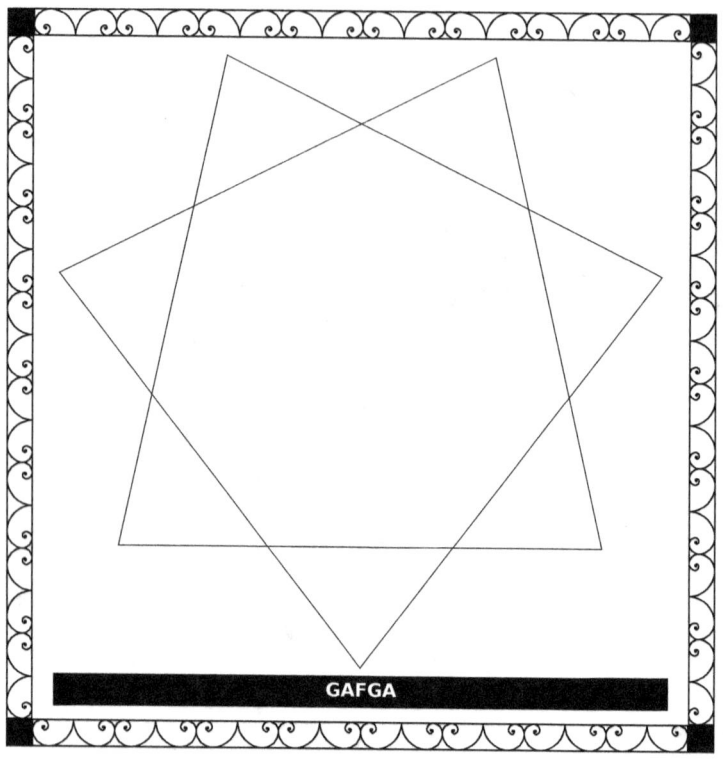

GAFGA

Mystery is the source of all true art and science.
The Adventures of Buckaroo Banzai Across the 8th Dimension

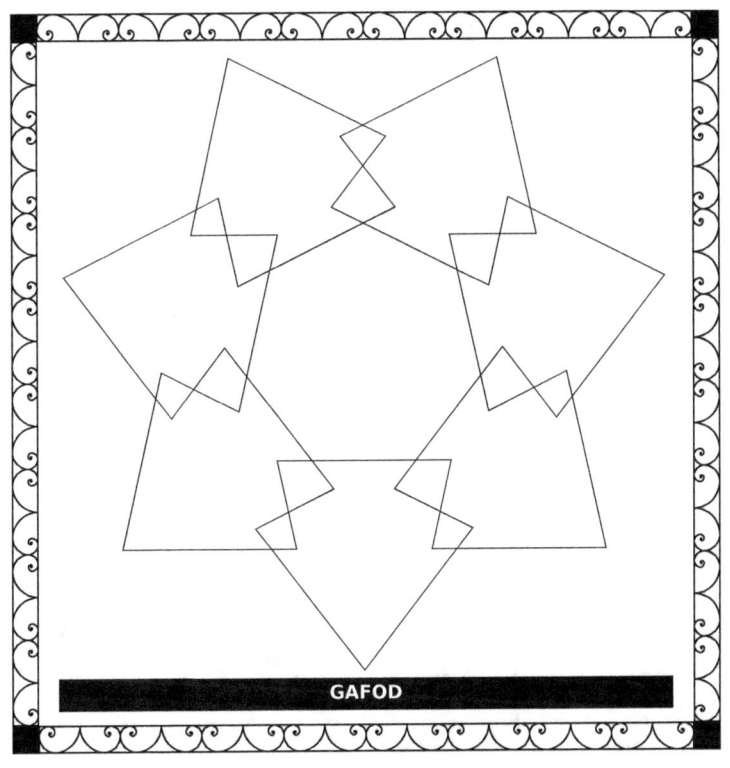

GAFOD

I am not an artist just someone who paints.

L. S. Lowry

61

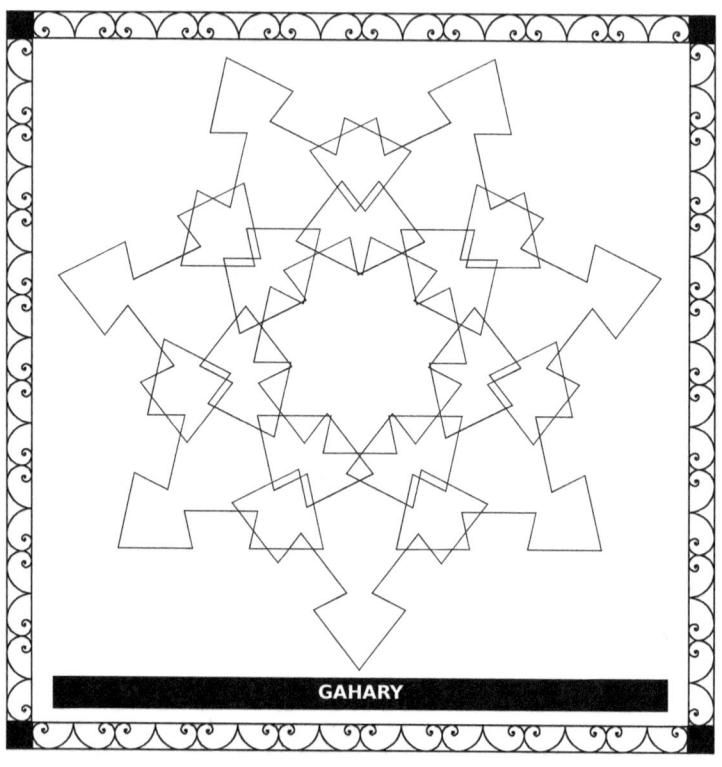

GAHARY

A work of art is a world in itself reflecting senses and emotions of the artist's world. Just as a flower, by virtue of its existence as a complete organism is both ornamental and self-sufficient as to color, form, and texture, so art, because of its singular existence is more than mere ornament.
Hans Hofmann

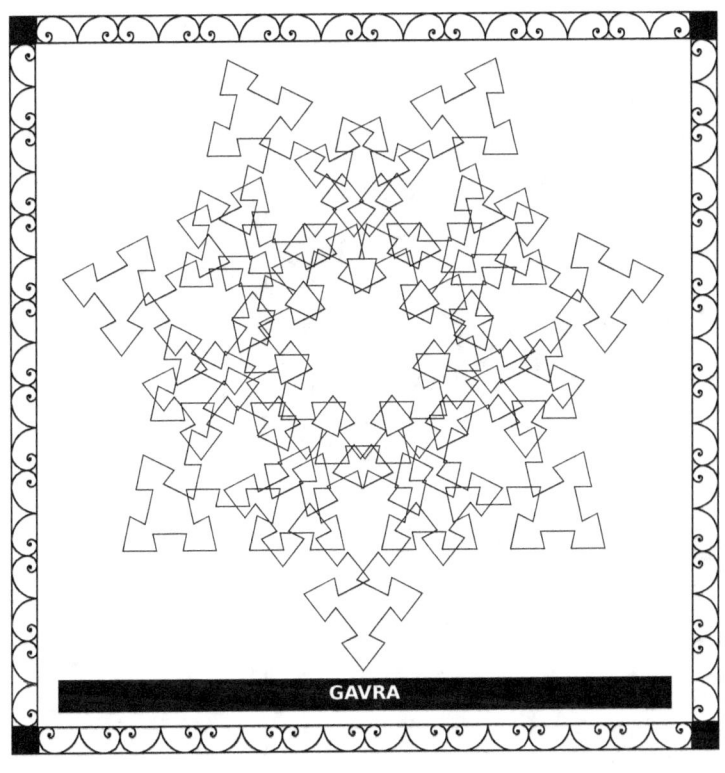

GAVRA

Be careless in your dress if you must, but keep a tidy soul.
Mark Twain

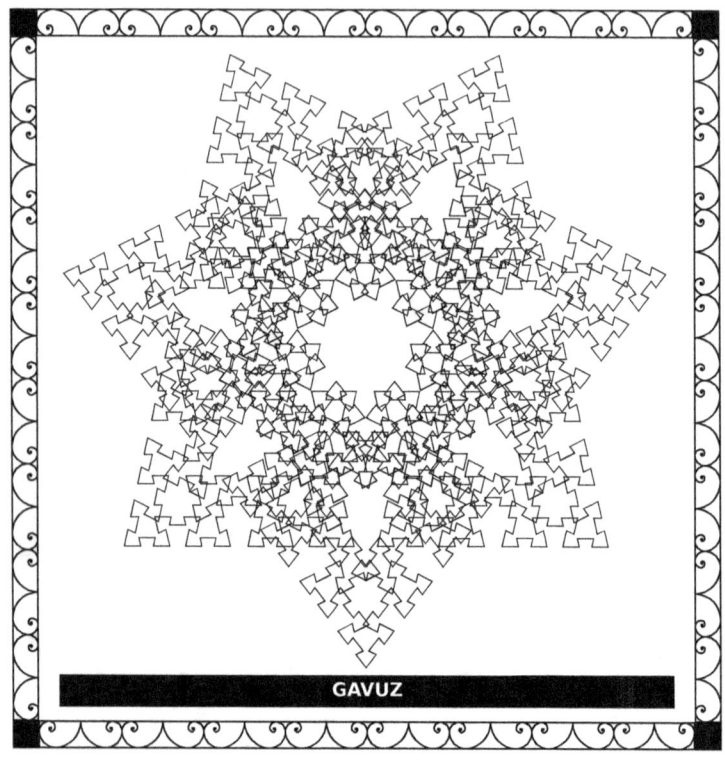

GAVUZ

The latter part of a wise man's life is taken up in curing the follies, prejudices, and false opinions he had contracted in the former.
Jonathan Swift

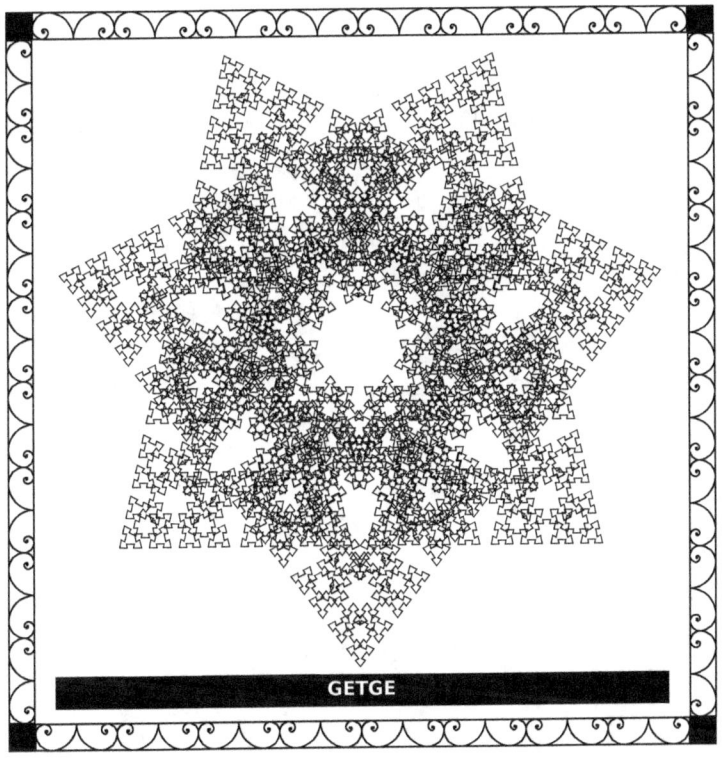

GETGE

Mathematics is one of the essential emanations of the human spirit, a thing to be valued in and for itself, like art or poetry.
Oswald Veblen

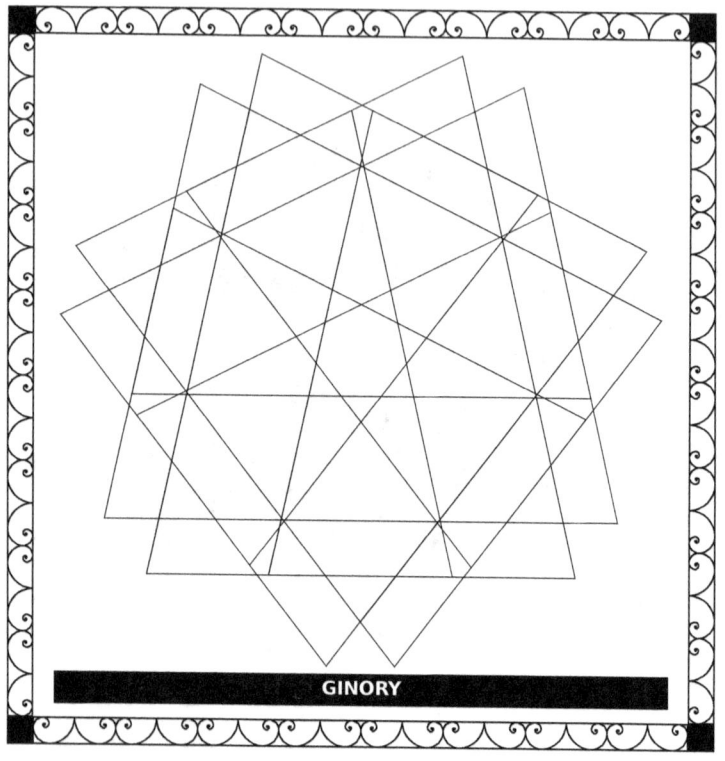

GINORY

Never trust the artist. Trust the tale. The proper function
of a critic is to save the tale from the artist who created it.
D. H. Lawrence

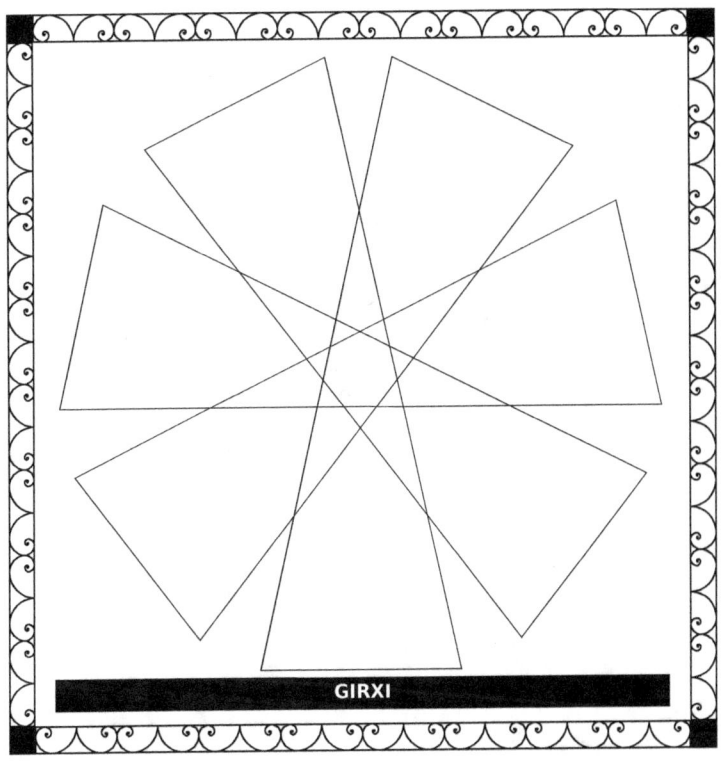

GIRXI

A man's style in any art should be like his dress — it should attract as little attention as possible.
Samuel Butler

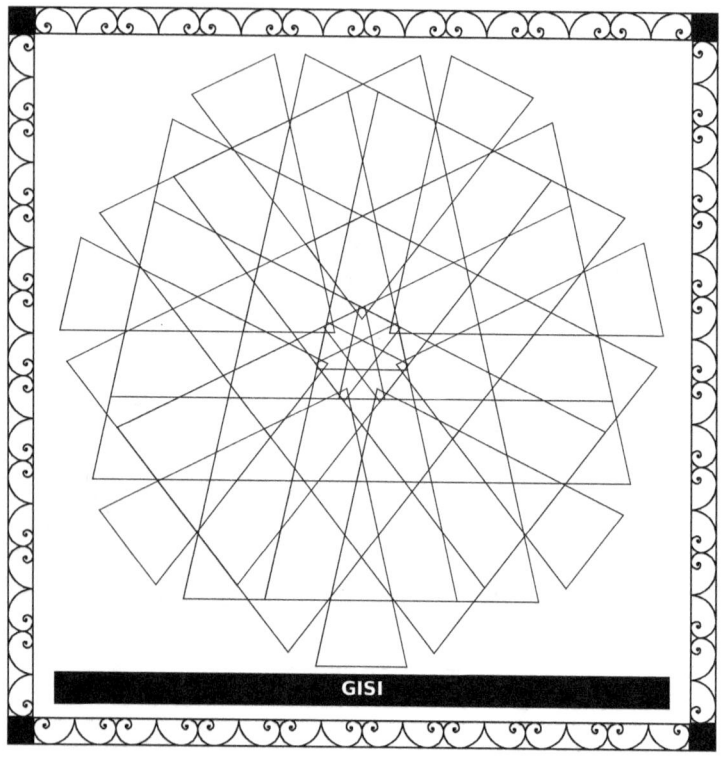

GISI

The great artist takes what he needs.
Kenneth Clark

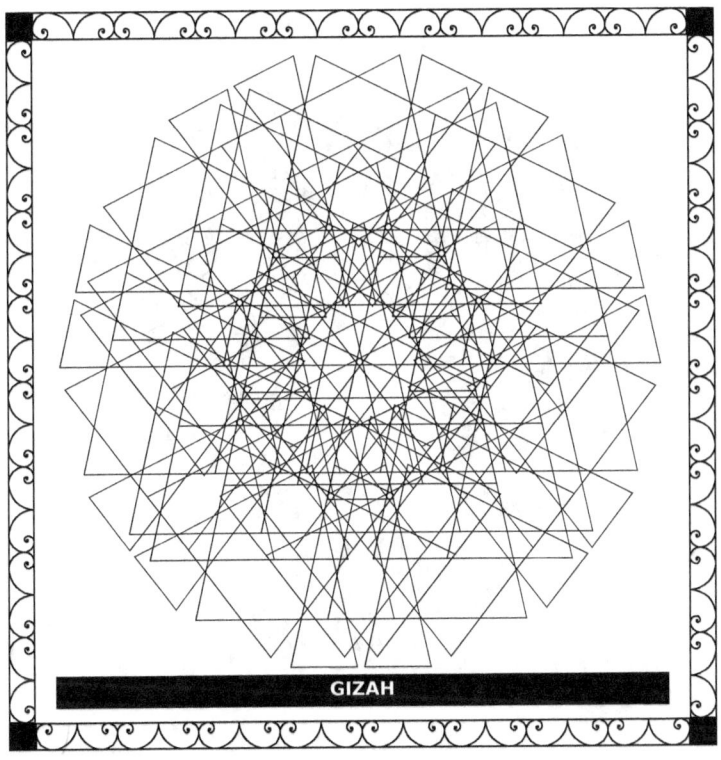

GIZAH

The current demoralization of the art world is attributable at least in part to museum interference, ideological and practical, with ongoing creation in art.

Harold Rosenberg

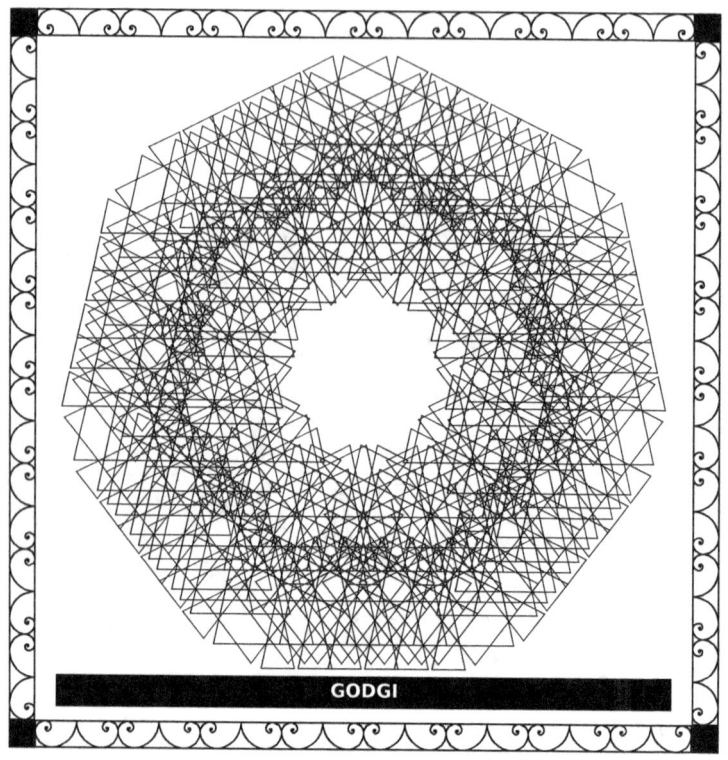

GODGI

All aesthetic judgment is really cultural evaluation.
Susan Sontag

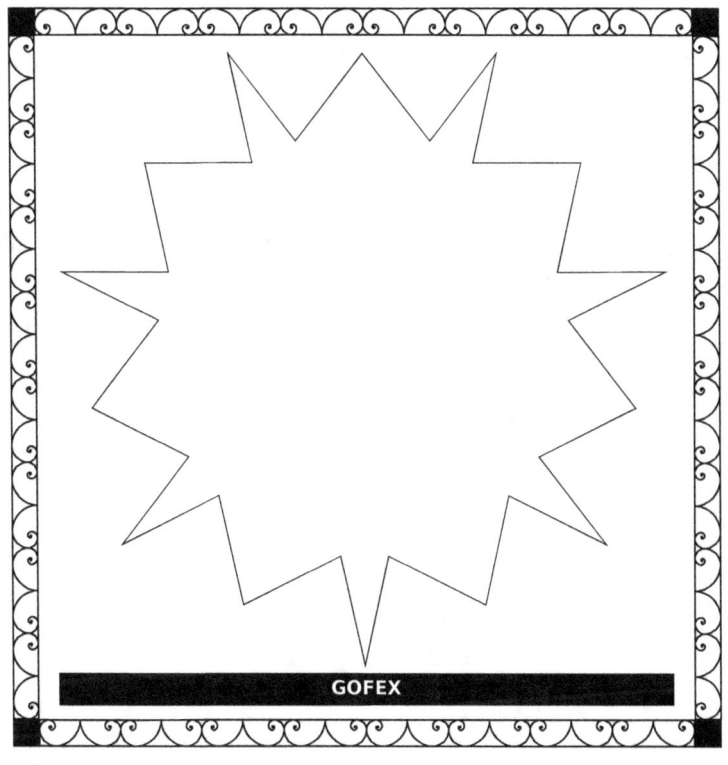

GOFEX

Bad art is more tragically beautiful than good art, because it documents human failure.
Henry Letham

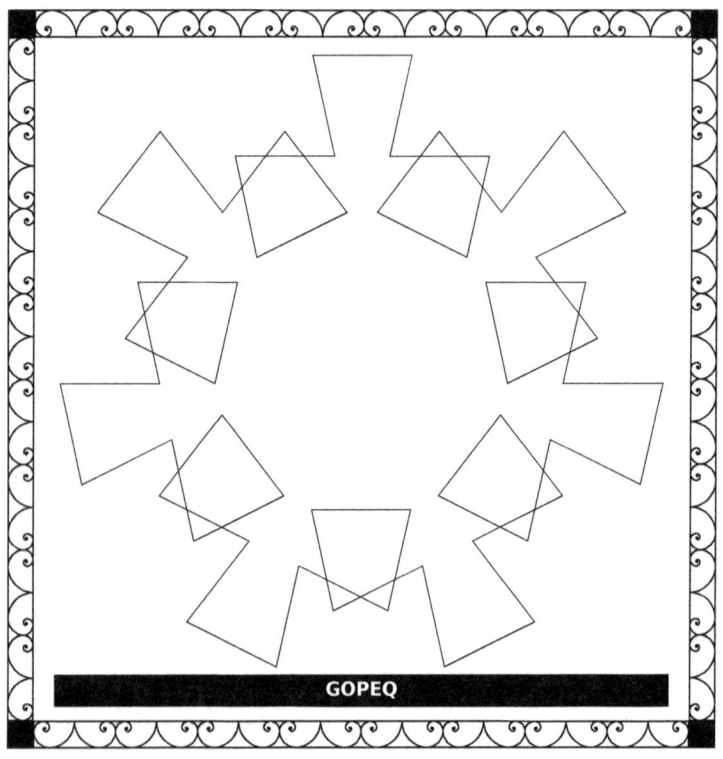

GOPEQ

Composition is the art of arranging in a decorative manner the diverse elements at the painter's command to express his feelings.
Henri Matisse

72

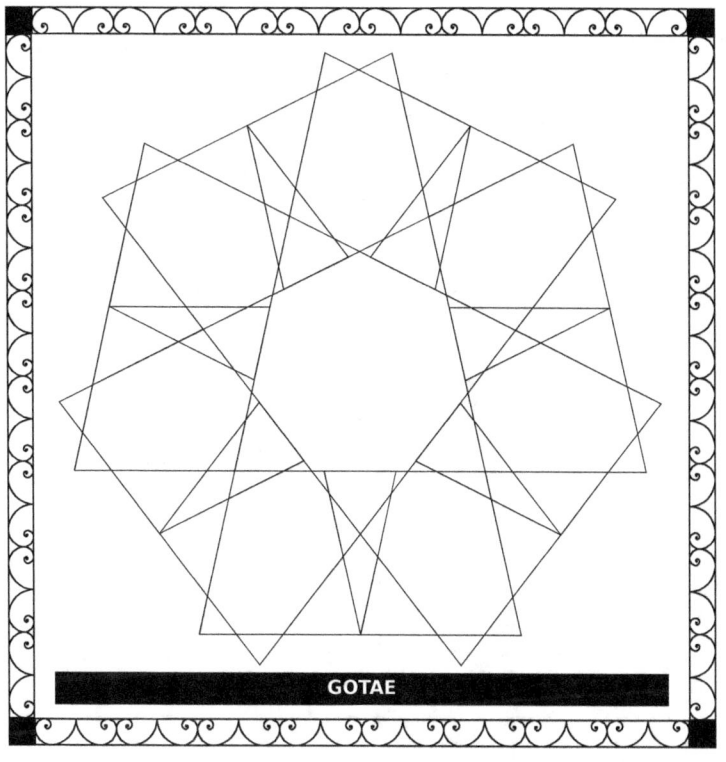

GOTAE

Every art and every faculty contemplates certain things as its principal objects.
Epictetus

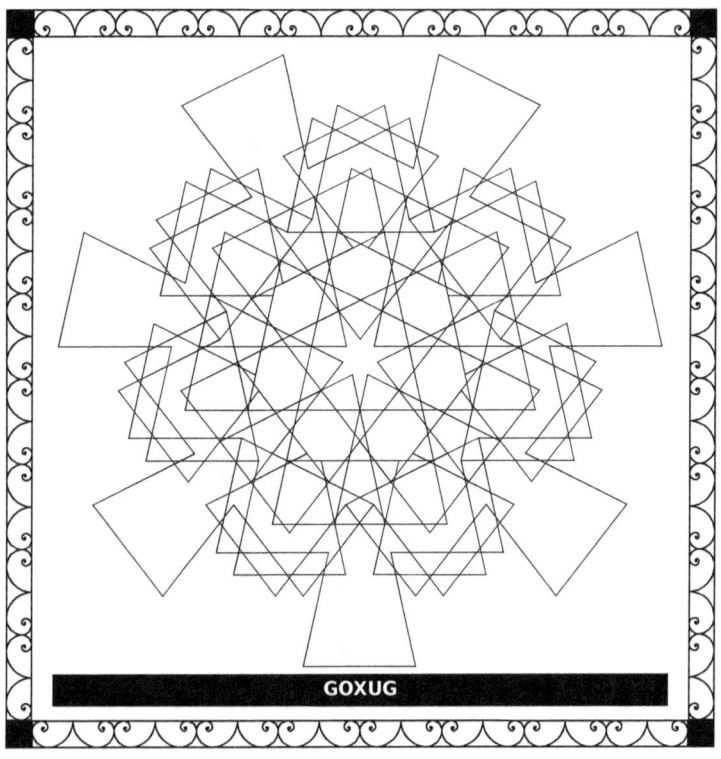

GOXUG

Those who contemplate the beauty of the earth find re-
serves of strength that will endure as long as life lasts.
Rachel Carson

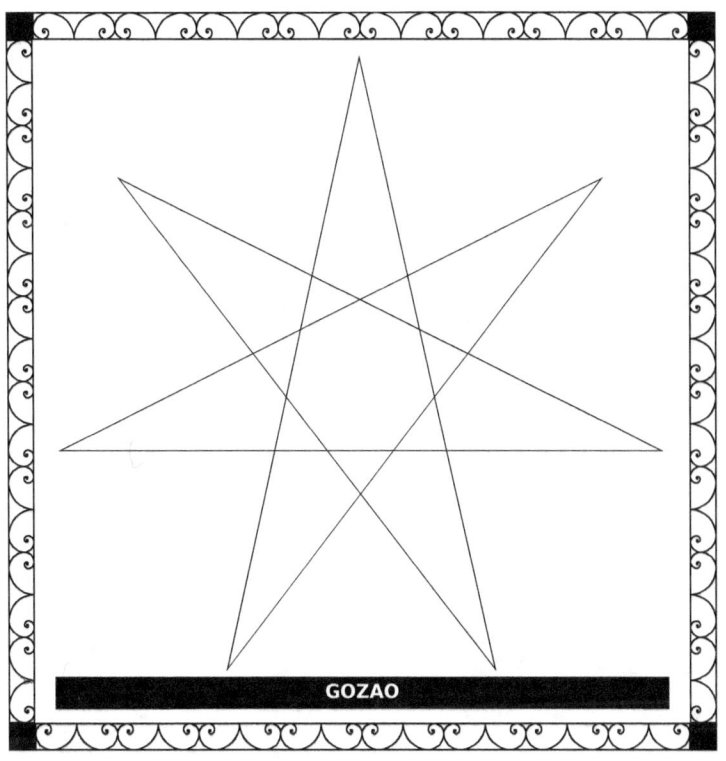

GOZAO

Life is earnest, art is gay.
Friedrich Schiller

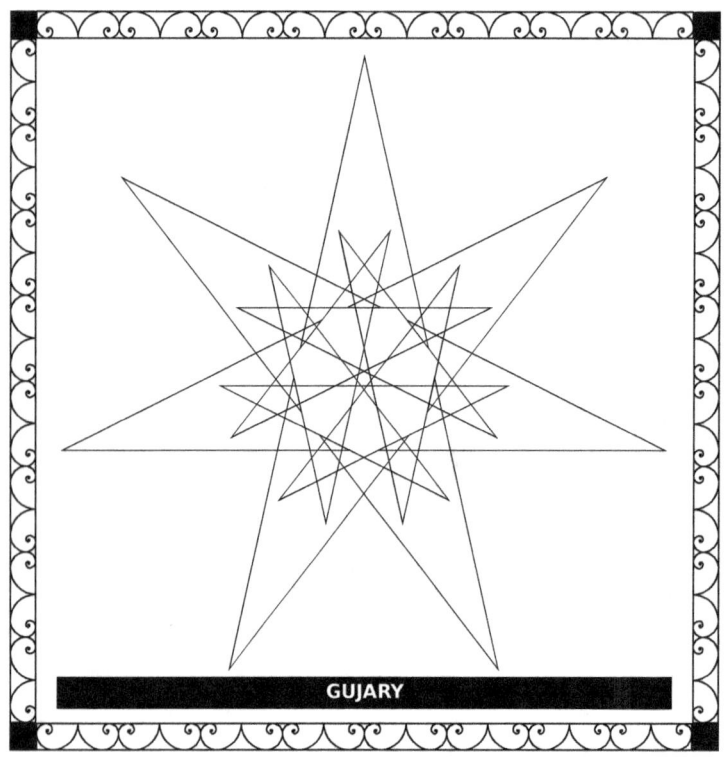

GUJARY

Beauty illustrates happiness: the wind in the grass, the glistening waves following each other, the flight of birds — all speak of happiness.

Agnes Martin, Beauty Is the Mystery of Life

76

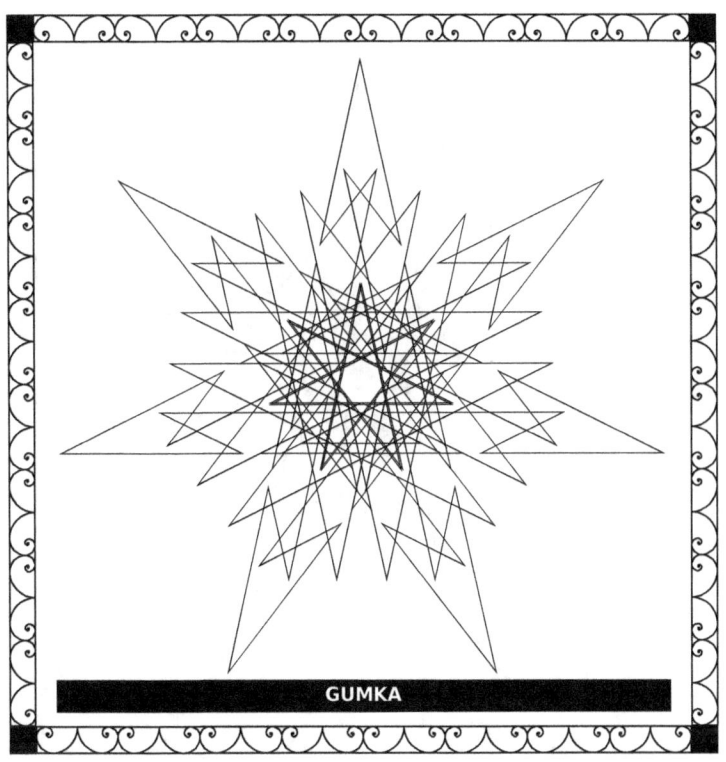

GUMKA

You are not controlling the storm, and you are not lost in it. You are the storm.
Sam Harris

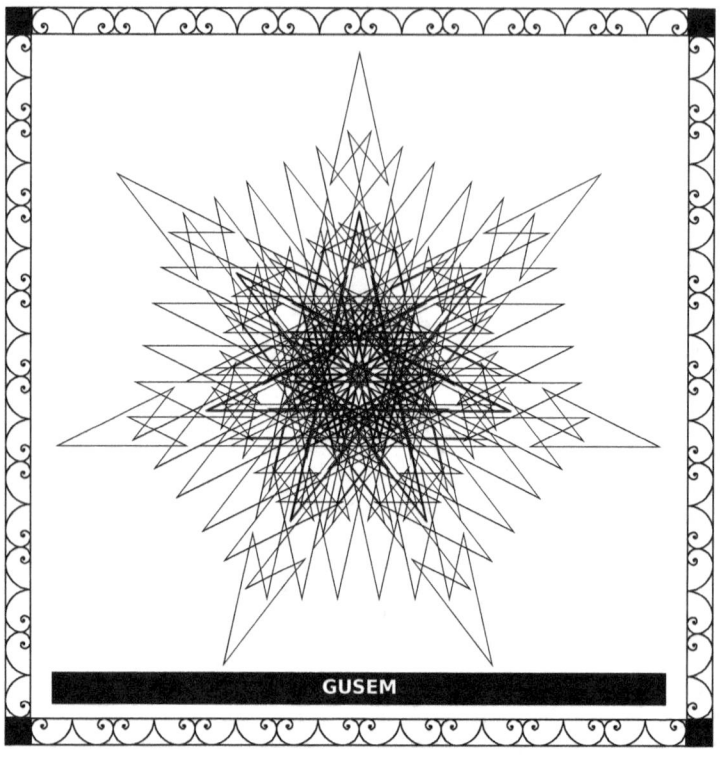

GUSEM

In their different ways, art and philosophy help us, in Schopen-hauer's words, to turn pain into knowledge.
Alain de Botton

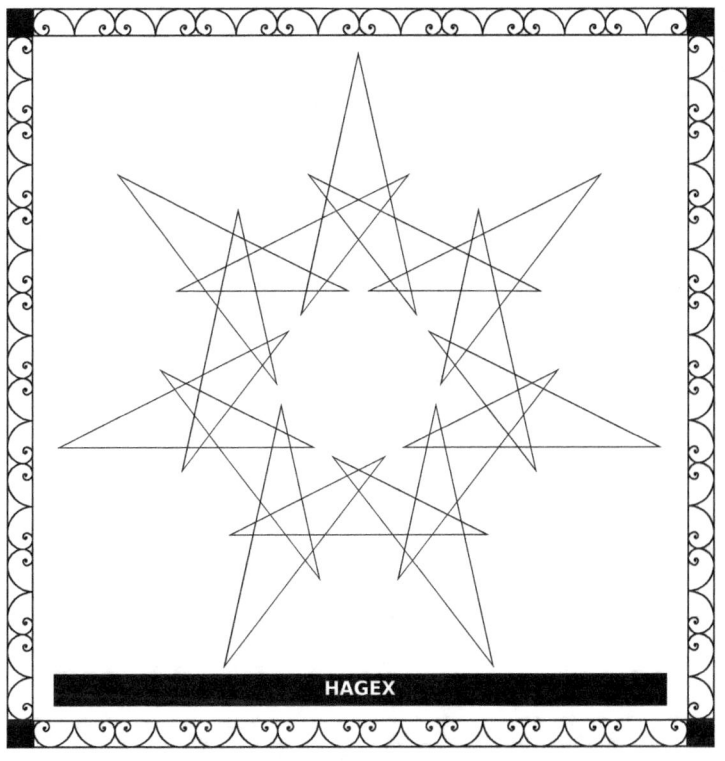

HAGEX

This vain presumption, of understanding everything, can have no other basis than never understanding anything. For anyone who had experienced just once the understanding of one single thing, thus truly tasting how knowledge is accomplished, would then recognize that of the infinity of other truths, he understands nothing.

Kim Stanley Robinson

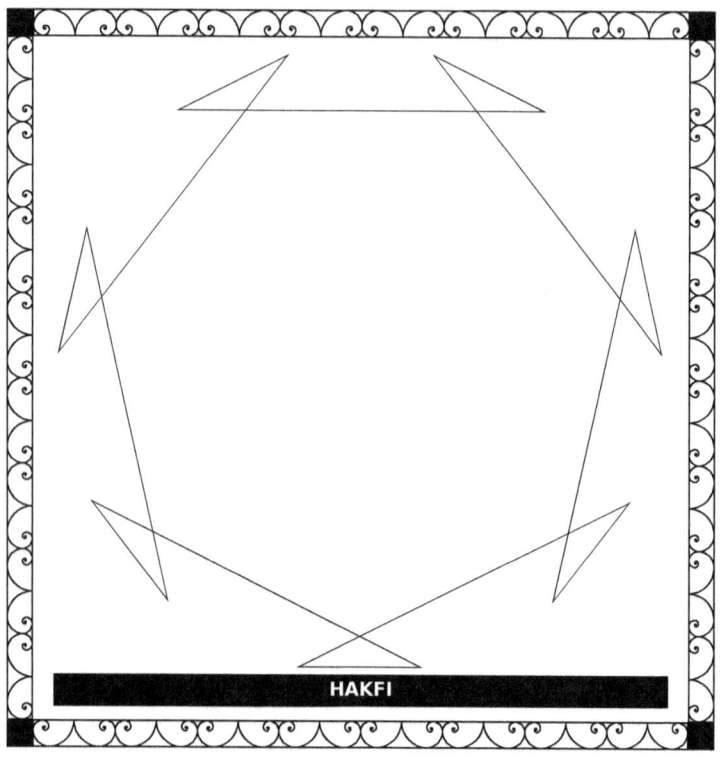

HAKFI

I travelled the world for inspiration and found it in a man who lives what he dreams.
Around the World in 80 Days (2004 film)

80

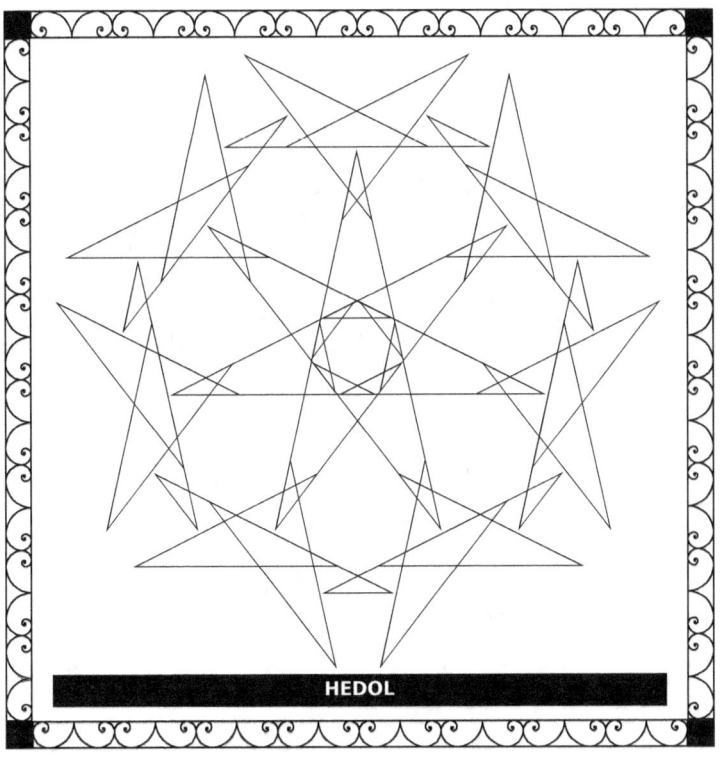

HEDOL

Greek art was extremely simple and direct; both in design and construction the Greek mind abhorred complication.
Ernest Flagg

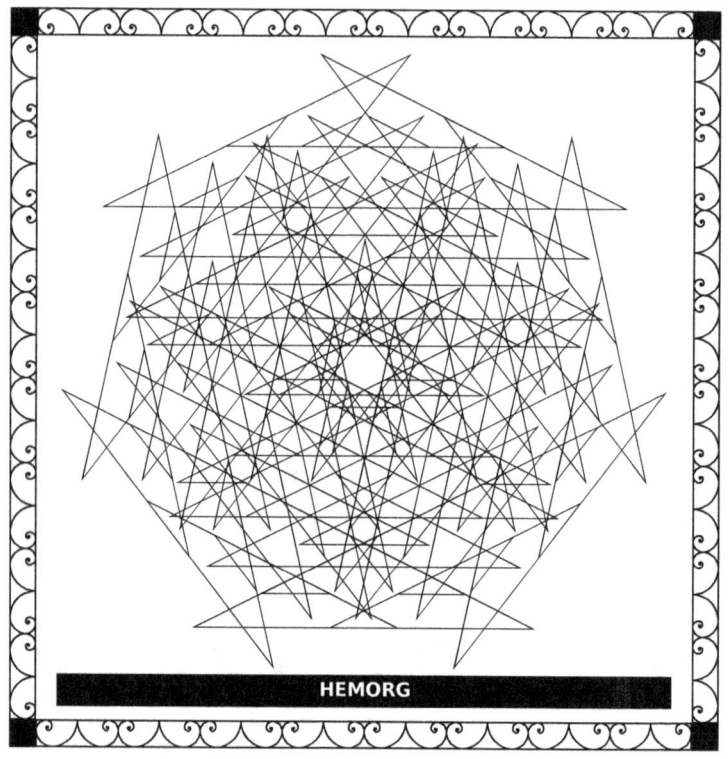

HEMORG

My concern is never art, but always what art can be used for.

Gerhard Richter

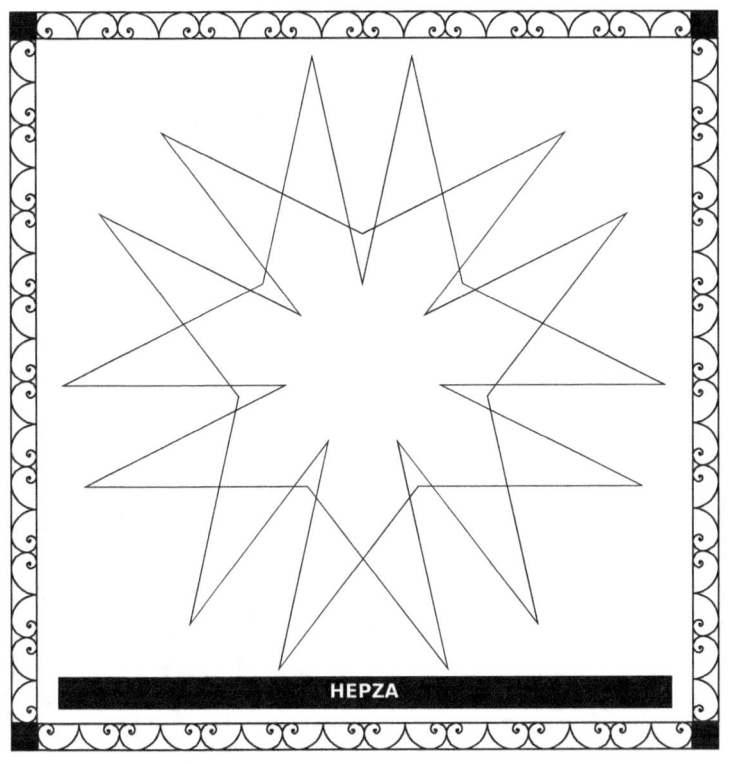

HEPZA

If you have been given a talent, exercise it freely and hap-
pily like the sun: give everyone from your splendour.
Paracelsus

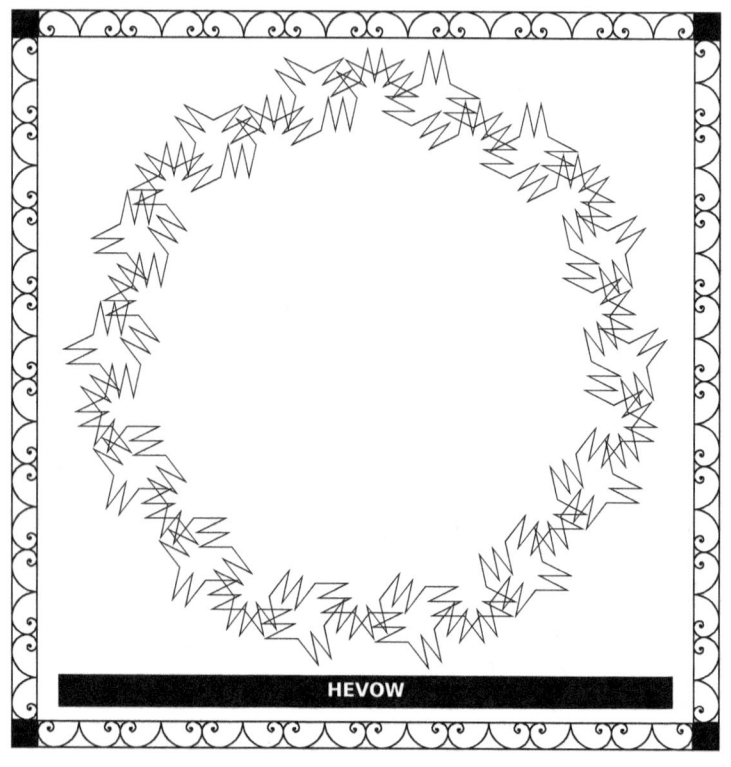

HEVOW

What you don't use, you loose.
Krishna Kant Shukla

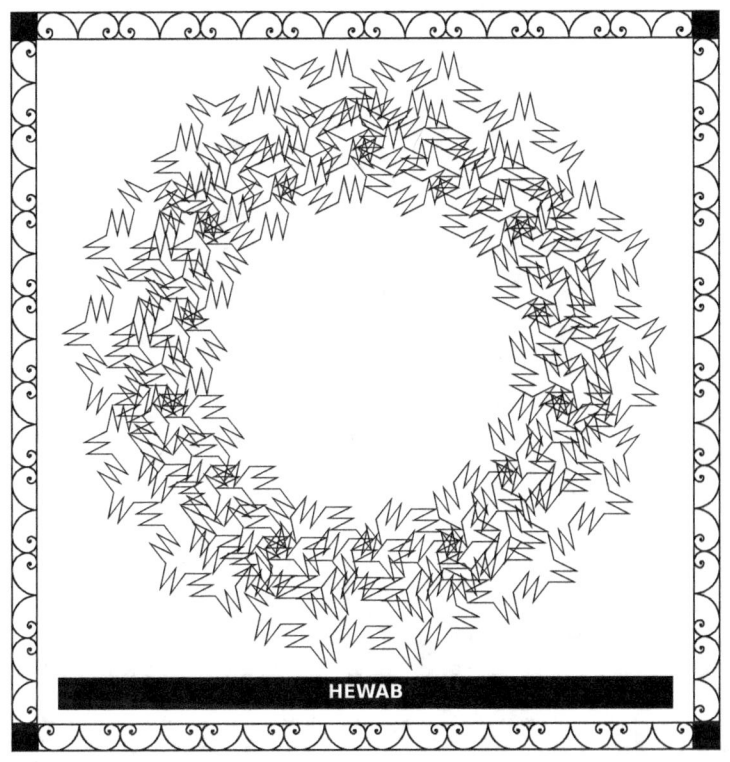

HEWAB

True art is above false honor.
Vladimir Nabokov

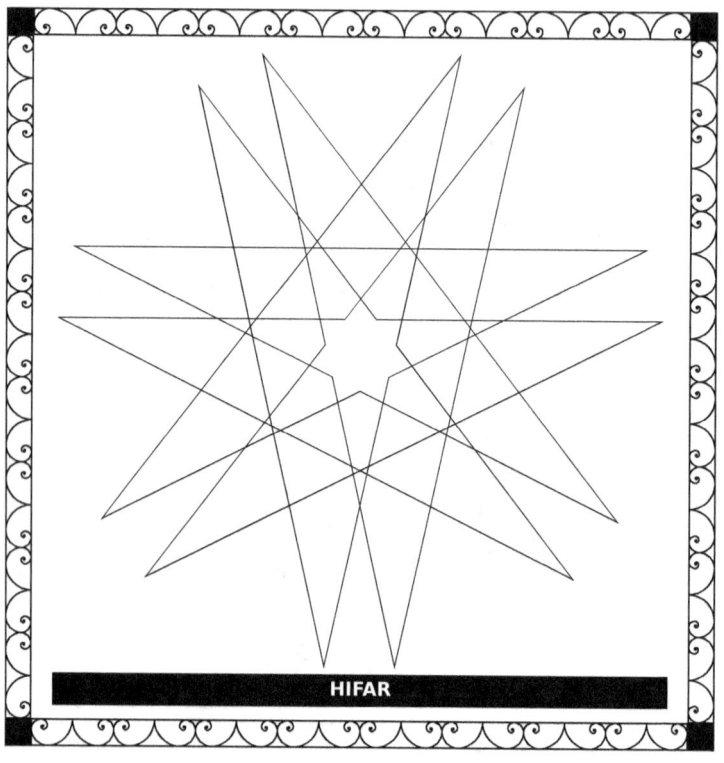

HIFAR

As art sinks into paralysis, artists multiply. This anomaly ceases to be one if we realize that art, on its way to exhaustion, has become both impossible and easy.
Emil Cioran

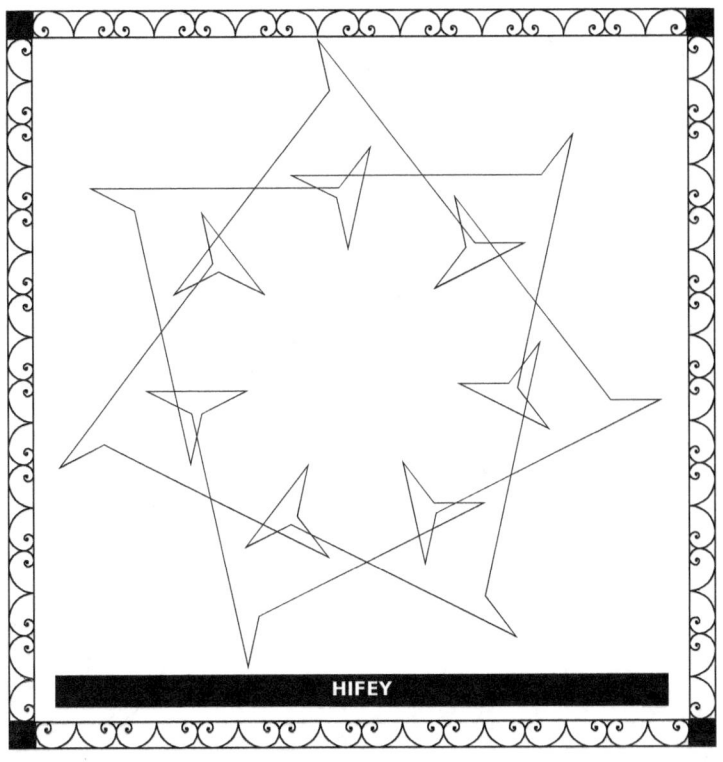

HIFEY

...art lies in the fine choice. The artist does not teach us to see facts: he teaches us to feel harmonies.
Arthur Wesley Dow

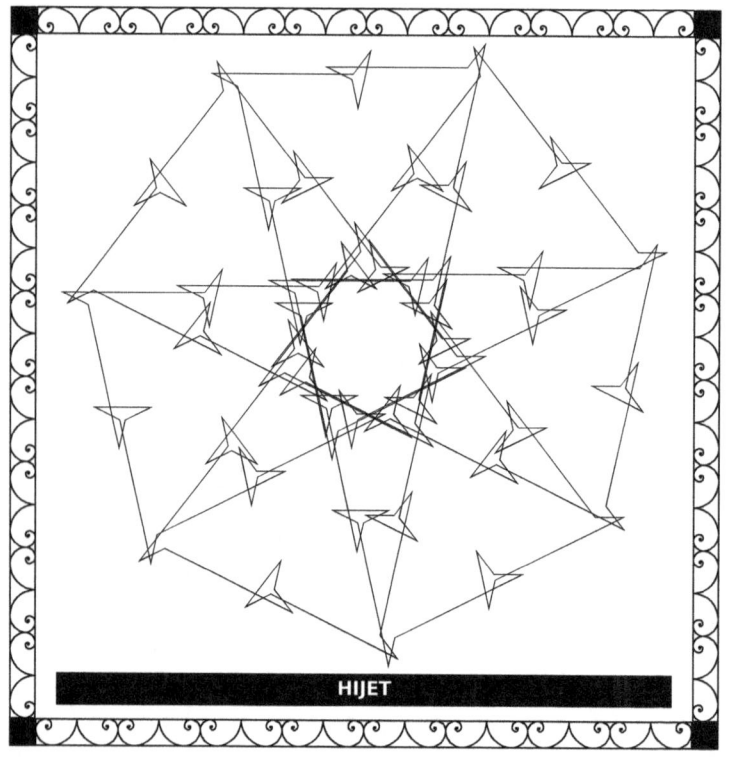

HIJET

That which we look on with unselfish love and true humility is surely ours, even as a lake looks at the stars above and makes within itself a heaven of stars.
Mary Gardiner Brainard

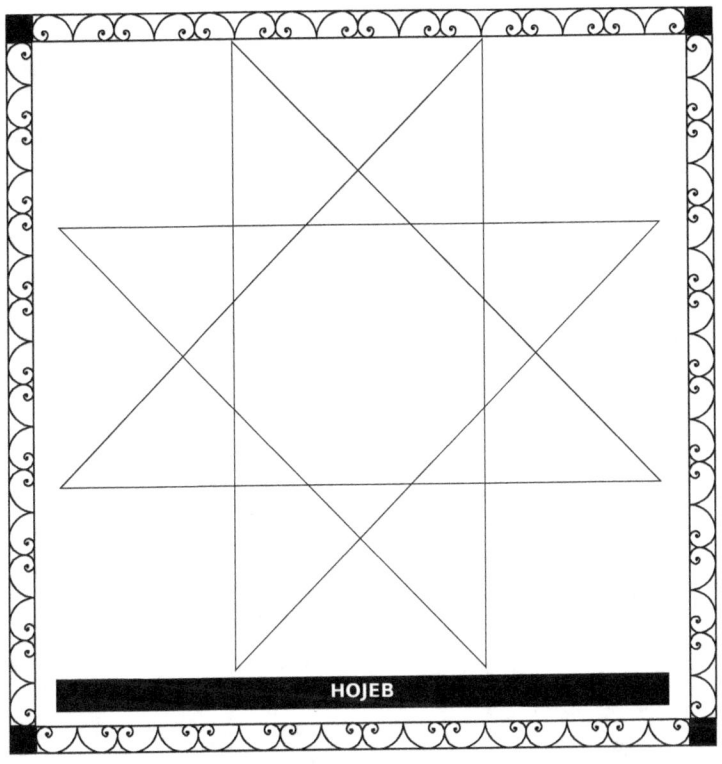

HOJEB

The human body is an instrument for the production of art in the life of the human soul.
Alfred North Whitehead

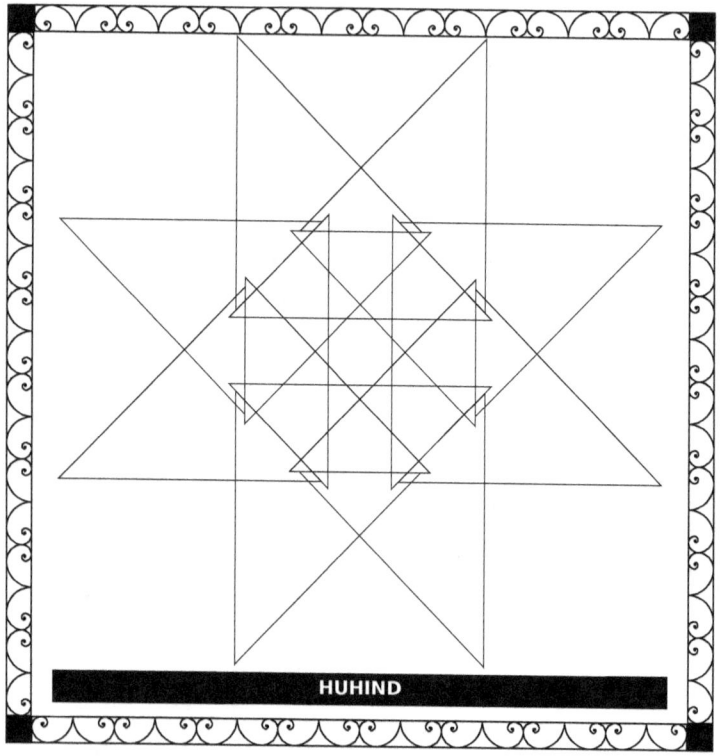

HUHIND

The moral life of man forms part of the subject-matter of the artist, but the morality of art consists in the perfect use of an imperfect medium.

Oscar Wilde, The Picture of Dorian Gray

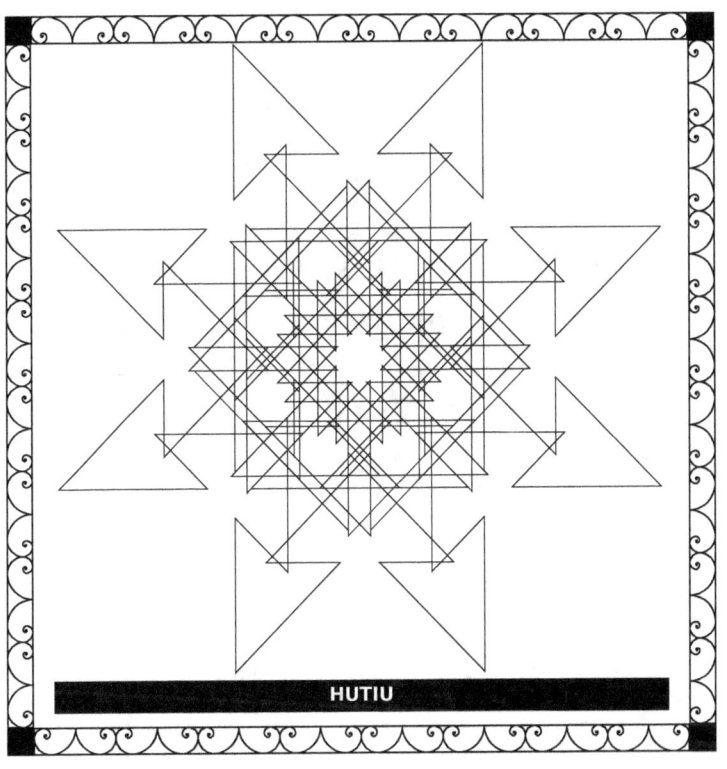

HUTIU

Could get a new art movement every month just by reading Scientific American.
Susan Sontag

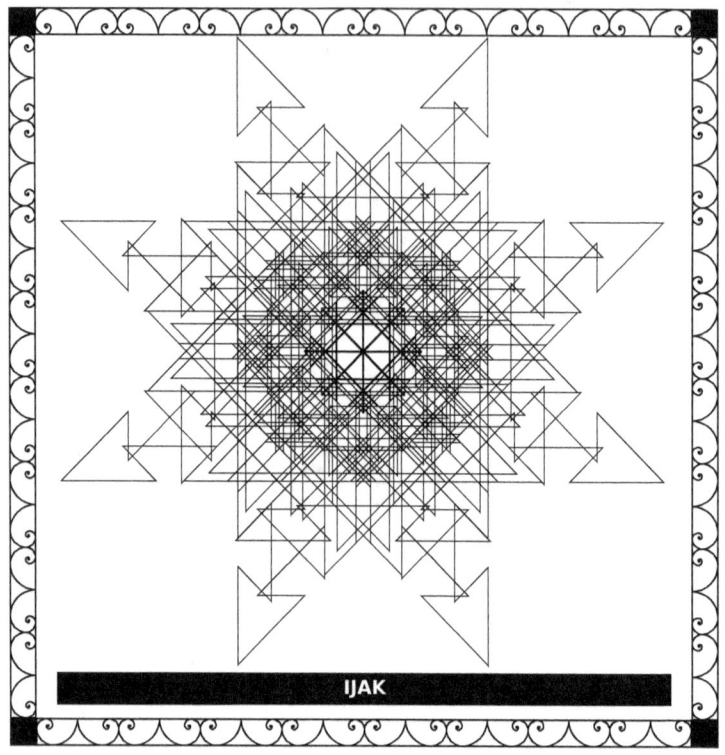

IJAK

All know the Way, but few actually walk it.
Bodhidharma

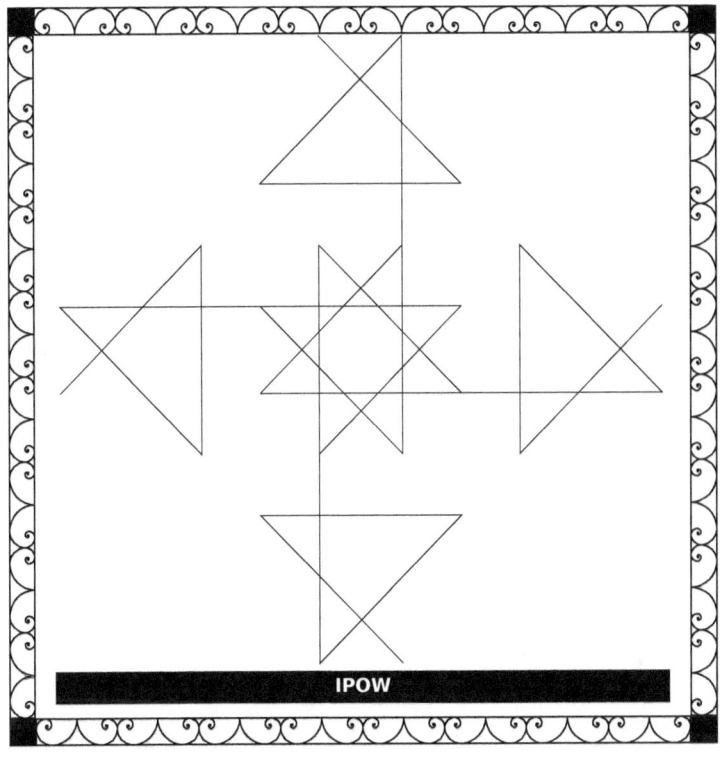

IPOW

Most works of art are, necessarily, bad...; one suffers through
the many for the few.
Randall Jarrell

93

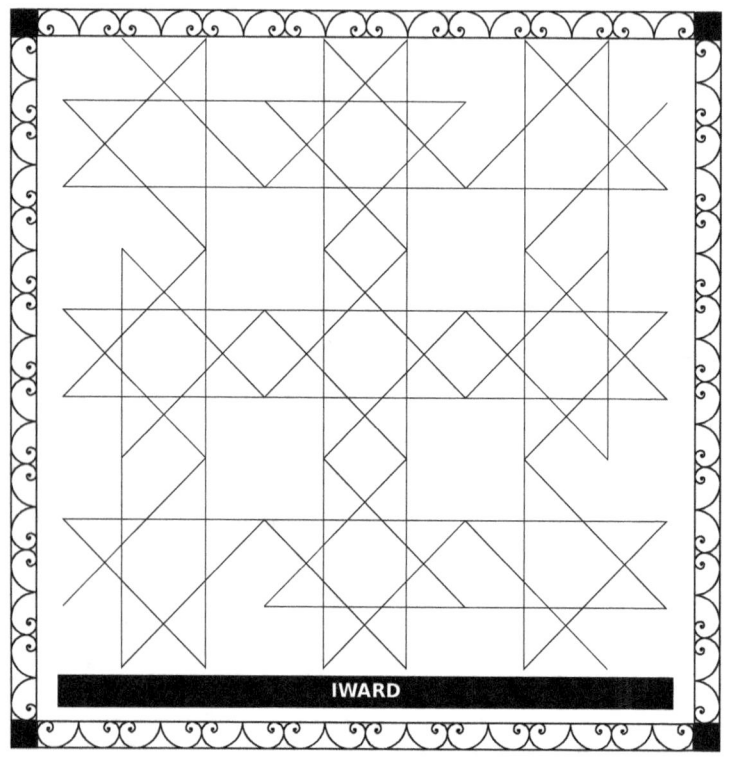

IWARD

An artist is a socially unattractive person whom socially attractive people make money out of.
Mignon McLaughlin

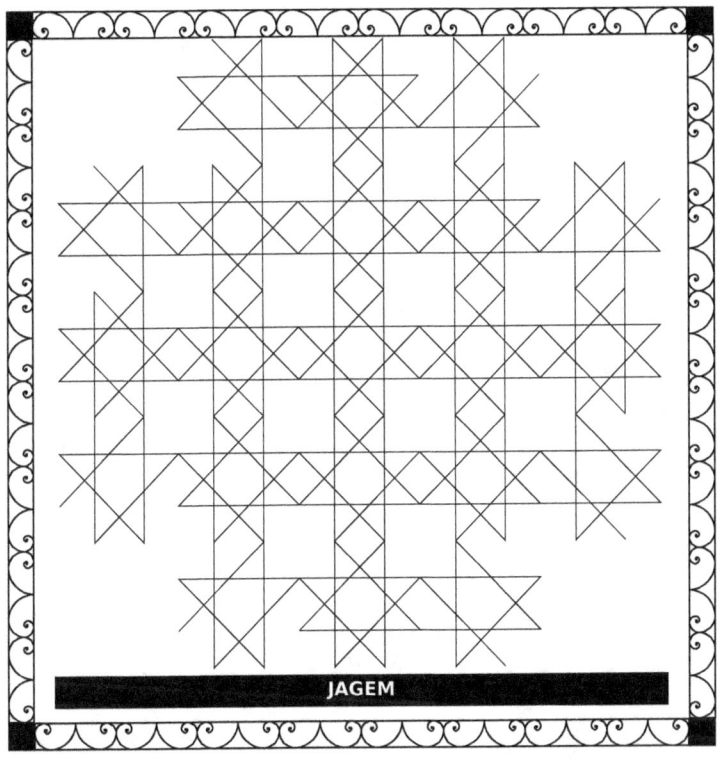

JAGEM

In art progress consists not in extension but in the knowledge of its limits.
Georges Braque

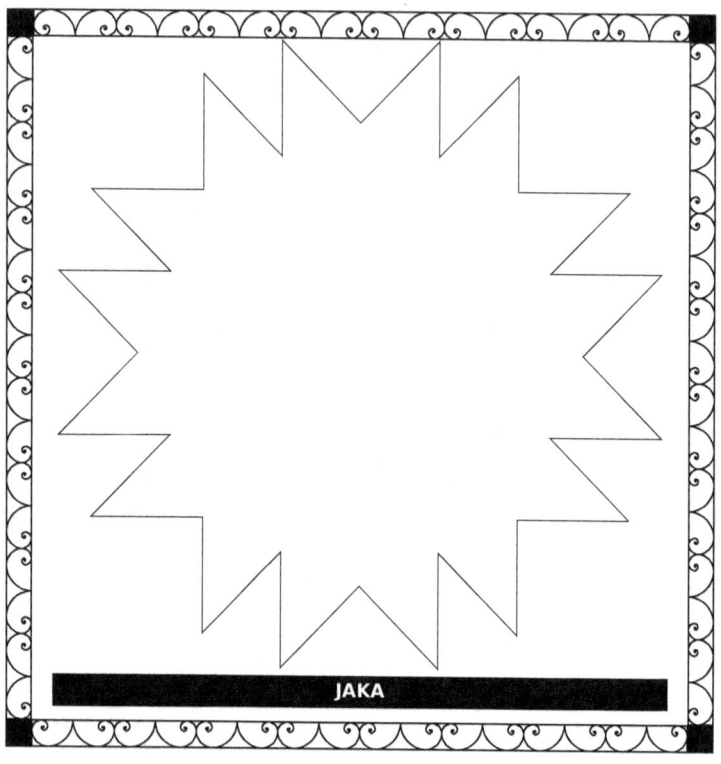

JAKA

If art does not enlarge men's sympathies, it does nothing morally.
George Eliot

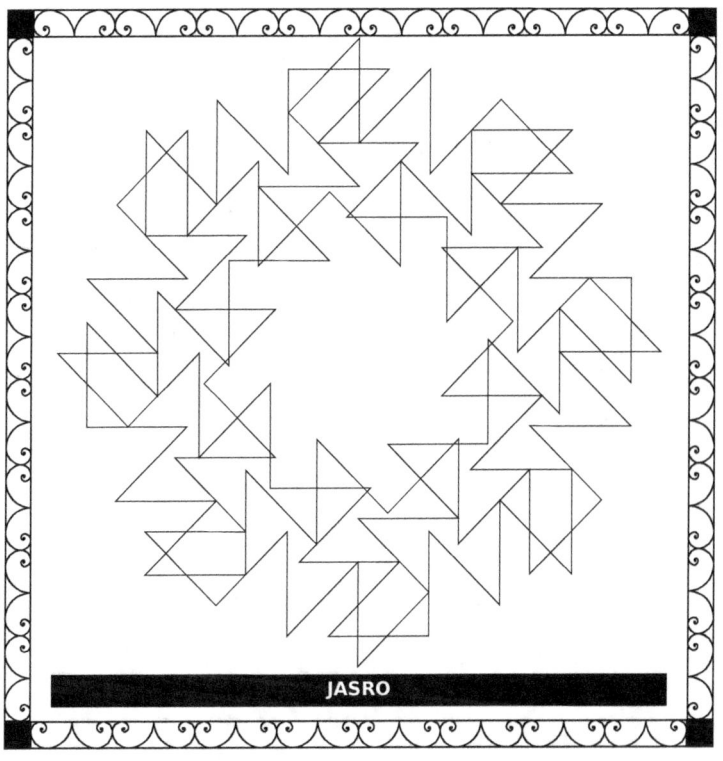

JASRO

In strategy your spiritual bearing must not be any different from normal. Both in fighting and in everyday life you should be determined though calm. Meet the situation without tenseness yet not recklessly, your spirit settled yet unbiased. Even when your spirit is calm do not let your body relax, and when your body is relaxed do not let your spirit slacken. *Miyamoto Musashi, The Book of Five Rings*

97

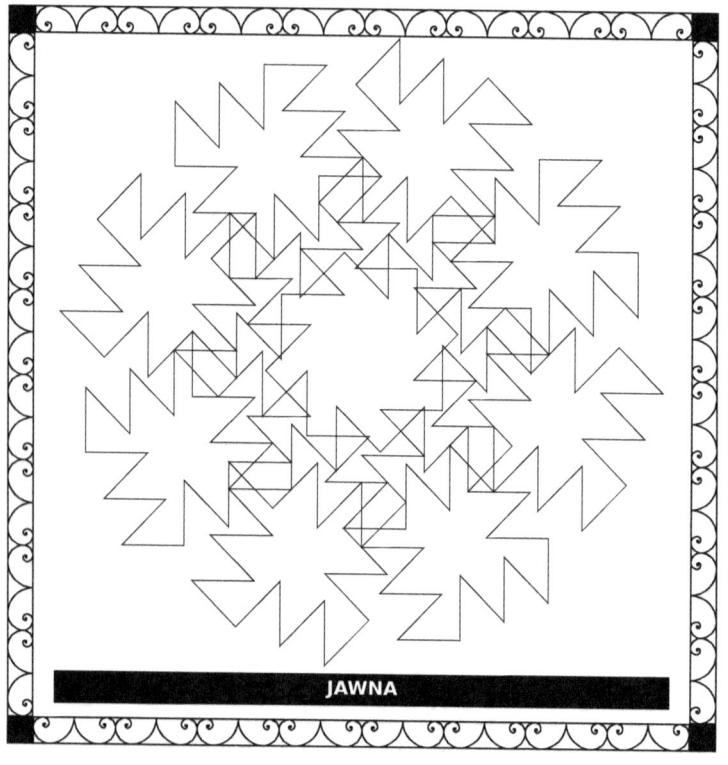

JAWNA

The truly radical work of art is the one that offers you something to hold on to in the midst of the flux of possibility.

Robert Hughes

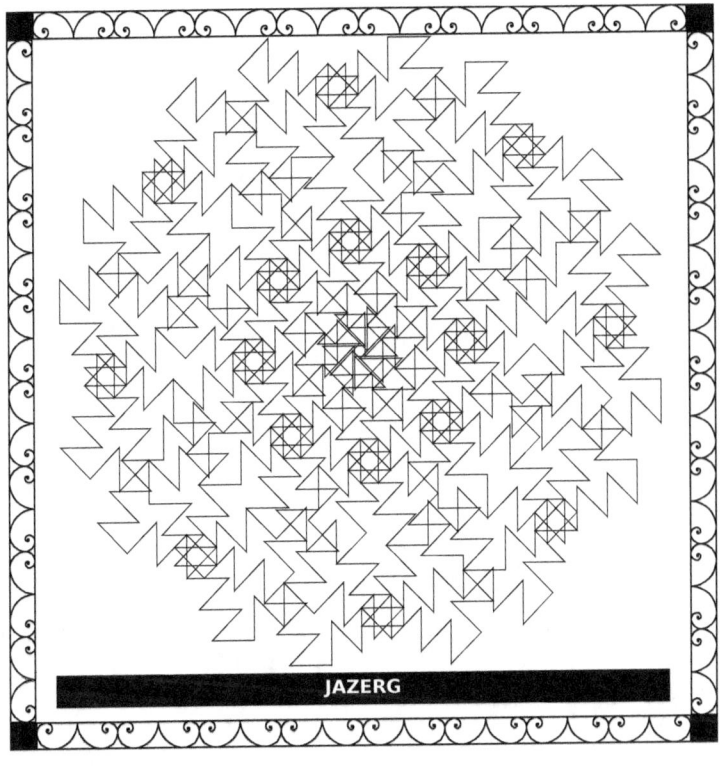

JAZERG

Every production of an artist should be the expression of an adventure of his soul.
W. Somerset Maugham

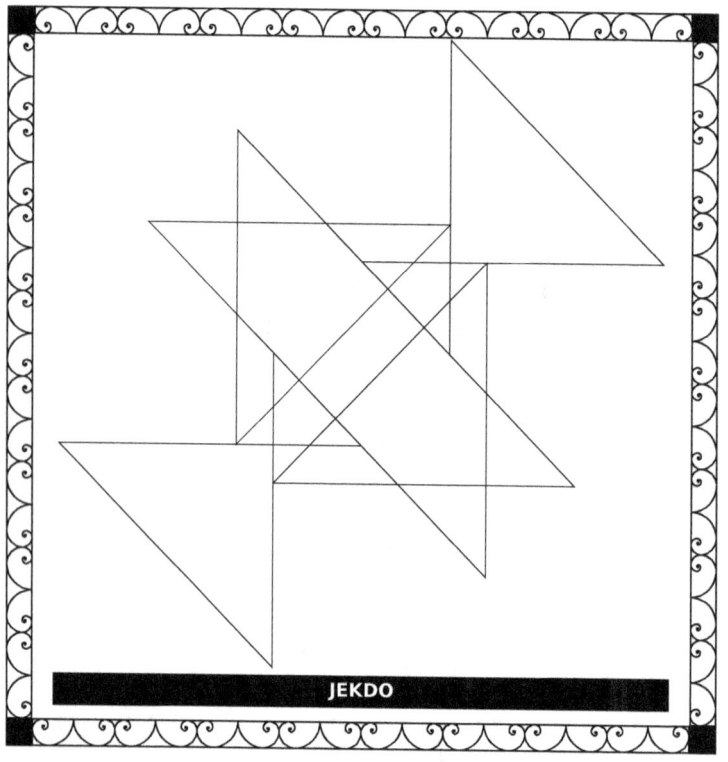

JEKDO

This spending of the best part of one's life earning money in order to enjoy a questionable liberty during the least valuable part of it reminds me of the Englishman who went to India to make a fortune first, in order that he might return to England and live the life of a poet.
Henry David Thoreau

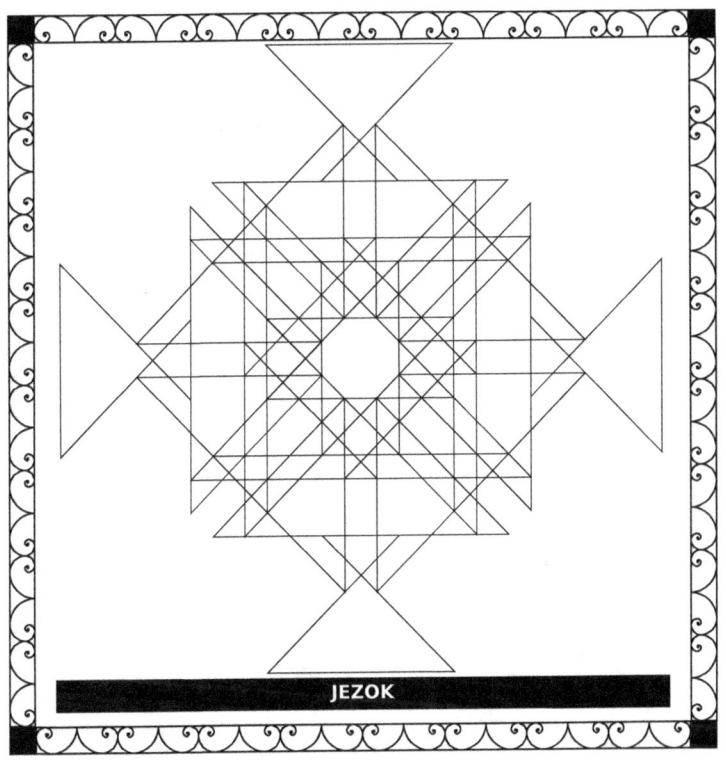

JEZOK

That adage about genius being 5 percent inspiration and
95 perspiration — it's true.
Yanni

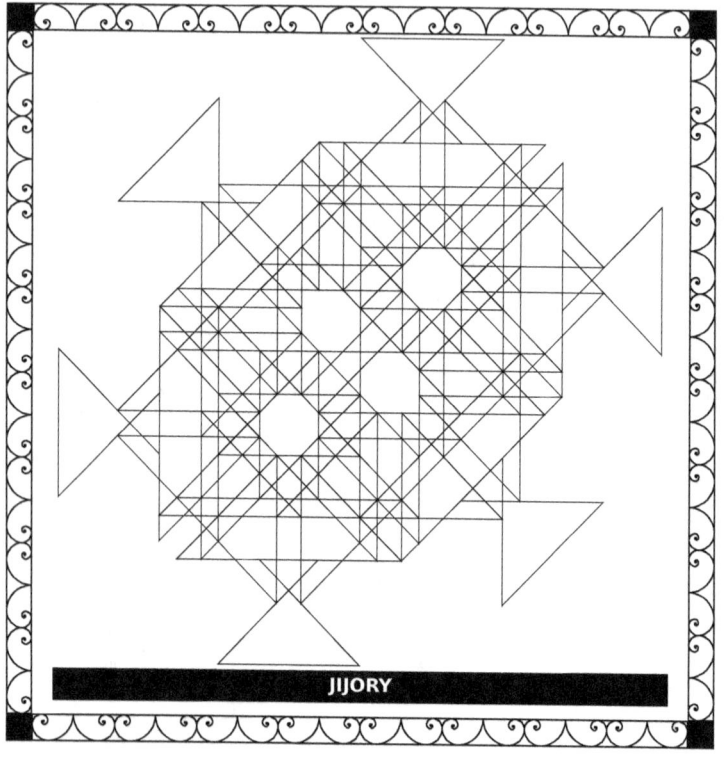

JIJORY

You must forget all your theories, all your ideas before the subject. What part of these is really your own will be expressed in your expression of the emotion awakened in you by the subject.

Henri Matisse

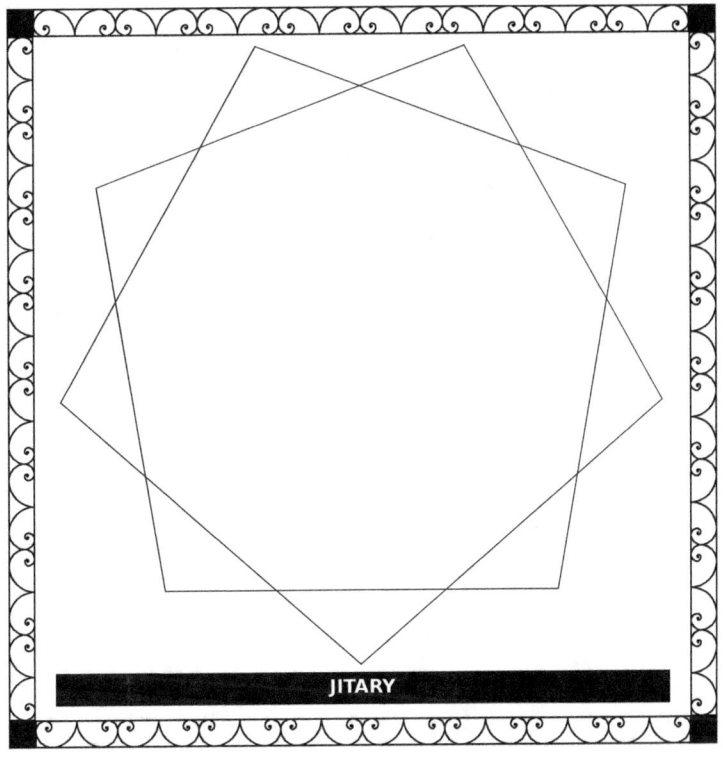

JITARY

Everybody needs beauty as well as bread, places to play in and pray in, where Nature may heal and cheer and give strength to body and soul alike.
John Muir

103

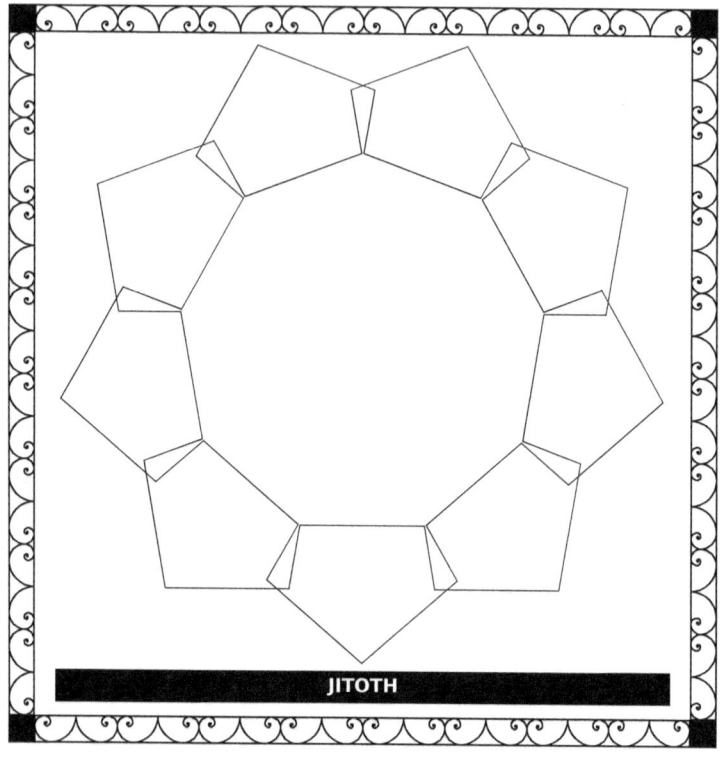

JITOTH

You study, you learn, but you guard the original naivete. It has to be within you, as desire for drink is within the drunkard or love is within the lover.
Henri Matisse

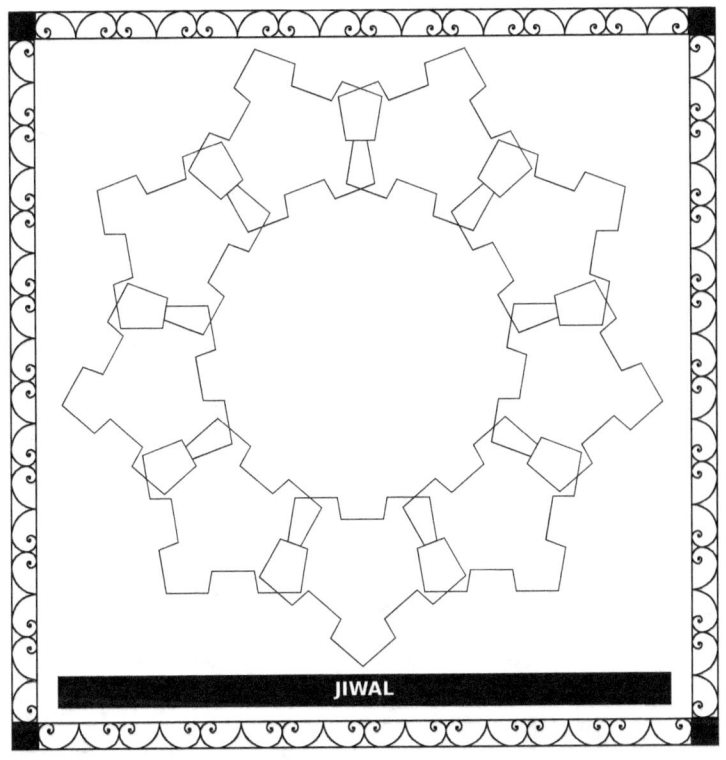

JIWAL

Only the impossible is worth the effort.

Jeanette Winterson

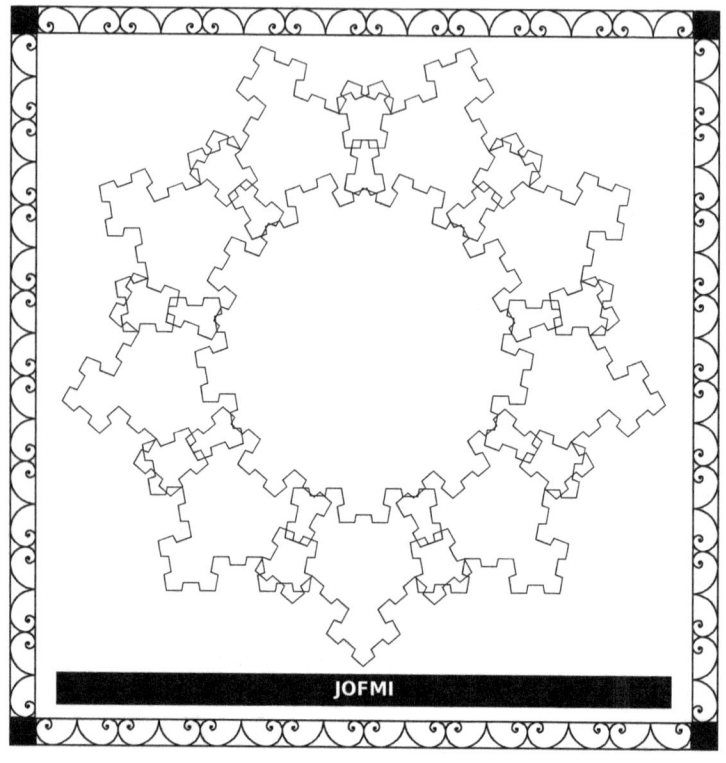

JOFMI

The condition every art requires is, not so much freedom from restriction, as freedom from adulteration and from the intrusion of foreign matter.
Willa Cather

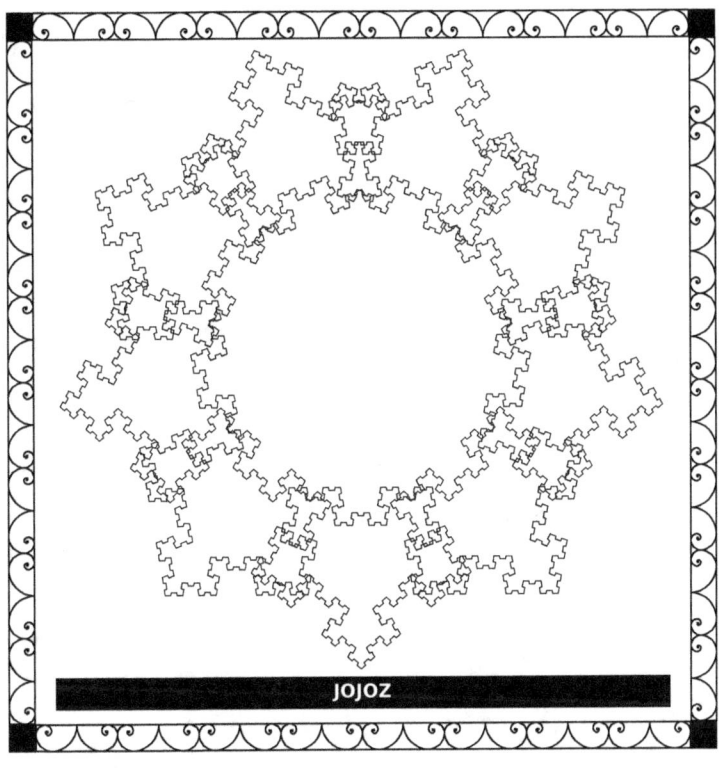

JOJOZ

One does not discover new lands without consenting to lose sight of the shore for a very long time.
Christopher Columbus

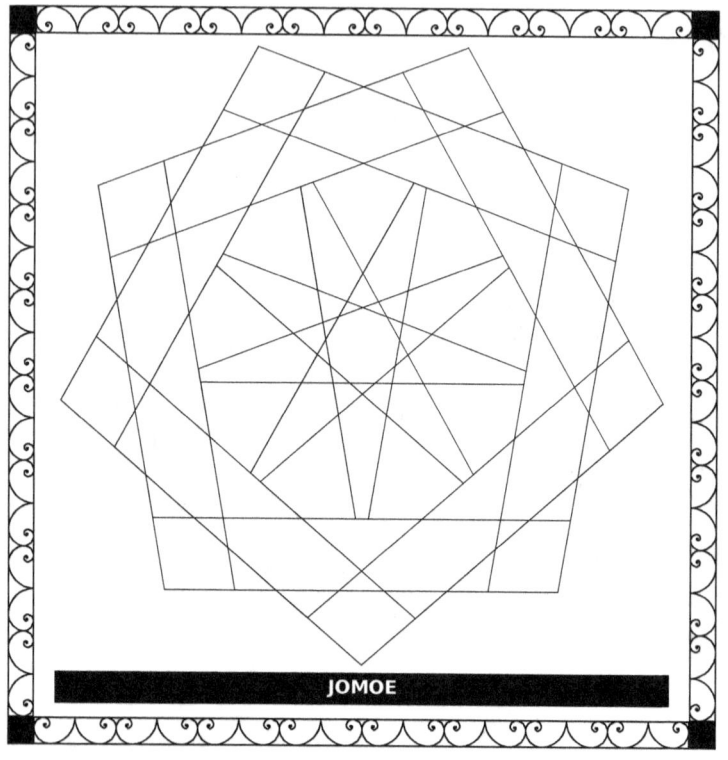

JOMOE

I have nothing to say and I am saying it and that is poetry.
John Cage

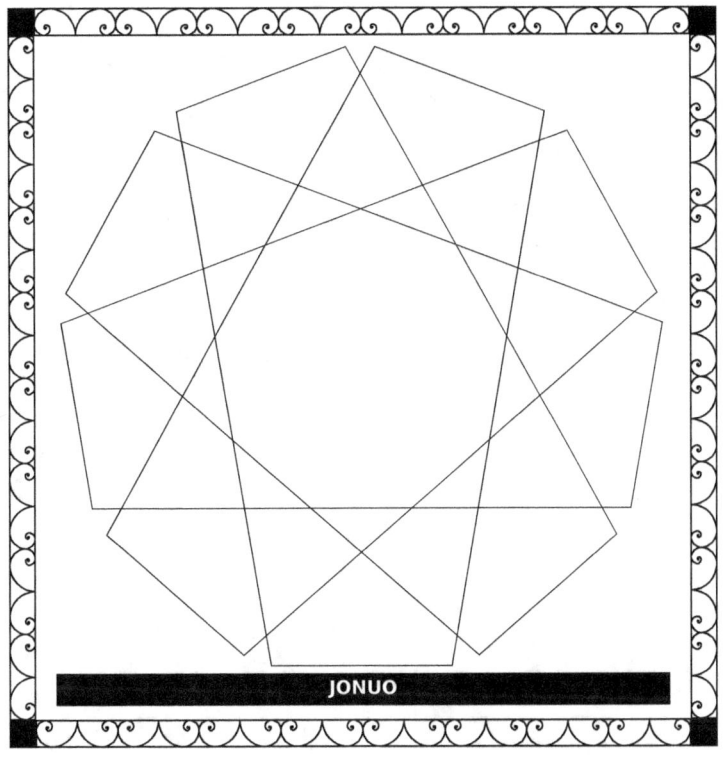

JONUO

Some new works of art have values of some kind or another. Others, the majority, have little or none. But newness as such, in art, is never a value.
Robert Hughes

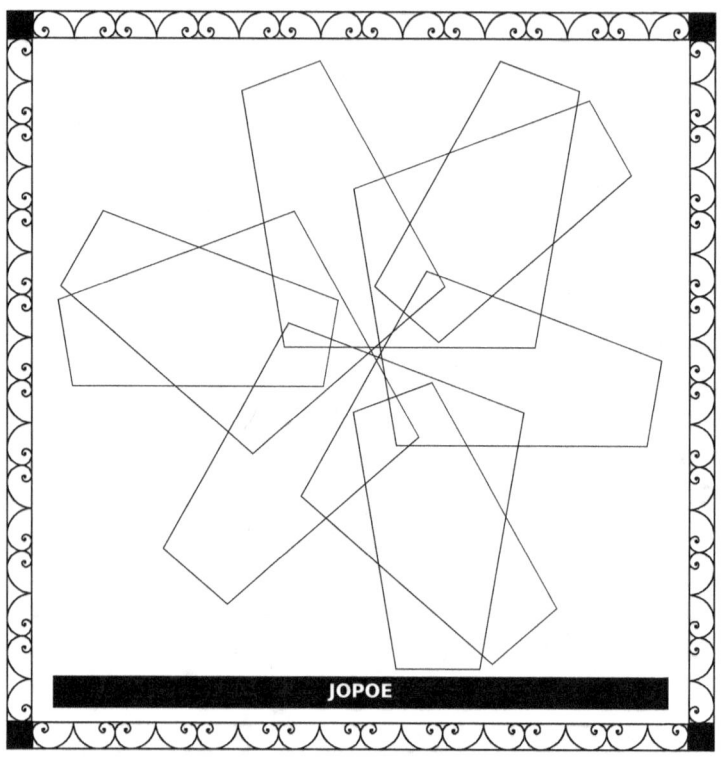

JOPOE

...it will refuse to bloom if I treat it simply as a routine exercise, instead of feeling it as an adventure.
Philippe Petit, Creativity: The Perfect Crime

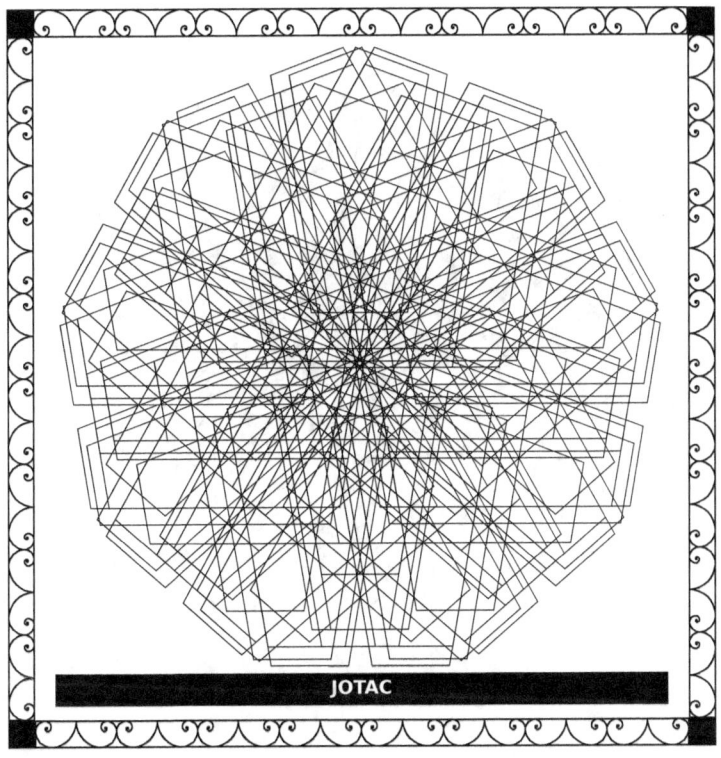

JOTAC

I think it's a responsibility for any artist to protect freedom of expression and to use any way to extend this power.
Ai Weiwei

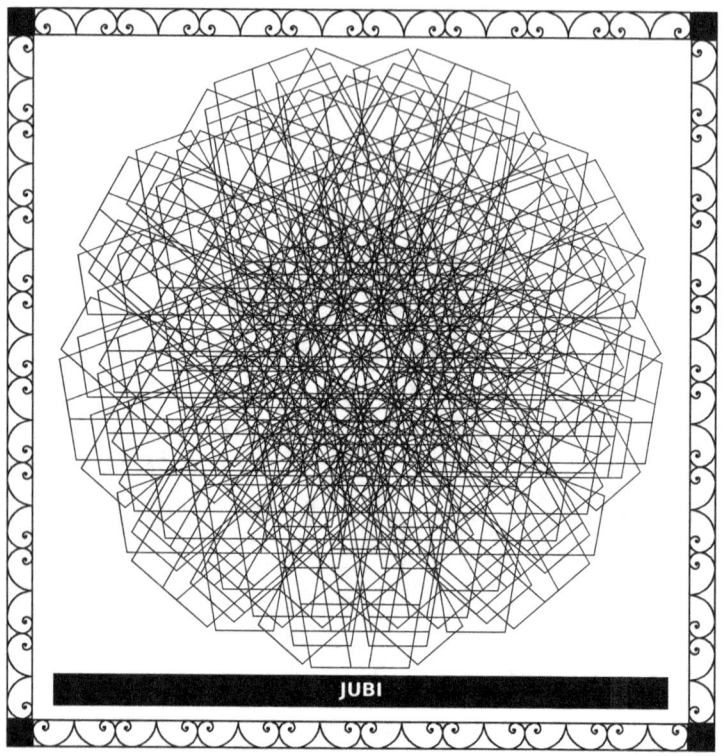

JUBI

Life is a creative endeavor. It is active, not passive. We are the yeast that leavens our lives into rich, fully baked loaves. When we experience our lives as flat and lackluster, it is our consciousness that is at fault. We hold the inner key that turns our lives from thankless to fruitful. That key is Blessing.

Julia Cameron

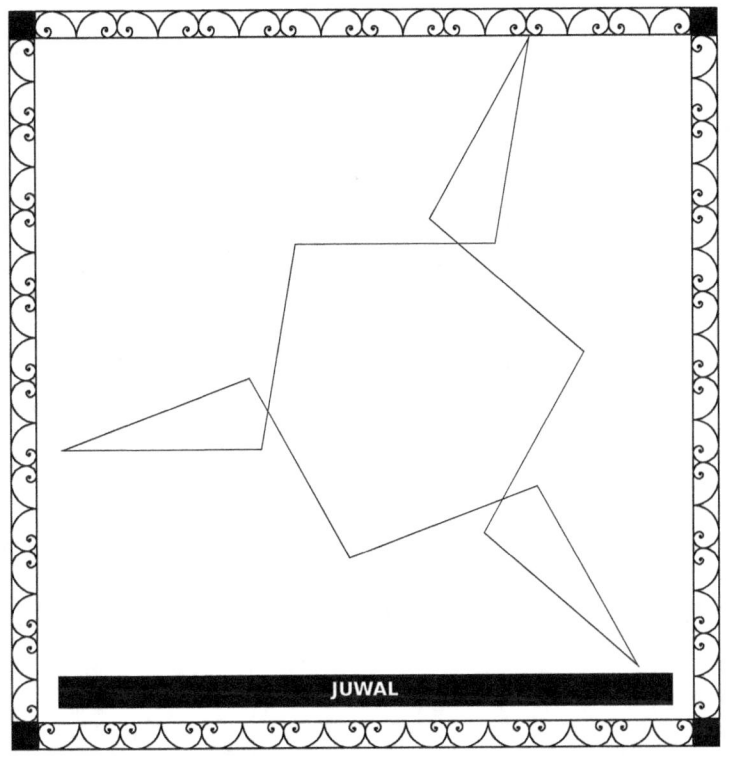

JUWAL

Life imitates art far more than art imitates life.
Oscar Wilde

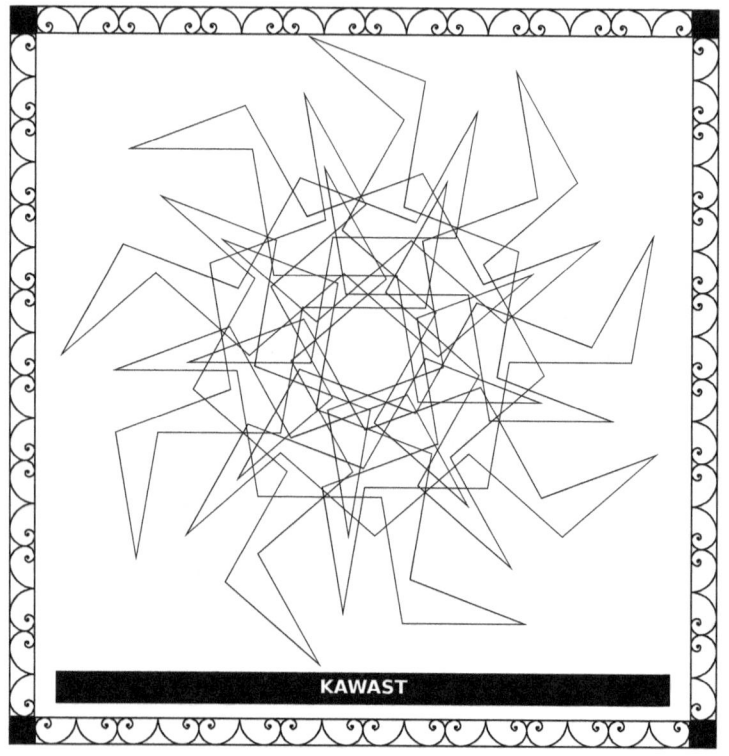

KAWAST

When a man becomes a writer, I think he takes on a sacred obligation to produce beauty and enlightenment and comfort at top speed.
Kurt Vonnegut

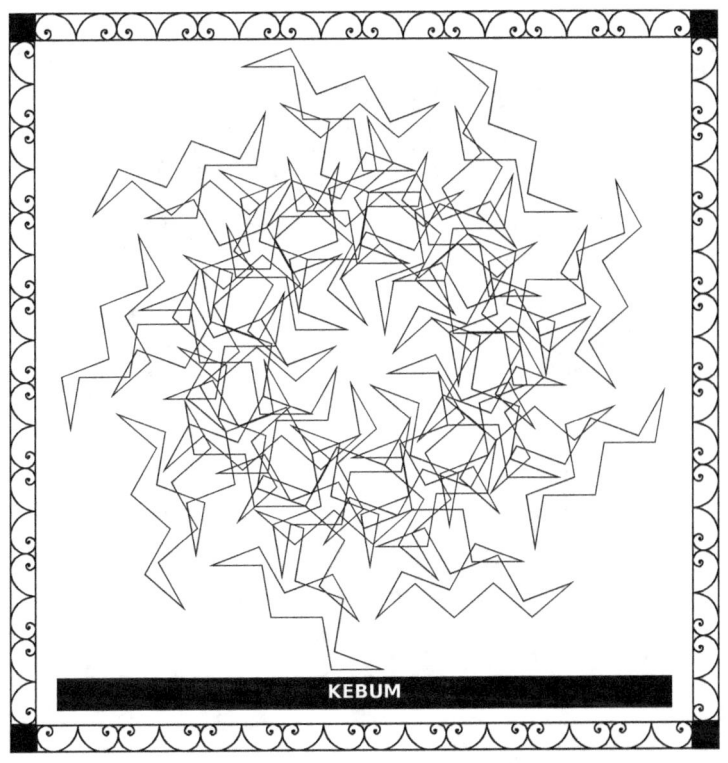

KEBUM

The artist is lonesome and admits his solitude.
Elfriede Jelinek

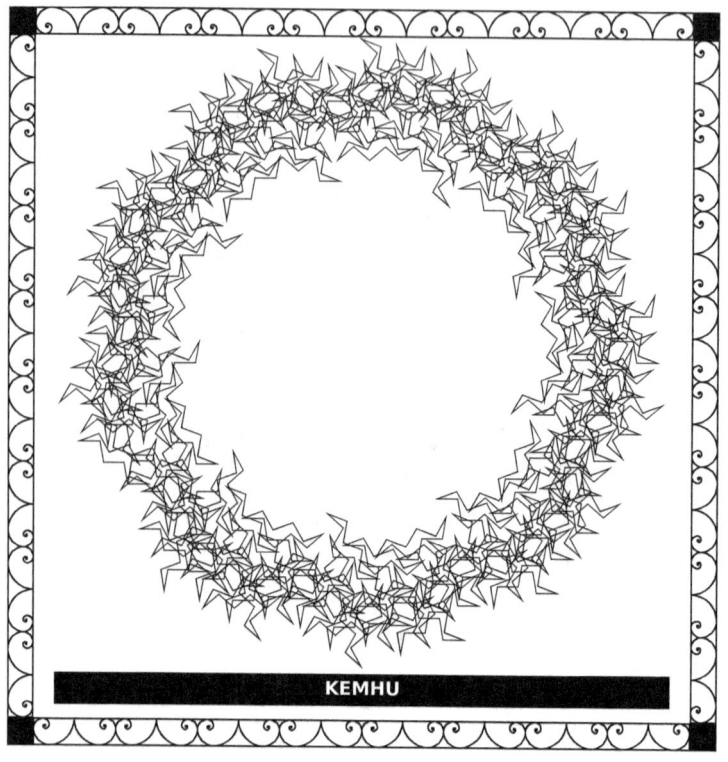

KEMHU

Film will only become an art when its materials are as inexpensive as pencil and paper.
Jean Cocteau

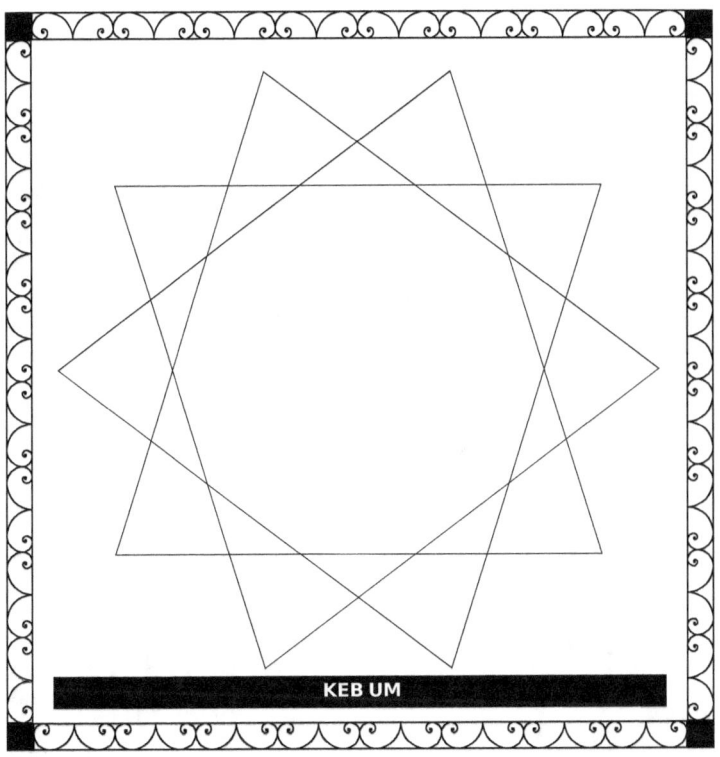

KEB UM

Ever since the Greeks, we have been drunk with language!
We have made a cage with words and shoved our God inside!

Morris West

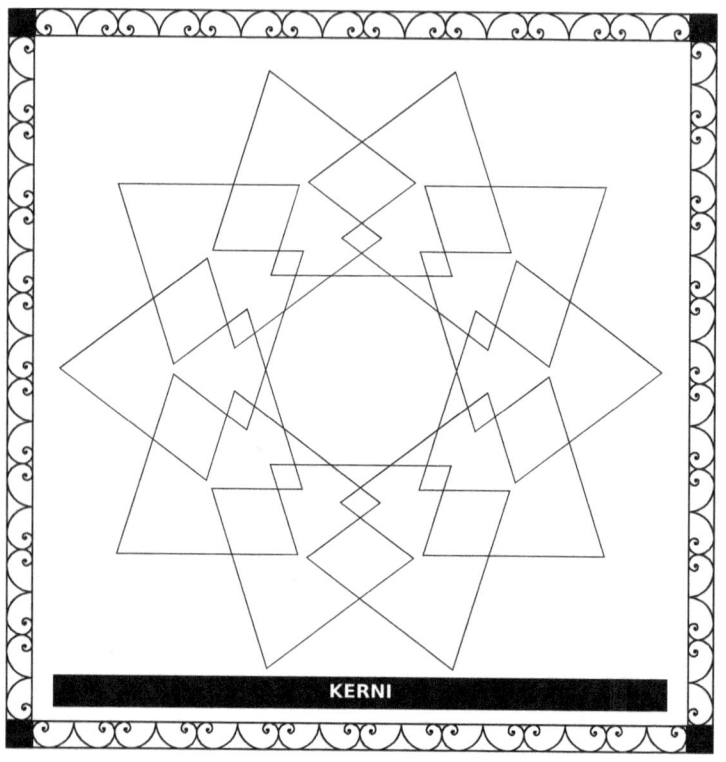

KERNI

The culture of a civilization is the art and literature through which it rises to consciousness of itself and defines its vision of the world.
Roger Scruton

118

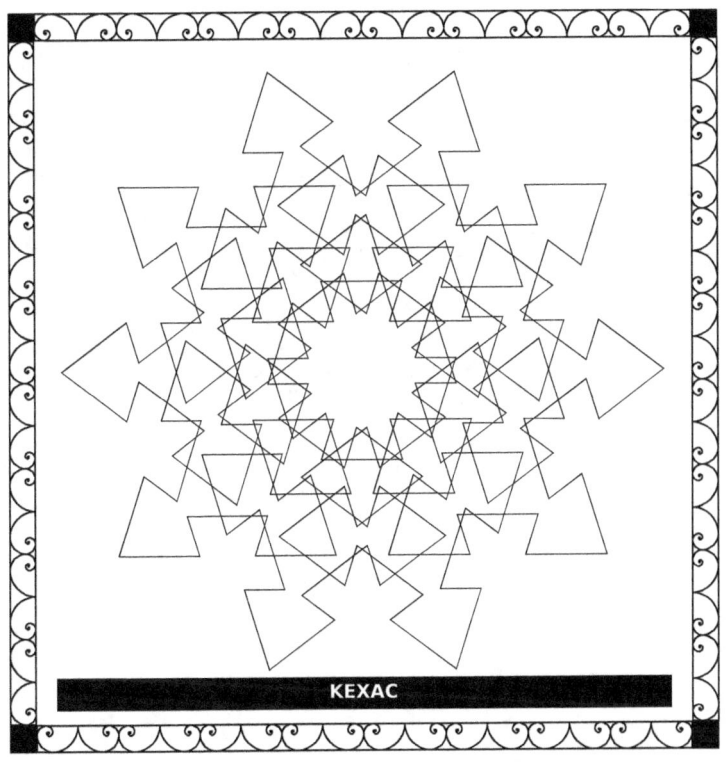

KEXAC

We consider the artist a special sort of person. It is more likely that each of us is a special sort of artist.
Elsa Gidlow

119

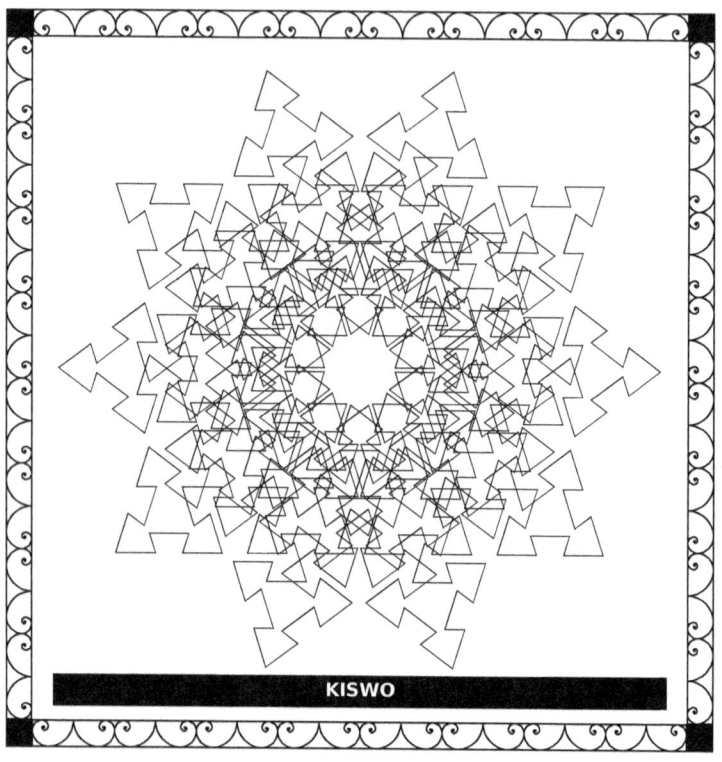

KISWO

The pursuit of beauty is much more dangerous nonsense than the pursuit of truth or goodness, because it affords a stronger temptation to the ego.
Northrop Frye

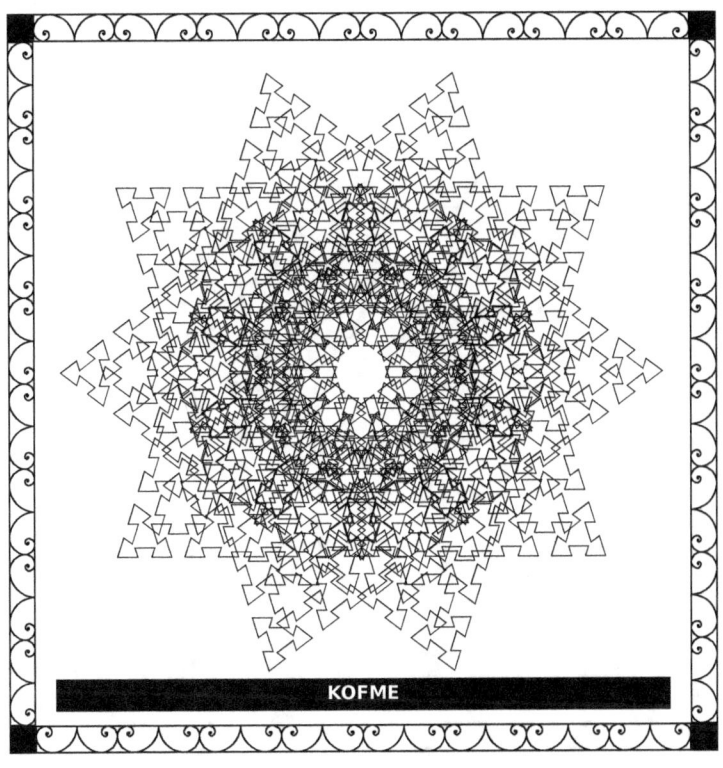

KOFME

In the haunted house of life, art is the only stair that doesn't creak.
Tom Robbins

121

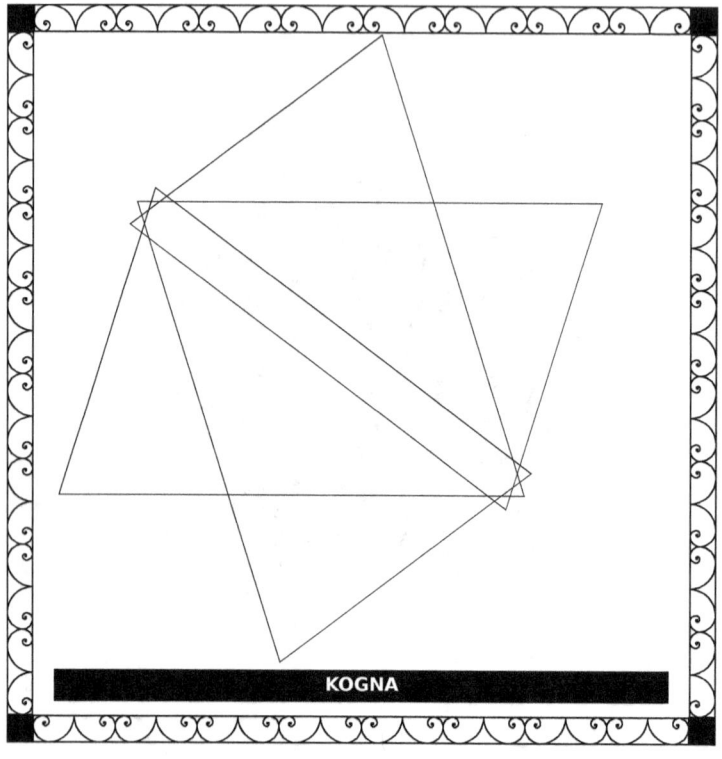

KOGNA

True art is by its nature moral. We recognize true art by its careful, thoroughly honest search for and analysis of values.

John Gardner

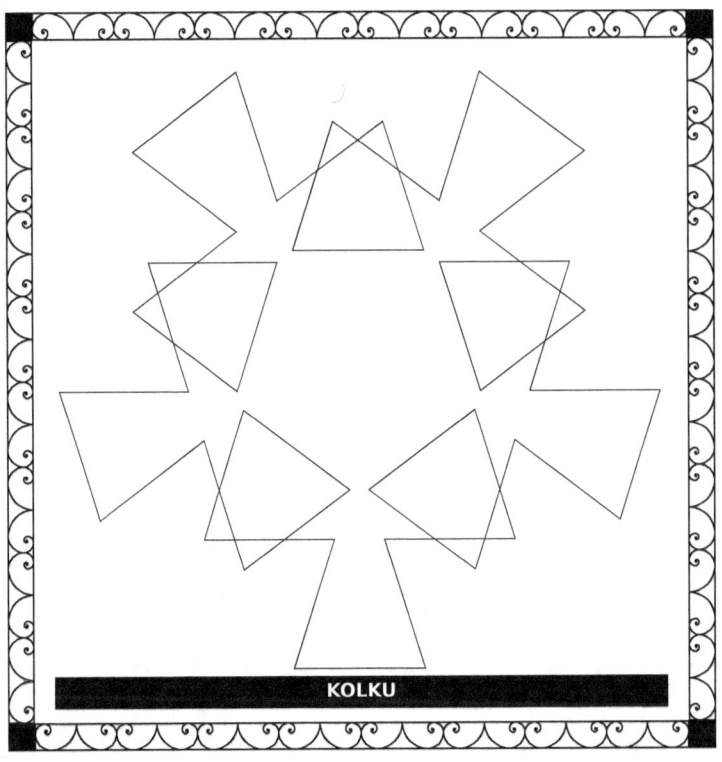

KOLKU

No doubt the artist is the child of his time; but woe to him if he is also its disciple, or even its favorite.
Friedrich Schiller

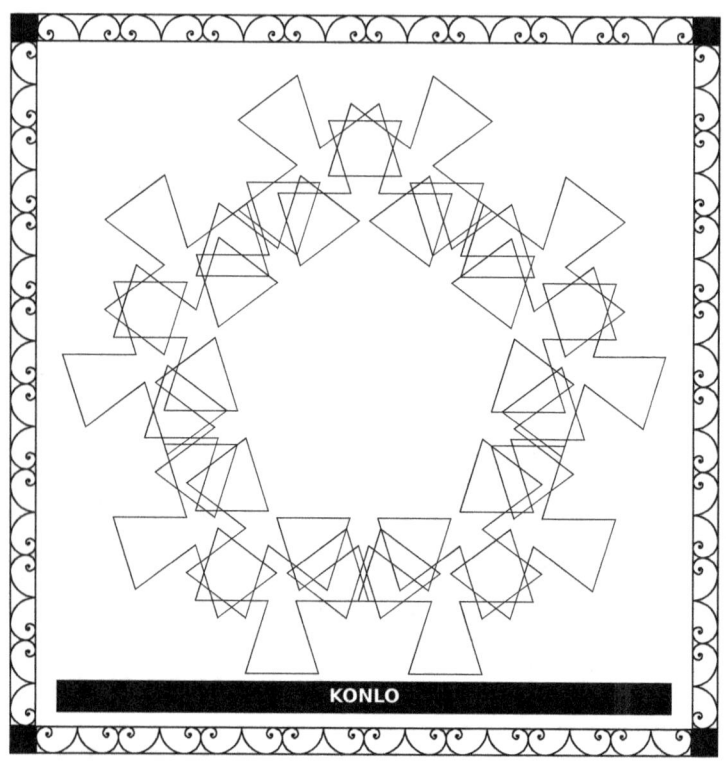

KONLO

The greatest foe to art is luxury, art cannot live in its atmosphere.
William Morris

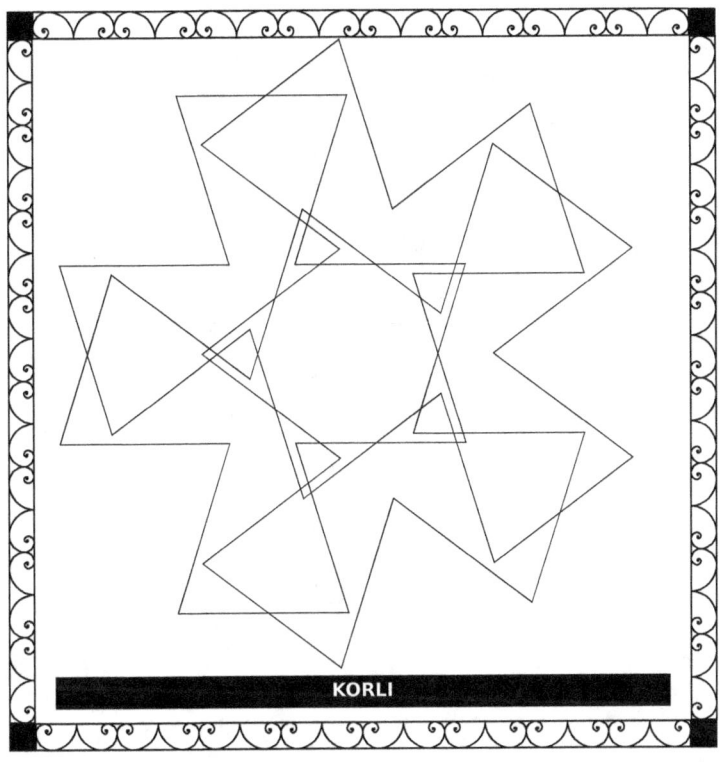

KORLI

We ought to view ourselves with the same curiosity and openness with which we study a tree, the sky or a thought, because we too are linked to the entire universe.

Henri Matisse

125

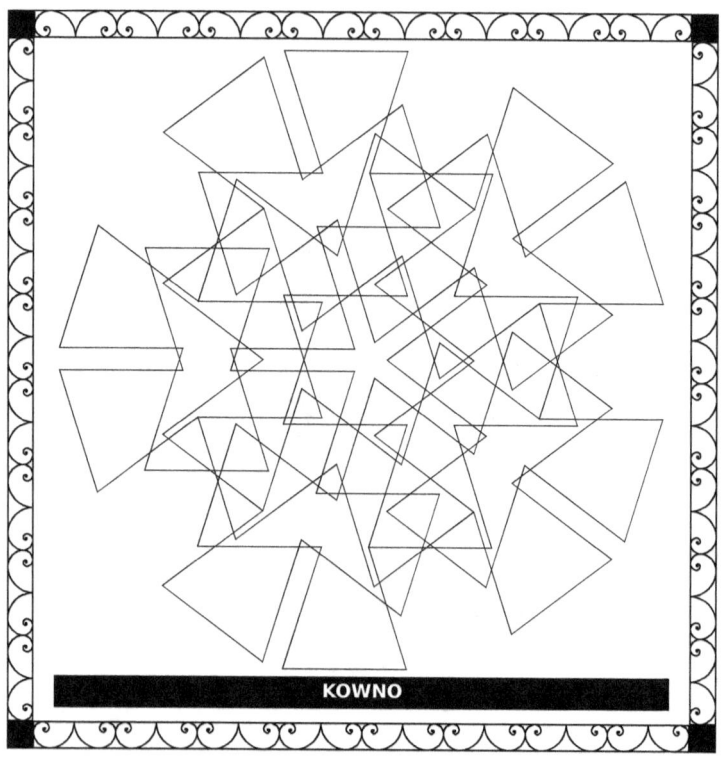

KOWNO

Misery is almost always the result of thinking.
Joseph Joubert

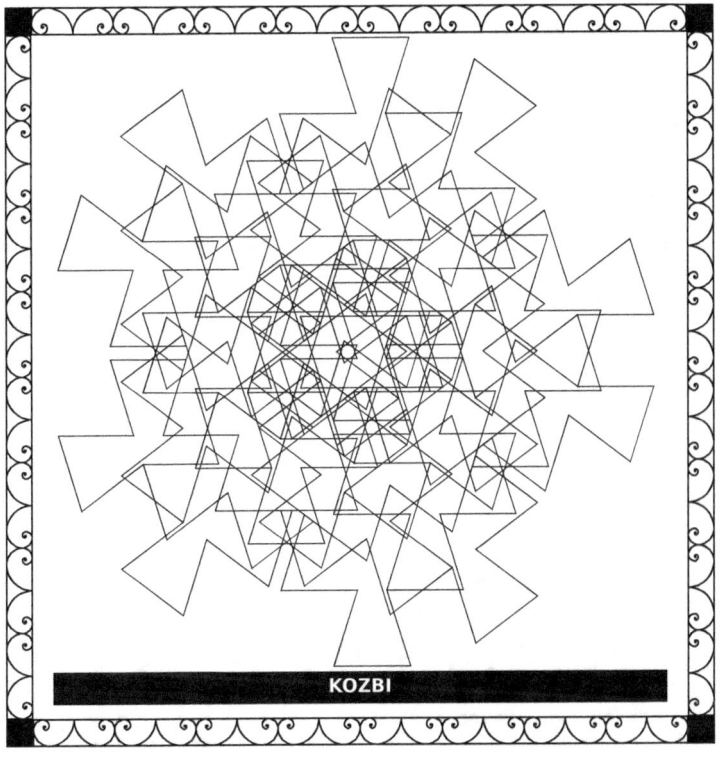

KOZBI

God is not a limited individual who sits alone up in the clouds on a golden throne. God is pure Consciousness that dwells within everything. Understanding this truth, learn to accept and love everyone equally.

Mata Amritanandamayi

127

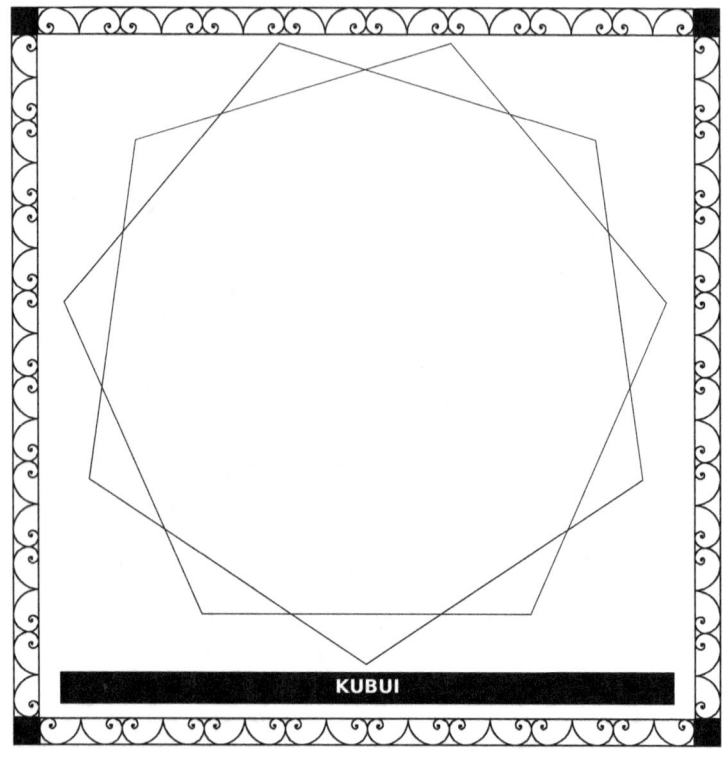

KUBUI

A painting is finished when the artist says it is finished.
Rembrandt

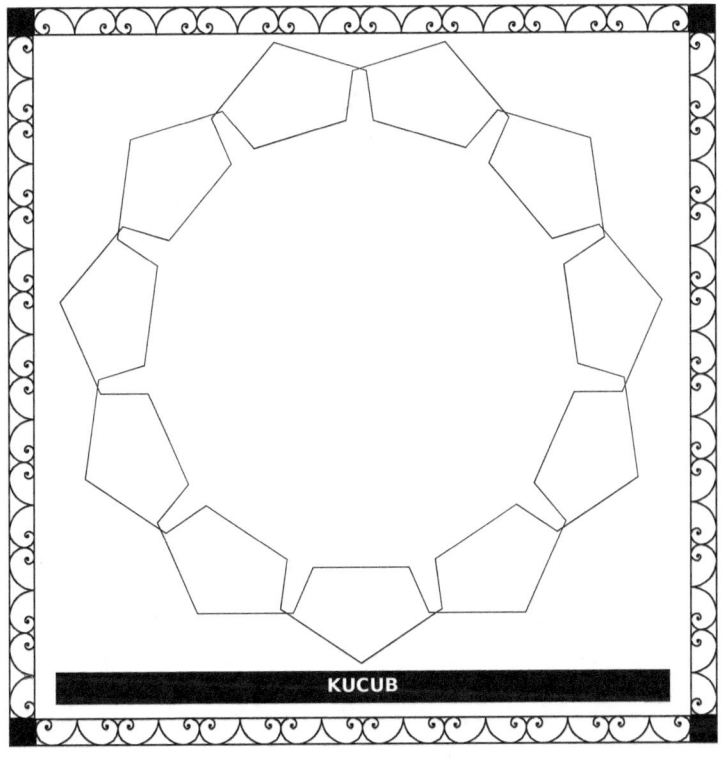

KUCUB

The primary distinction of the artist is that he must actively cultivate that state which most men, necessarily, must avoid: the state of being alone.

James Baldwin

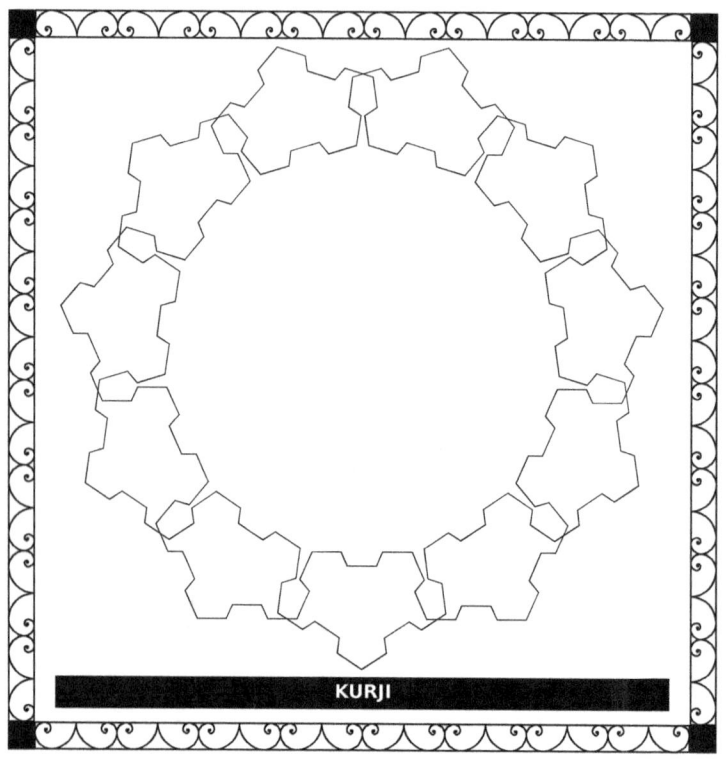

KURJI

The wealthy are always surrounded by hangers-on; science and art are as well.
Anton Chekhov

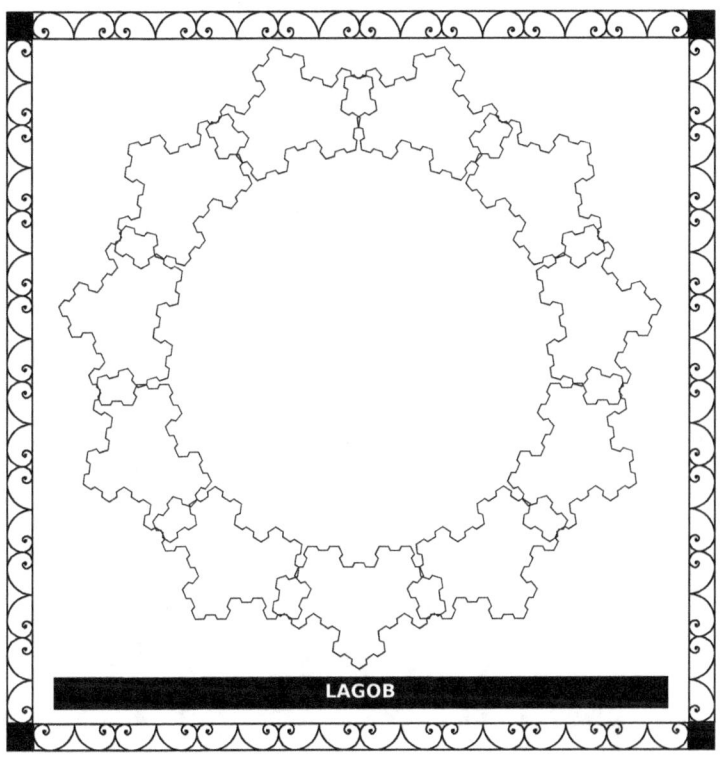

LAGOB

Being an artist means seeing things and never having the
ability to shut your eyes.
Keariene Muizz

131

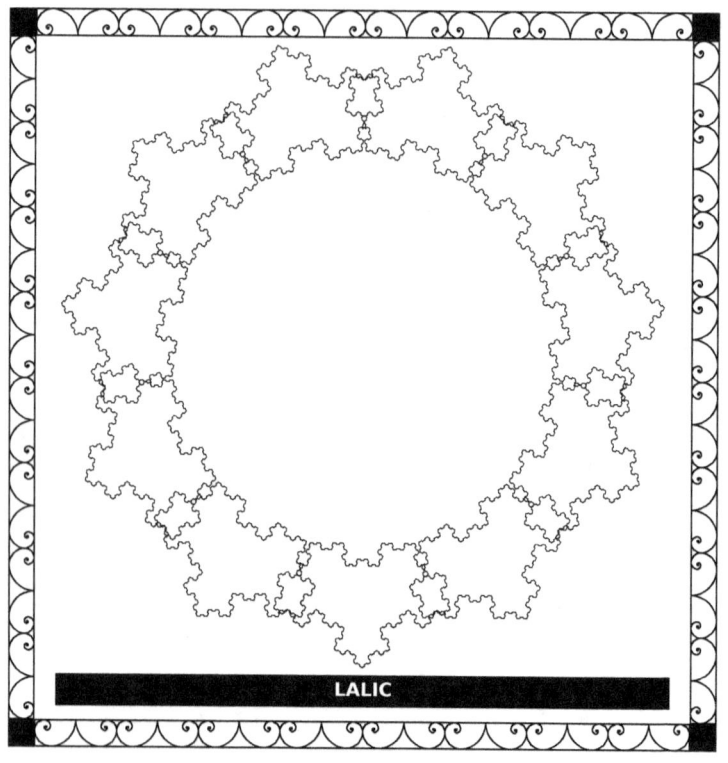

LALIC

One of the most striking signs of the decay of art is the intermixing of different genres.
Johann Wolfgang von Goethe

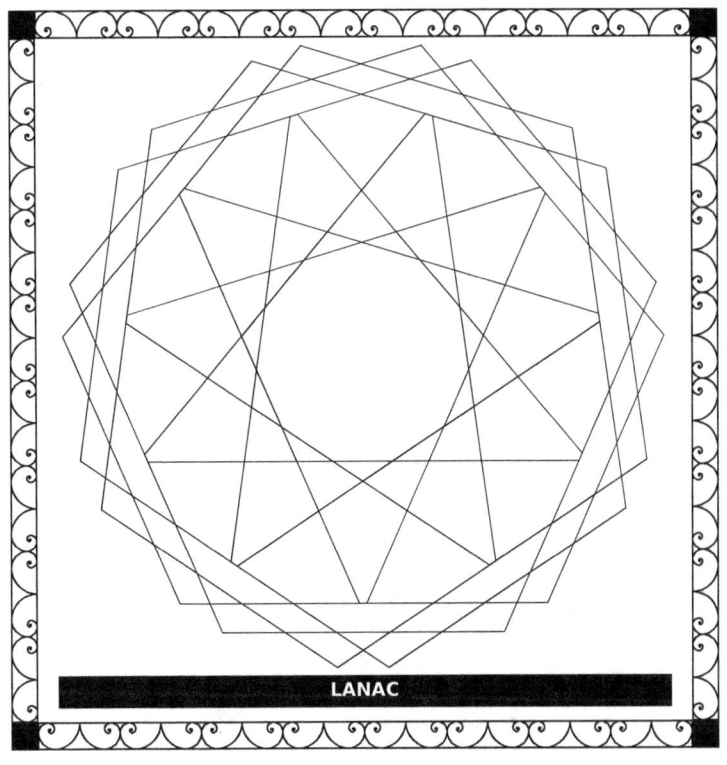

LANAC

Injure a businessman and he'll try to make you sorry; injure
an artist and he'll try to make you immortal.
Mignon McLaughlin

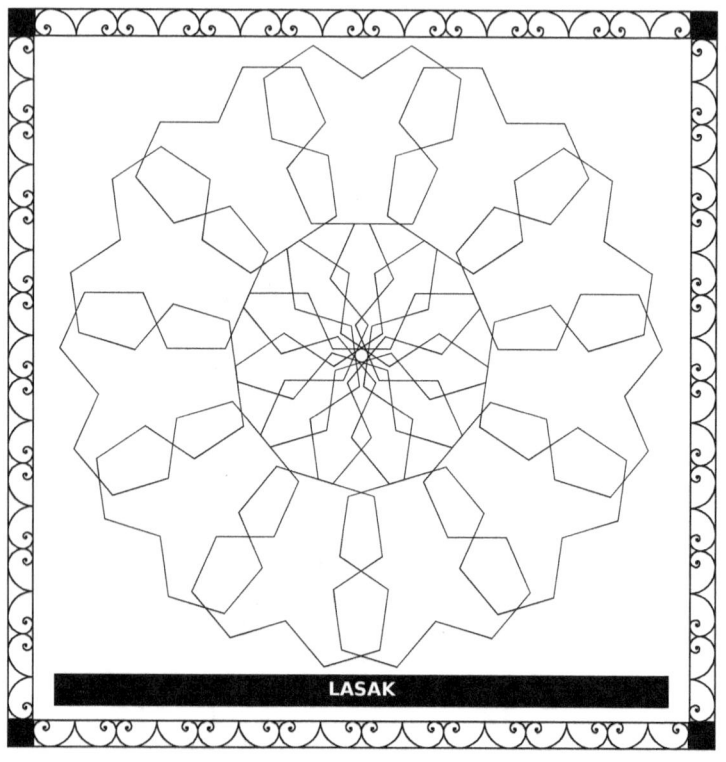

LASAK

Every artist is a cannibal, every poet is a thief. All kill for
inspiration and sing about their grief.
Bono

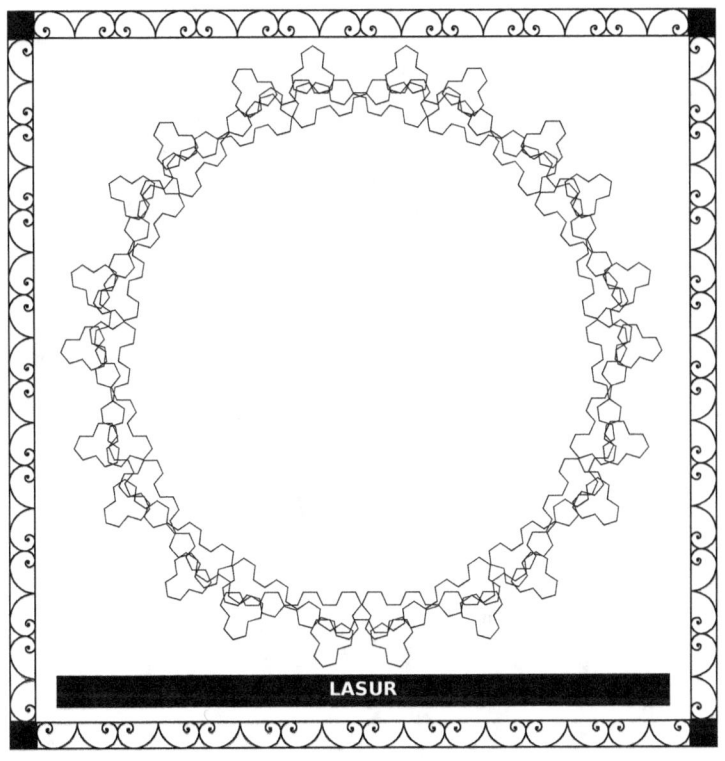

LASUR

A community's art is its spiritual vision.
Northrop Frye

135

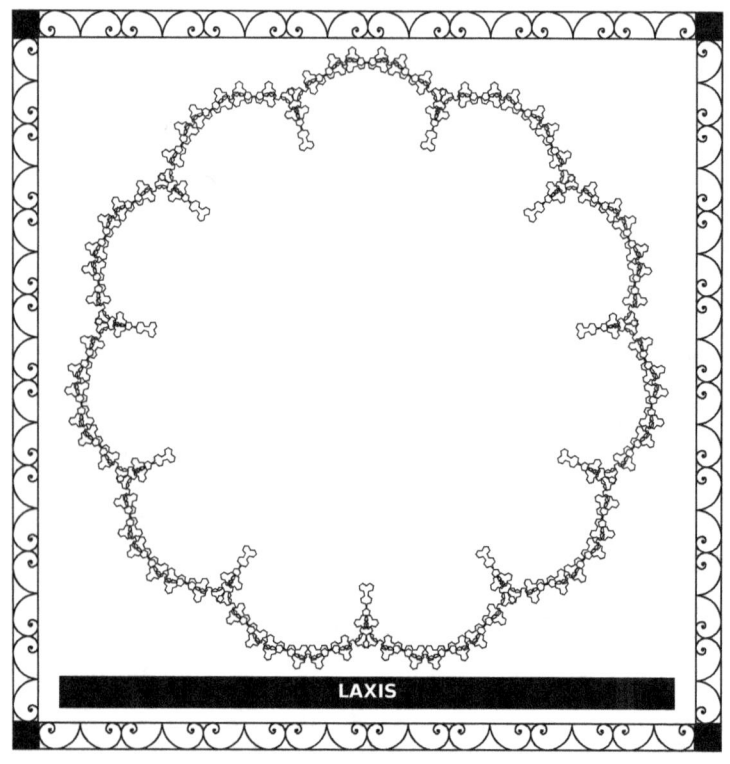

LAXIS

You are not what you were born, but what you have it in
yourself to be.
William Monahan, Kingdom of Heaven

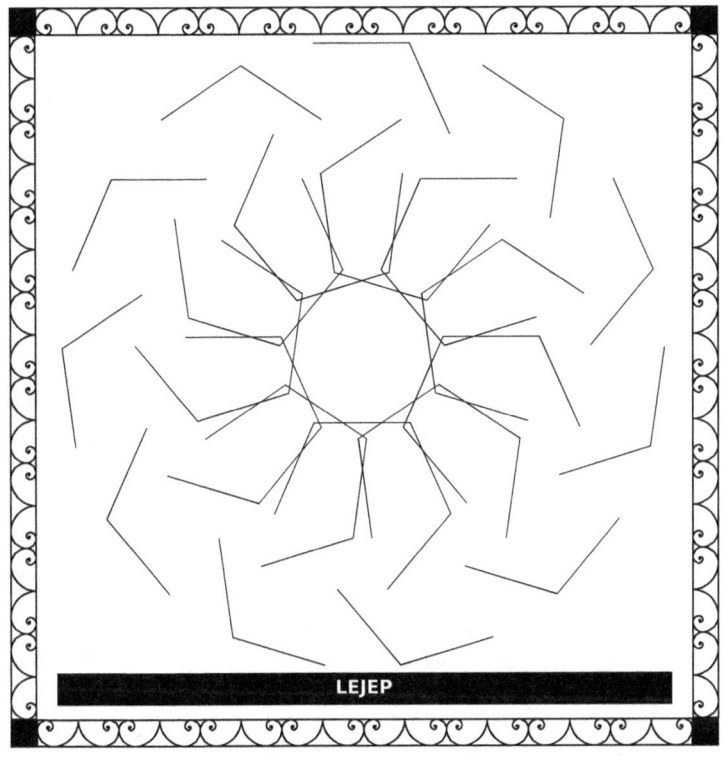

LEJEP

I can choose either to be a victim of the world or an adventurer in search of treasure. It's all a question of how I view my life.
Paulo Coelho

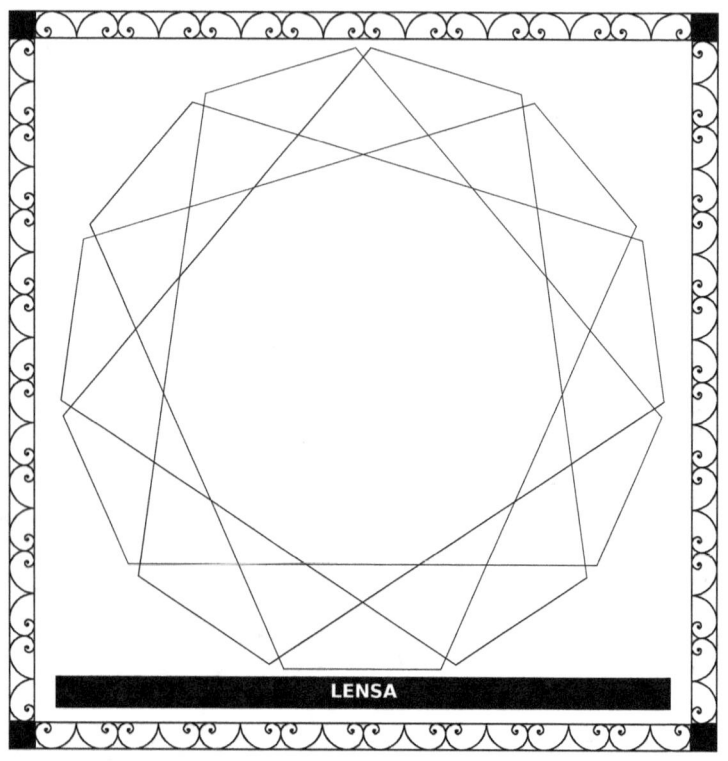

LENSA

Art is for all — and the greatest art proves it.
William Soutar

138

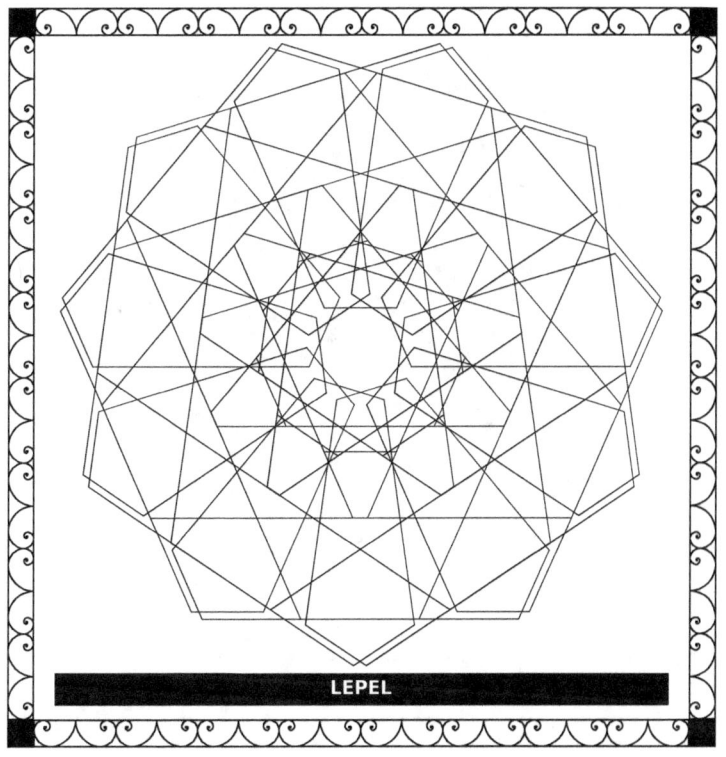

LEPEL

For us of the minority, the opportunity to see geese is more important than television, and the chance to find a pasque-flower is a right as inalienable as free speech.
Aldo Leopold

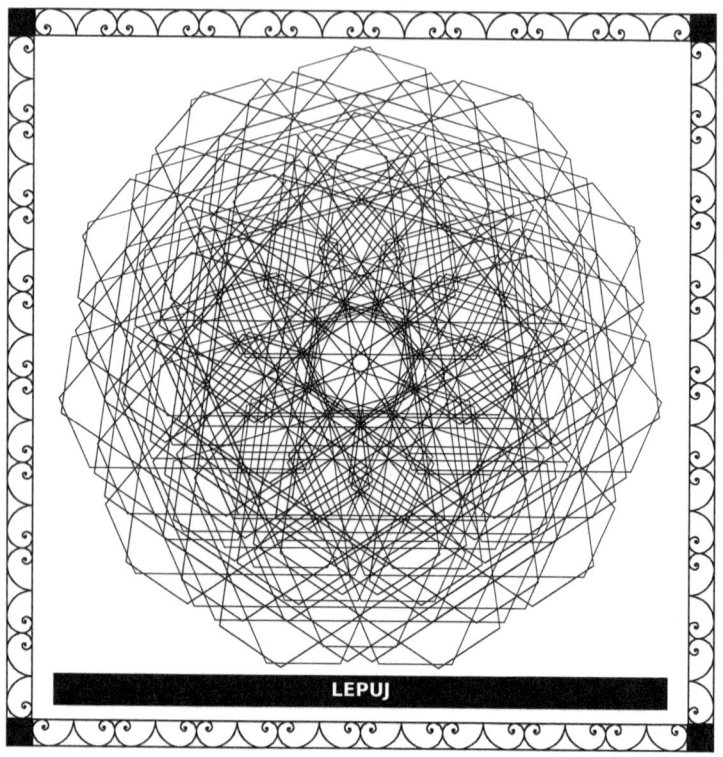

LEPUJ

Gratitude enhances your ability to see beauty. It's like seeing beauty in HD.
Steve Maraboli

140

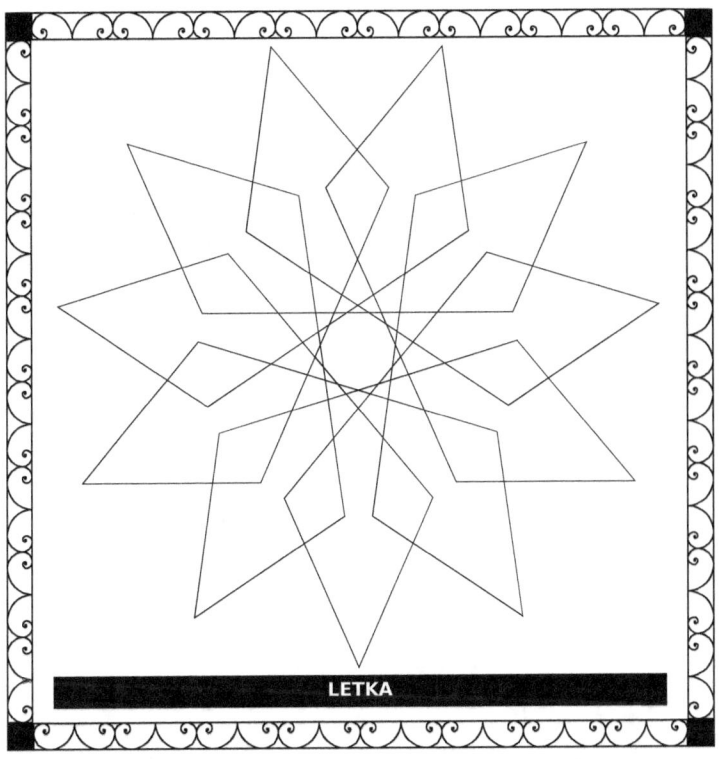

LETKA

There is poetry as soon as we realize that we possess nothing.
John Cage

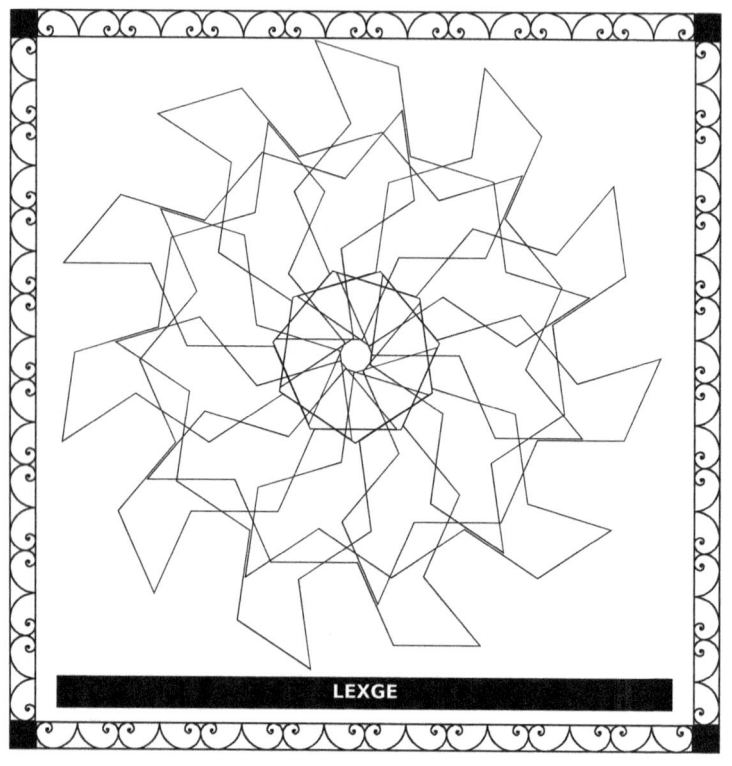

LEXGE

If I were not Alexander, I should wish to be Diogenes.
Alexander the Great to Diogenes

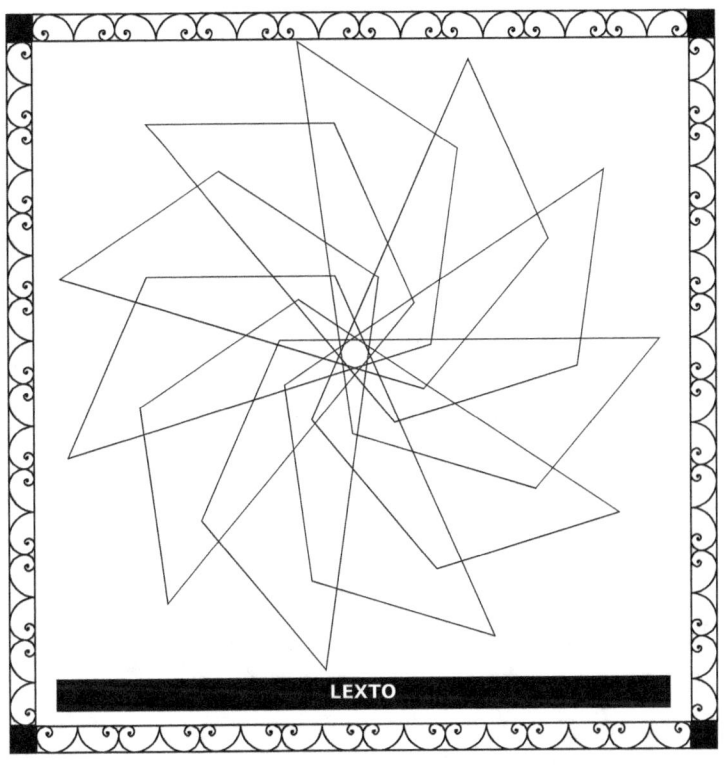

LEXTO

Only believe, only believe. All things are possible, only believe.
Smith Wigglesworth

143

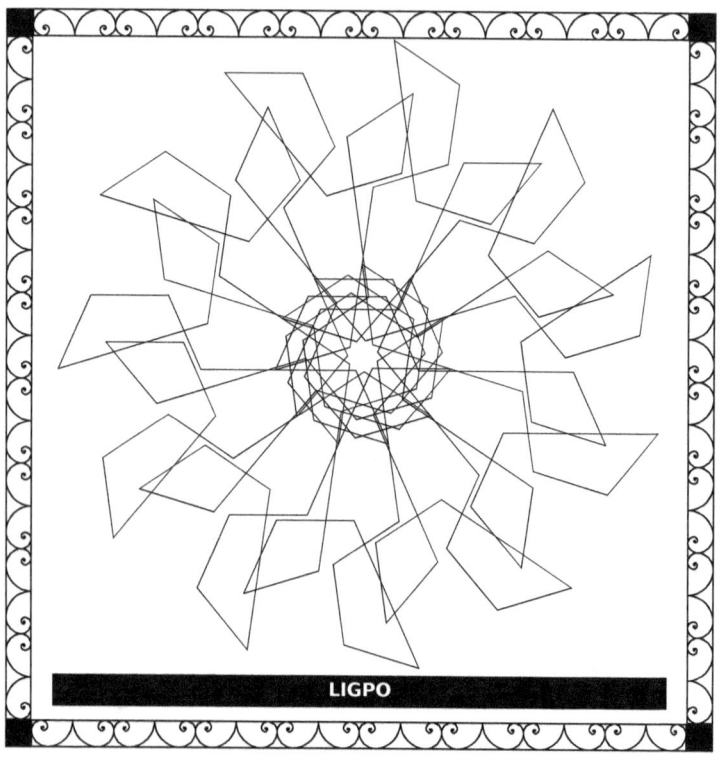

LIGPO

The beauty of a move lies not in its appearance but in the thought behind it.

Aron Nimzowitsch

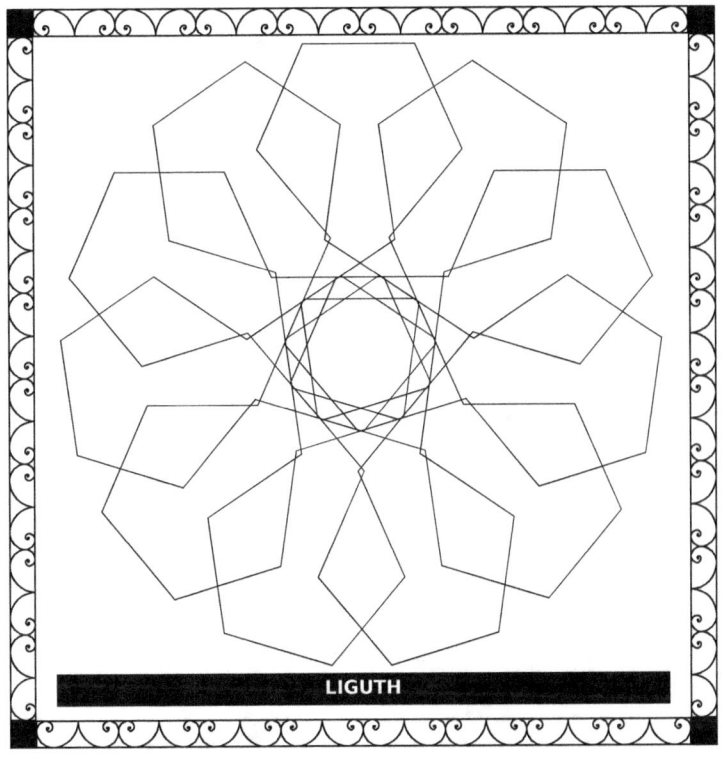

LIGUTH

The tragedy of human history is decreasing happiness in the midst of increasing comforts.
Chinmayananda Saraswati

145

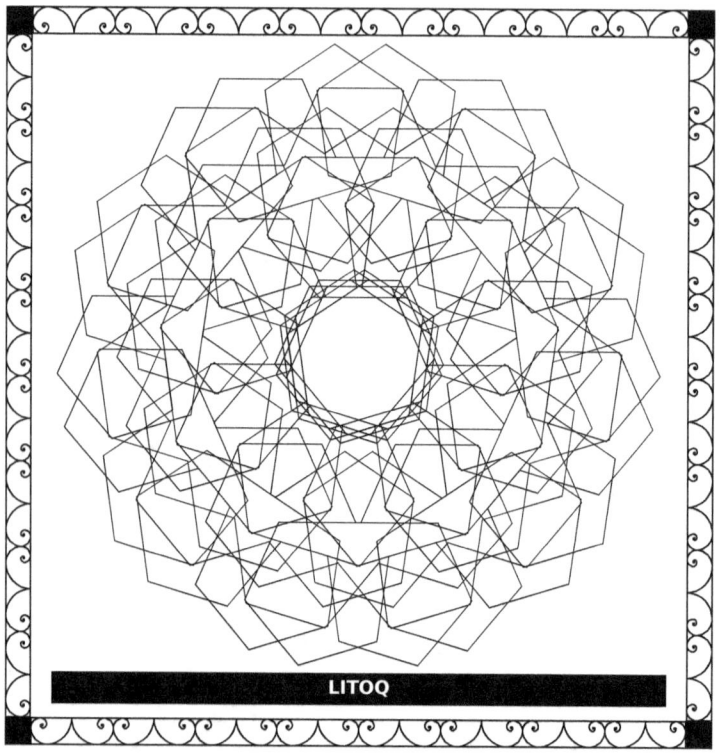

LITOQ

All too willingly man sees himself as the centre of the universe, as something not belonging to the rest of nature but standing apart as a different and higher being. Many people cling to this error and remain deaf to the wisest command ever given by a sage, the famous KNOW THYSELF inscribed in the temple of Delphi.

Konrad Lorenz

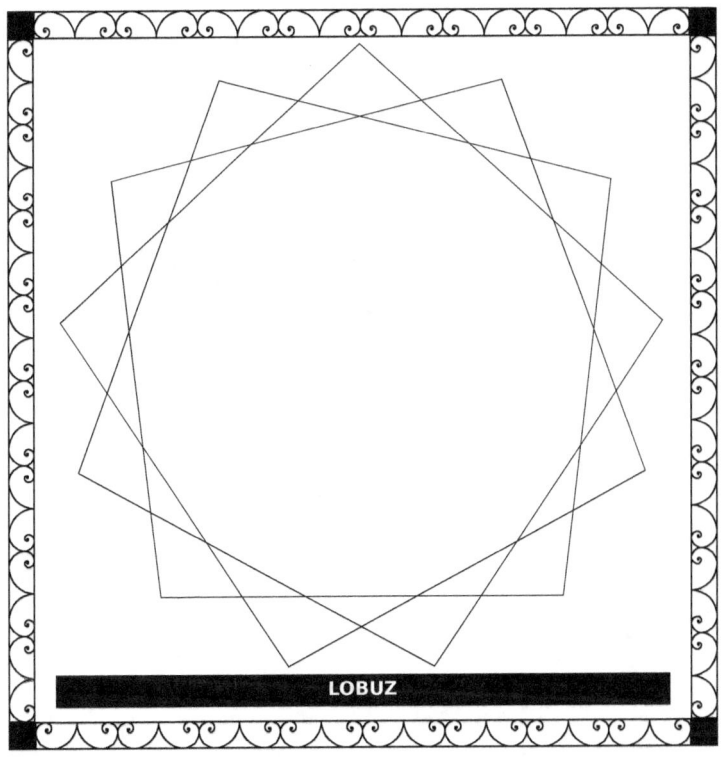

LOBUZ

Every artist makes himself born. It is very much harder than the other time, and longer.
Willa Cather

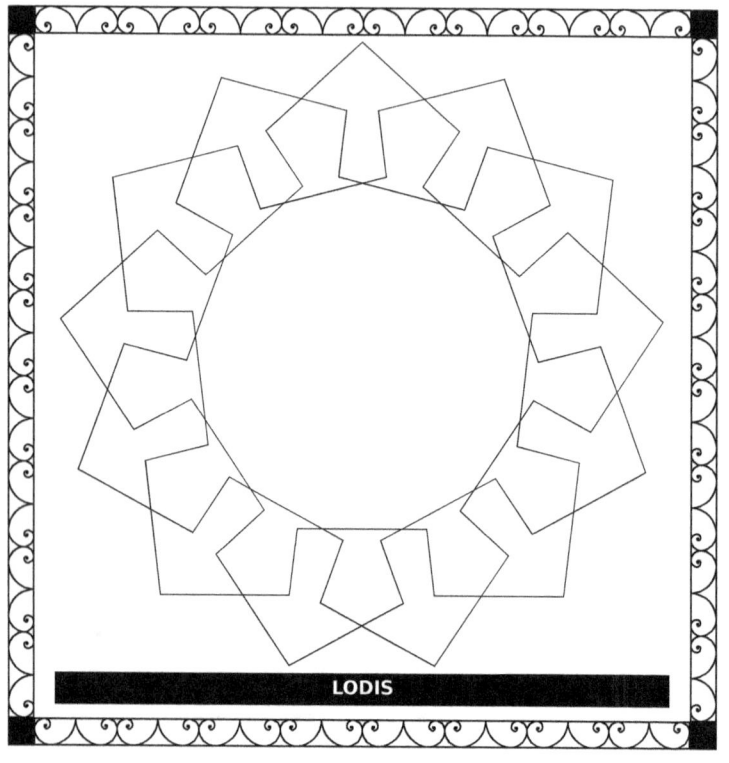

LODIS

My own mystic bent leads me to believe that musical variations, collage, reiteration and process, or evolution, are beautiful. Life is worth living and beauty is worth making.
Beth Anderson

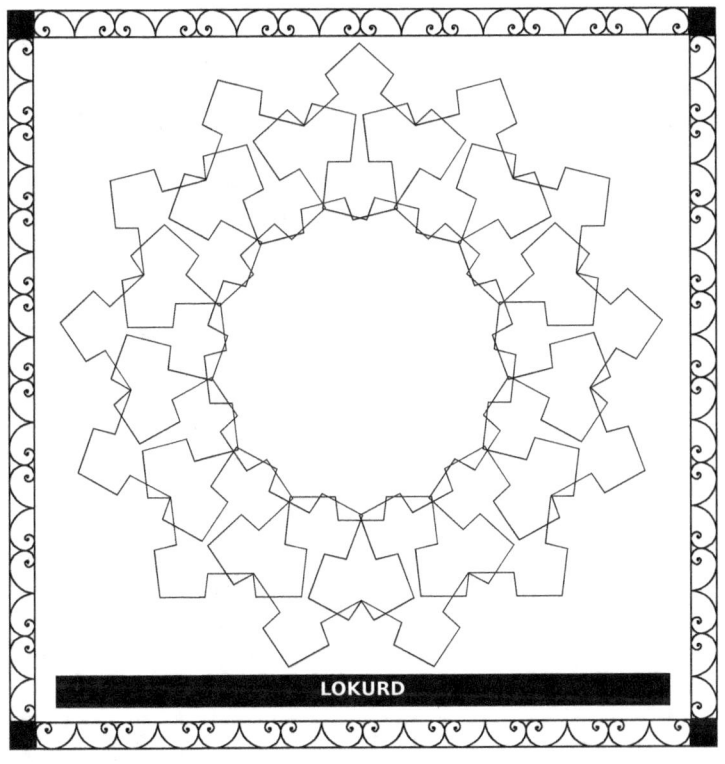

LOKURD

A society that does not recognize that each individual has values of his own which he is entitled to follow can have no respect for the dignity of the individual and cannot really know freedom.

Friedrich Hayek

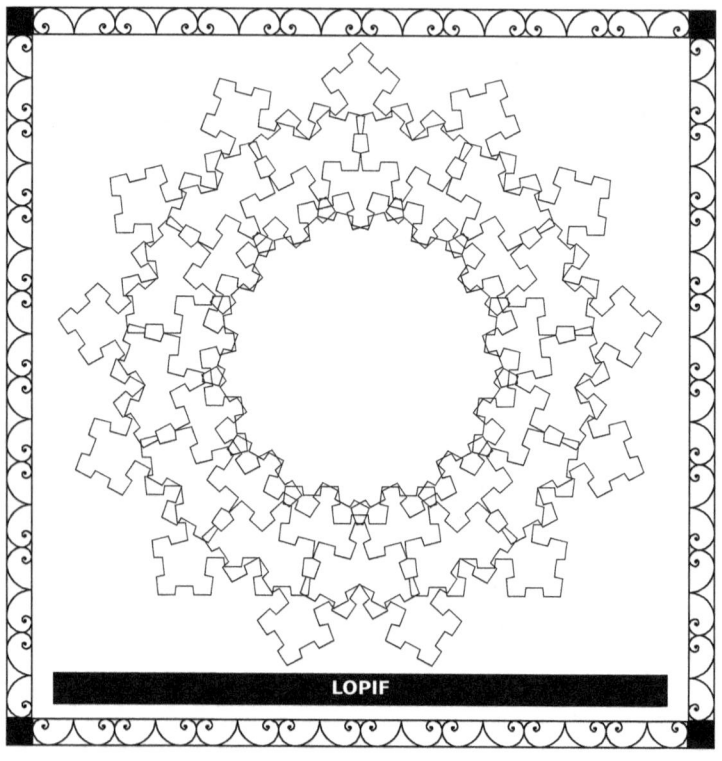

LOPIF

If they think that an artist can destroy their faith, then their faith is rather fragile.

Marilyn Manson

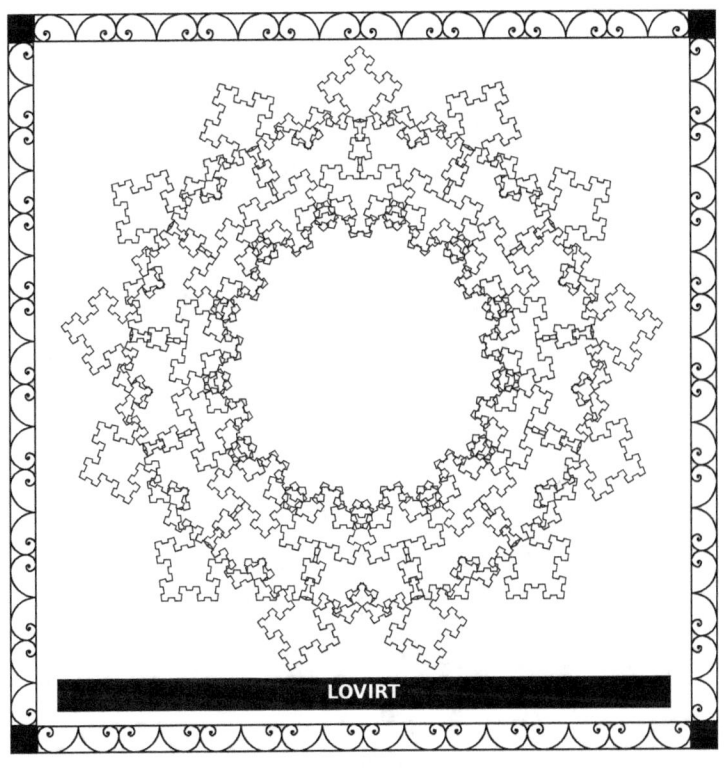

LOVIRT

The world cannot live at the level of its great men.

James Frazer

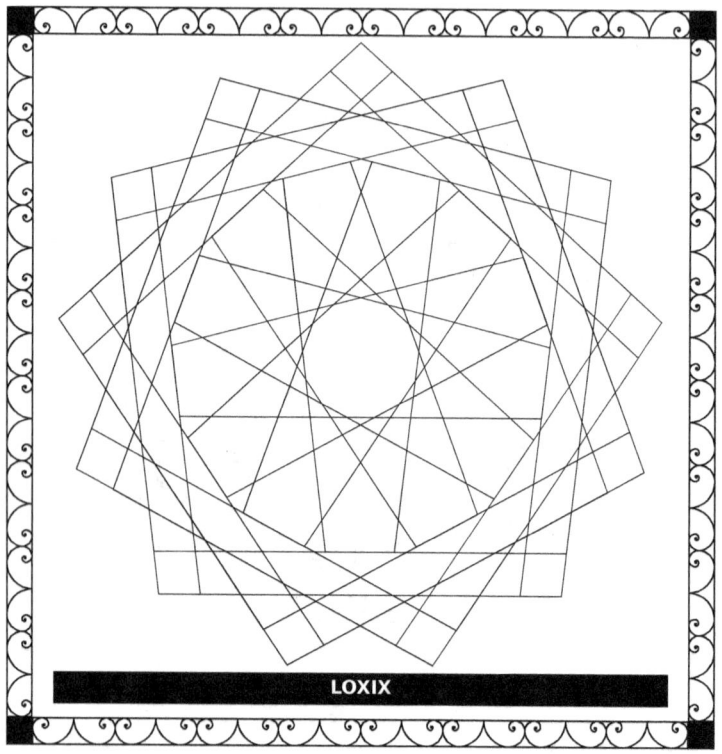

LOXIX

The artist is nothing without the gift, but the gift is nothing without work.
Emile Zola

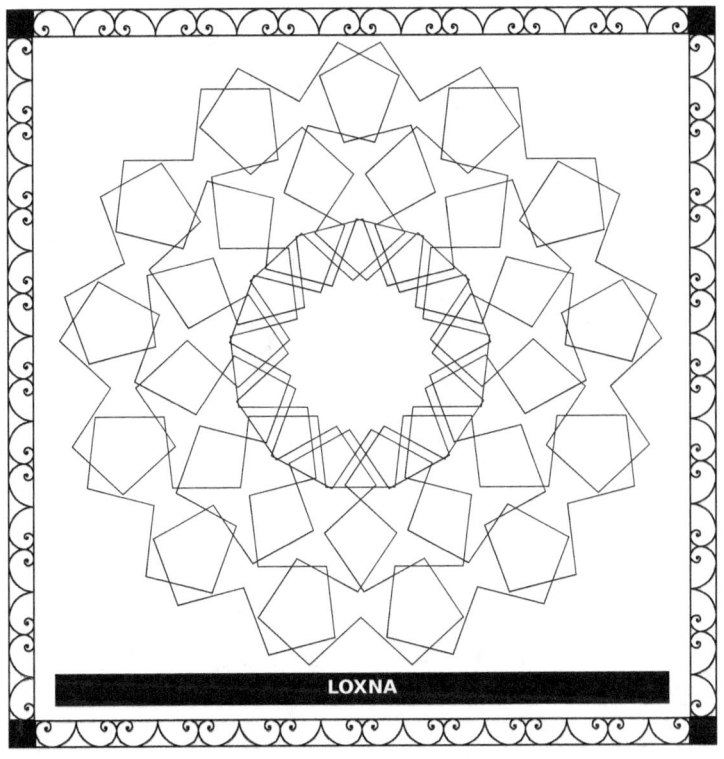

LOXNA

The mind alone was one with the universe, clear and untroubled, like the reflection of the moon in a pond amidst the ragings of a typhoon. To reach this sublime immobility is the supreme achievement.

Eiji Yoshikawa, Musashi

153

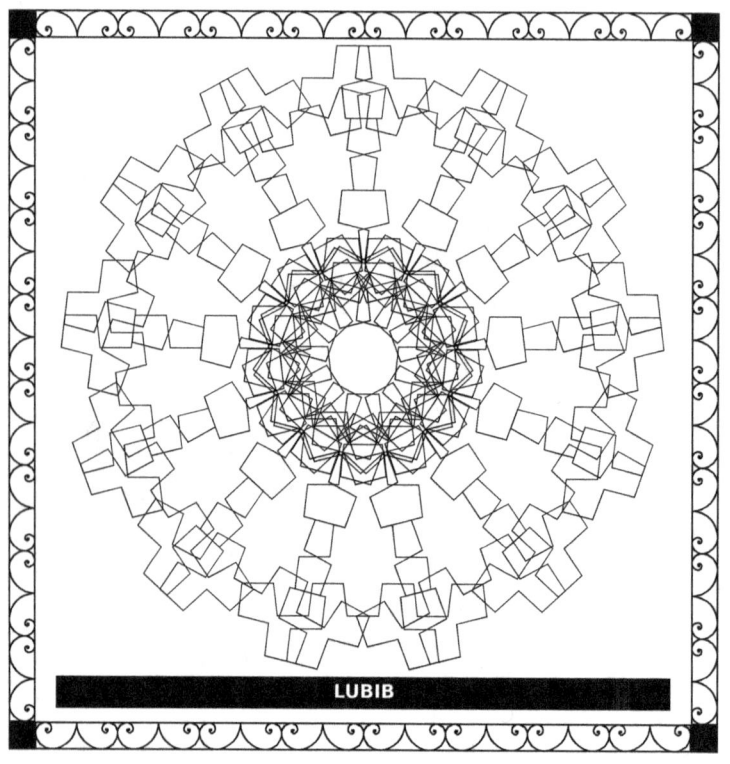

LUBIB

We have to give our opinion, we have to say something, or we are a part of it. As an artist I am forced to say something.
Ai Weiwei

154

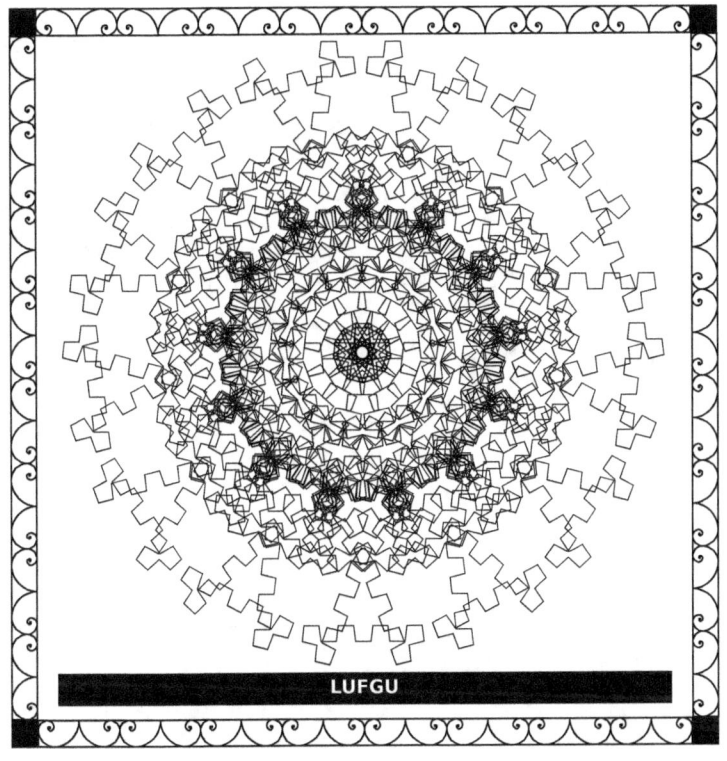

LUFGU

The role of art is to give food for thought, to act as a stimulant, to entice the onlooker to inspect things, people, emotions, from a new point of view.

Jim Ede

155

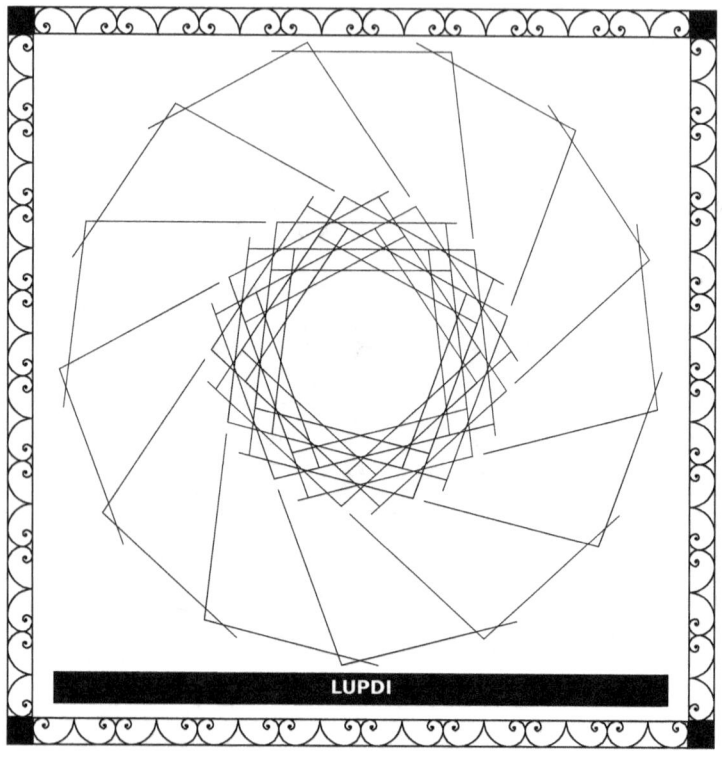

LUPDI

The art of substantiating shadows, and of lending existence to nothing.

Edmund Burke, Burke's description of poetry

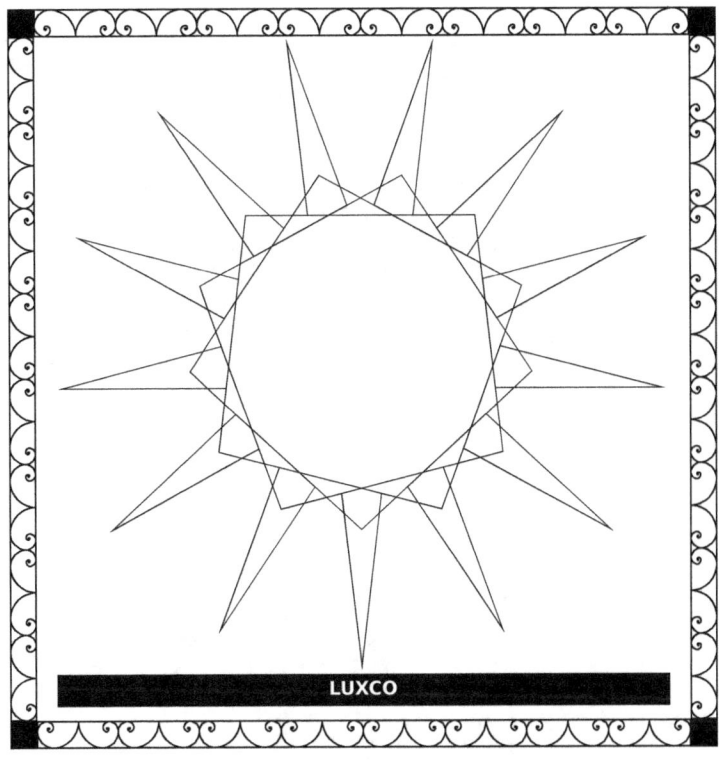

LUXCO

The soul active sees absolute truth; and utters truth, or creates.
Ralph Waldo Emerson

157

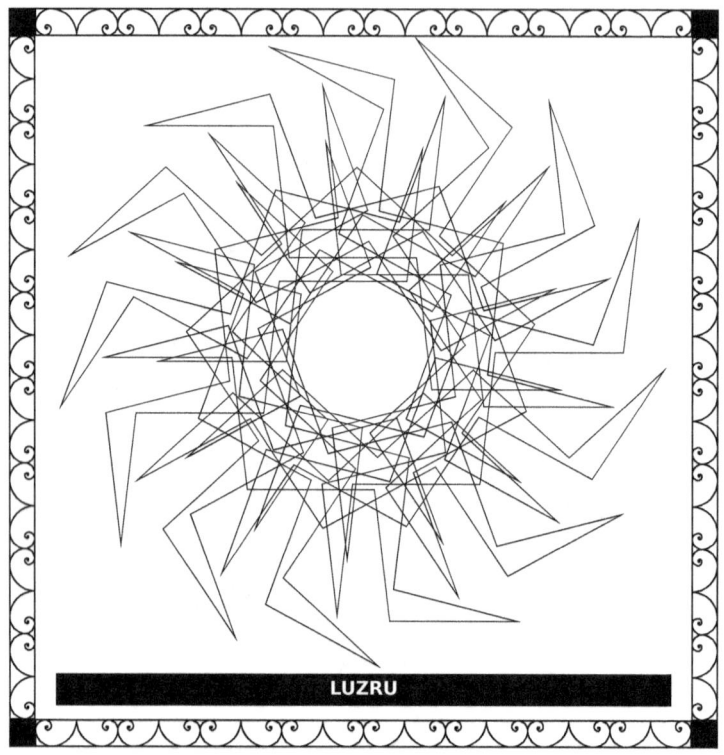

LUZRU

All of the philosophers put together are not worth a single saint.
Emil Cioran

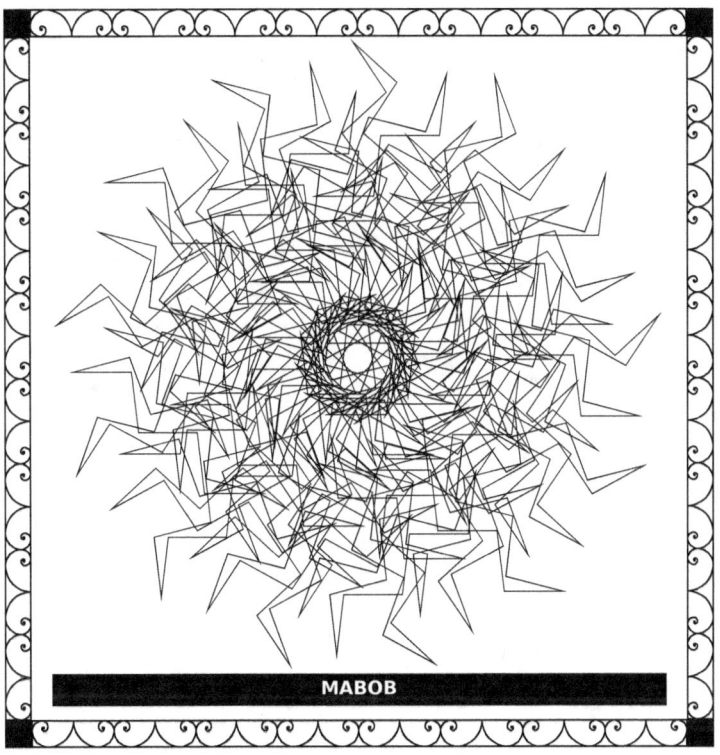

MABOB

Science looks and observes and art sees and foresees. Every great scientist has experienced a moment when the artist in him saved the scientist.
Naum Gabo

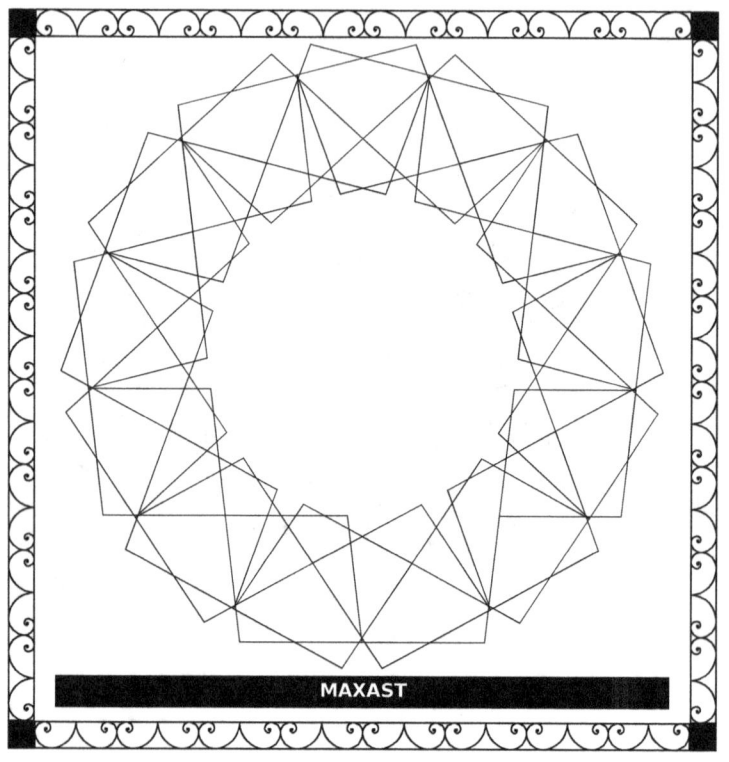

MAXAST

The production of a work of art is determined by the material and intellectual climate in which a man lives and dies.
Hippolyte Taine

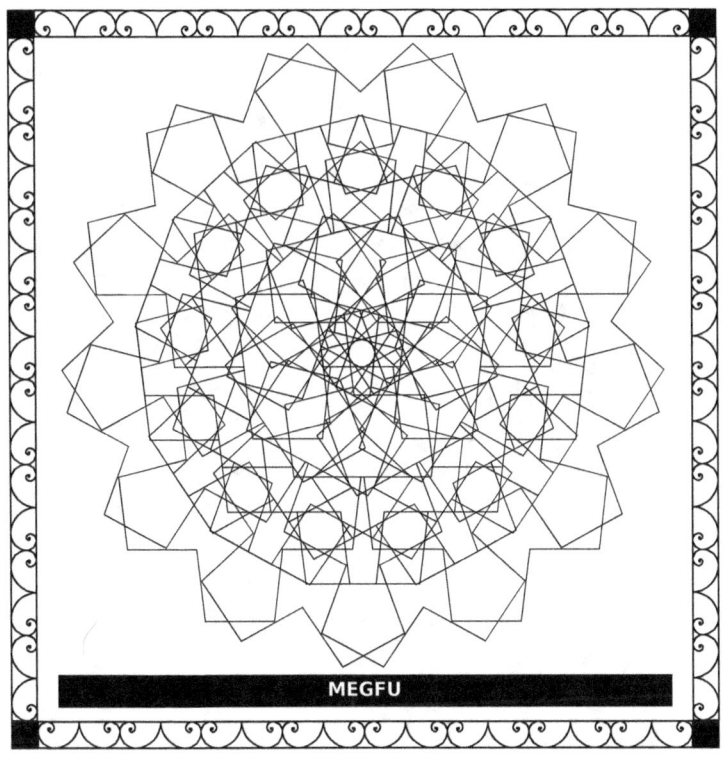

MEGFU

Whether naive on my part or not, it seemed worth taking the time to try to convince others that their lives possessed beauty and meaning worth preserving and honoring.

Aberjhani

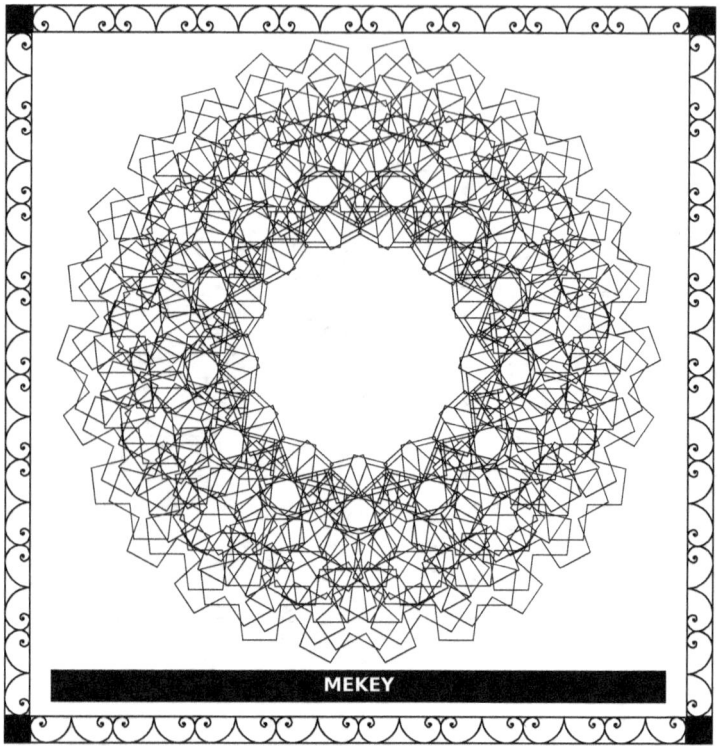

MEKEY

Why do you not do as I do? Letting go of your thoughts as though they were the cold ashes of a long dead fire?
John Cage

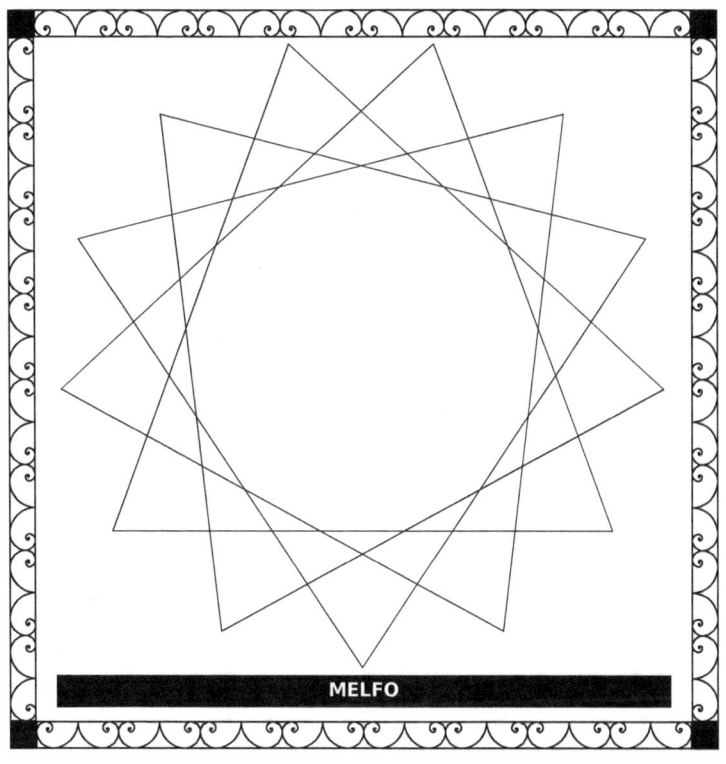

MELFO

Our desires are never wholly transparent, even to ourselves.
Mark Kingwell

163

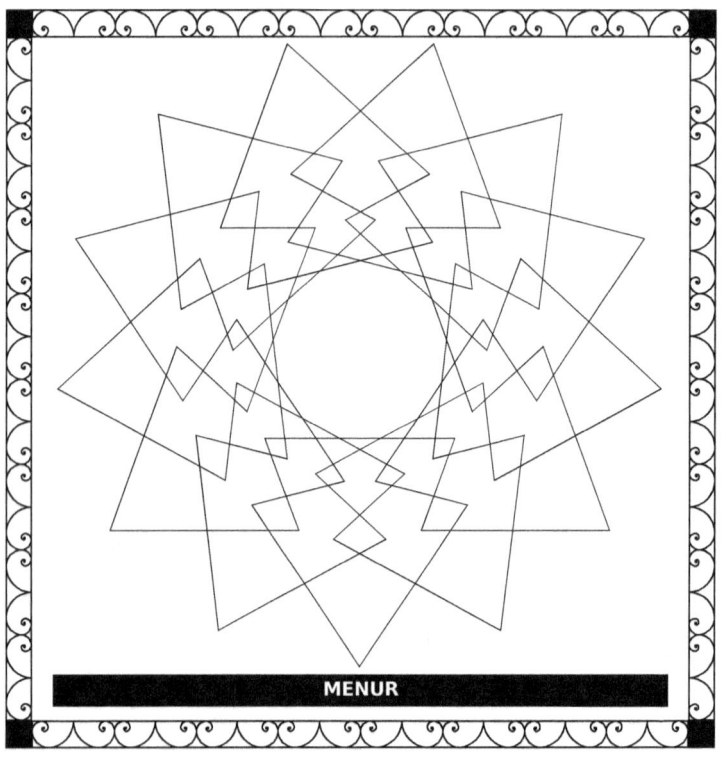

MENUR

The first question I ask myself when something doesn't seem to be beautiful is why do I feel it's not beautiful? And very shortly you discover there is no reason.
John Cage

164

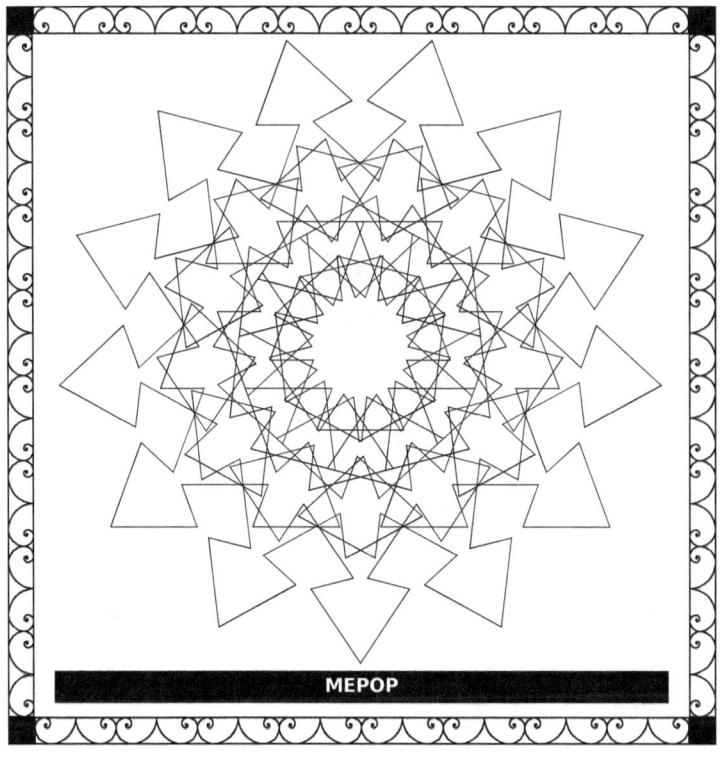

MEPOP

A man is an artist only at certain moments, by an effort of will. Objects have the same appearance for everybody.
Edgar Degas

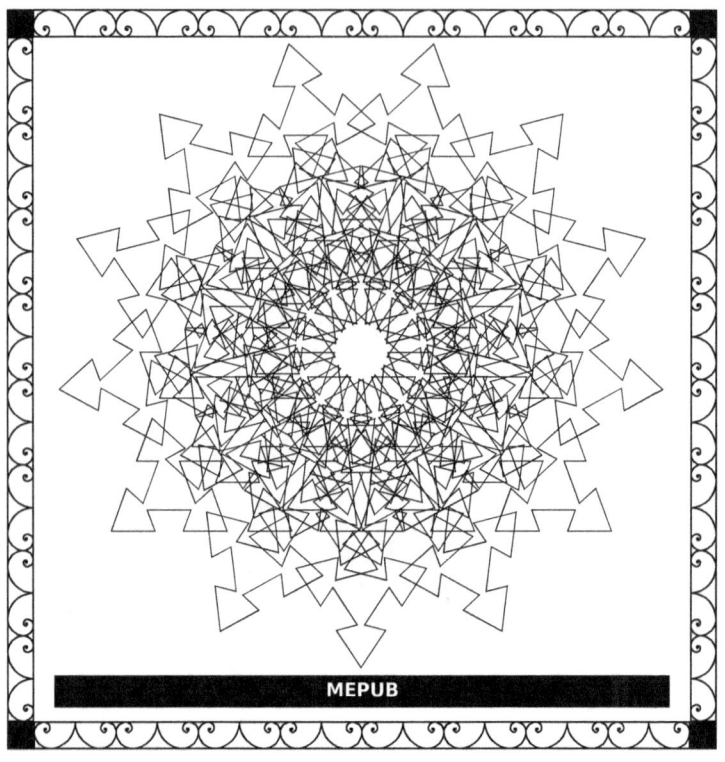

We live in an age where the artist is forgotten. He is a researcher. I see myself that way.
David Hockney

166

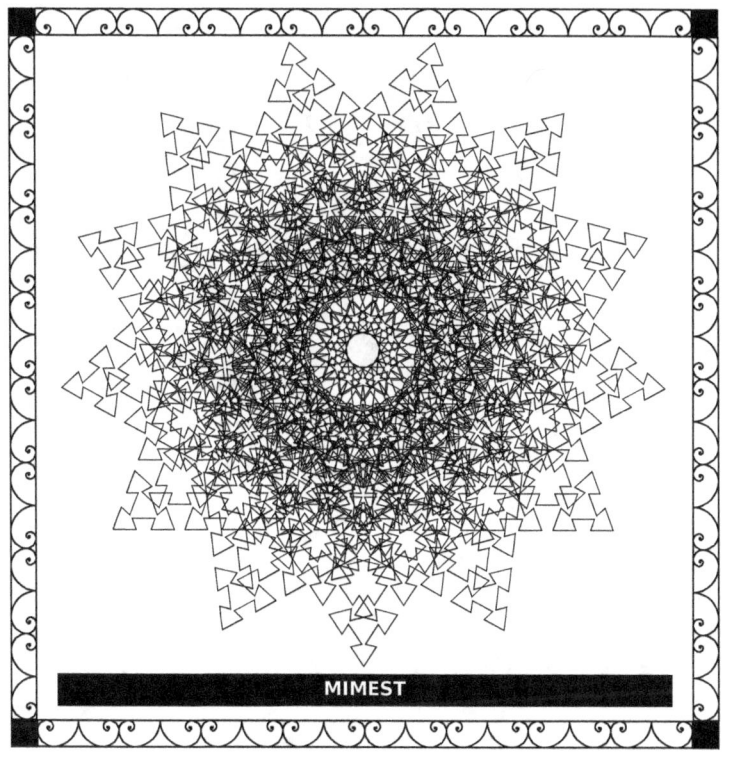

MIMEST

The simplest means are those which best enable an artist to express himself. His means of expression must derive almost all of necessity from his temperament.
Henri Matisse

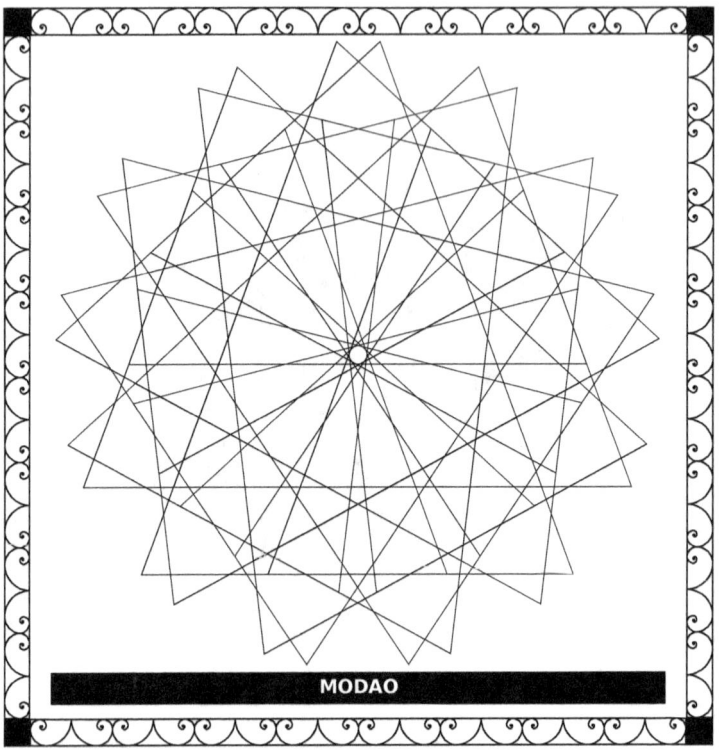

MODAO

Method is much, technique is much, but inspiration is even more.
Benjamin N. Cardozo

168

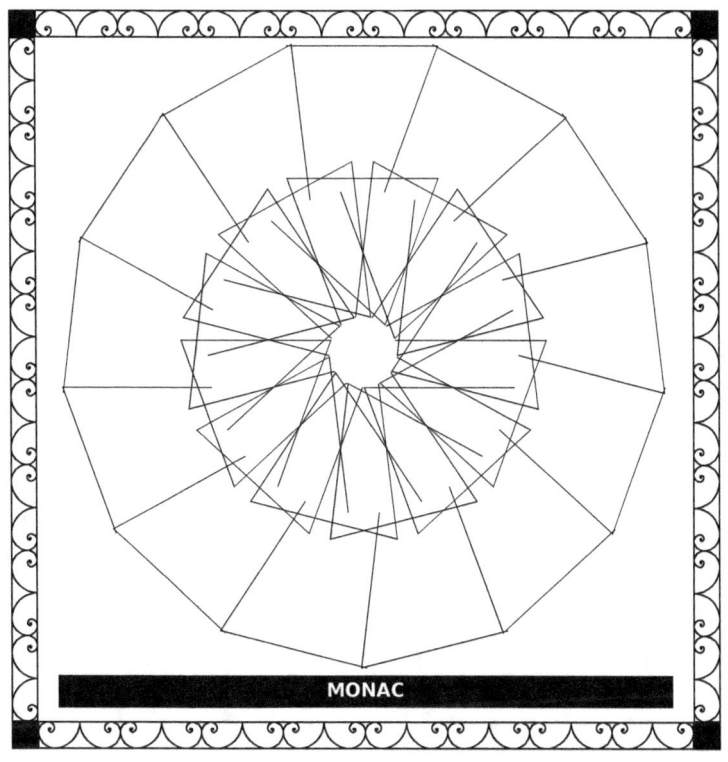

MONAC

Life with no music would be a mistake
Garegin Nzhdeh

169

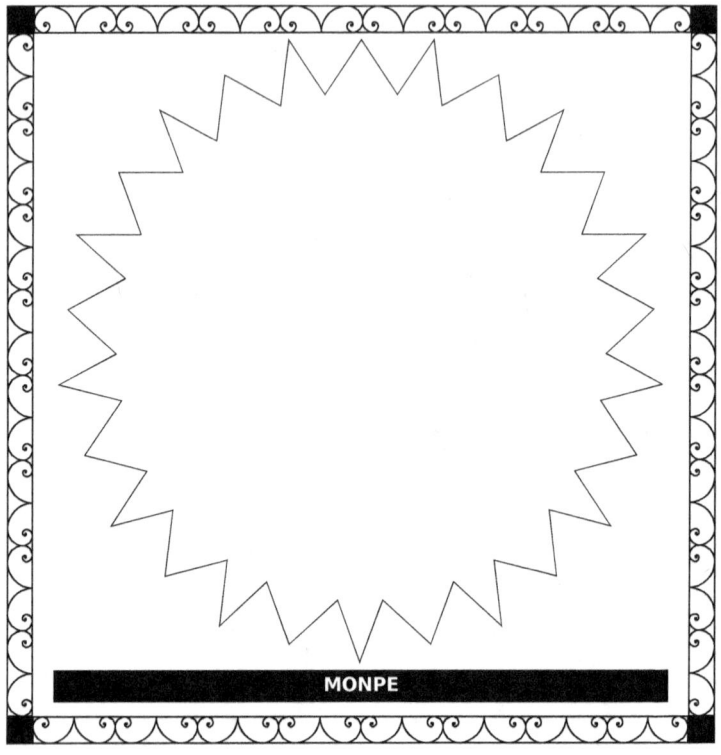

MONPE

Well, art is reality, art is a muse if it helps us to realise the truth. It is the major guiding element which helps you to realise the truth.
S.H. Raza

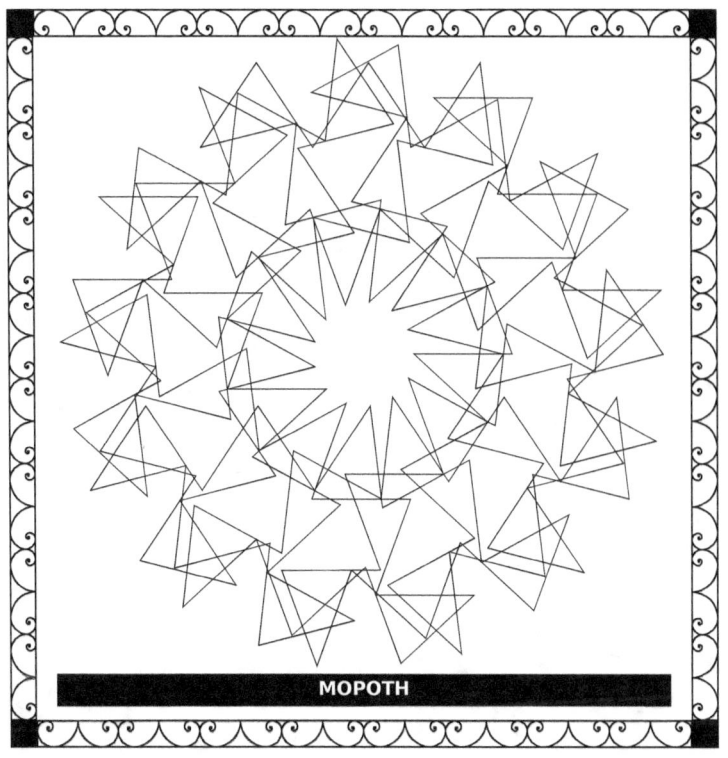

MOPOTH

We do not come into this world, we come out of it, as leaves from a tree. As the ocean waves, the universe peoples. Every individual is an expression of the whole realm of nature, a unique action of the total universe. This fact is rarely, if ever, experienced by most individuals.

Alan Watts

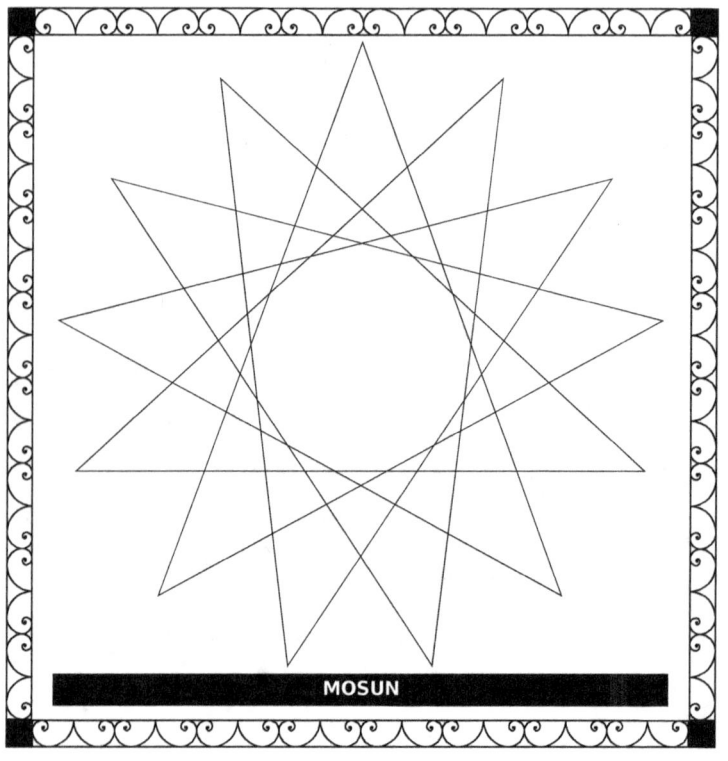

MOSUN

I feel that music is the art which can best express the emotions which flow within us. It conveys something bigger than it is.

Andrew Sega

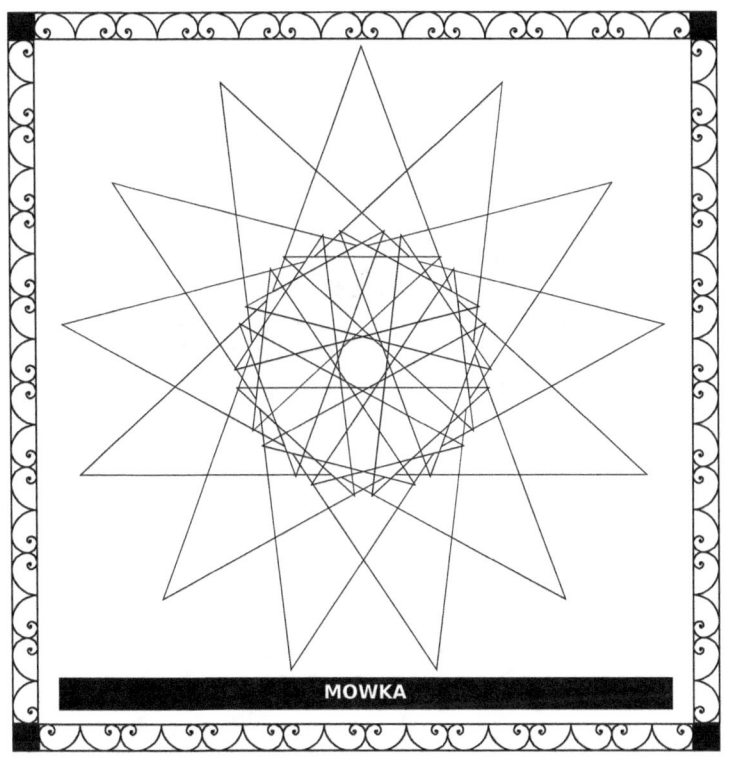

MOWKA

If the world were clear, art would not exist.
Albert Camus

173

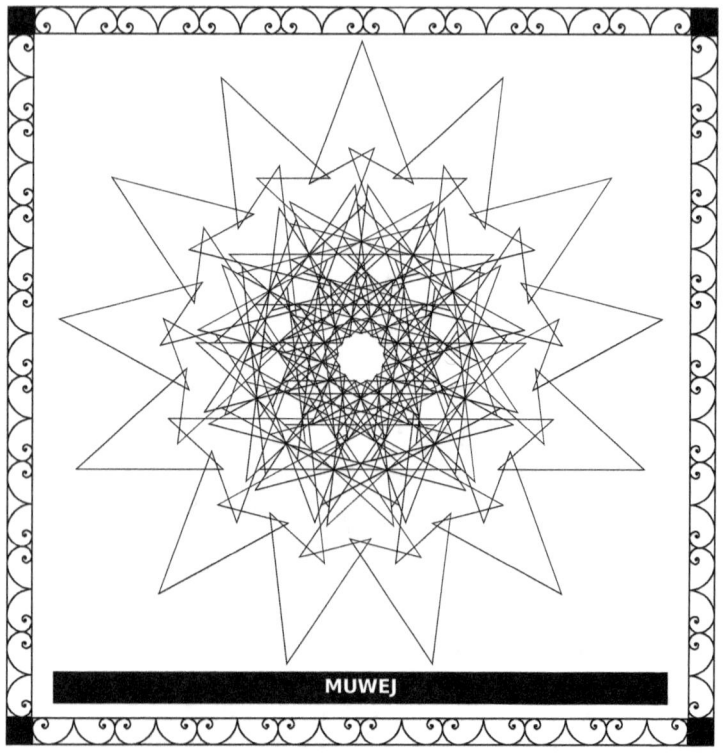

MUWEJ

Every great work of art ... is a celebration, an act of insubordination against the betrayals, horrors and infidelities of
life.
Azar Nafisi

174

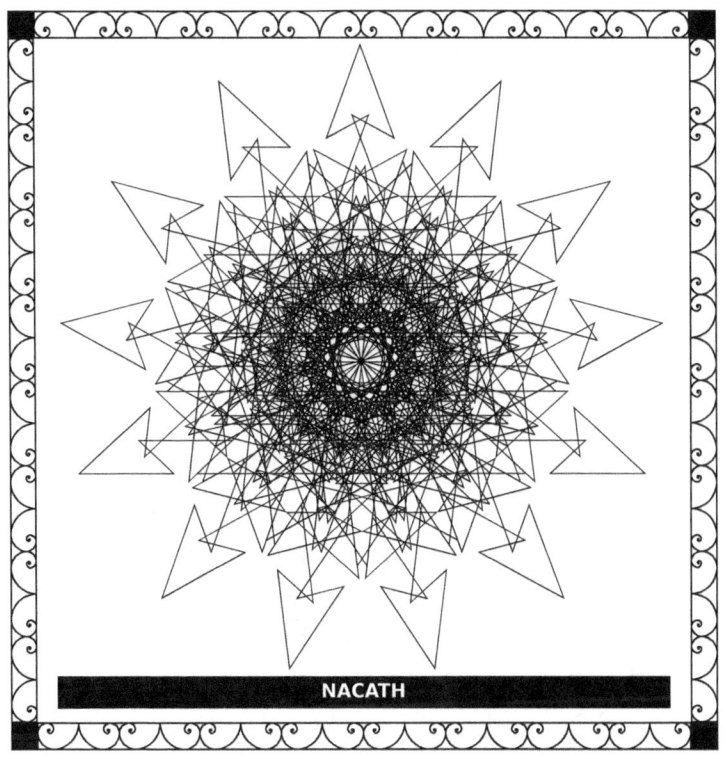

NACATH

If a work of art is to explore new environments, it is not to be regarded as a blueprint but rather as a form of action-painting.
Marshall McLuhan

175

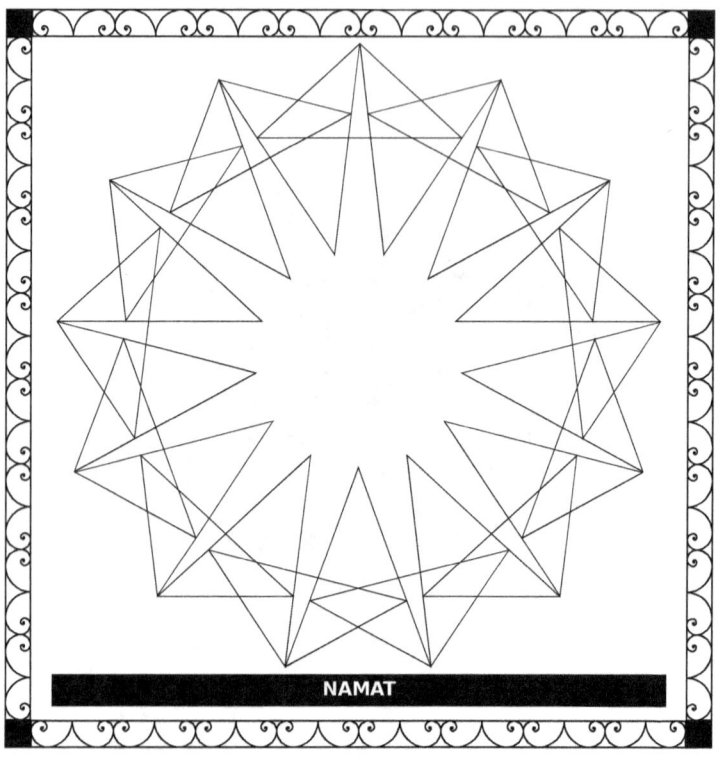

NAMAT

What is art but a way of seeing?
Saul Bellow

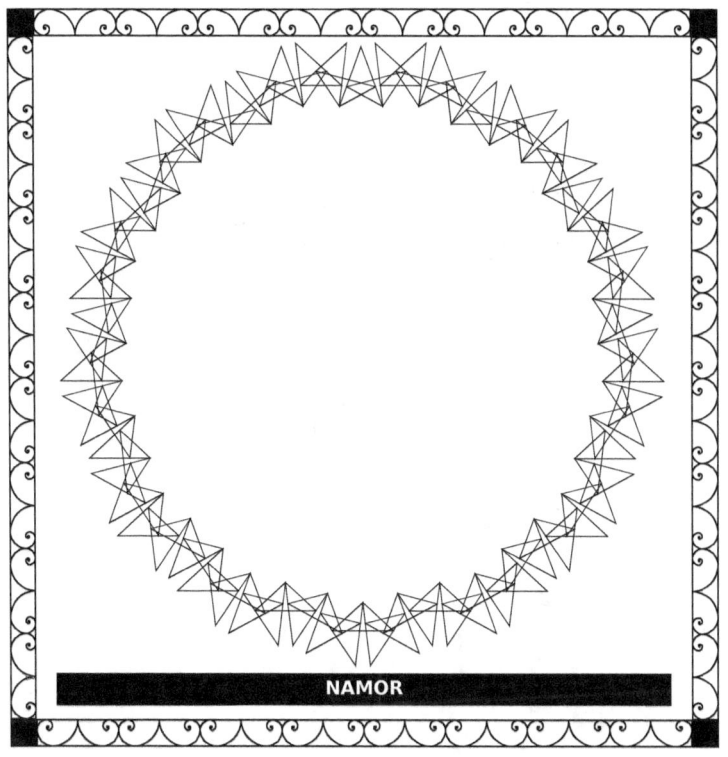

NAMOR

The man of genius whether as artist or thinker requires a mass of accidental variations to select from and a rigidly selective process of attention.

Boris Sidis

177

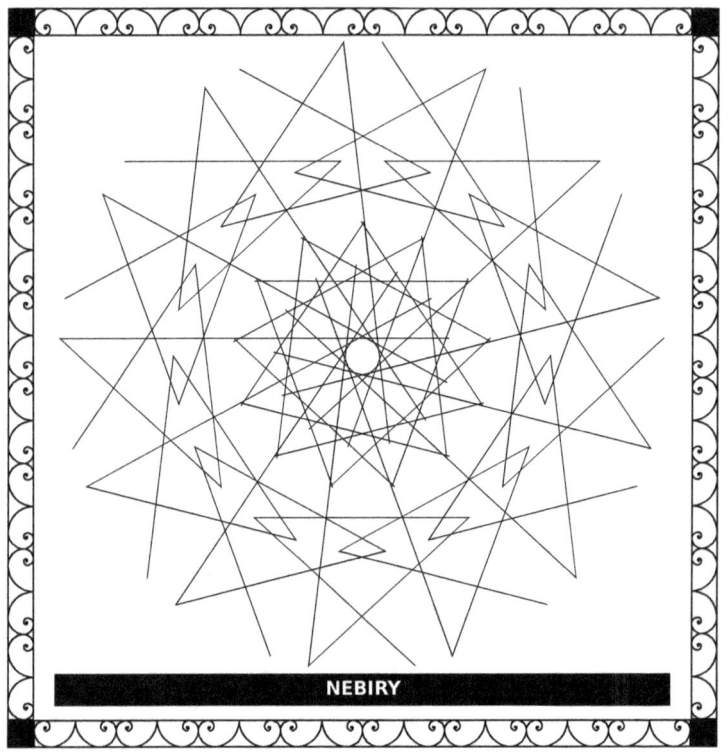

NEBIRY

Observe intently the birds of heaven, because they do not sow seed or reap or gather into storehouses; still your heavenly Father feeds them. Are you not worth more than they are?

Jesus

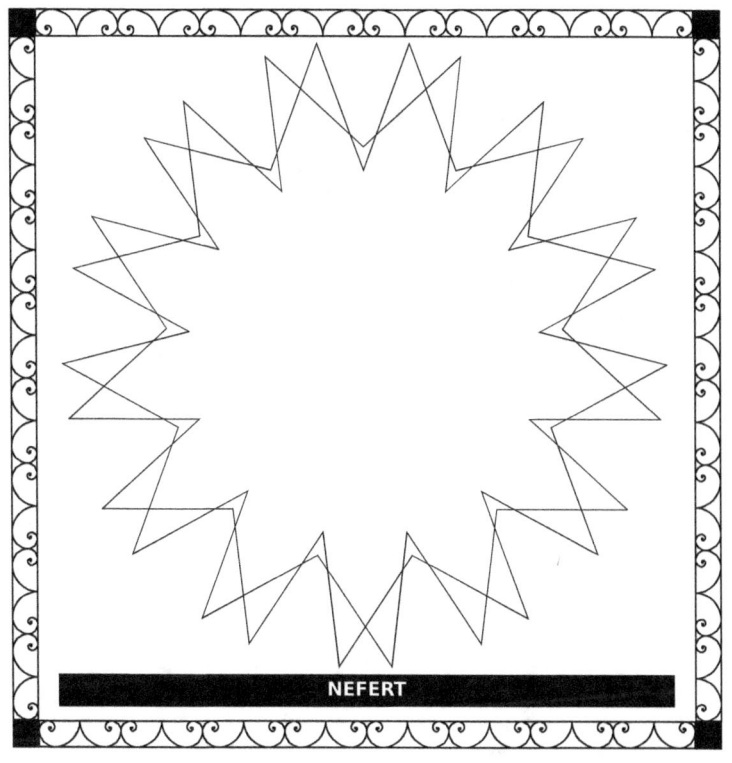

NEFERT

You are right to demand that an artist engage his work consciously, but you confuse two different things: solving the problem and correctly posing the question.
Anton Chekhov

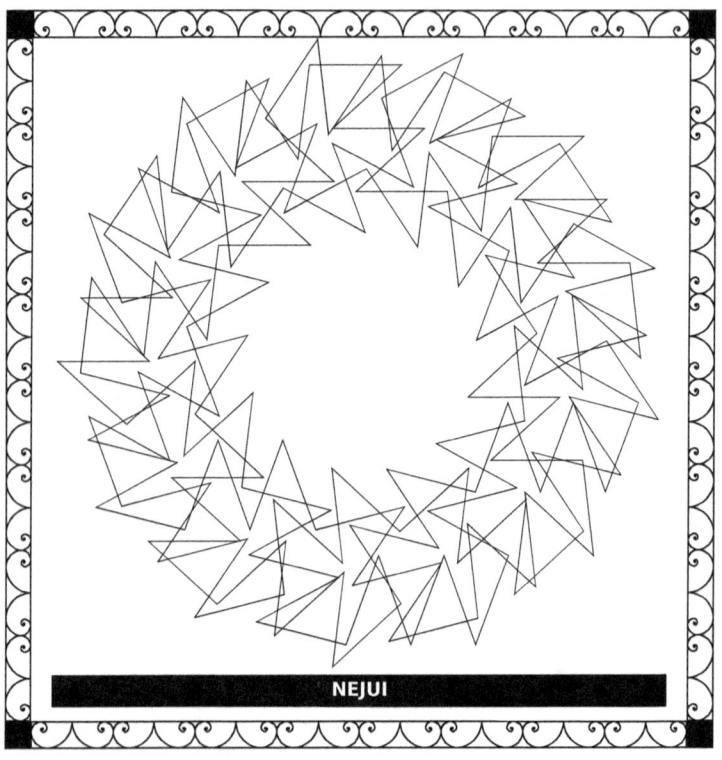

NEJUI

I lean against the wind, pretend that I am weightless, and in this moment I am happy.
Brandon Boyd

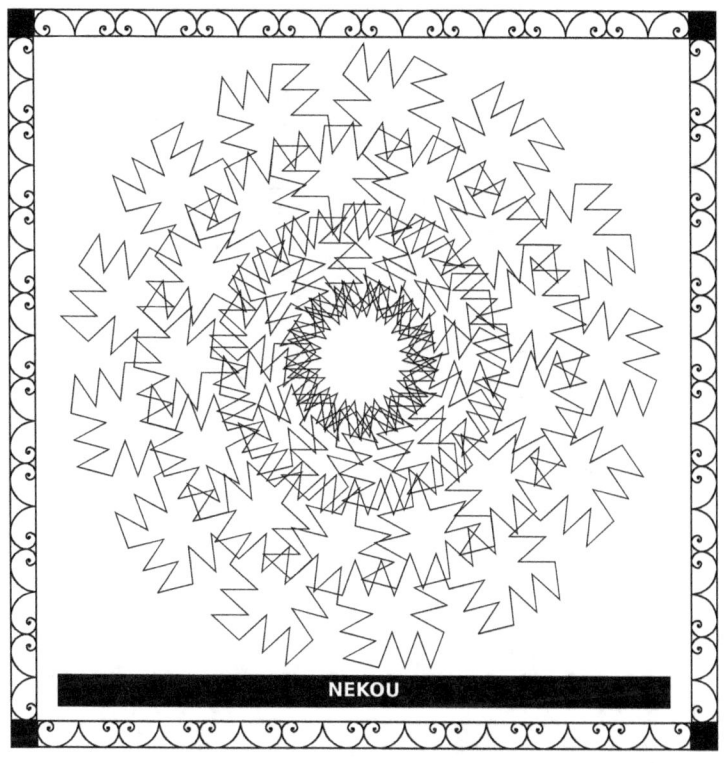

NEKOU

A picture lives by companionship, expanding and quickening in the eyes of the sensitive observer. It dies by the same token. It is therefore risky to send it out into the world. How often it must be impaired by the eyes of the unfeeling and the cruelty of the impotent.
Mark Rothko

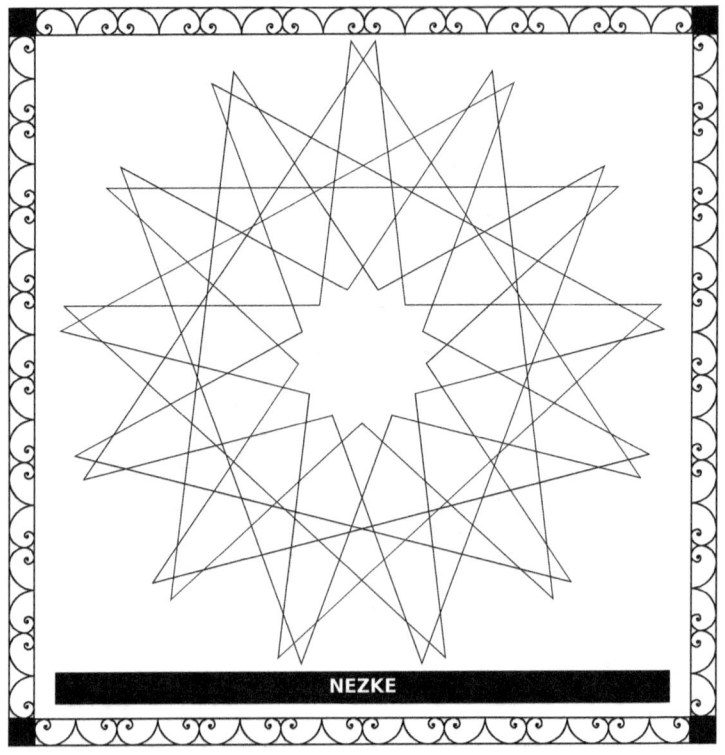

NEZKE

If we crave some cosmic purpose, then let us find ourselves a worthy goal.
Carl Sagan

182

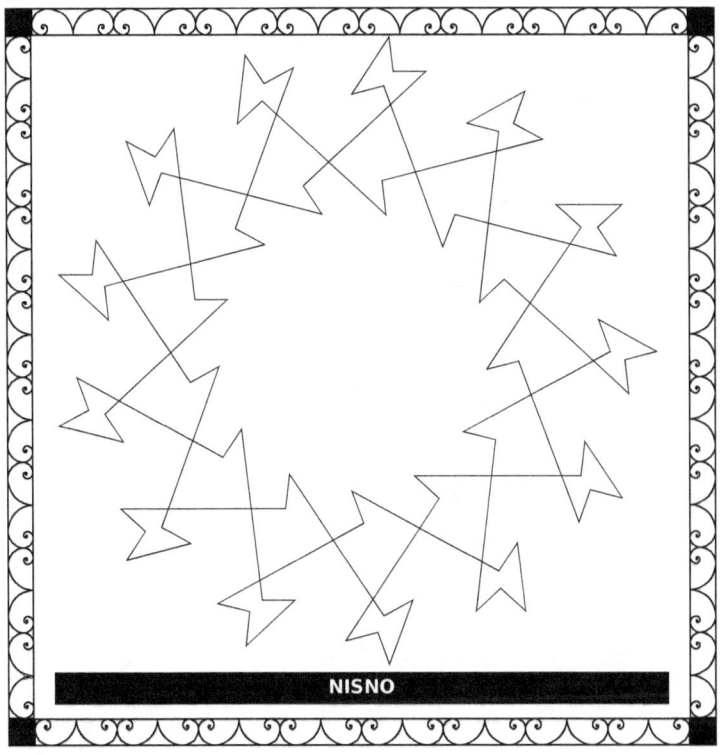

NISNO

The mural artist is concerned with bringing to life dead surfaces by the application of colour.
Fernand Leger

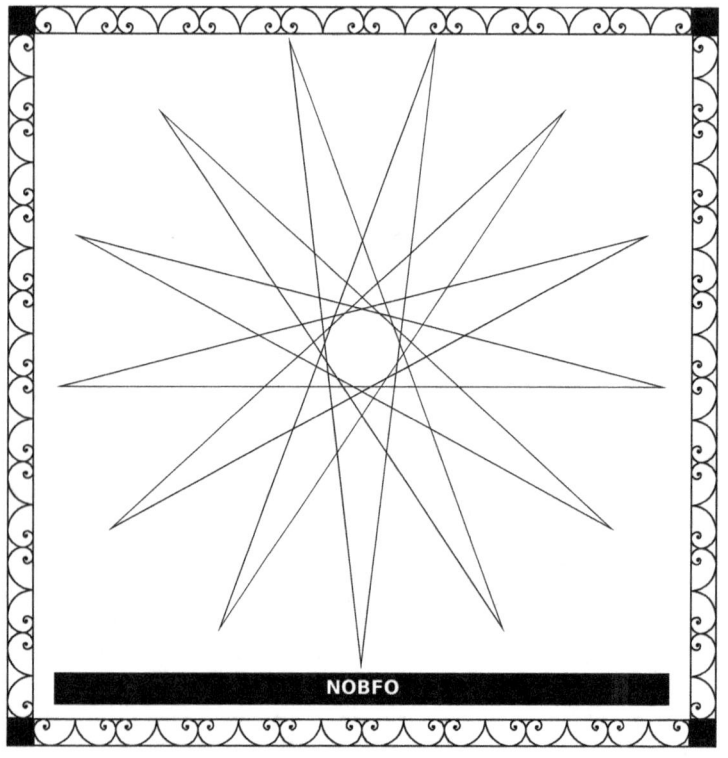

NOBFO

An investment in knowledge pays the best interest.
Benjamin Franklin

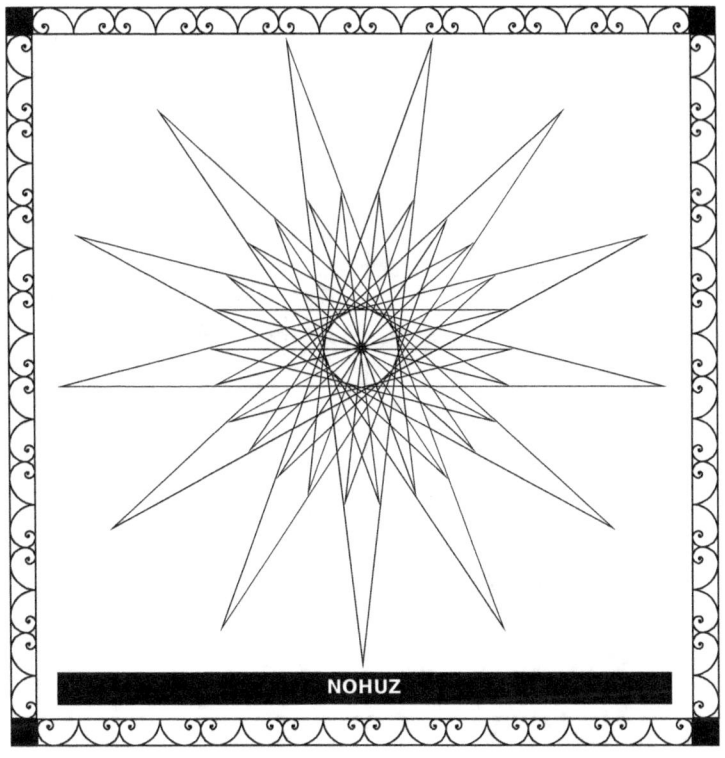

NOHUZ

While our art cannot, as we wish it could, save us from wars, privation, envy, greed, old age, or death, it can revitalize us amidst it all.

Ray Bradbury

185

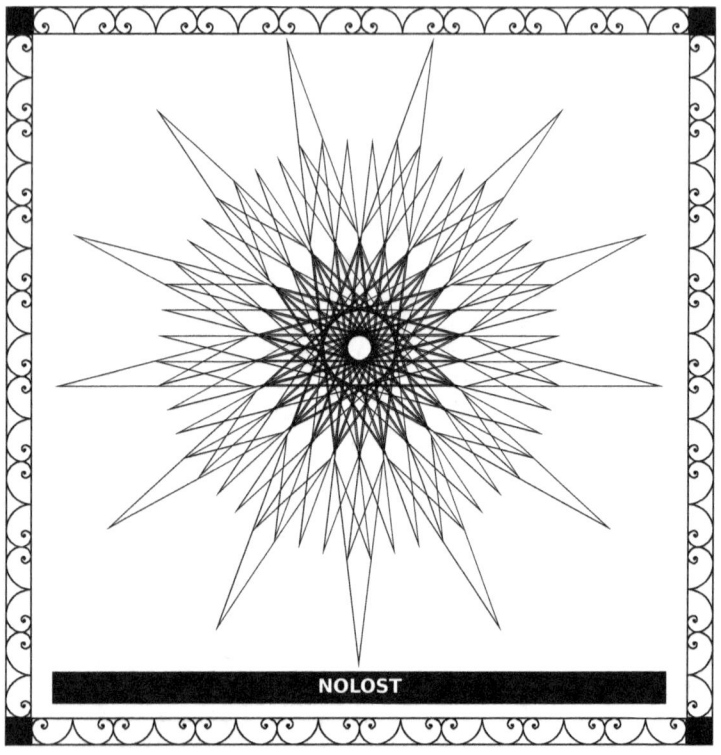

NOLOST

Against the assault of laughter nothing can stand.
Mark Twain

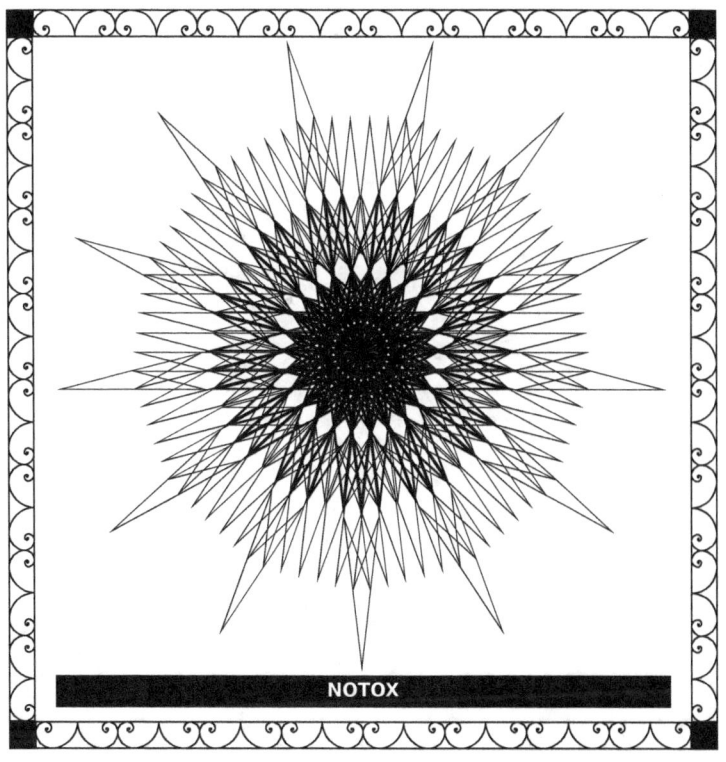

NOTOX

The more horrible this world (as today, for instance), the more abstract our art, whereas a happy world brings forth an art of the here and now.
Paul Klee

187

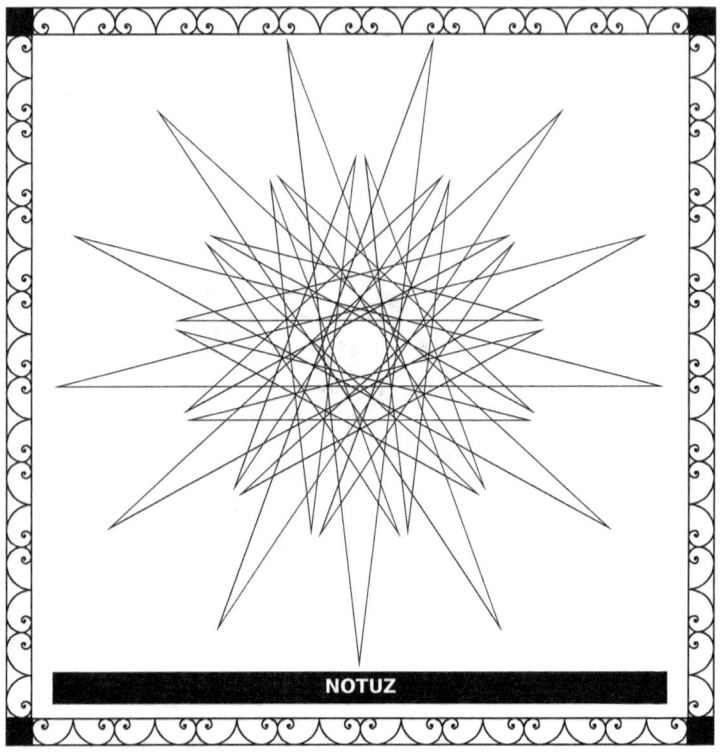

NOTUZ

If art were to redeem man, it could do so only by saving him from the seriousness of life and restoring him to an unexpected boyishness.
John Lennon

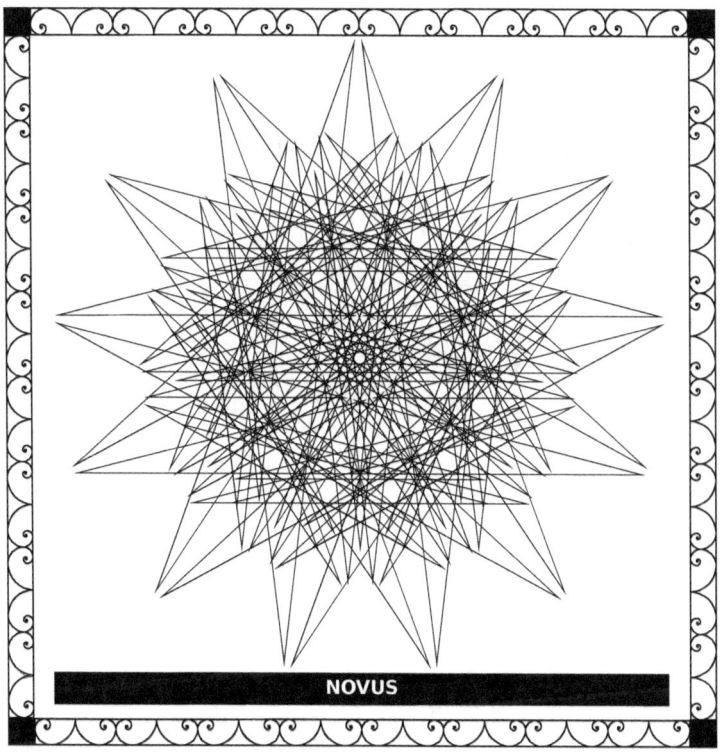

NOVUS

Great is the art of beginning, but greater the art is of ending; Many a poem is marred by a superfluous verse.
Henry Wadsworth Longfellow

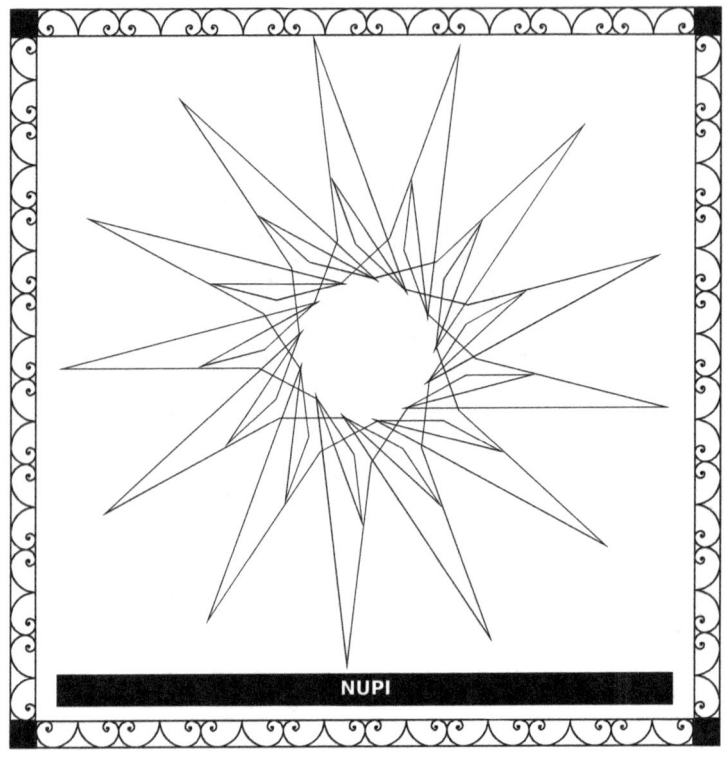

NUPI

The highest purpose is to have no purpose at all. This puts one in accordance with nature, in her manner of operation.
John Cage

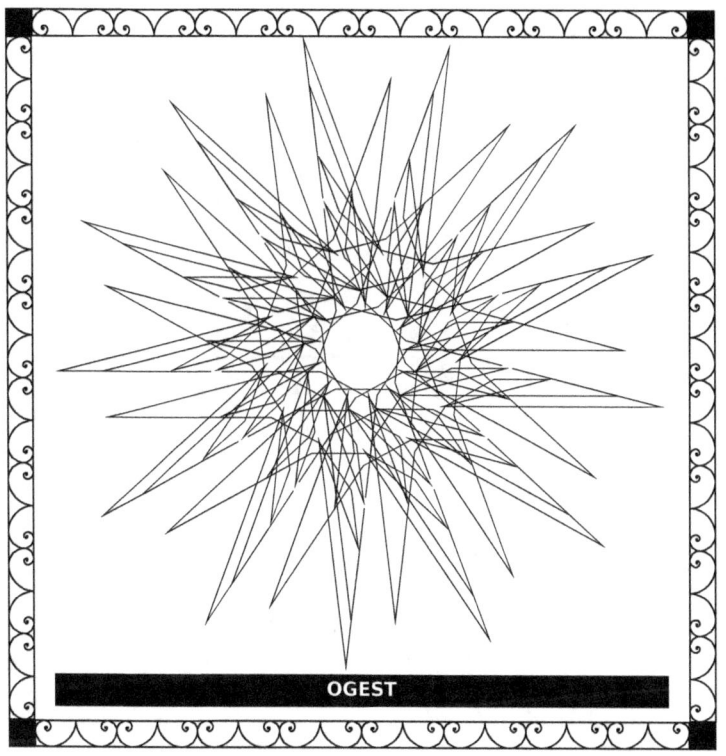

OGEST

I am unable to make any distinction between the feeling
I get from life and the way I translate that feeling into
painting.
Henri Matisse

191

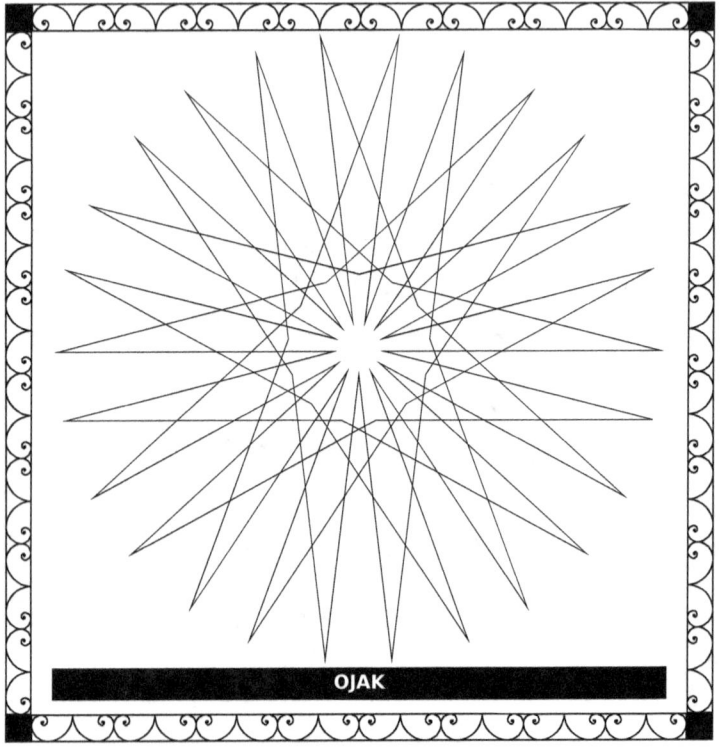

OJAK

He opened the door that so many of us went through, the door of possibility, by saying anything an artist makes is art.

Peter Blake

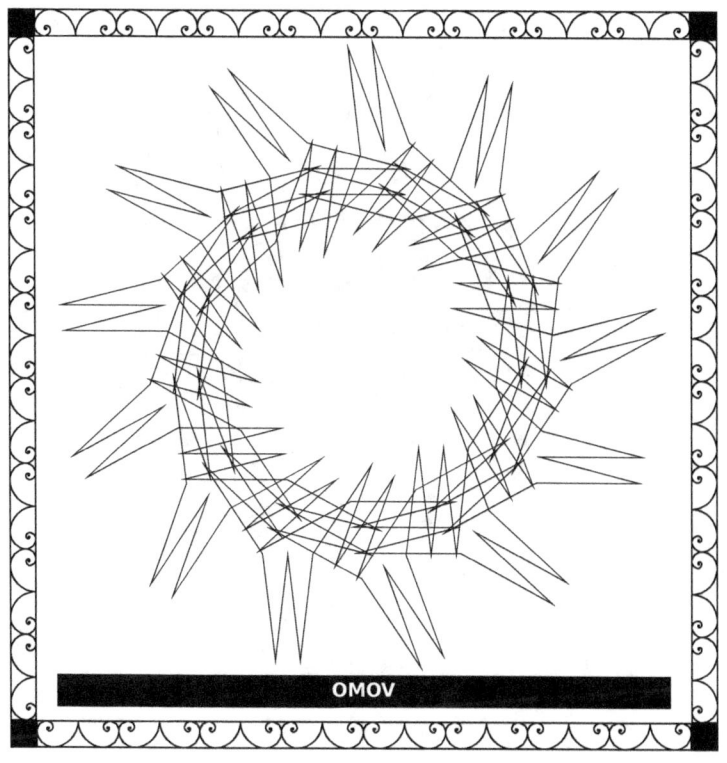

OMOV

An artist reveals his naked soul in his work - and so, gentle
reader, do you when you respond to it.
Ayn Rand

193

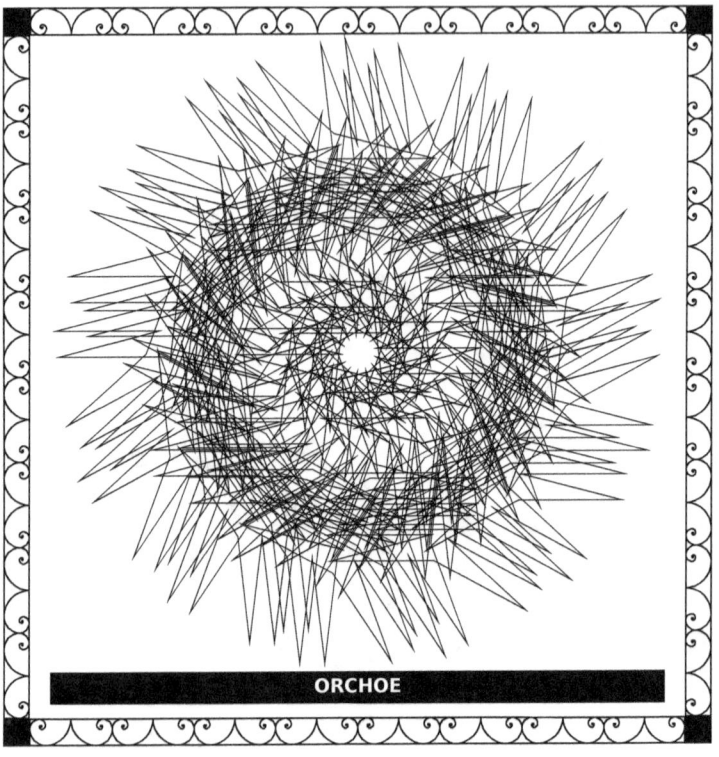

ORCHOE

We should not be simply fighting evil in the name of good, but struggling against the certainties of people who claim always to know where good and evil are to be found.
Tzvetan Todorov

194

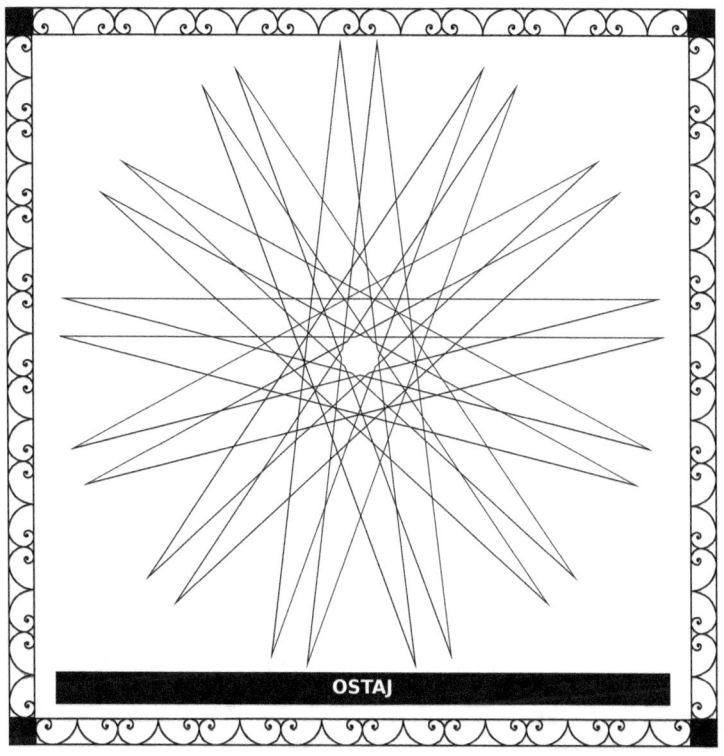

OSTAJ

Whether I make them or not, there are always sounds to be heard and all of them are excellent.
John Cage

195

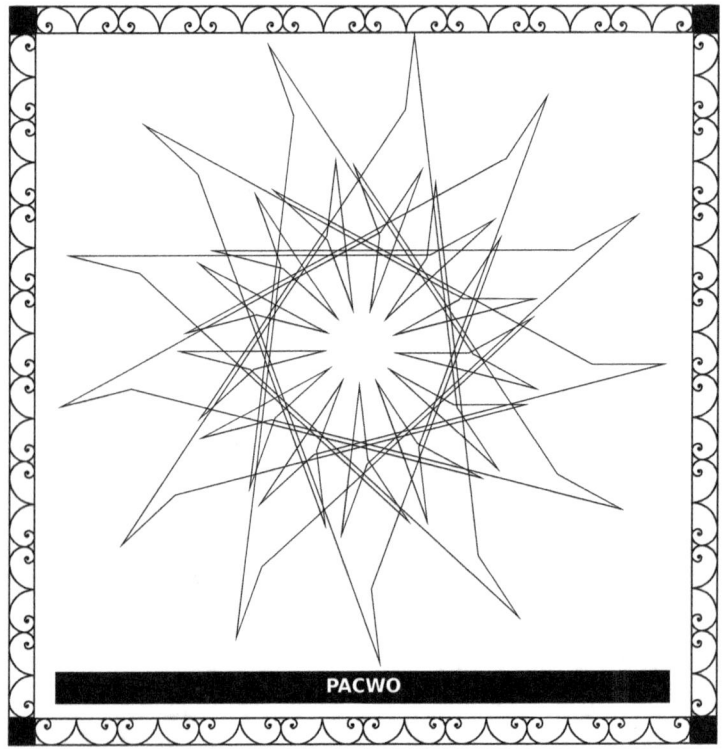

PACWO

When one looks into the window of a store which sells devotional art objects, one can't help wishing the iconoclasts had won.

W. H. Auden

196

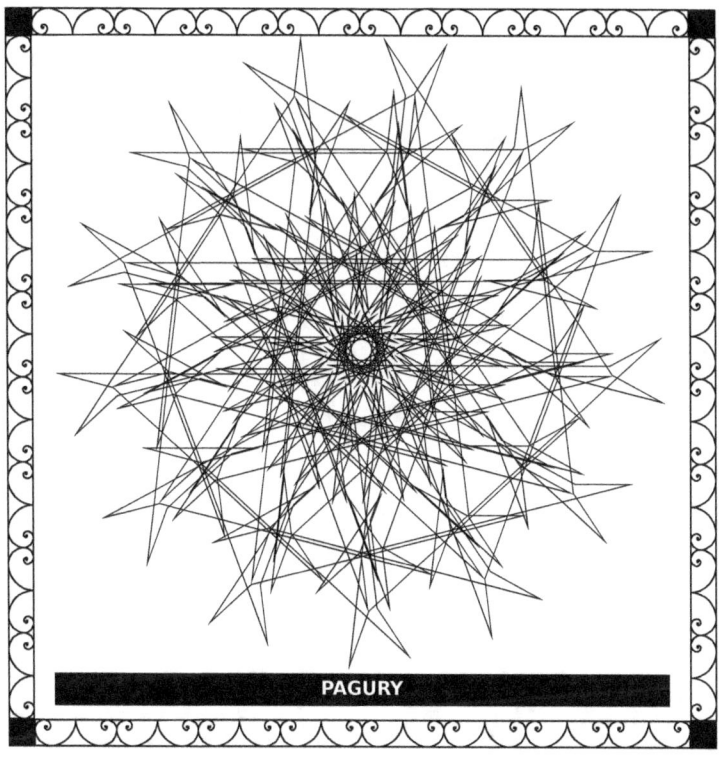

PAGURY

There is no more sombre enemy of good art than the pram in the hall.
Cyril Connolly

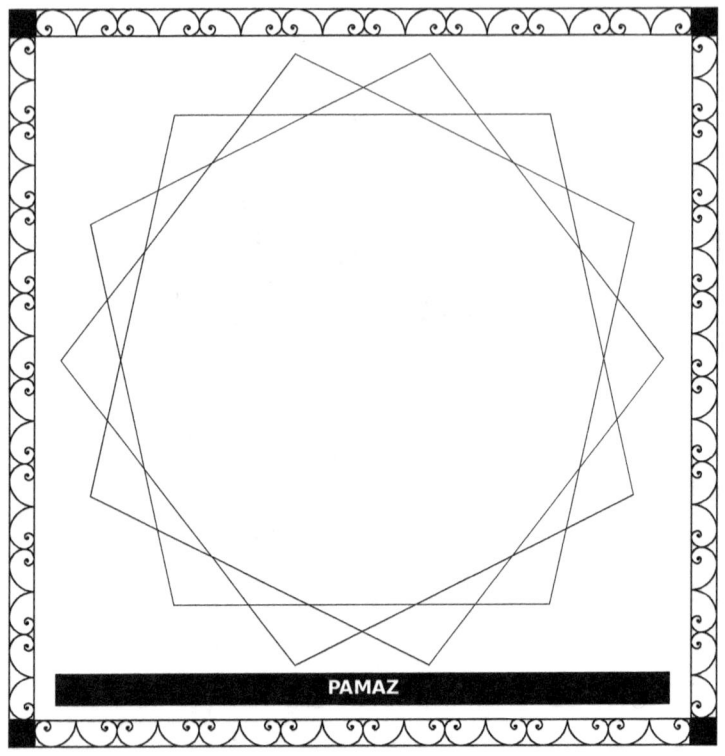

PAMAZ

Greatness in art is always a by-product.
Harold Rosenberg

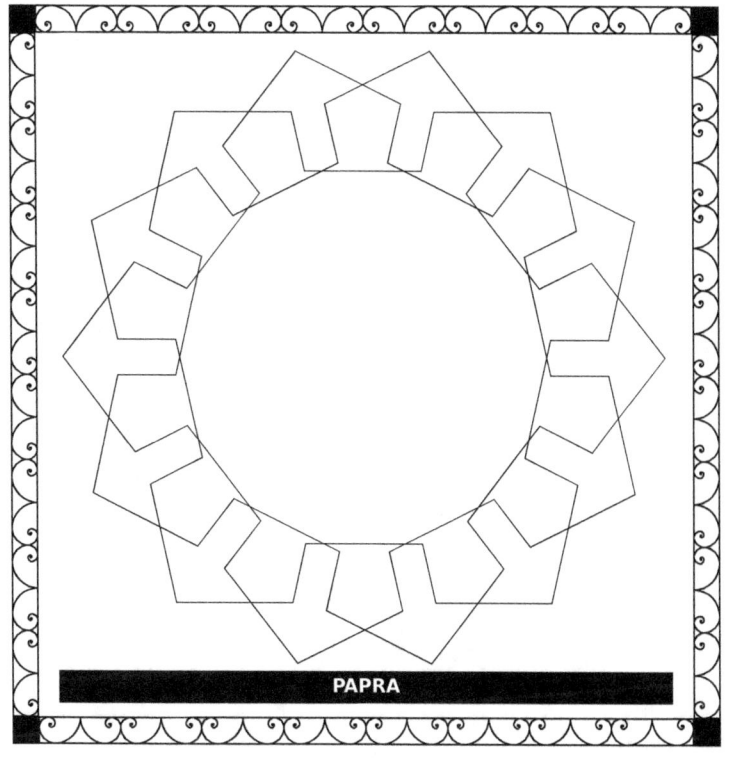

PAPRA

Inspiration is never genuine if it is known as inspiration at the time. True inspiration always steals on a person; its importance not being fully recognised for some time.
Samuel Butler

199

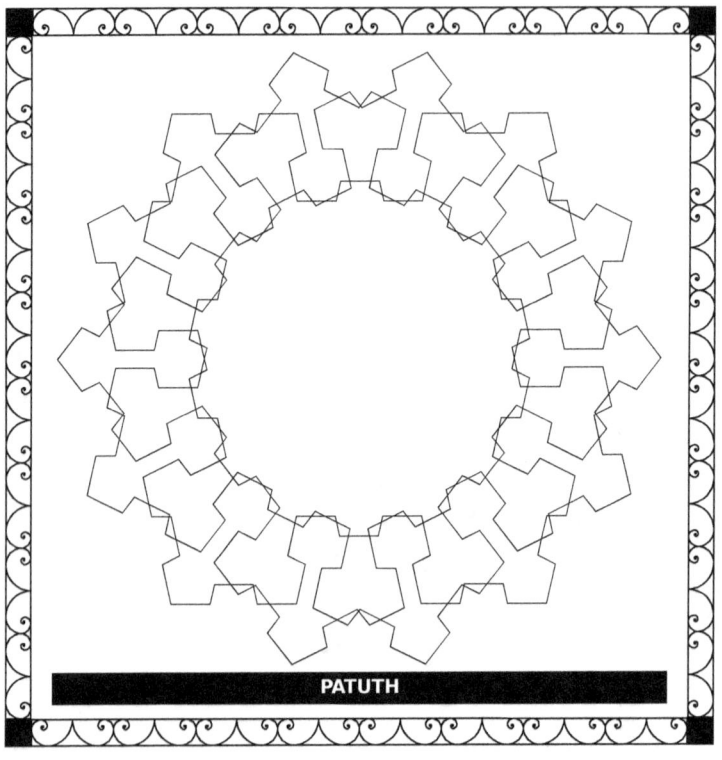

PATUTH

I love to experiment with all styles, and do not have any particular prejudice or bias towards any specific style. These works appear, and they turn out, the way they should. I do not decide in what style I want to paint. I am only experimenting. Even Picasso, when he arrived at Cubism, had already experimented with a lot of other styles.

Guity Novin

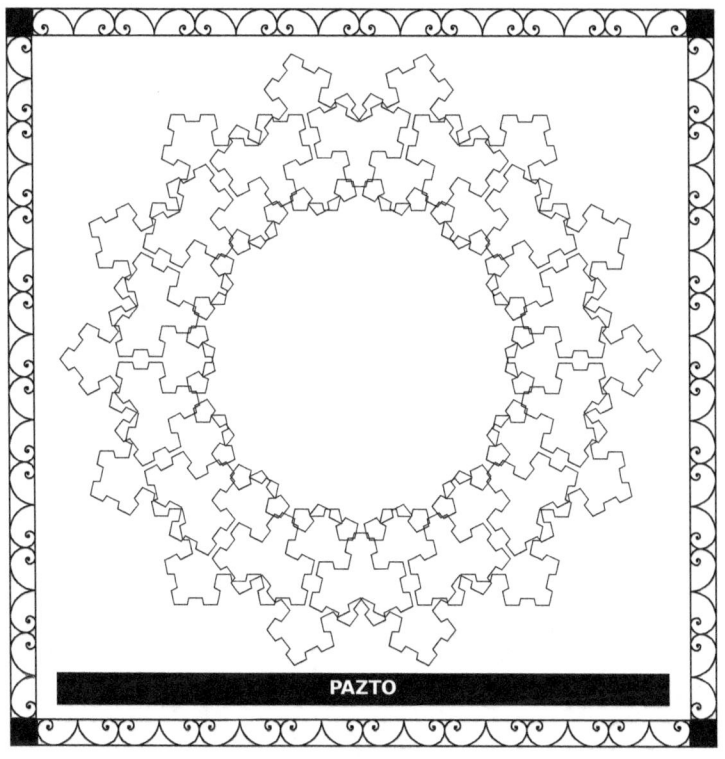

PAZTO

The magic happens only when the artist serves with love
and the listener receives with the same spirit.
Ravi Shankar

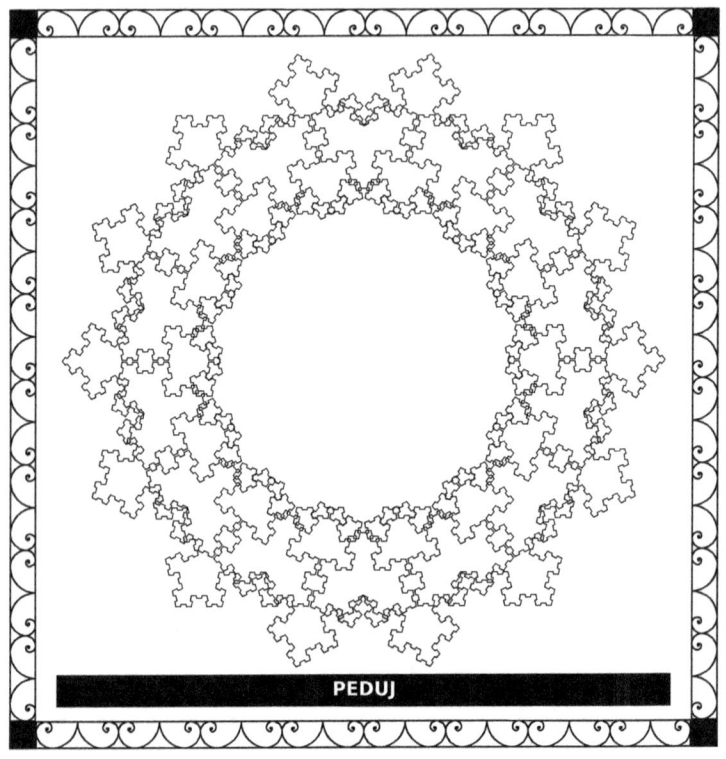

PEDUJ

Many people live habitually as if the present moment were an obstacle that they need to overcome in order to get to the next moment, and imagine living your whole live like that. Always, this moment is not quite good enough because you need to get to the next one.

Eckhart Tolle

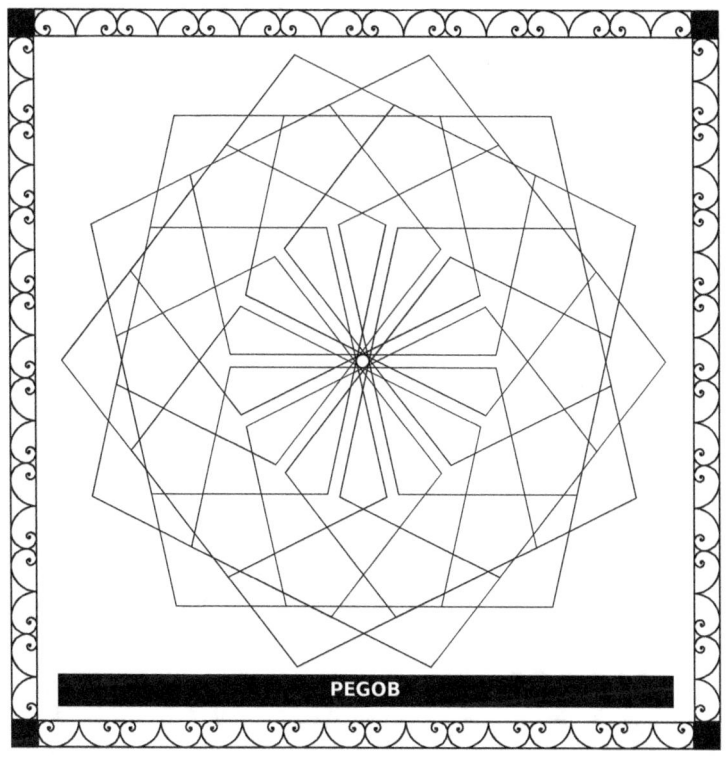

PEGOB

The artist has never been a dictator, since he understands better than anybody else the variations in human personality.
Heywood Broun

203

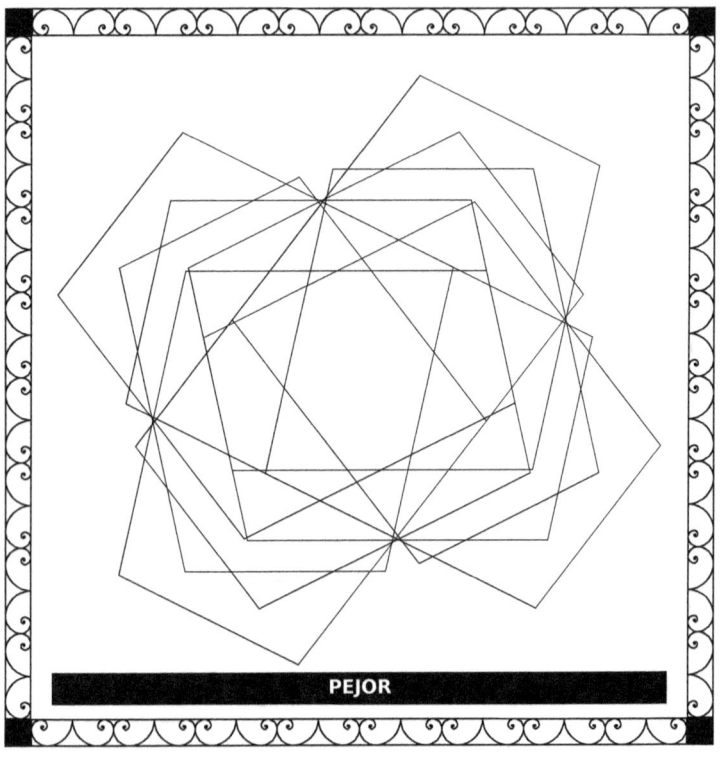

PEJOR

The notes I handle no better than many pianists. But the pauses between the notes — ah, that is where the art resides.
Artur Schnabel

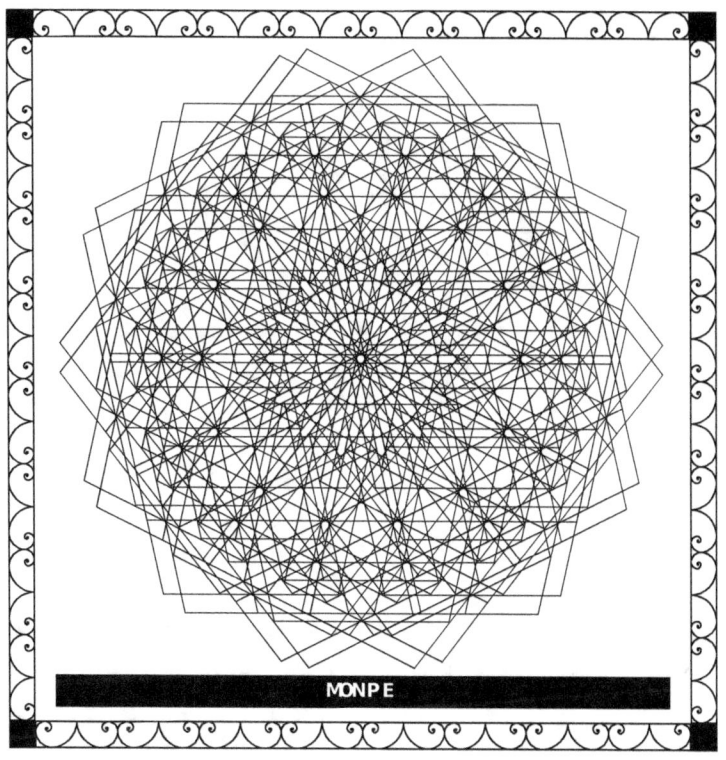

MONPE

Dead he is not, but departed, for the artist never dies.
Henry Wadsworth Longfellow

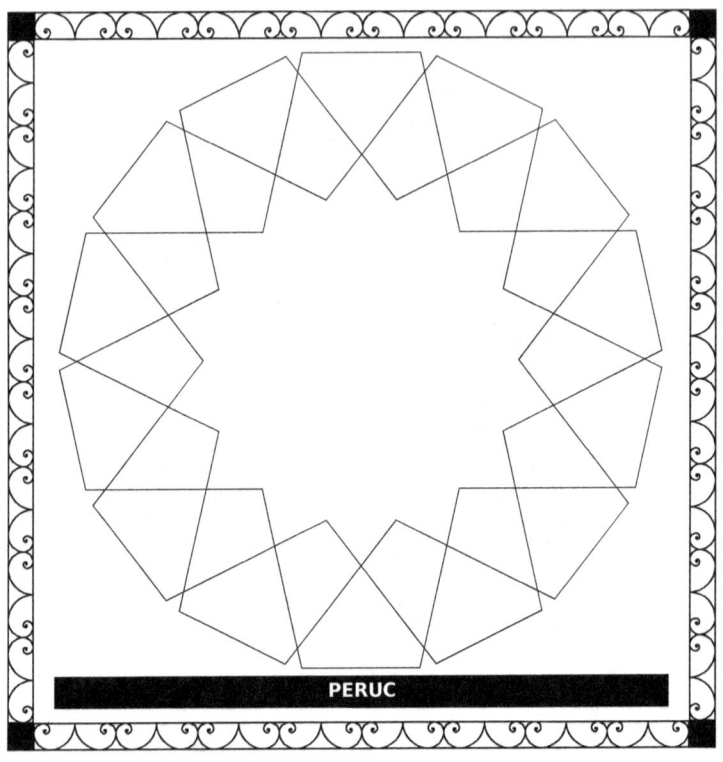

PERUC

The function of art is to struggle against obligation.
Amedeo Modigliani

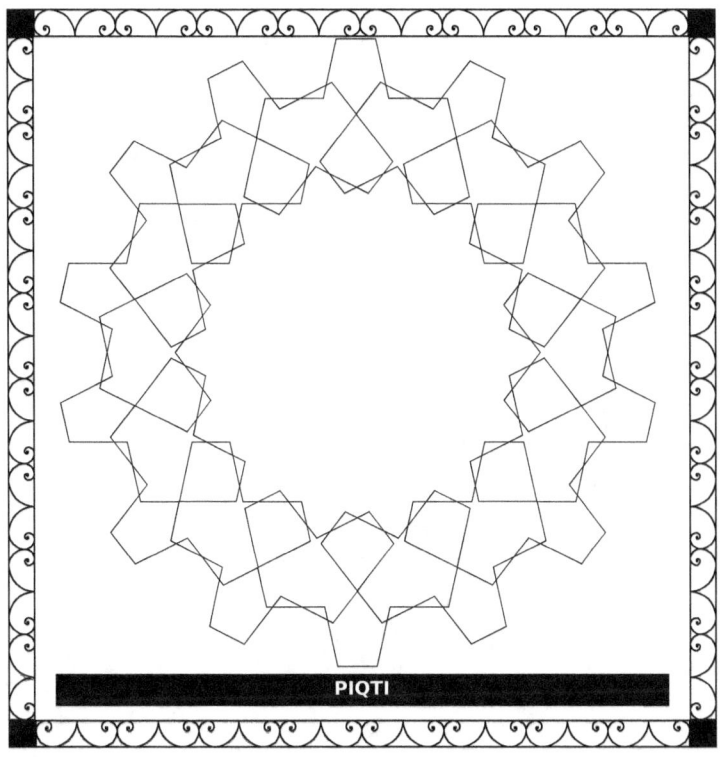

PIQTI

Why is art beautiful? Because it's useless. Why is life ugly? Because it's all ends and purposes and intentions.
Fernando Pessoa

207

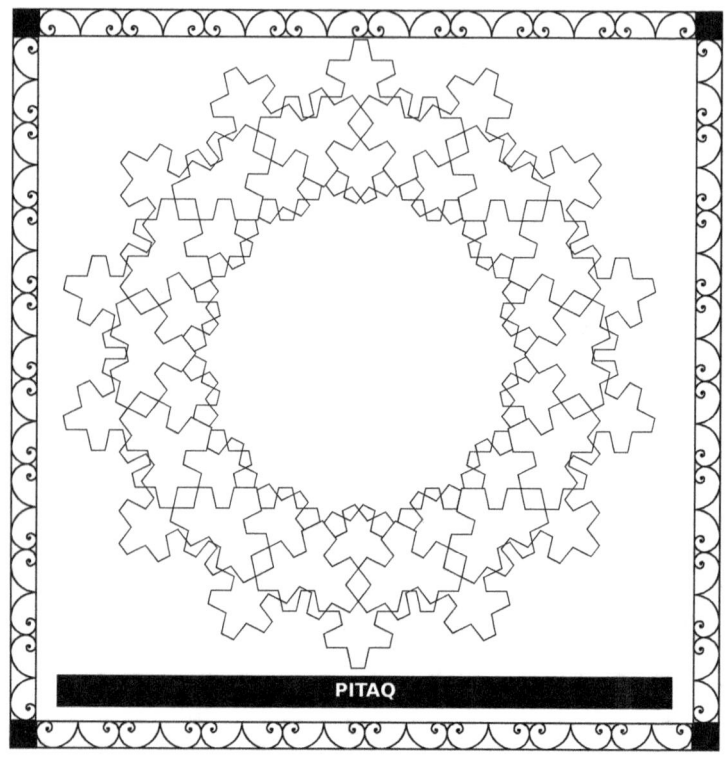

PITAQ

They will explain themselves — as all poems should do
without any comment.
John Keats

208

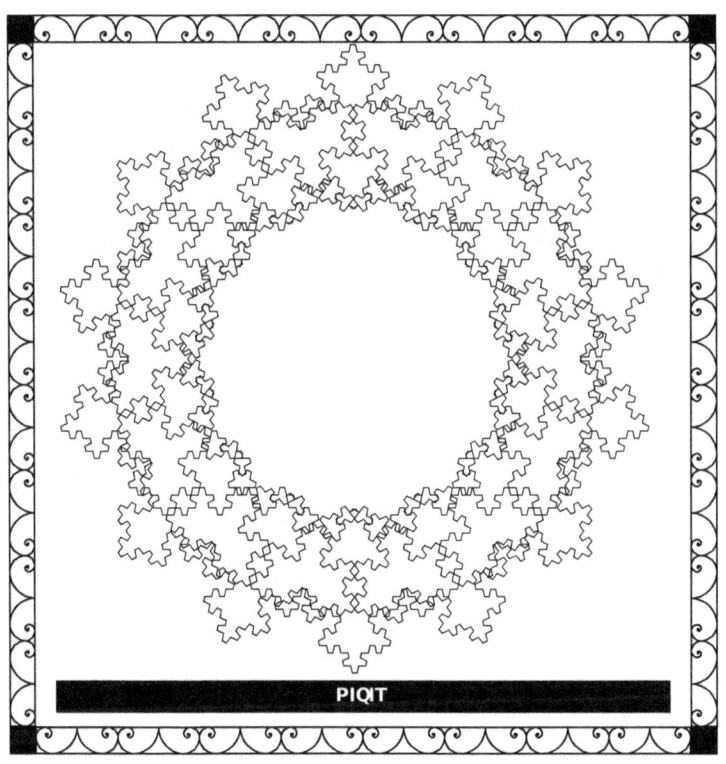

PIQT

A work of art makes a great impression on us only when it gives us something which, even with all the efforts of our intellect, we cannot understand completely.
Arthur Schopenhauer

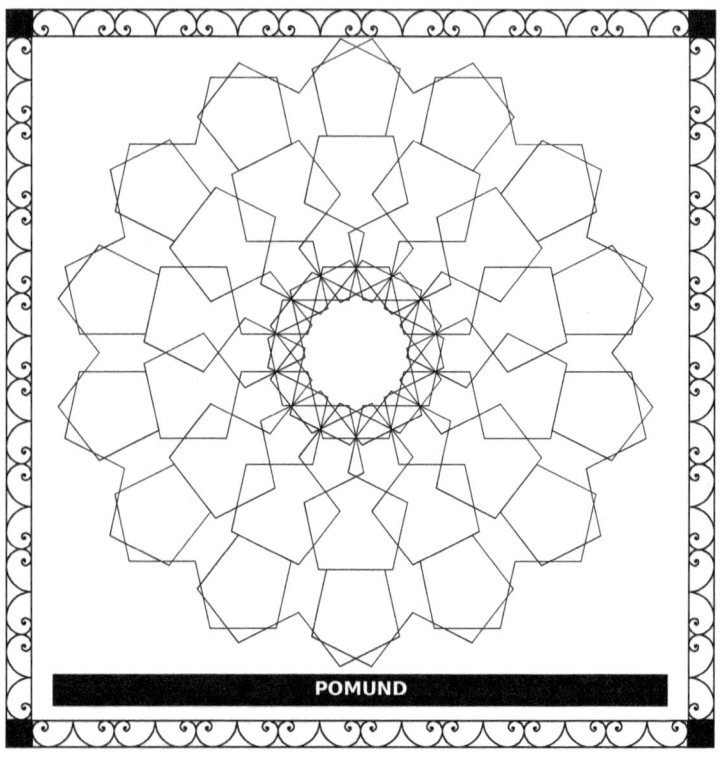

POMUND

It was Pythagoras who first called heaven kosmos, because it is perfect, and adorned with infinite beauty and living beings.

Anonymous ancient author of "The Life of Pythagoras"

210

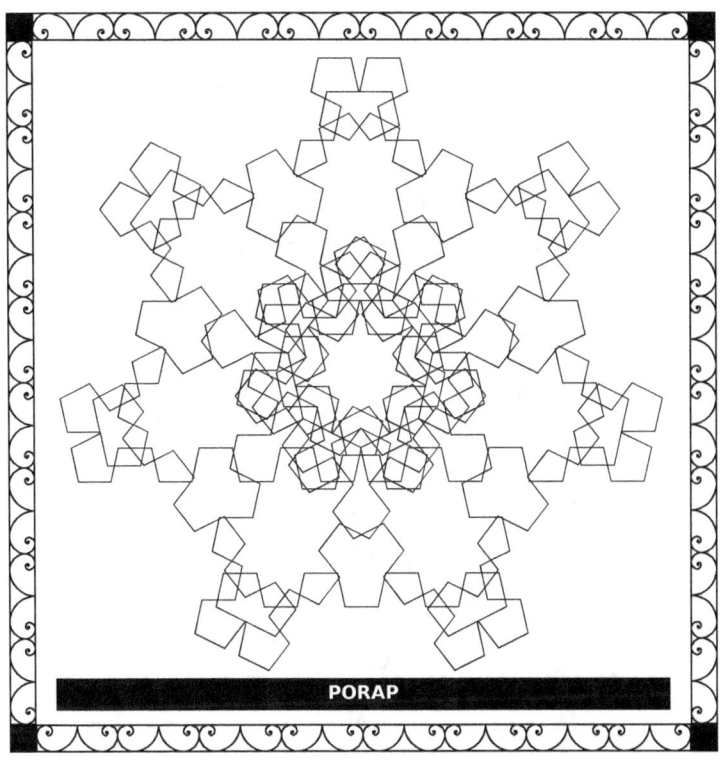

PORAP

So many gods, so many creeds; so many paths that wind and wind, while just the art of being kind is all the sad world needs.

Ella Wheeler Wilcox

211

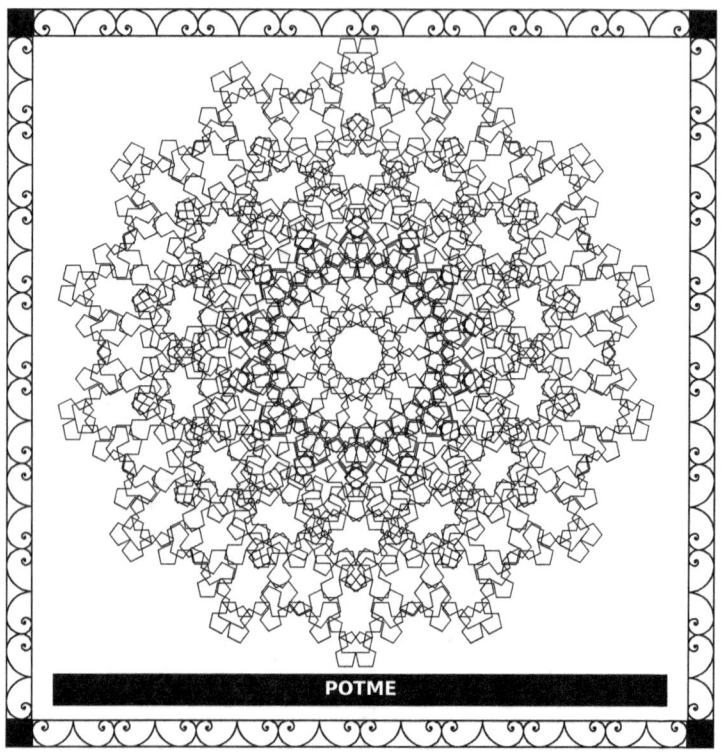

POTME

I think the art of filmmaking is something you learn through actions, by doing it, not by learning theories. And as you do it, your mind starts to change.
Alejandro Jodorowsky

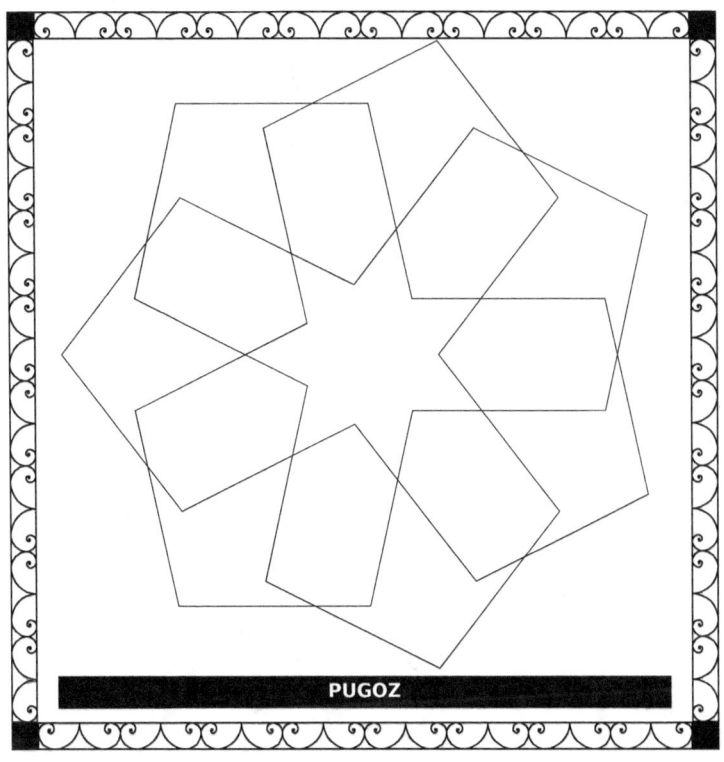

PUGOZ

Realistic, naturalistic art had dissembled the medium, using art to conceal art; Modernism used art to call attention to art.

Clement Greenberg

213

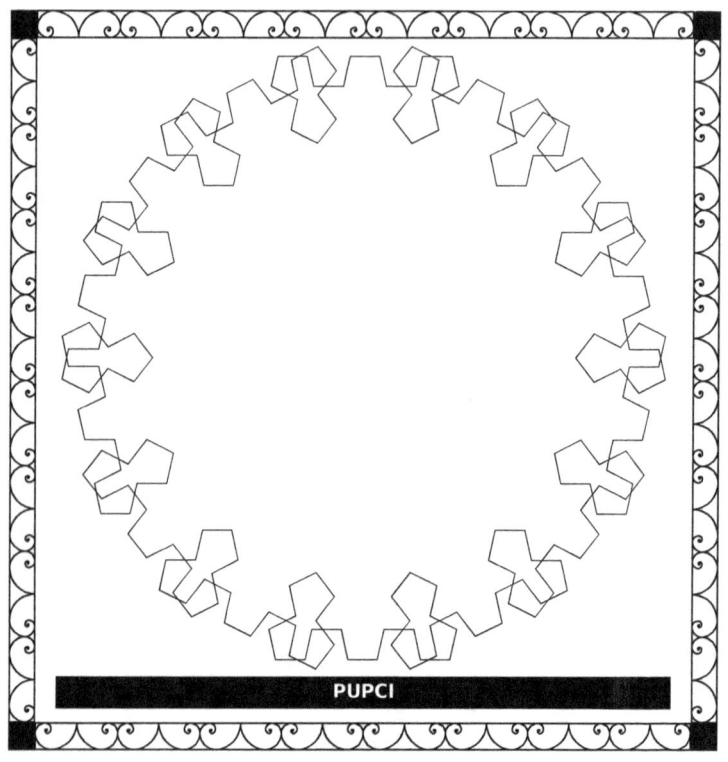

PUPCI

Achilles exists only through Homer. Take away the art of writing from this world, and you will probably take away its glory.

Francois-Rene de Chateaubriand

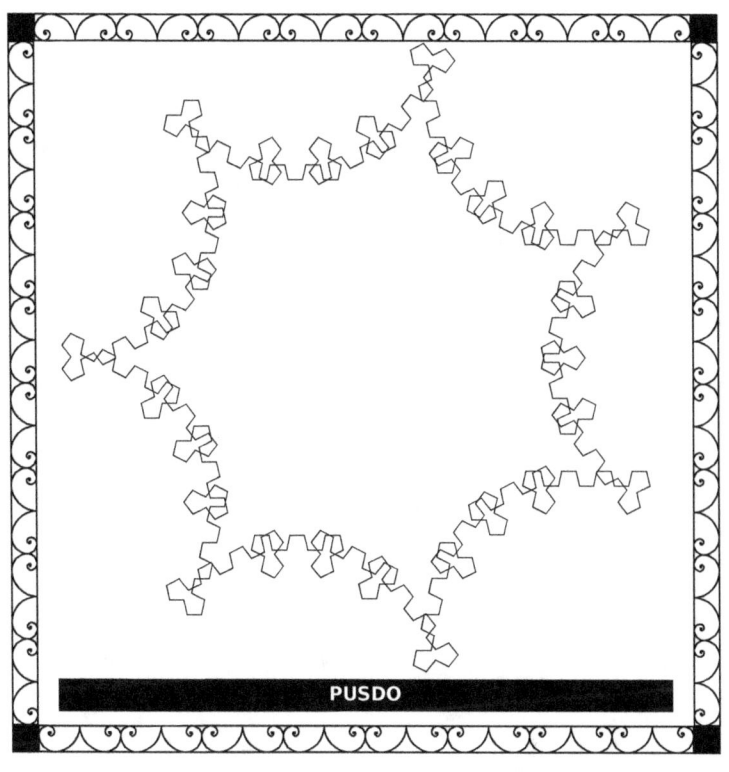

PUSDO

Great artists have no country.
Alfred de Musset

215

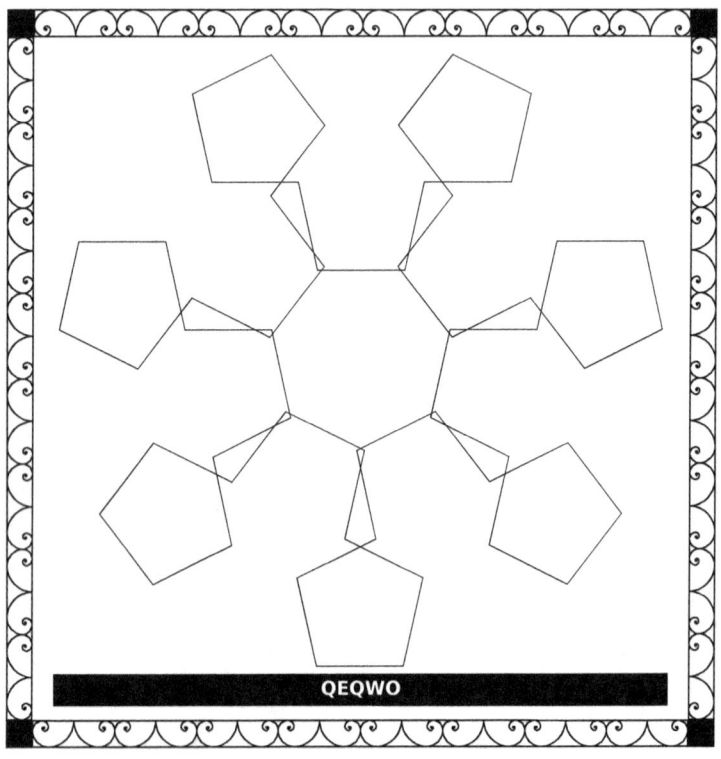

QEQWO

Art is something absolute, something positive, which gives power just as food gives power. While creative science is a mental food, art is the satisfaction of the soul.
Hans Hofmann

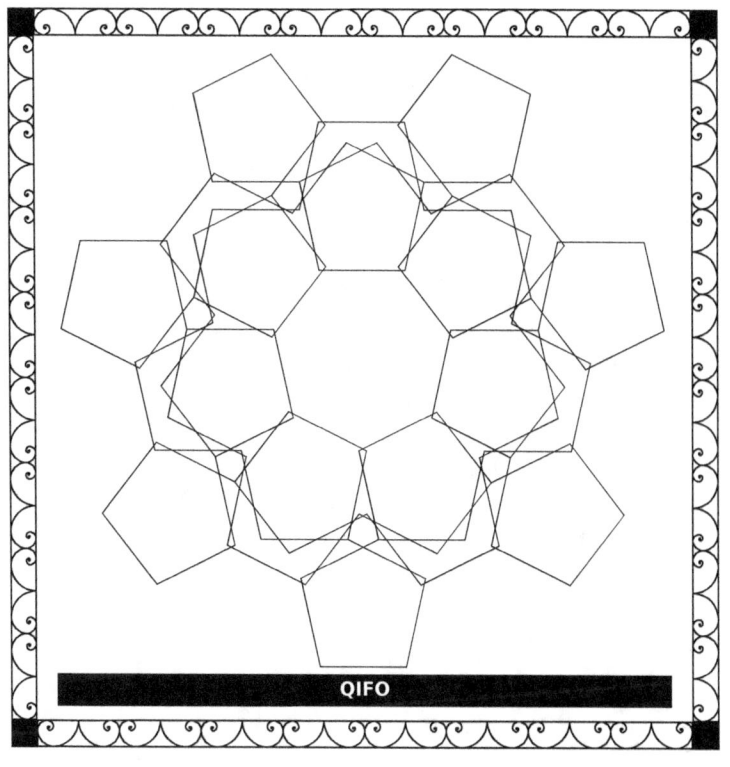

QIFO

Experience isn't interesting until it begins to repeat itself
— in fact, till it does that, it hardly is experience.
Elizabeth Bowen

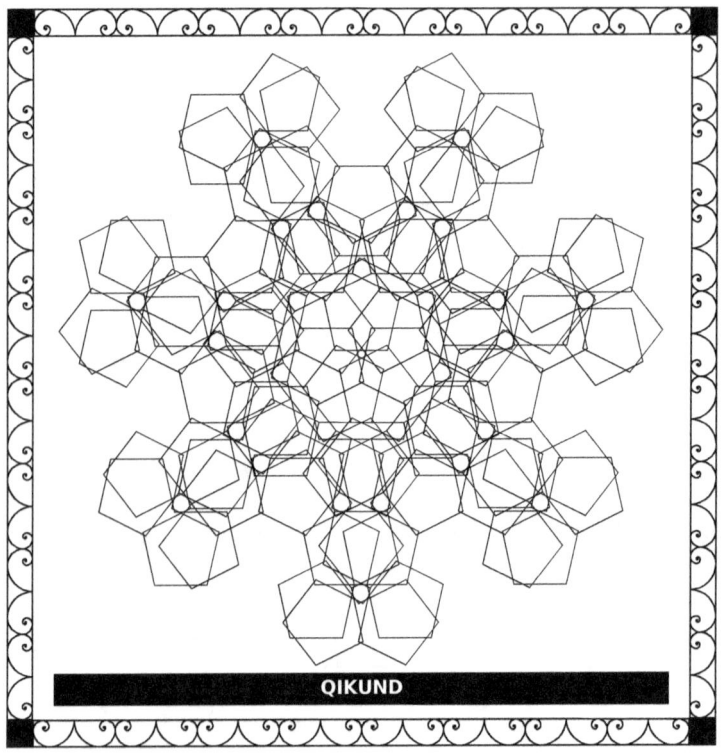

QIKUND

Our intention is to affirm this life, not to bring order out of chaos, nor to suggest improvements in creation, but simply to wake up to the very life we're living, which is so excellent once one gets one's mind and desires out of its way and lets it act of its own accord.

John Cage

218

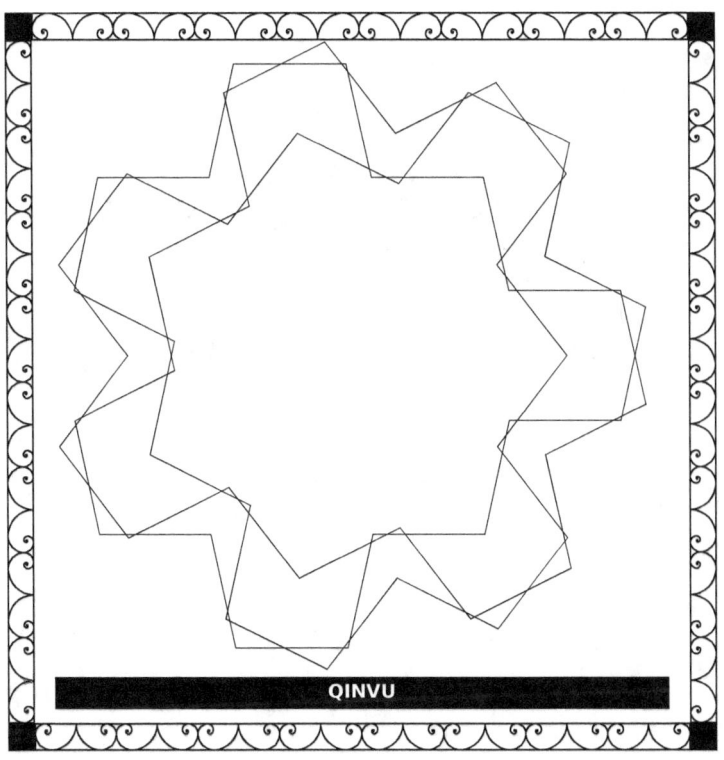

QINVU

Your mind is like this water my friend, when it is agitated it becomes difficult to see. But if you allow it to settle, the answer becomes clear.
Kung Fu Panda

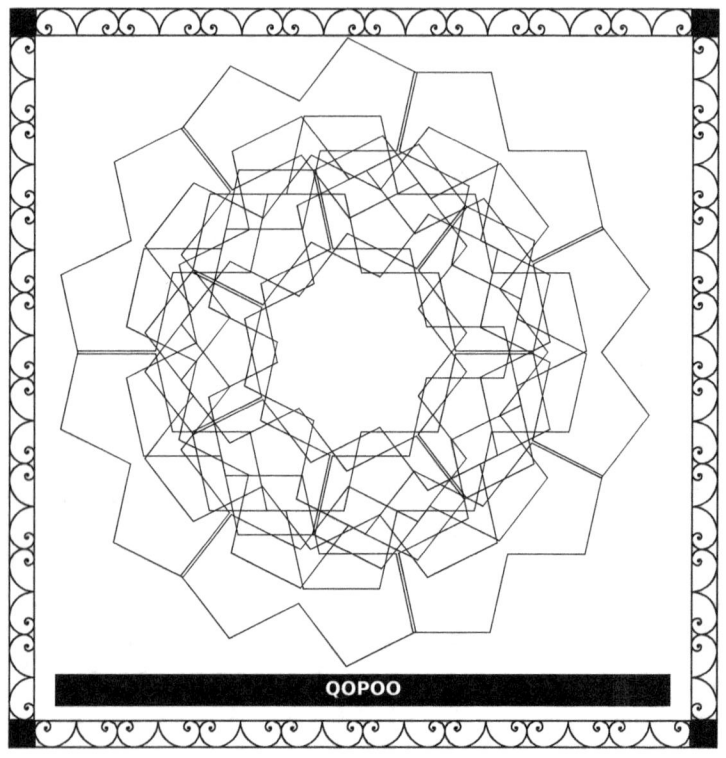

QOPOO

Let people alone. Let them find their way. Let them find
their level and you may sometimes be delighted and aston-
ished at the extraordinary high level to which they'll rise
if they're let alone.
Robertson Davies

220

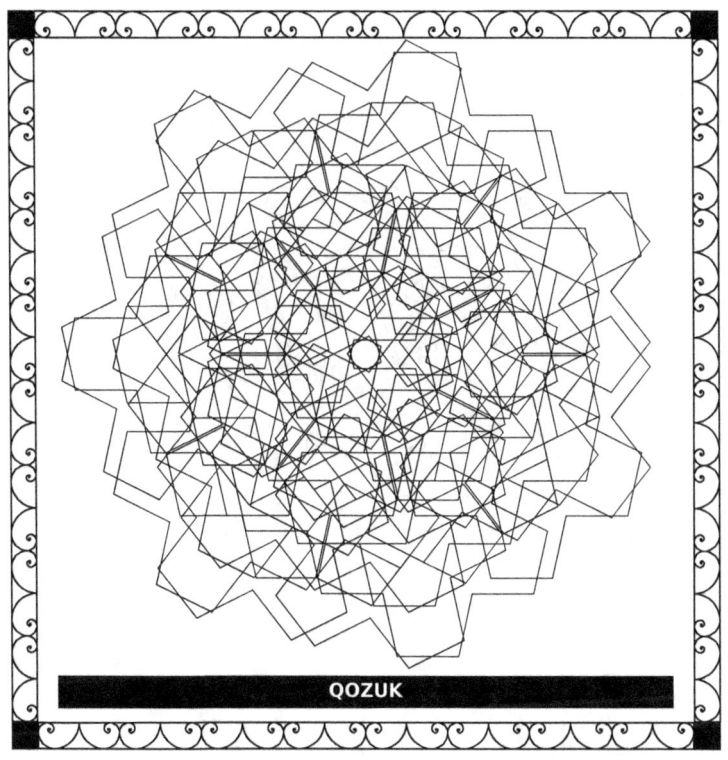

QOZUK

My activism is a part of me. If my art has anything to do with me, then my activism is part of my art.
Ai Weiwei

221

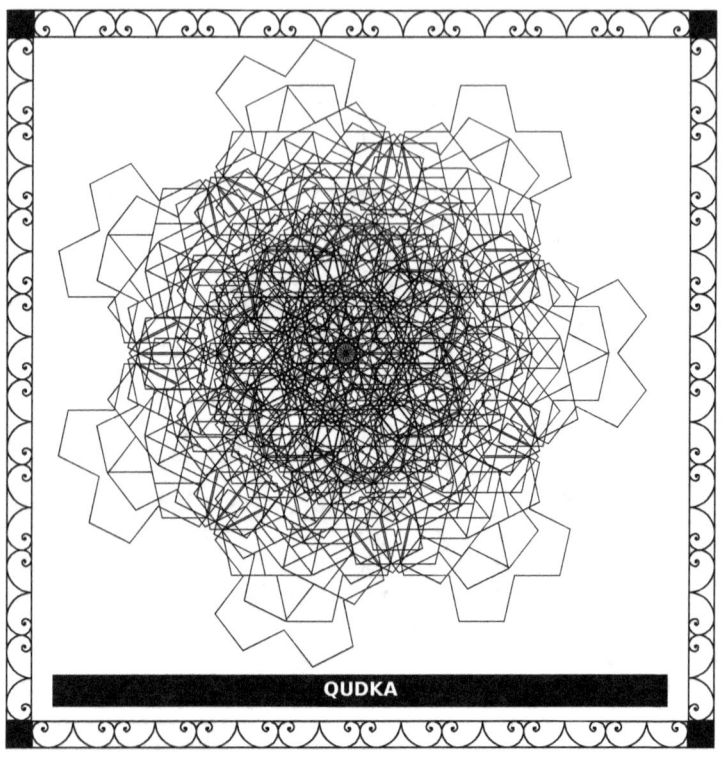

QUDKA

Every artist was first an amateur.
Ralph Waldo Emerson

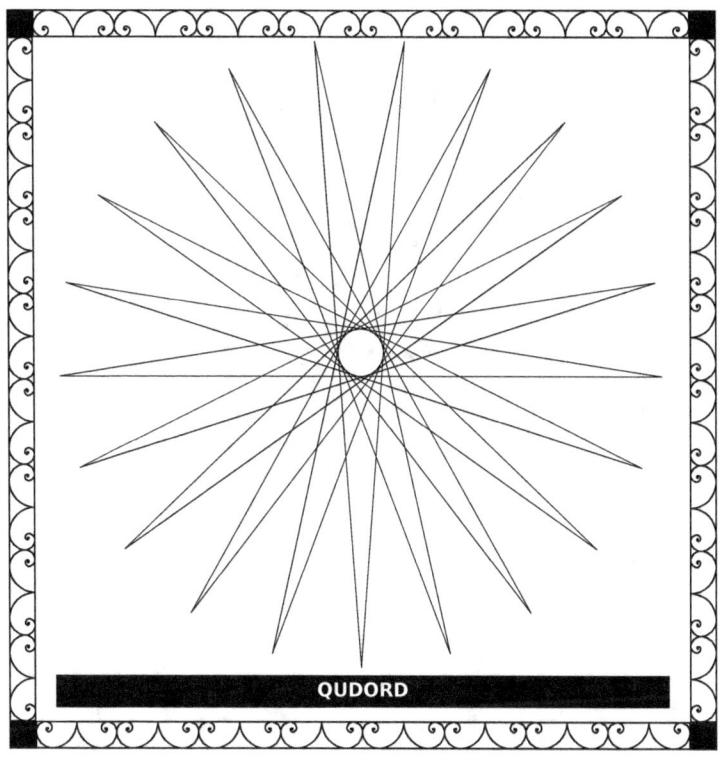

QUDORD

A burglar who respects his art always takes his time before taking anything else.

O. Henry

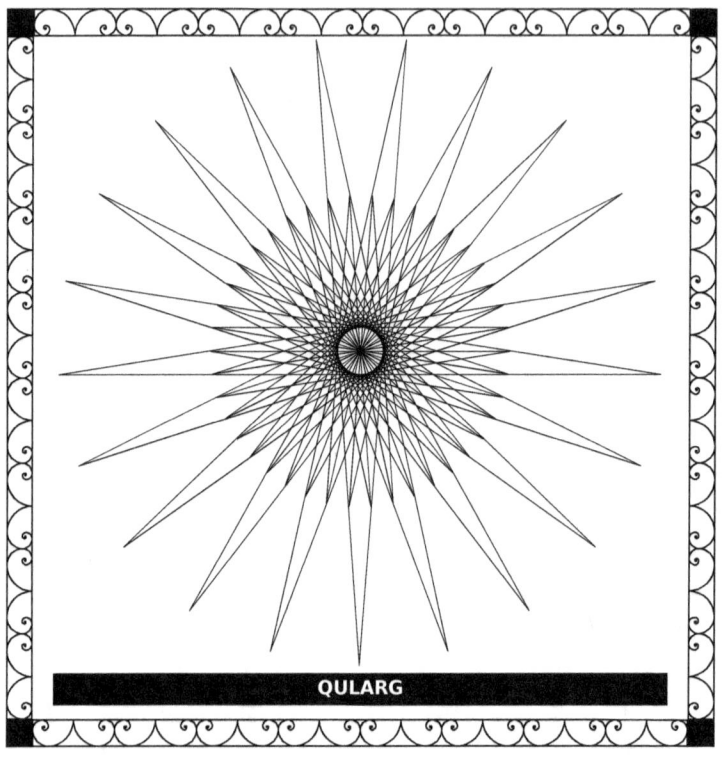

QULARG

To do an evil action is base; to do a good action without incurring danger is common enough; but it is the part of a good man to do great and noble deeds, though he risks every thing.

Plutarch

224

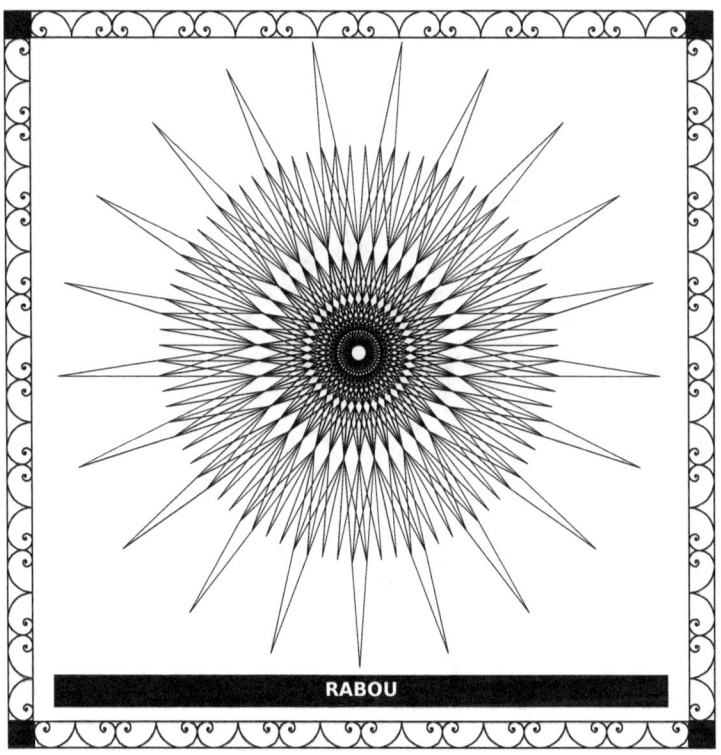

RABOU

Knowing that certain nights whose sweetness lingers will keep returning to the earth and sea after we are gone, yes, this helps us to die.

Albert Camus

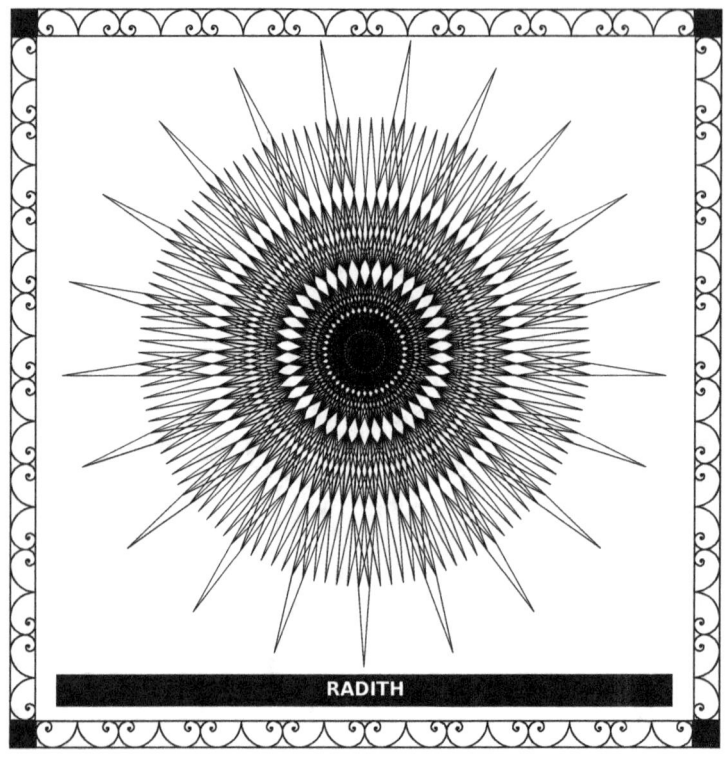

RADITH

Only he is an artist who can make a riddle out of a solution.
Karl Kraus

226

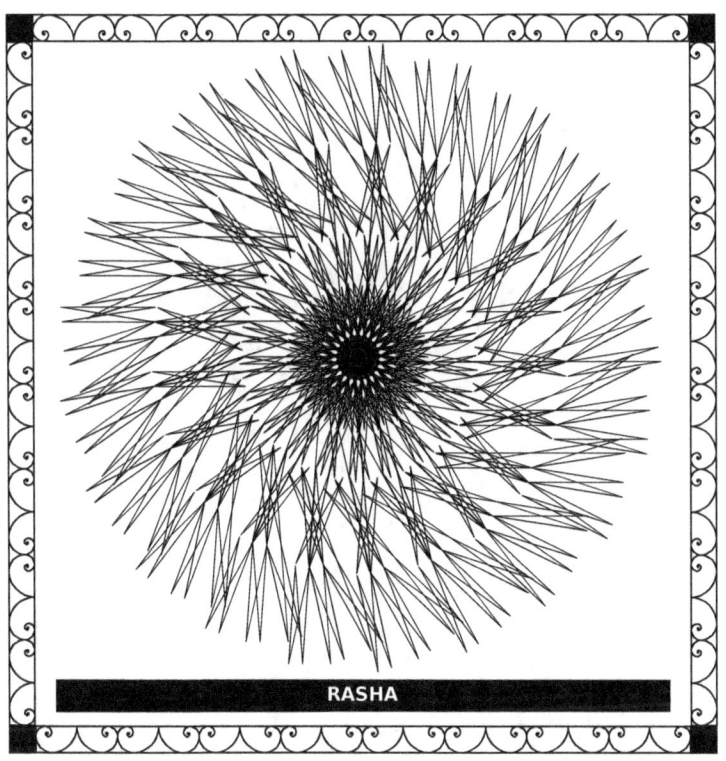

RASHA

Both art and the artist lack identity and define themselves
only through their encounter with each other.
Harold Rosenberg

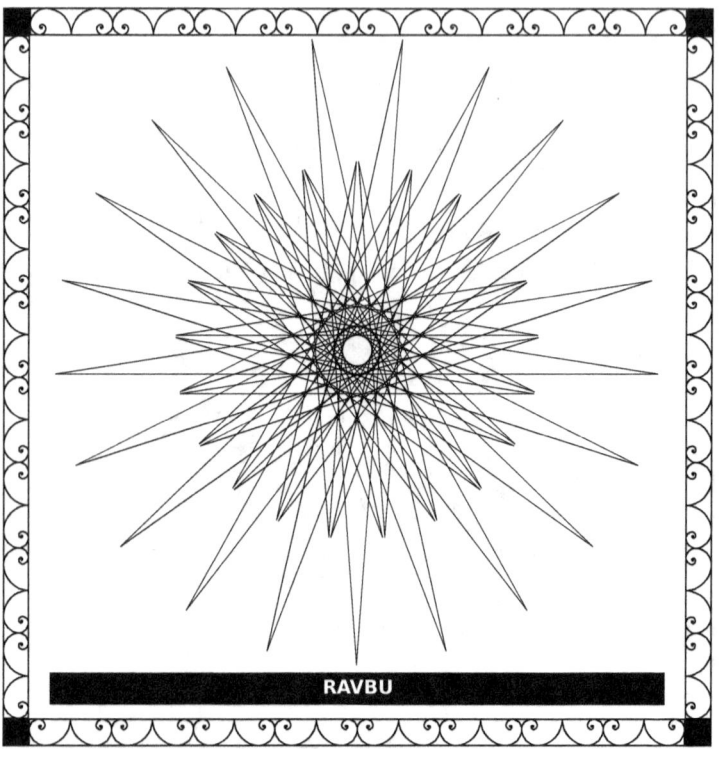

RAVBU

I am enough of an artist to draw freely upon my imagination. Imagination is more important than knowledge. Knowledge is limited. Imagination encircles the world.
Albert Einstein

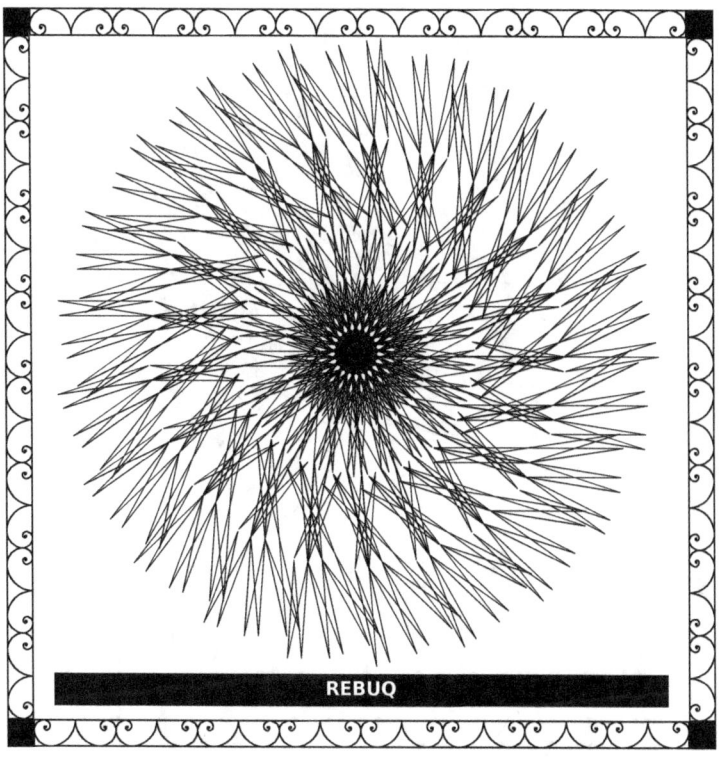

REBUQ

When pride in some form is lost we feel very different. We feel the victory over pride, and we feel very different being for a few moments free of pride. We feel a moment of perfection that is indescribable, a sudden joy in living.
Agnes Martin, On the Perfection Underlying Life

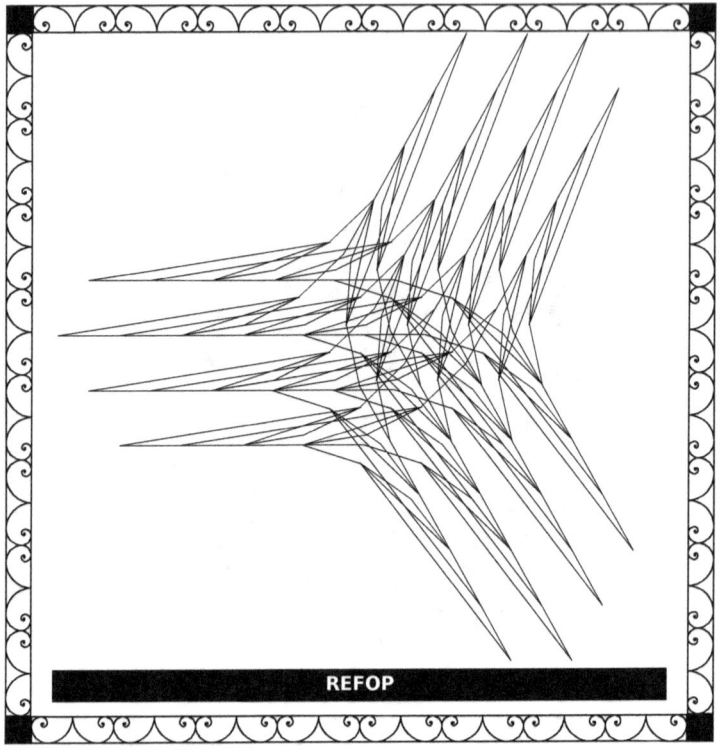

REFOP

I've described my usual writing process as scrambling from peak to peak on inspiration through foggy valleys of despised logic. Inspiration is better — when you can get it.
Lois McMaster Bujold

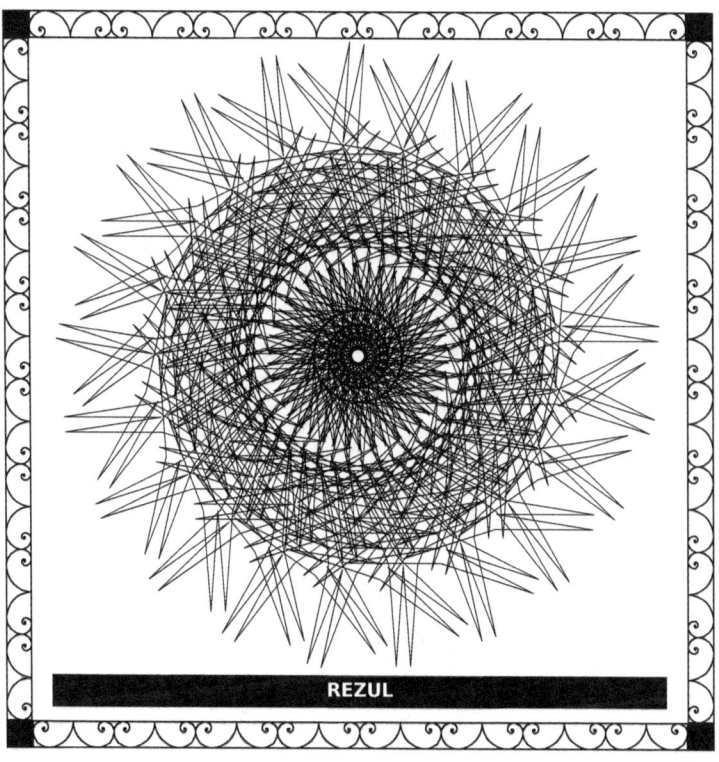

REZUL

I have never seen a greater monster or miracle in the world than myself.
Michel de Montaigne

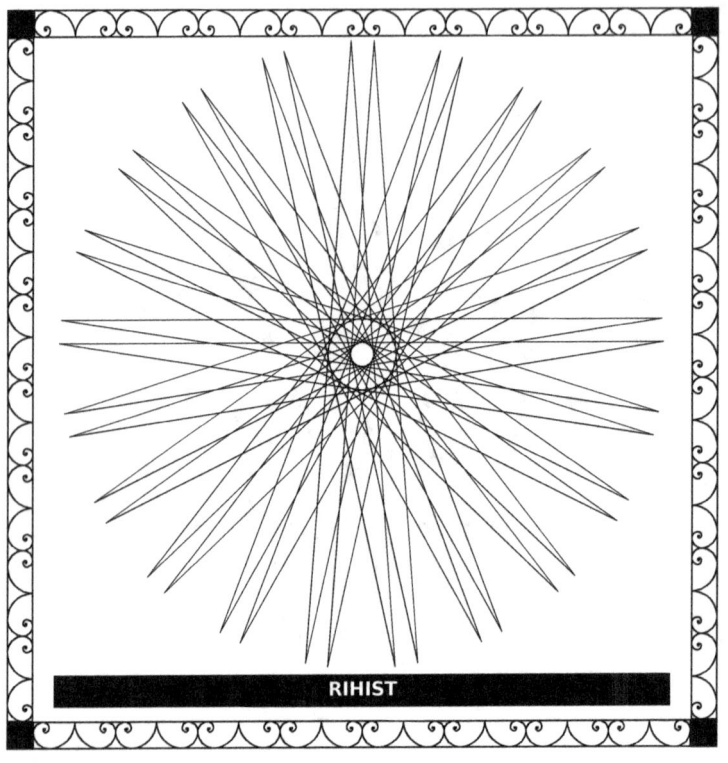

RIHIST

Everything written about art is profoundly unimportant.
Patrick Swift

232

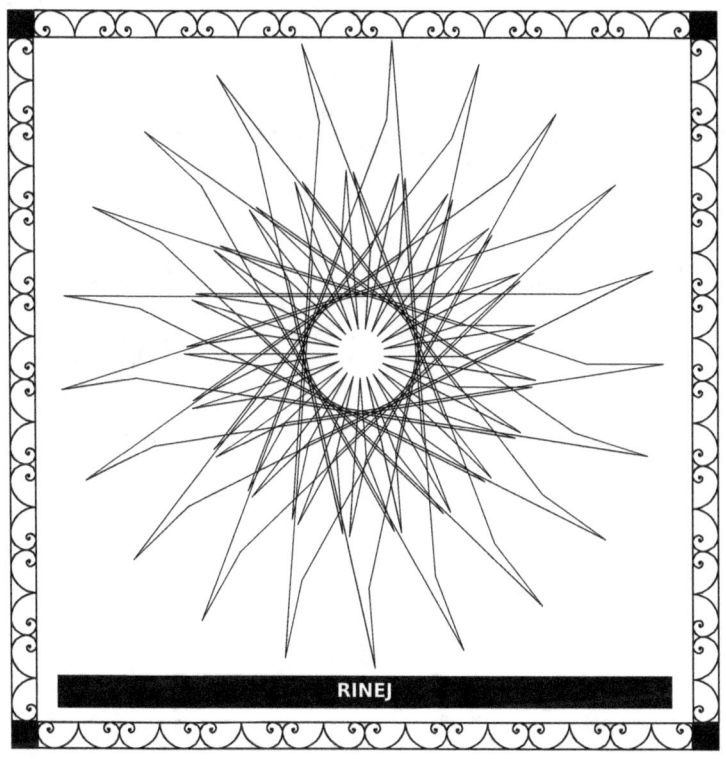

RINEJ

The works of abstract art are subtle creations of order out of simple contrasting elements.
Jan Tschichold

233

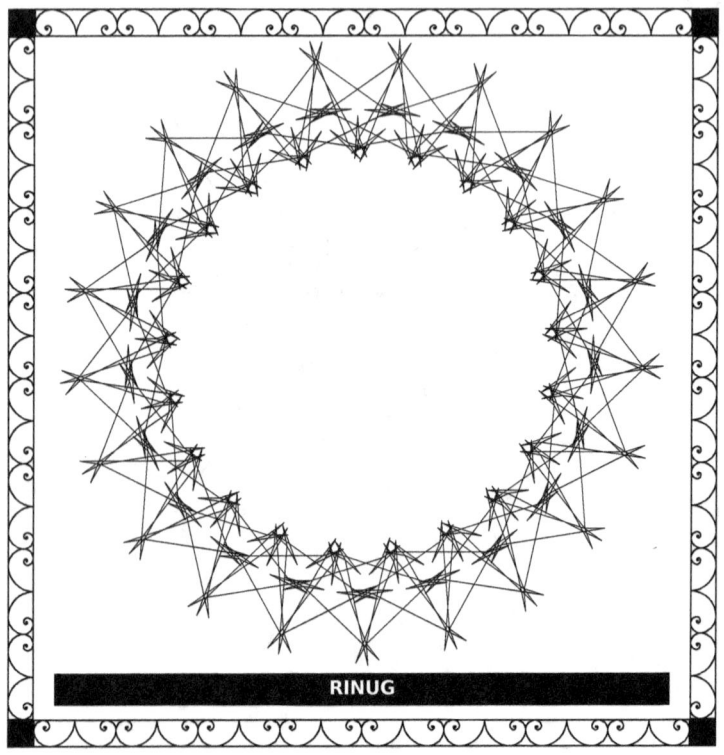

RINUG

The sole art that suits me is that which, rising from unrest, tends toward serenity.
Andre Gide

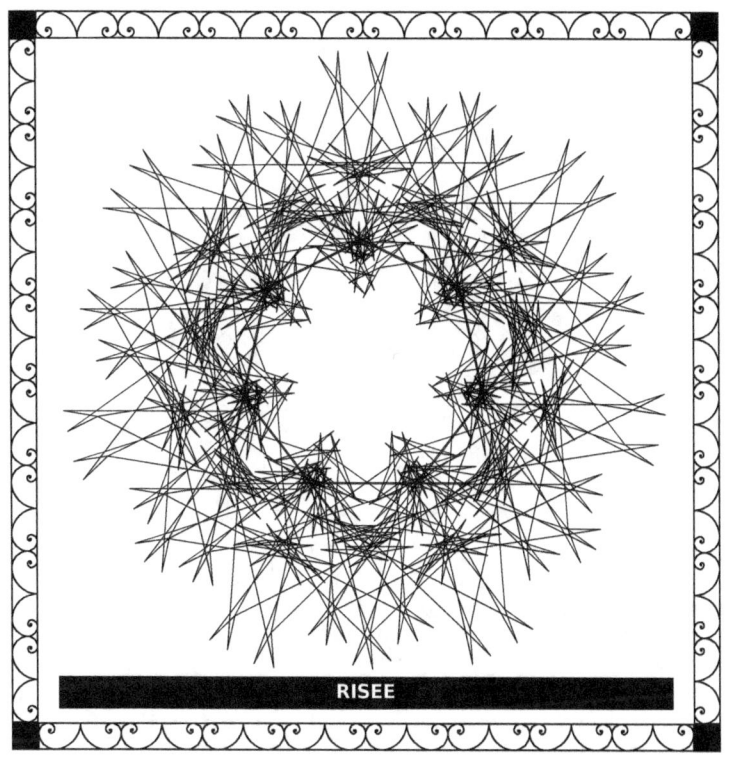

RISEE

The artist begins with a vision — a creative operation requiring effort. Creativity takes courage.
Henri Matisse

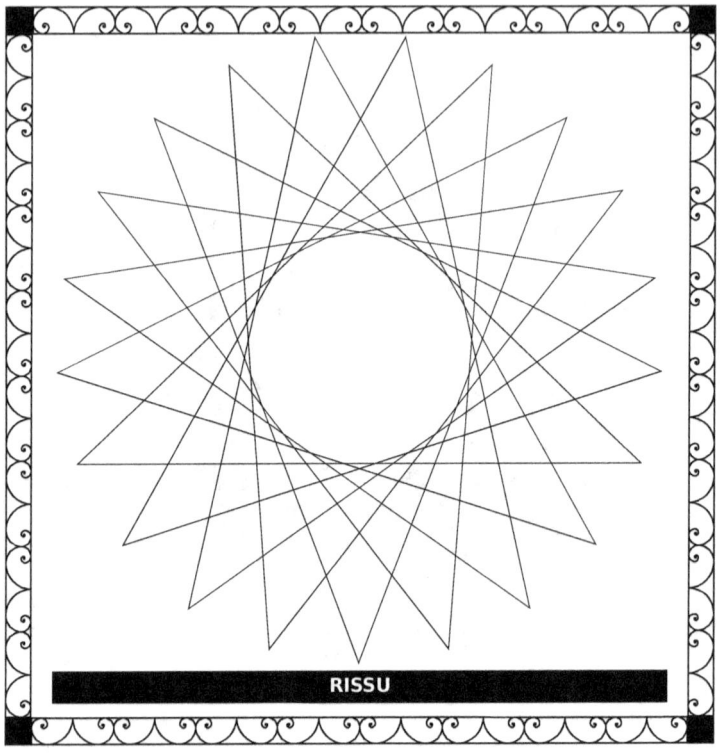

RISSU

The art always wins. Anything can happen to me, but the art will stay.
Ai Weiwei

236

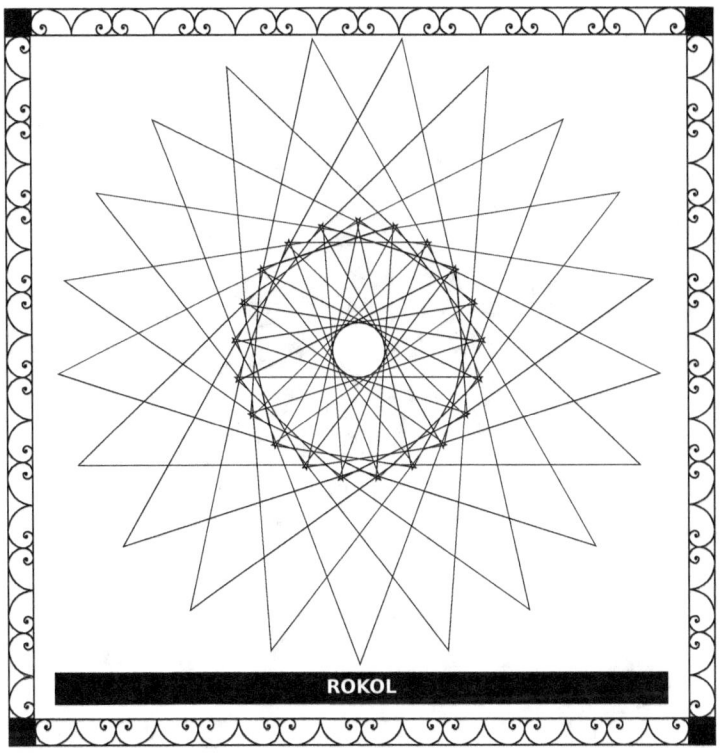

ROKOL

The magic happens only when the artist serves with love and the listener receives with the same spirit.

M. S. Swaminathan

237

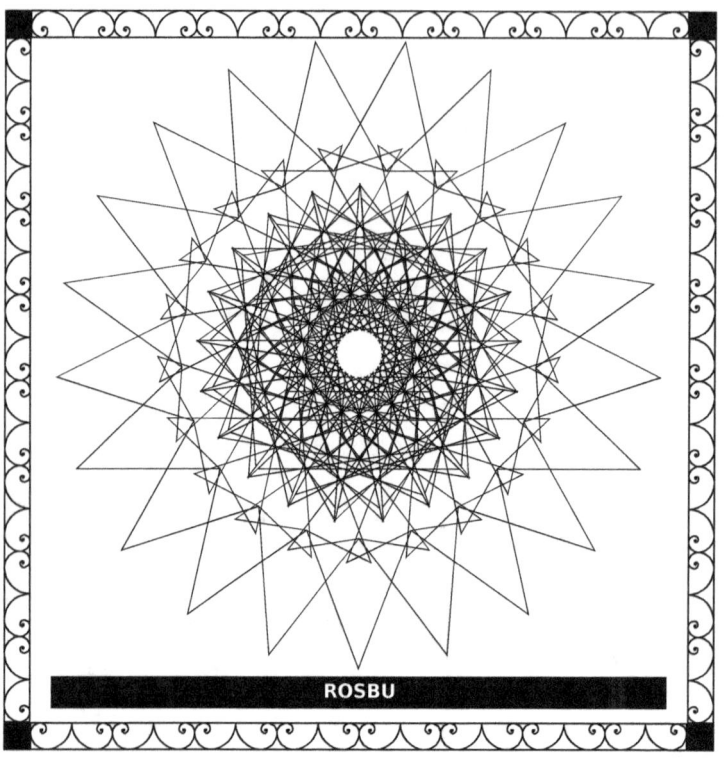

ROSBU

No man thinks there is much ado about nothing when the ado is about himself.
Anthony Trollope

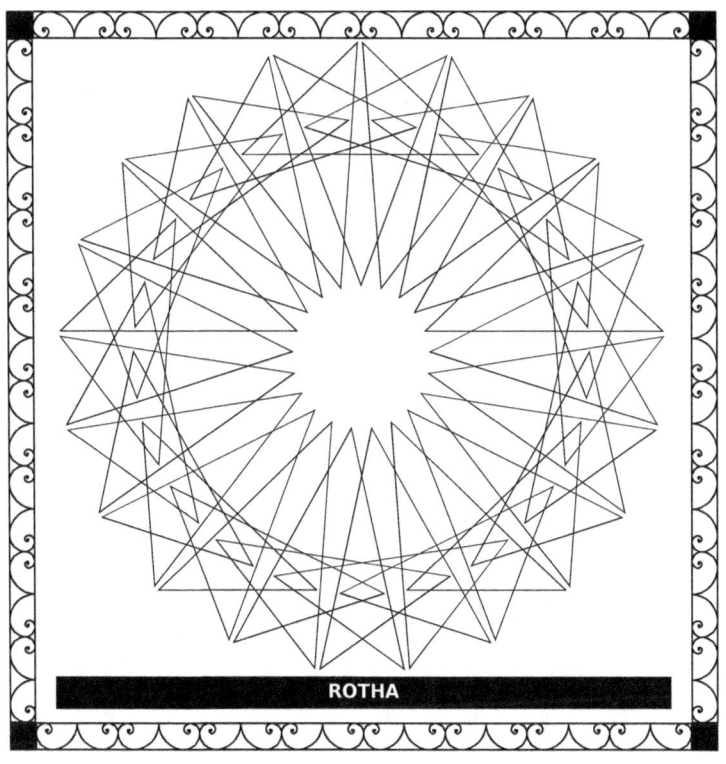

ROTHA

The artist is the creator of beautiful things. To reveal art
and conceal the artist is art's aim.

Oscar Wilde, The Picture of Dorian Gray

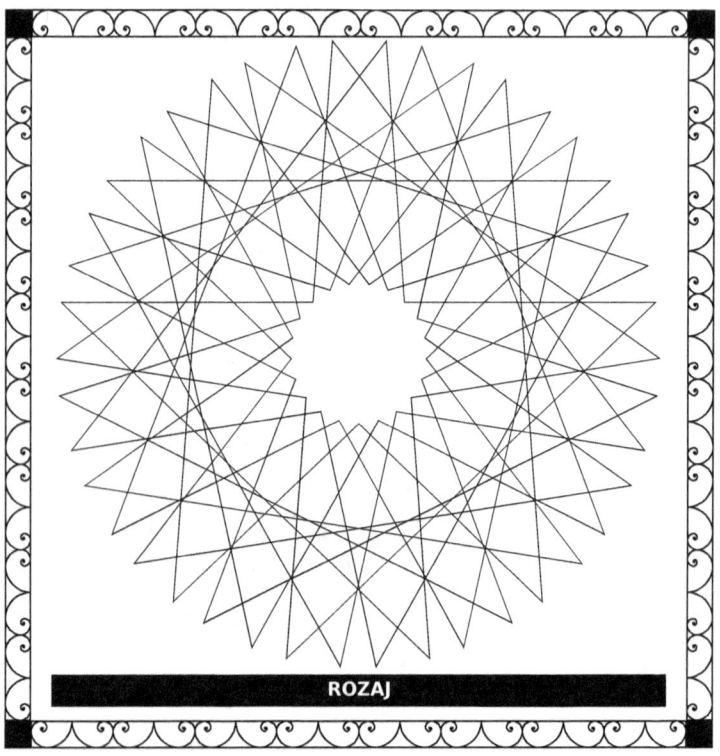

ROZAJ

The saying that beauty is but skin deep is but a skin-deep saying.
Herbert Spencer

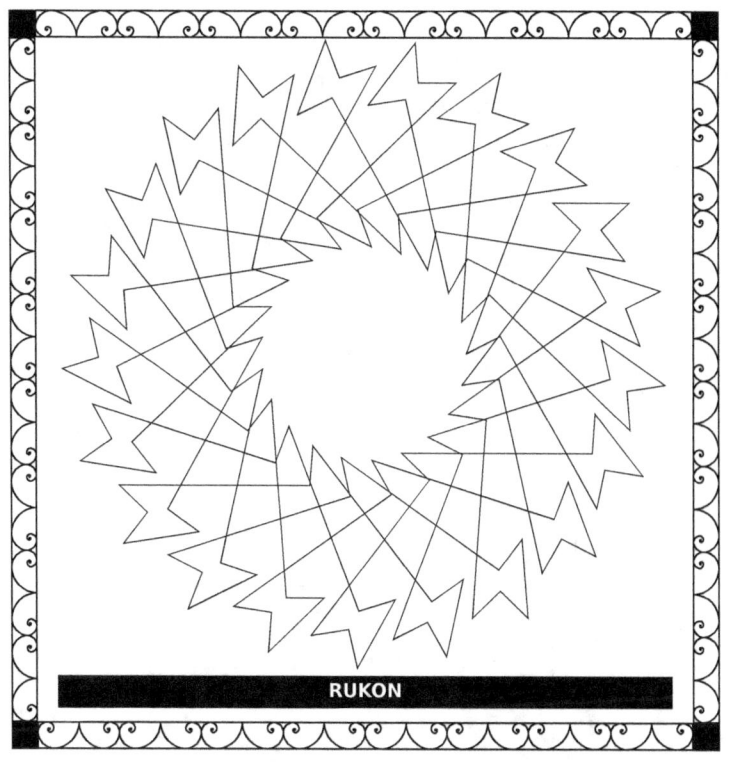

RUKON

Let the beauty of what you love be what you do.
Rumi

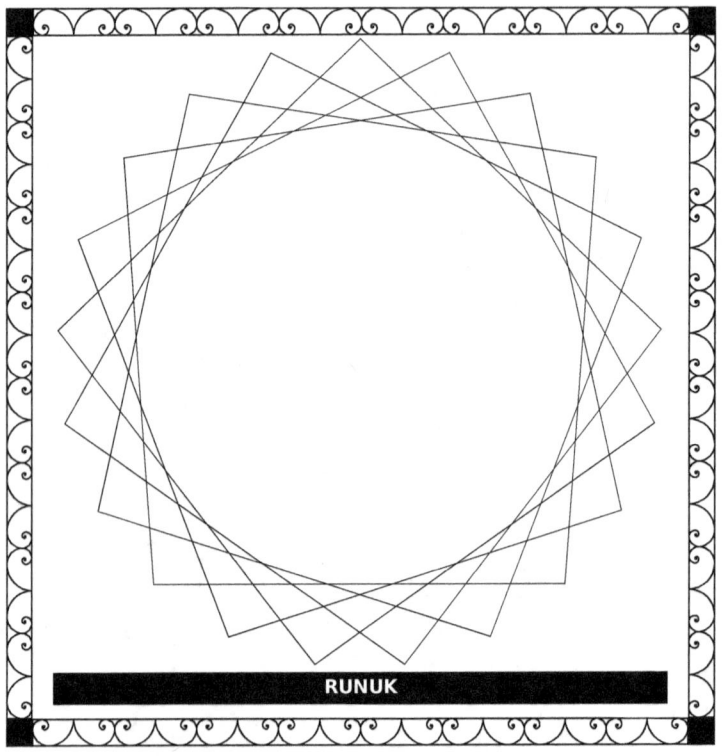

RUNUK

Success or achievement is not the final goal. It is the spirit in which you act that puts the seal of beauty upon your life.
Chinmayananda Saraswati

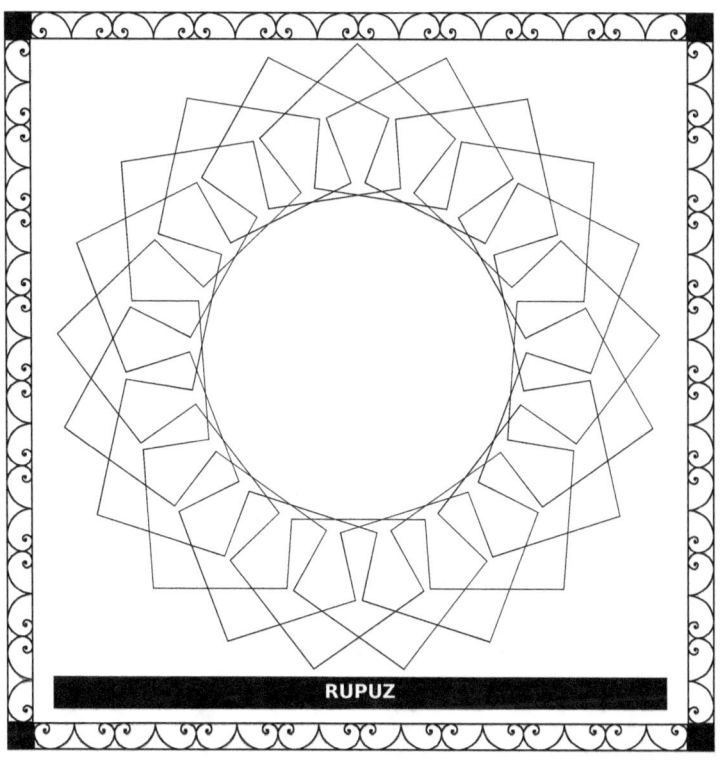

RUPUZ

The true artist will let his wife starve, his children go bare-foot, his mother drudge for his living at seventy, sooner than work at anything but his art.
George Bernard Shaw

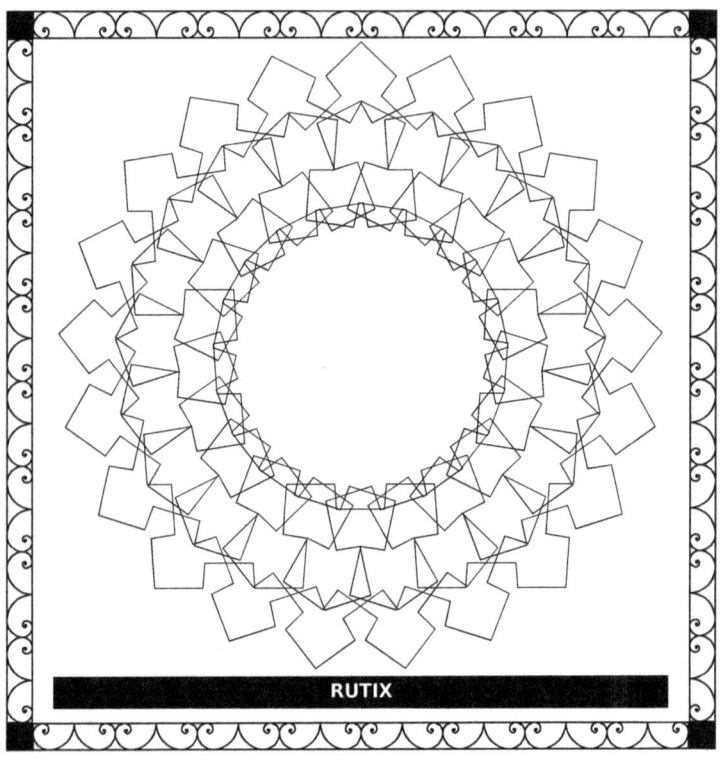

RUTIX

There is an artist imprisoned in each one of us. Let him loose to spread joy everywhere.
Bertrand Russell

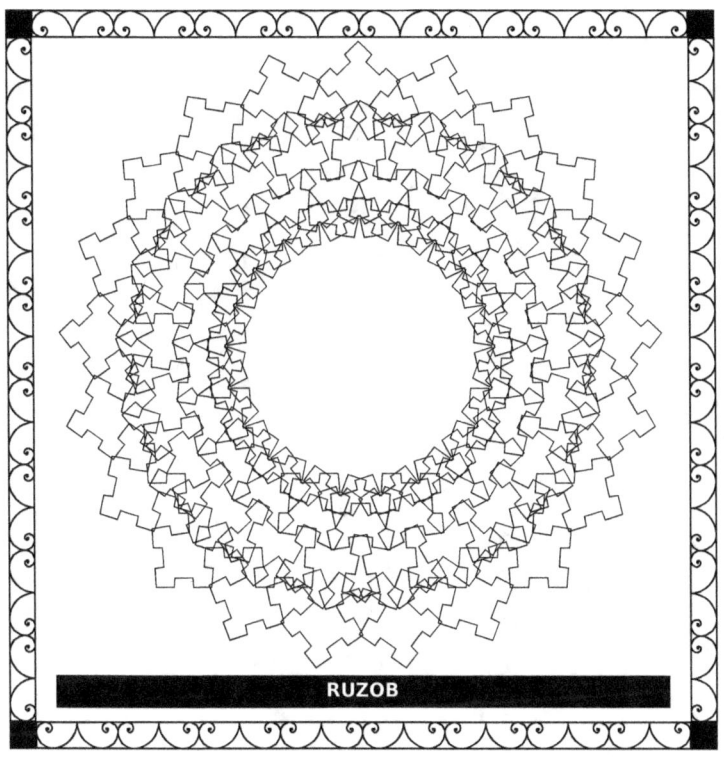

RUZOB

The real voyage of discovery consists not in seeking new landscapes but in having new eyes.
Marcel Proust

245

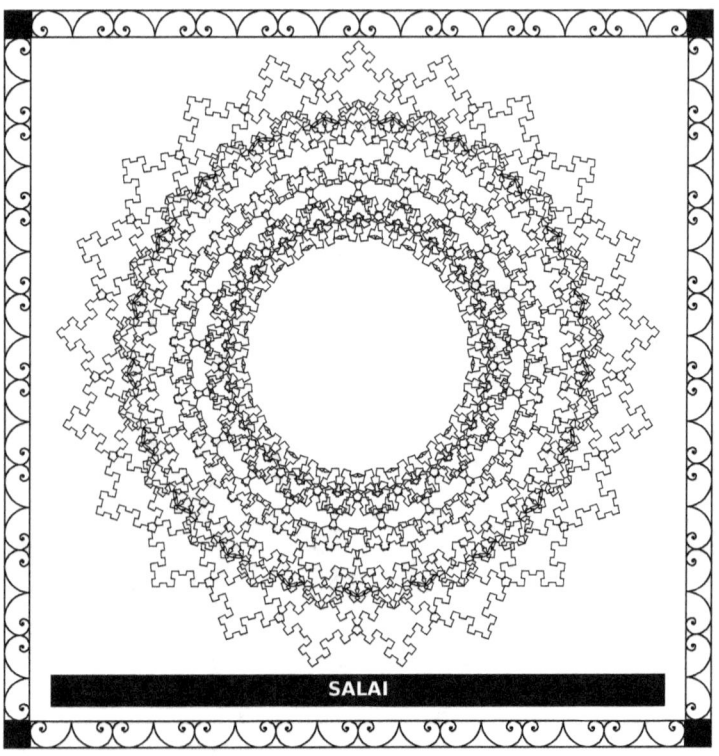

SALAI

Works of art make rules but rules do not make works of art.
Claude Debussy

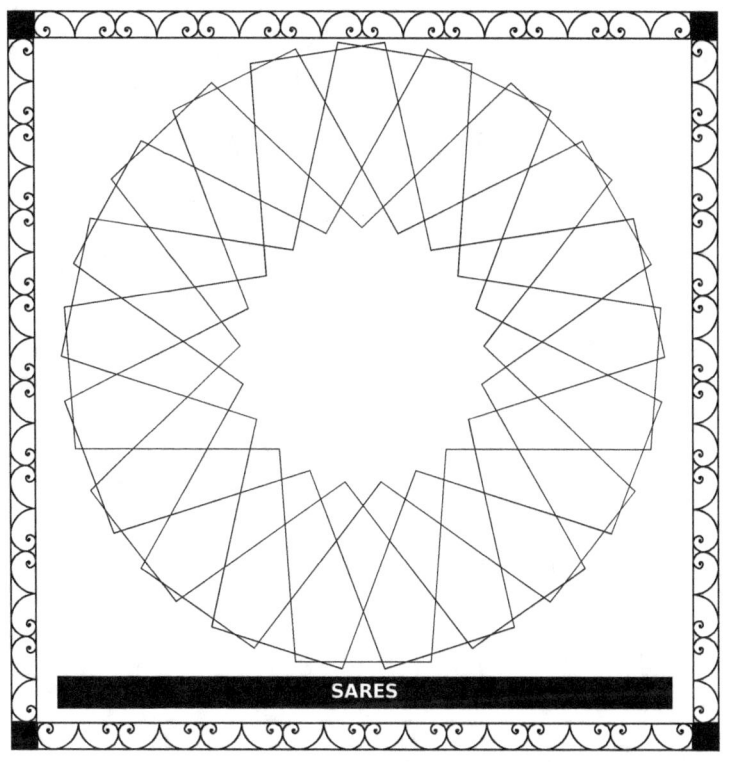

SARES

You become an artist to upset your family.
Gunter Brus

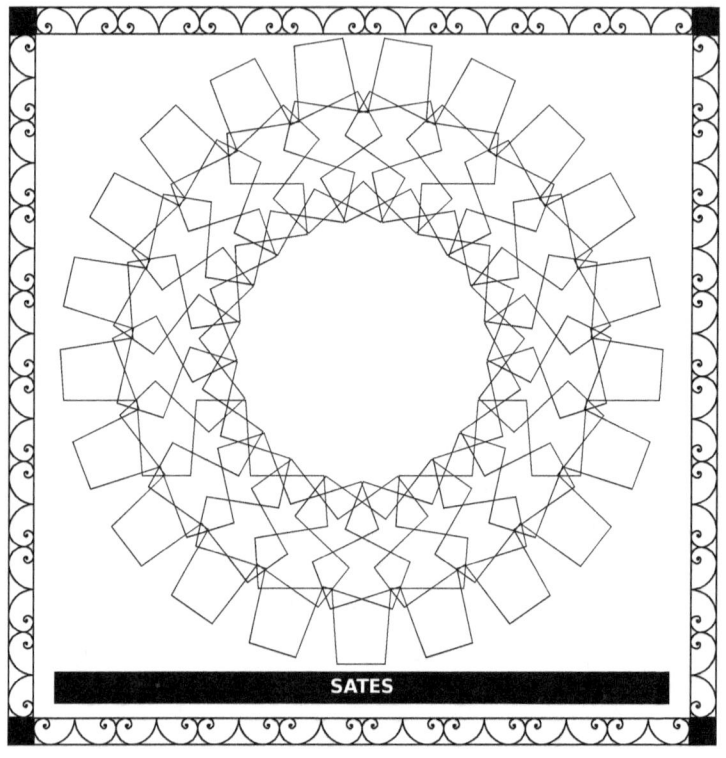

SATES

The criteria of art are the imponderable, the immeasurable.
Elfriede Jelinek

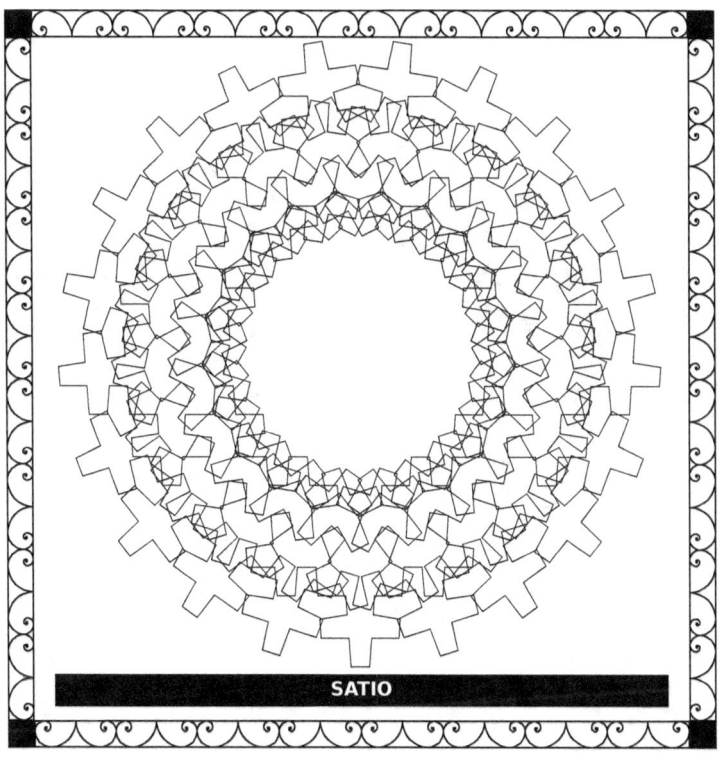

SATIO

Another unsettling element in modern art is that common symptom of immaturity, the dread of doing what has been done before.

Edith Wharton

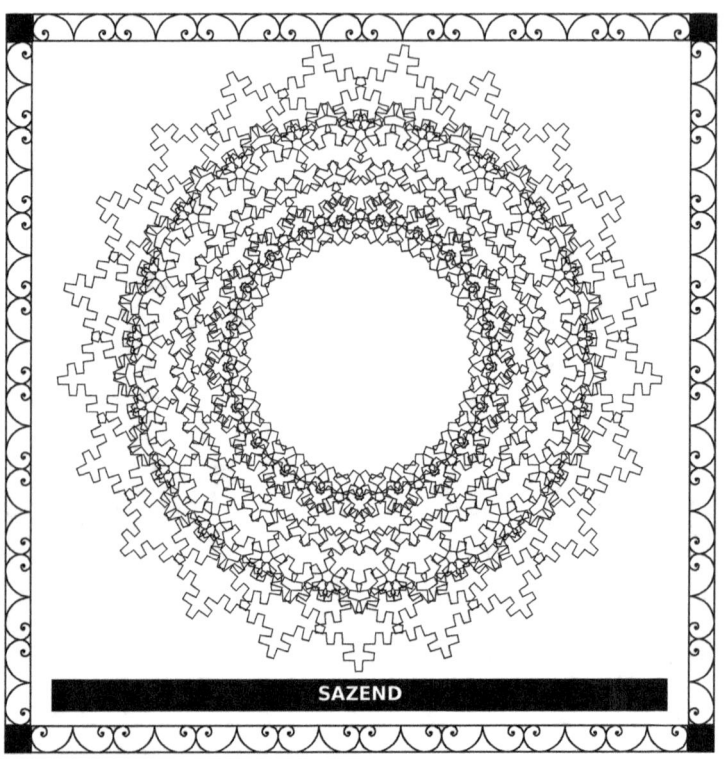

SAZEND

Creation always involves building upon something else. There
is no art that doesn't reuse. And there will be less art if
every reuse is taxed by the appropriator.
Lawrence Lessig

250

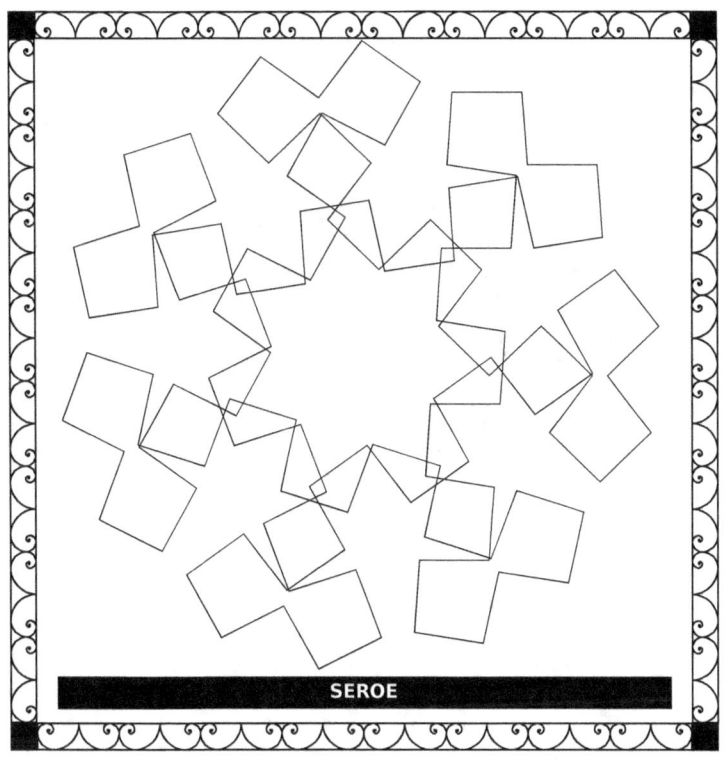

SEROE

Through Kurt [Cobain] I saw the beauty of minimalism and the importance of music that's stripped down.
Dave Grohl

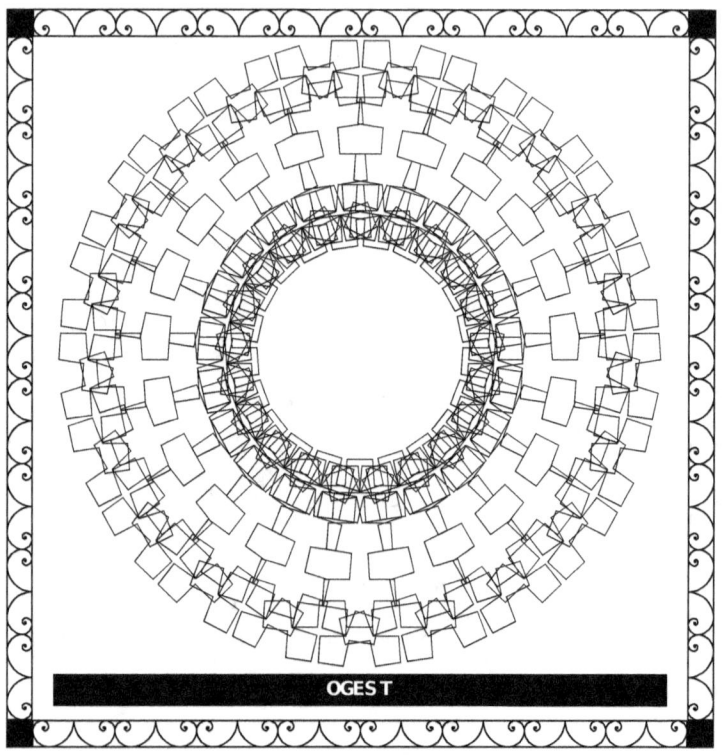

OGES T

The more I look at most of the art movements, it's all occultism, when you get down to it. The Surrealists were openly talking about being magicians.
Alan Moore

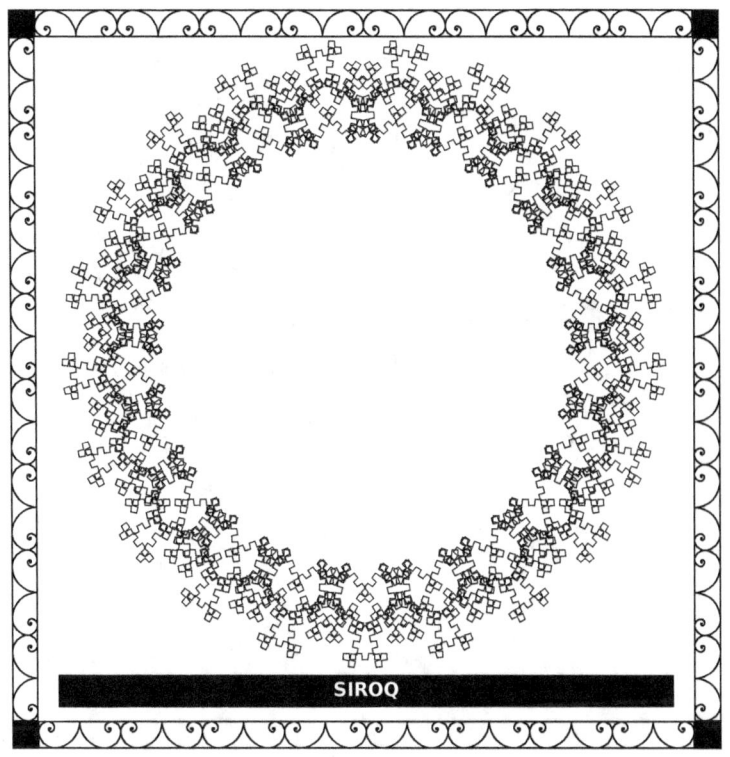

SIROQ

Very few people know why art sells so high. I don't even know.
Ai Weiwei

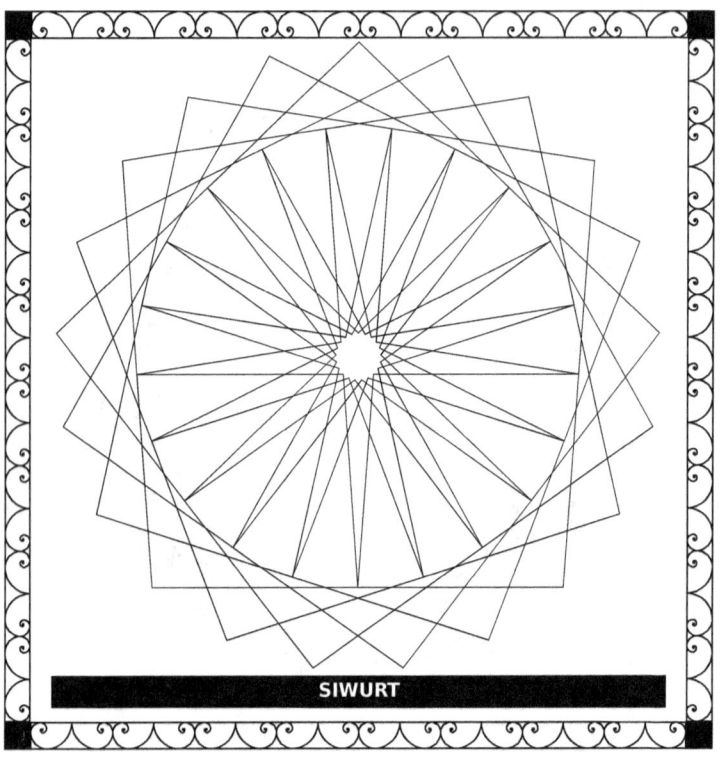

SIWURT

Every person is worthy of an infinite wealth of love - the beauty of his soul knows no limit.
Rabindranath Tagore

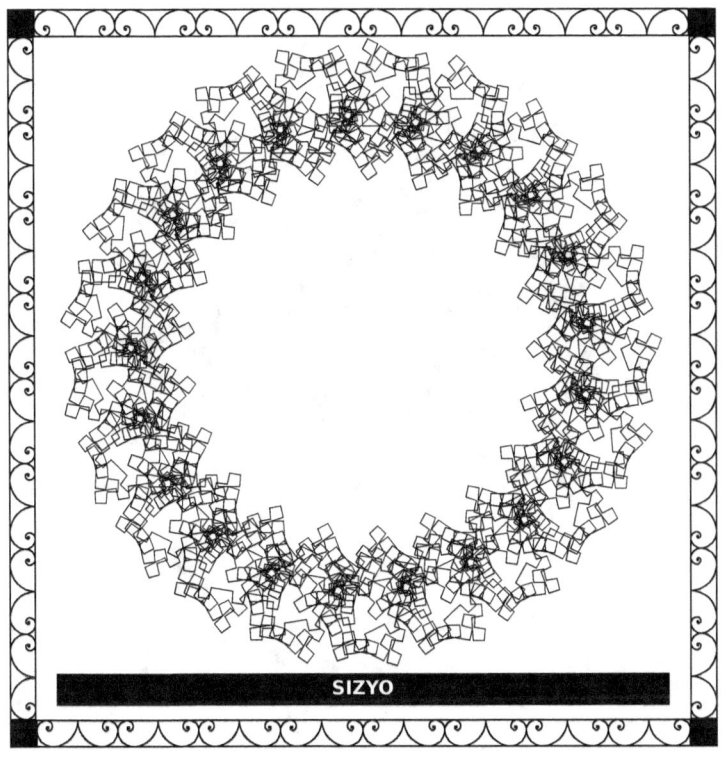

SIZYO

Great art is an instant arrested in eternity.
James Huneker

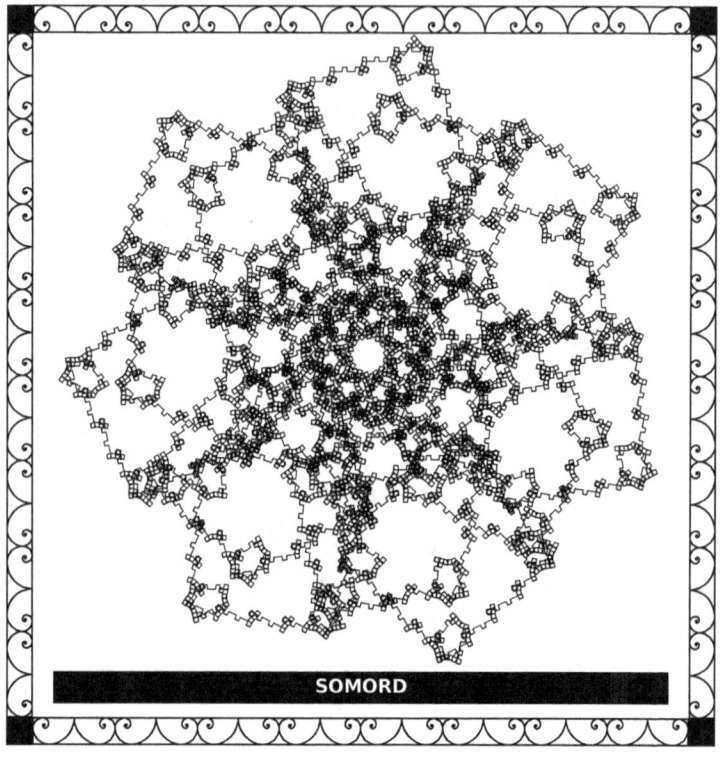

SOMORD

I don't want to make plop art — sculpture that just gets plopped down in places. I wouldn't want to litter every corner of the world with my sculpture.

Rachel Whiteread

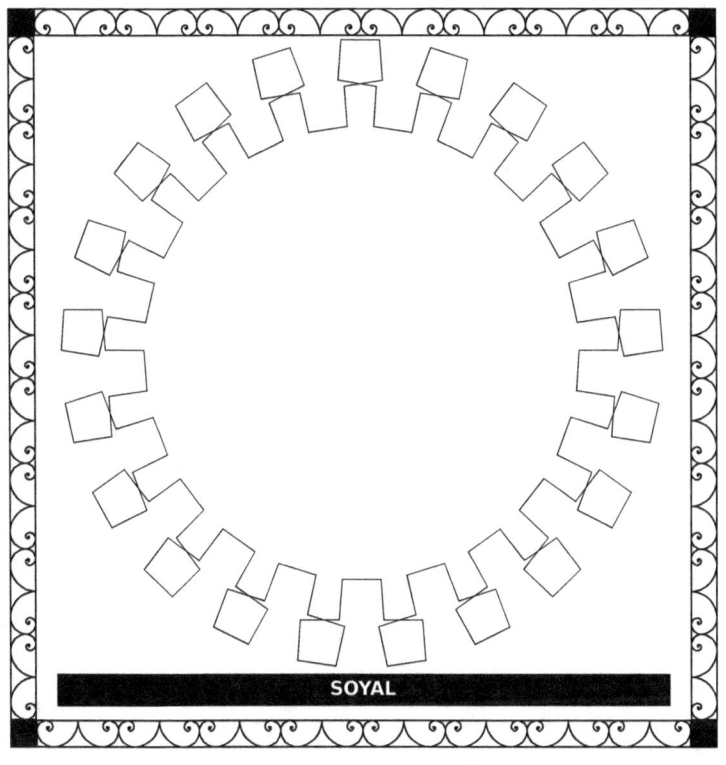

SOYAL

The relation of feeling toward art and its bringing-forth can be one of production or one of reception and enjoyment.
Martin Heidegger

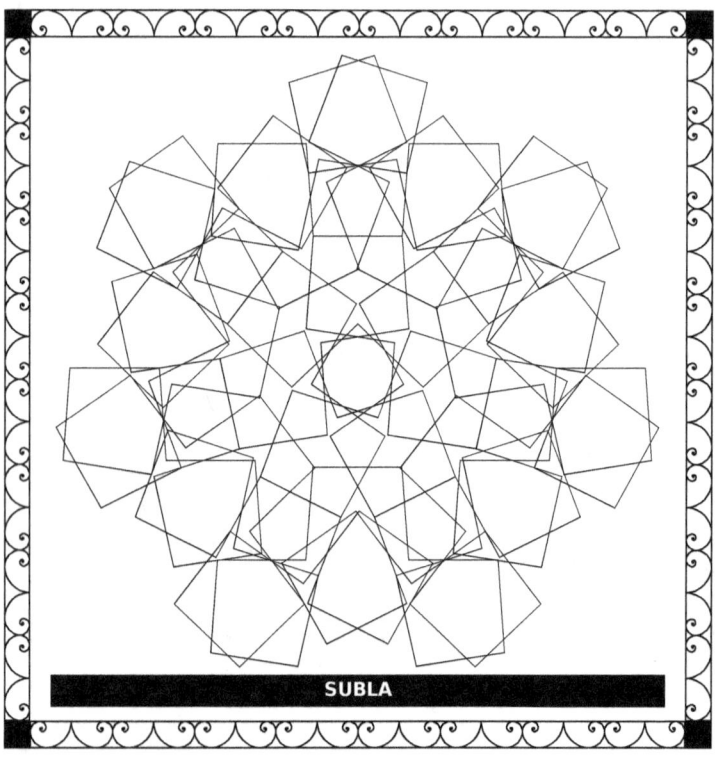

SUBLA

When you start working, everybody is in your studio —
the past, your friends, enemies, the art world, and above
all, your own ideas — all are there. But as you continue
painting, they start leaving, one by one, and you are left
completely alone. Then, if you are lucky, even you leave.
John Cage

258

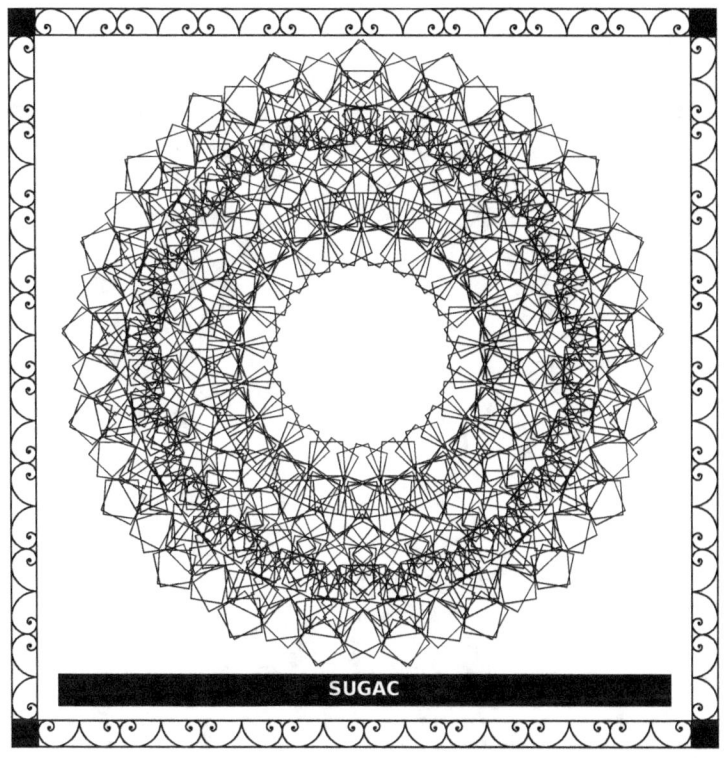

SUGAC

Music is the space between the notes.
Claude Debussy

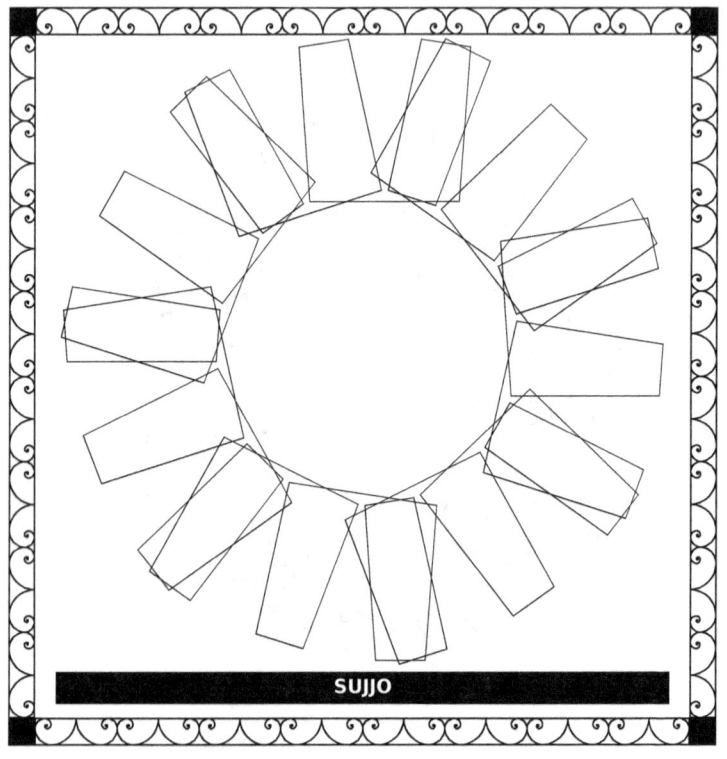

SUJJO

A great artist is always before his time or behind it.
George Moore

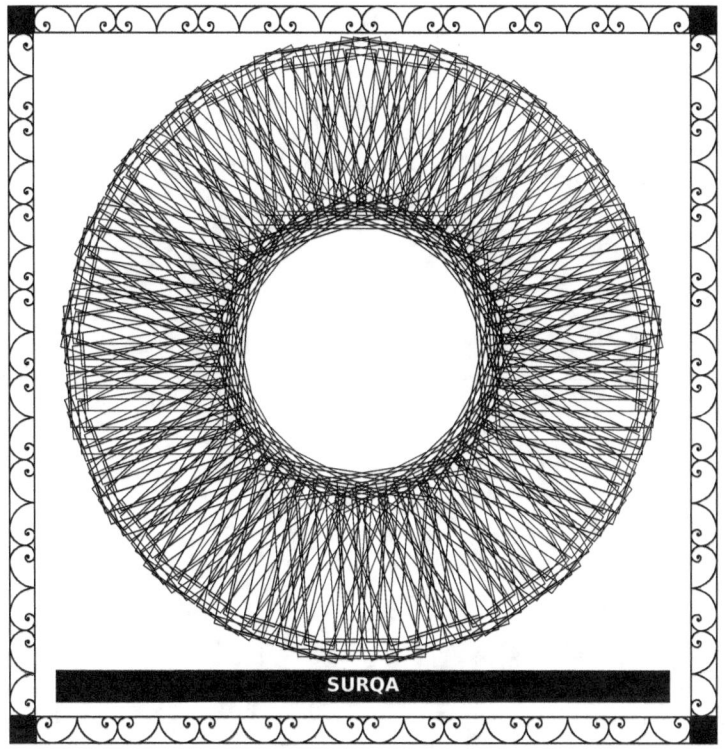

SURQA

A scientist can pretend that his work isn't himself, it's merely the impersonal truth. An artist can't hide behind the truth. He can't hide anywhere.
Ursula K. Le Guin

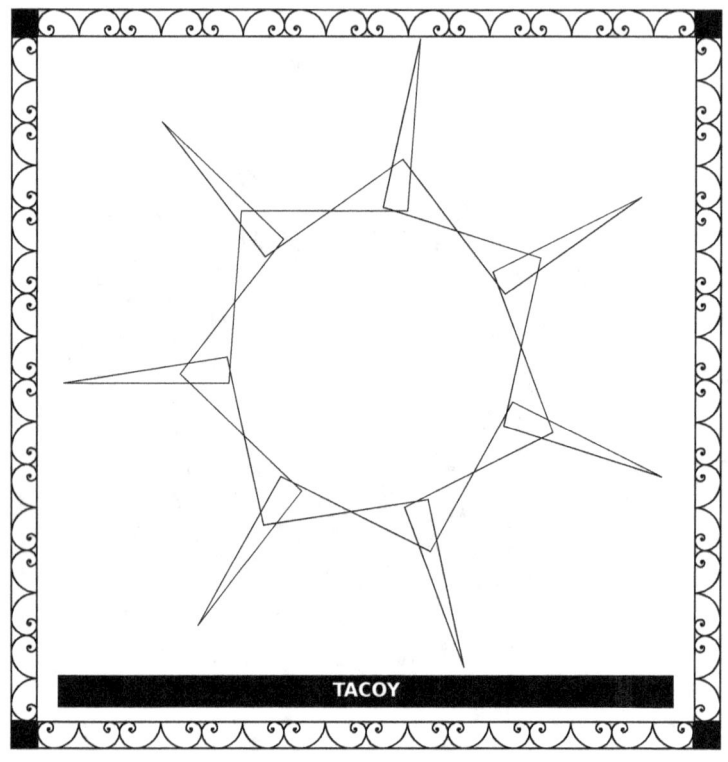

TACOY

At a crisis in my youth he taught me the wisdom of choice:
To try and fail is at least to learn; to fail to try is to suffer
the inestimable loss of what might have been.
Chester Barnard

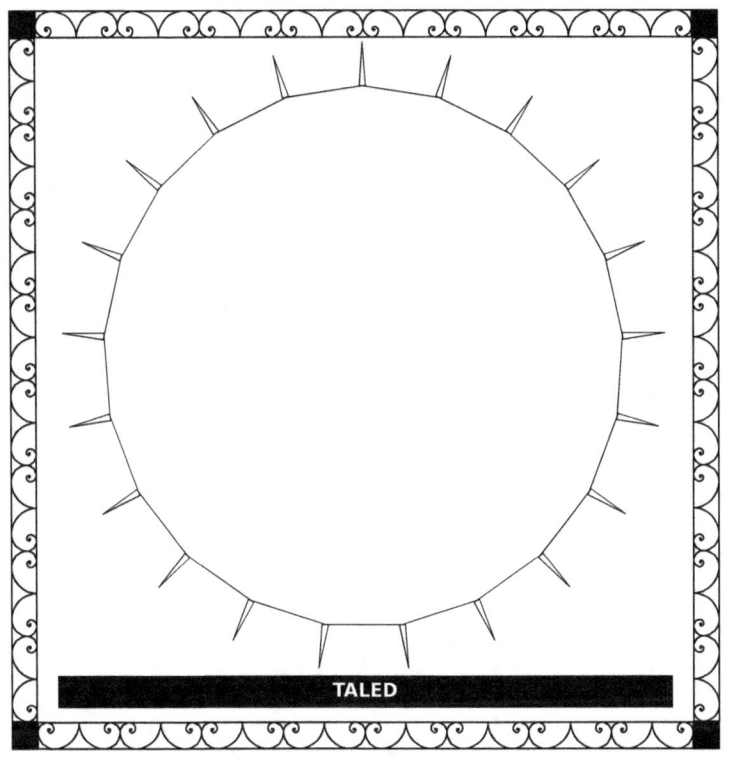

TALED

Rarely do great beauty and great virtue dwell together.
Petrarch

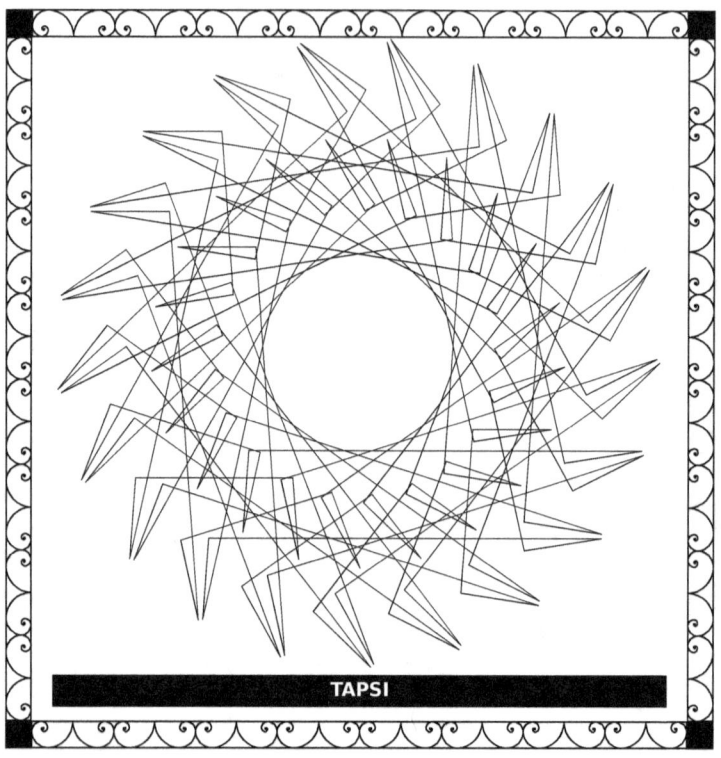

TAPSI

The world is always full of brilliant youth which fades into grey and embittered middle age: the first flowering takes everything. The great men are those who have developed slowly, or who have been able to survive the glamour of their early florescence and to go on learning from life.
Willa Cather

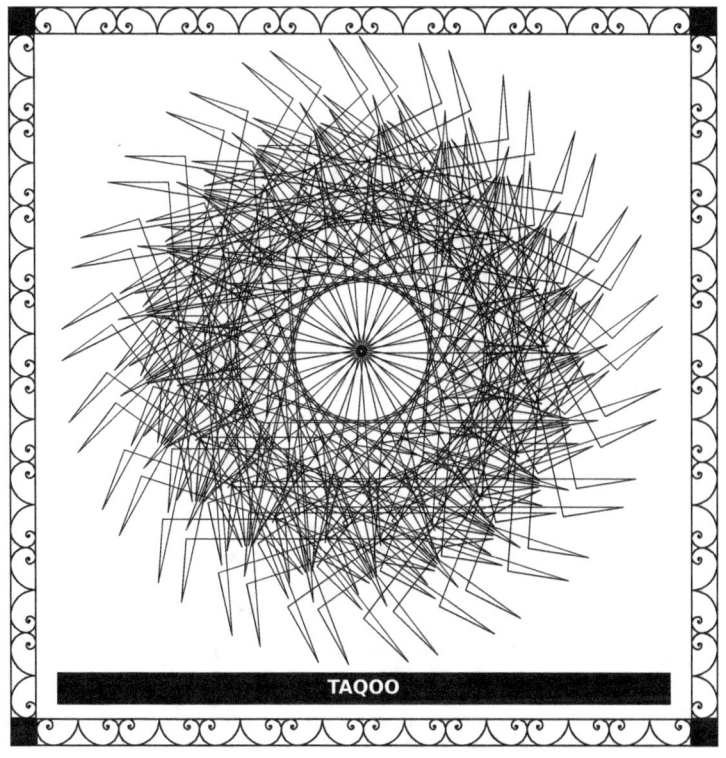

TAQOO

The truth of art keeps science from becoming inhuman, and the truth of science keeps art from becoming ridiculous.
Raymond Chandler

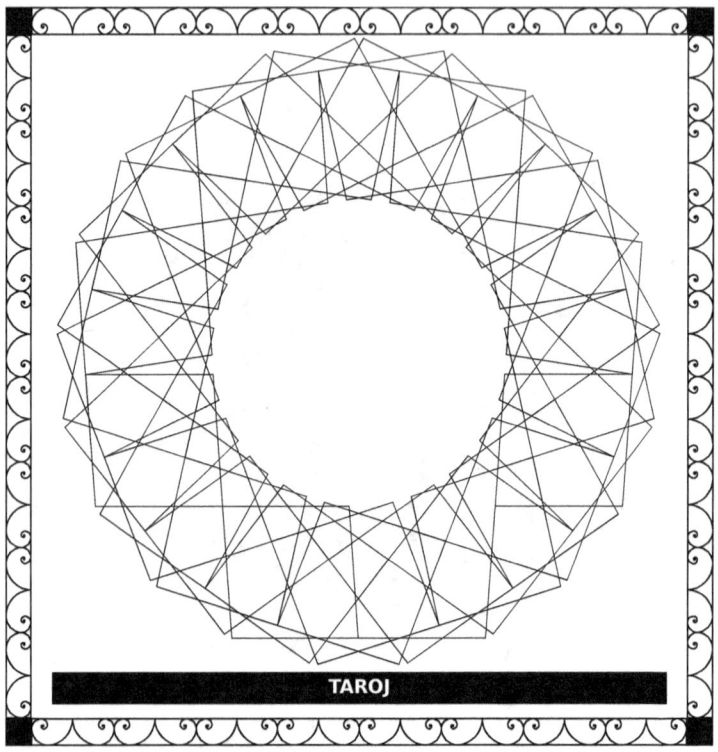

TAROJ

A work of art must carry within itself its complete signifi-
cance and impose that upon the beholder before he recog-
nises the subject matter.
Henri Matisse

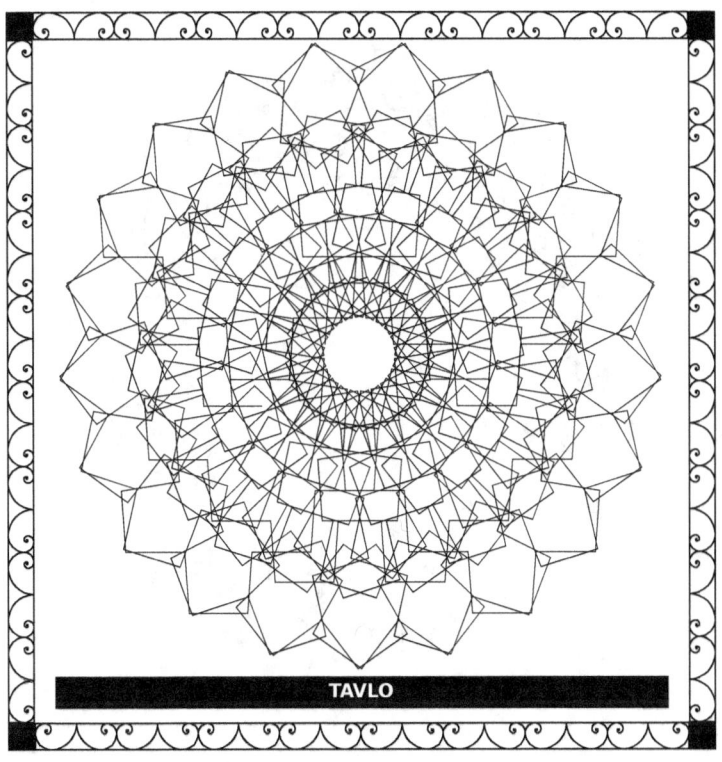

TAVLO

I am for richness of meaning rather than clarity of meaning;
for the implicit function as well as the explicit function.
Robert Venturi

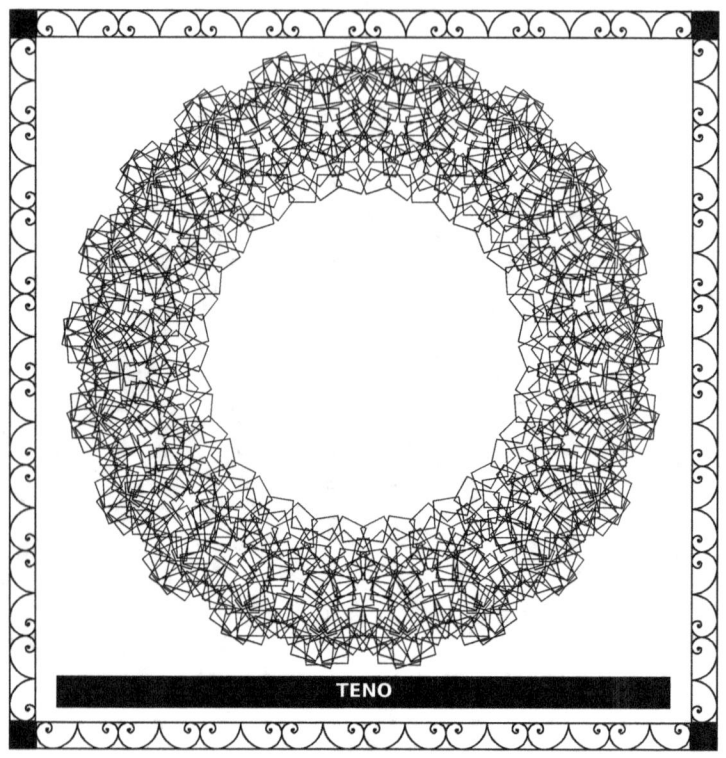

TENO

In this life, you're either a man or an actor, there's nothing in between.
Andrea Pirlo

268

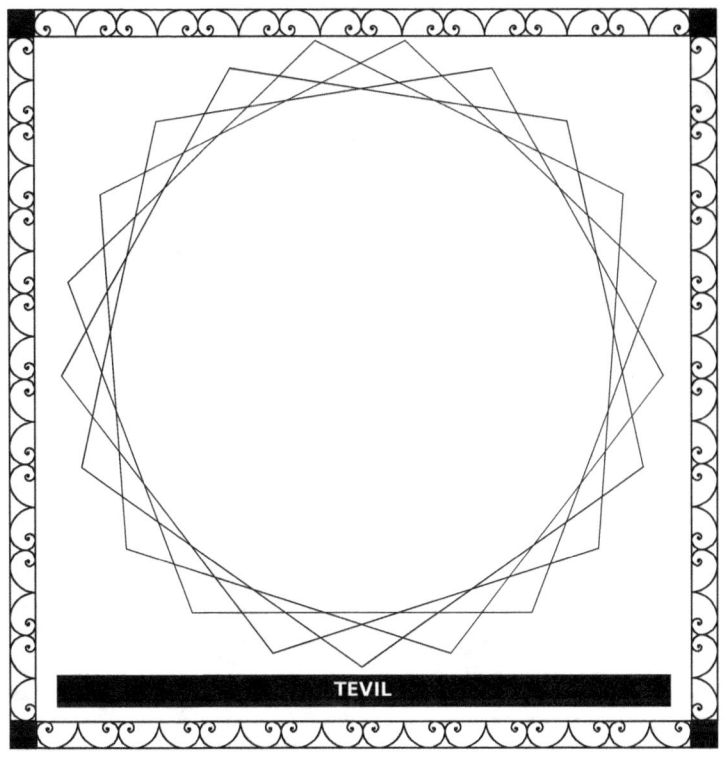

TEVIL

Faith...is the art of holding on to things your reason has once accepted in spite of your changing moods.
C. S. Lewis

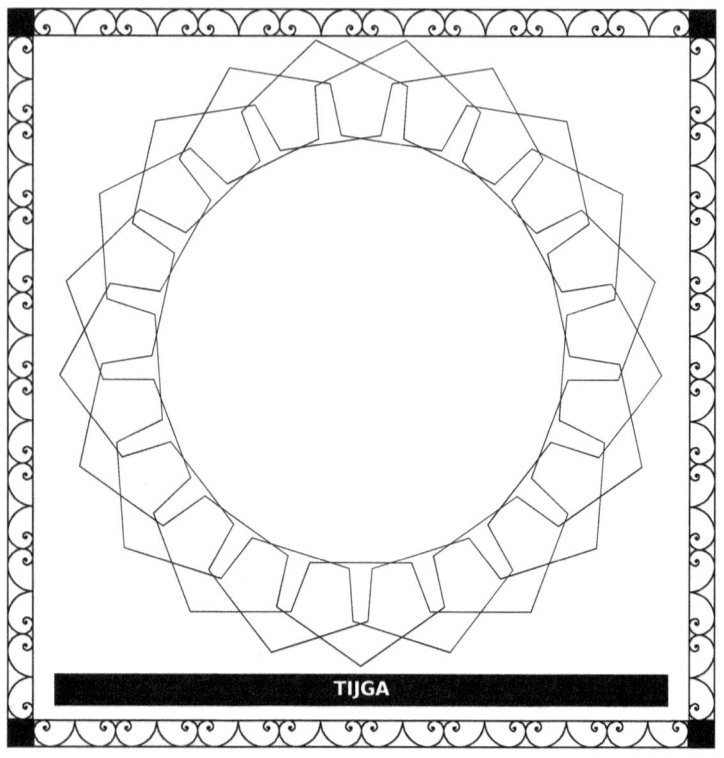

TIJGA

The desire to be loved is really death when it comes to art.
David Cronenberg

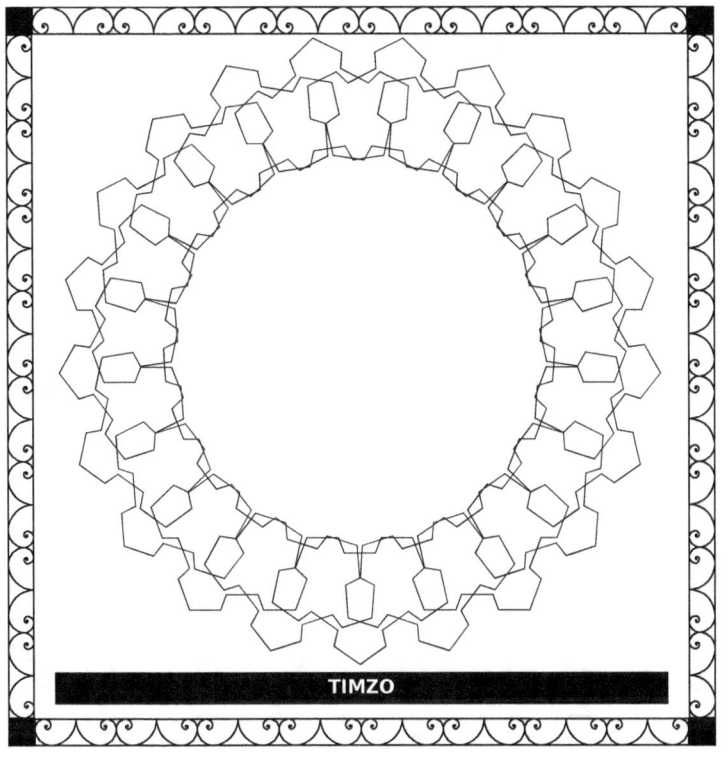

TIMZO

Try not to change the world. You will fail. Try to love the world. Lo, the world is changed. Changed forever.
Sri Chinmoy

271

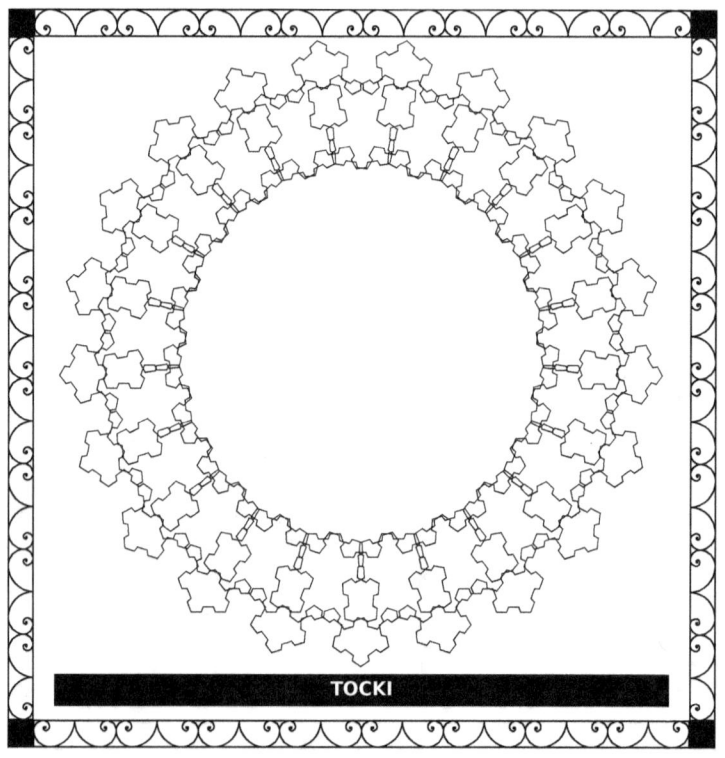

TOCKI

An art thief is a man who takes pictures.
George Carlin

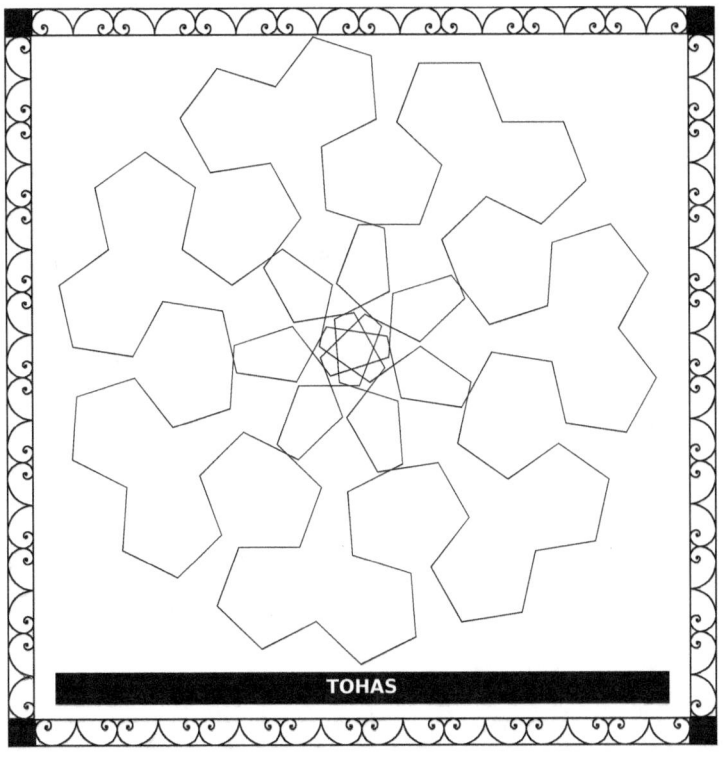

TOHAS

Once you know what people really want, you can't hate them anymore. You can fear them, but you can't hate them, because you can always find the same desires in your own heart.

Orson Scott Card, Speaker for the Dead

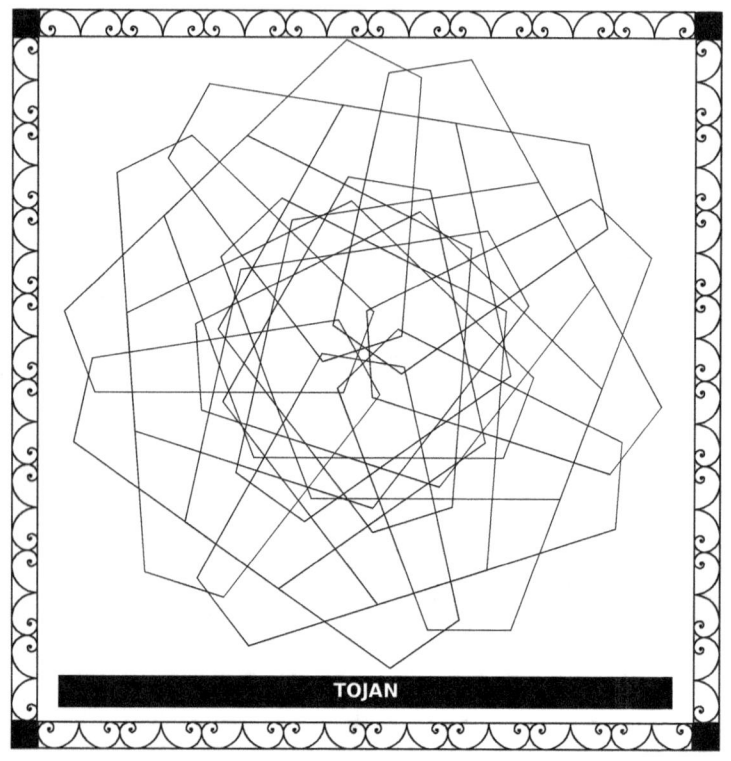

TOJAN

Not to do what you feel like doing is freedom.
Chinmayananda Saraswati

274

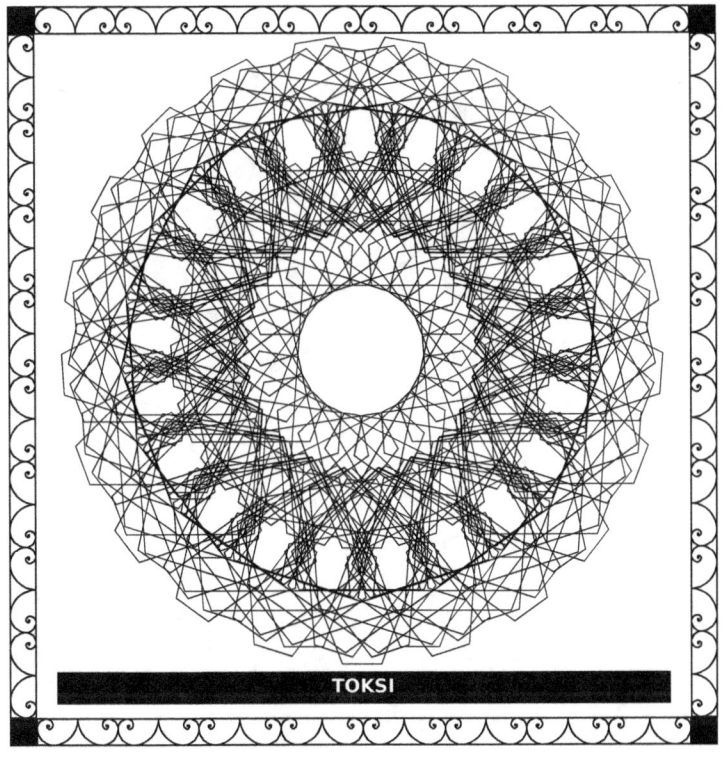

TOKSI

As far as consistency of thought goes, I prefer inconsistency.
John Cage

275

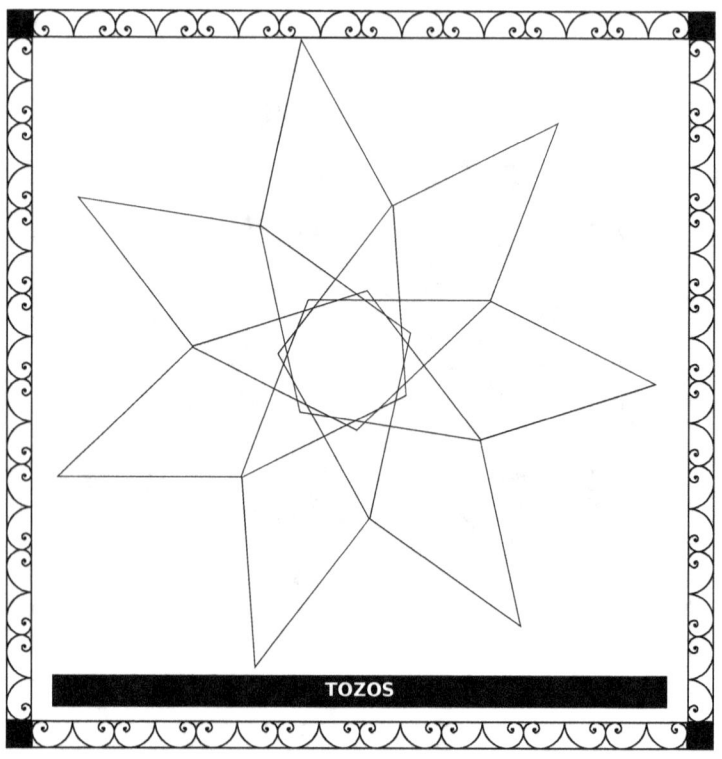

TOZOS

Supermarket tabloids and celebrity gossip shows are not just innocently shallow entertainment, but a fundamental part of a much larger movement that involves apathy, greed and hierarchy. Celebrity doesn't have anything to do with art or craft. It's about being rich and thinking that you're better than everybody else.

Joseph Gordon-Levitt

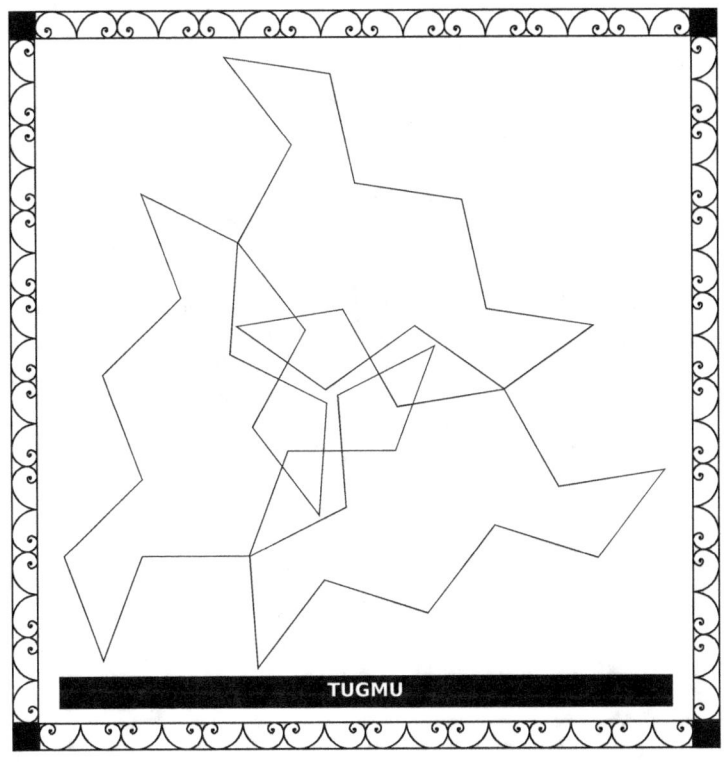

TUGMU

A book is never finished; it's abandoned.
Gene Fowler

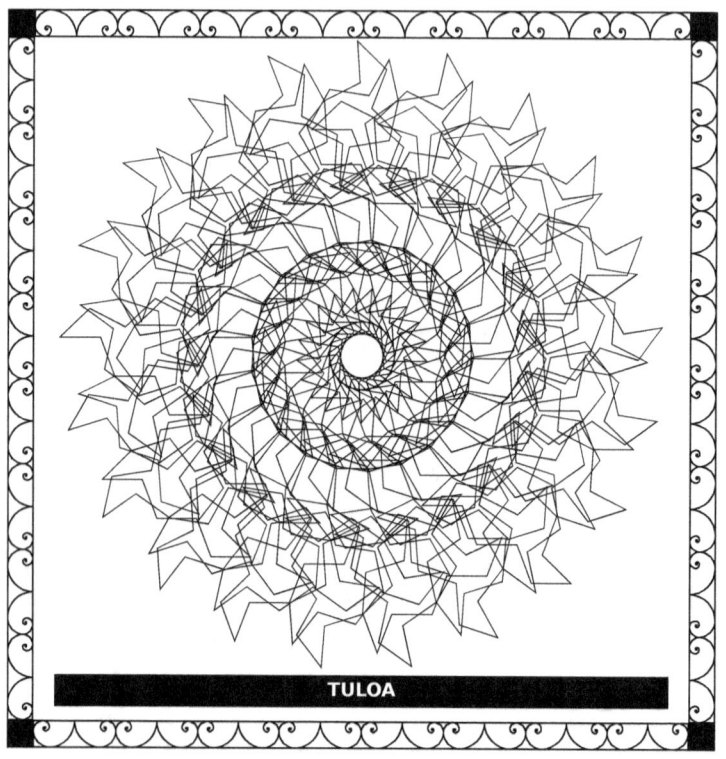

TULOA

The rules of art do not exist, because what makes art art
is the fact that it obeys no rules at all.
Elfriede Jelinek

278

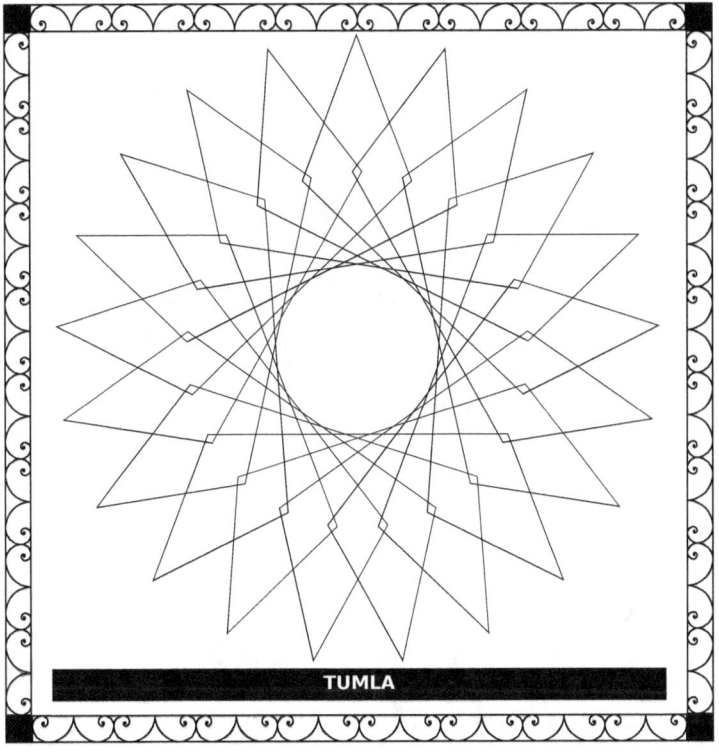

TUMLA

The best art, and the only art which will ever lead to great results, must have for its basis the interpretation of beauty in nature.

Ernest Flagg

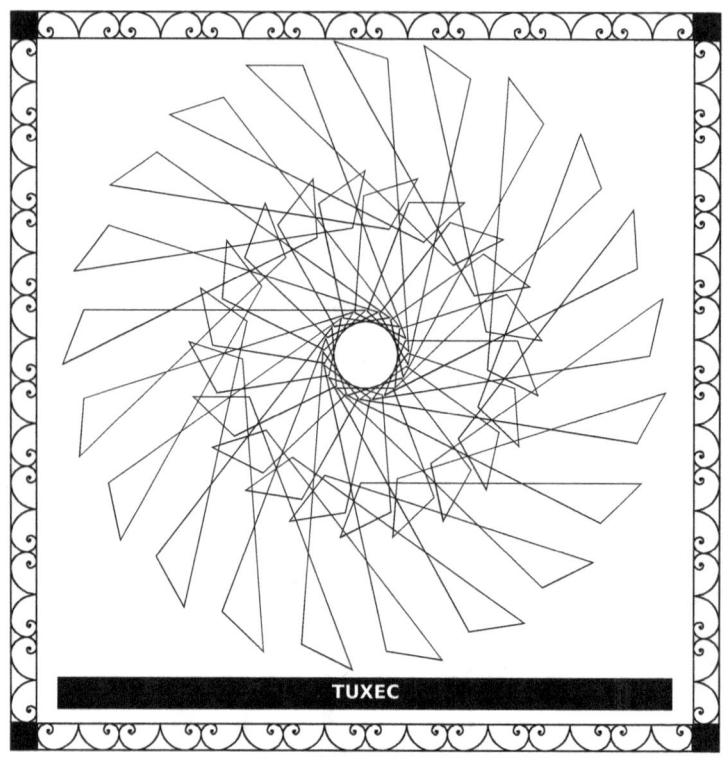

TUXEC

In art as in love, instinct is enough.
Anatole France

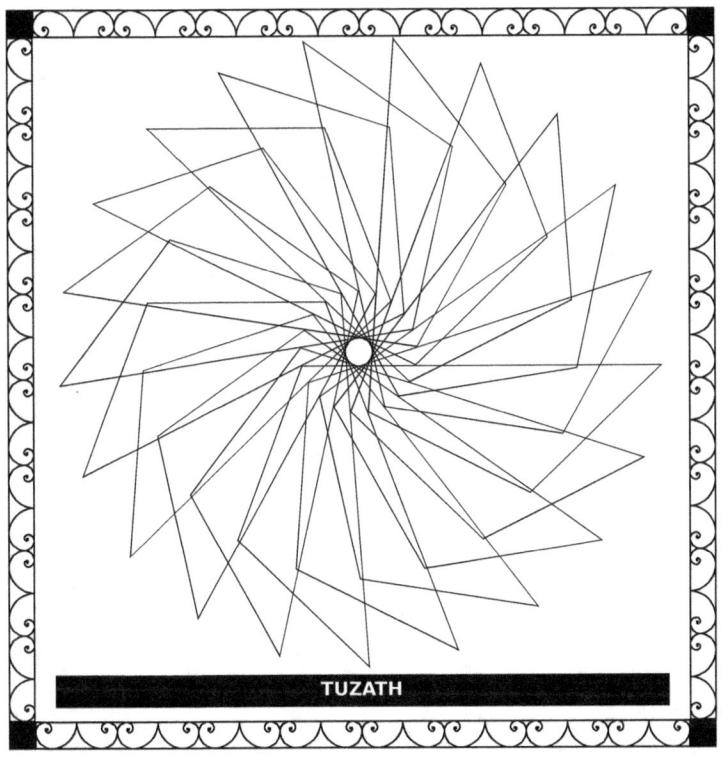

TUZATH

Teach yourself by your own mistakes; people learn only by error. The good artist believes that nobody is good enough to give him advice.

William Faulkner

281

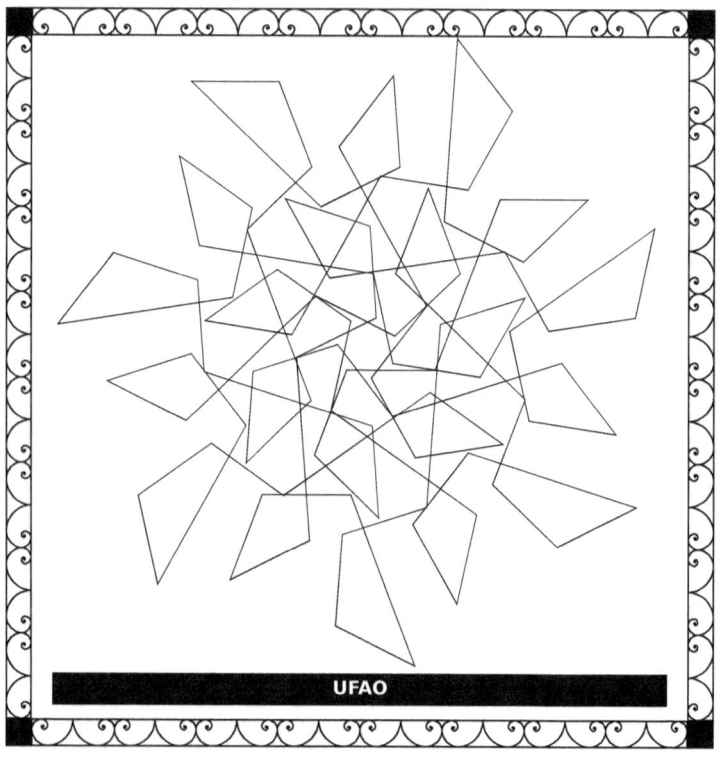

UFAO

We make artwork as something that we have to do, not knowing how it will work out. When it is finished we have to see if it is effective. Even if we obey inspiration we cannot expect all the work to be successful. An artist is a person who can recognize failure.

Agnes Martin, Beauty Is the Mystery of Life

282

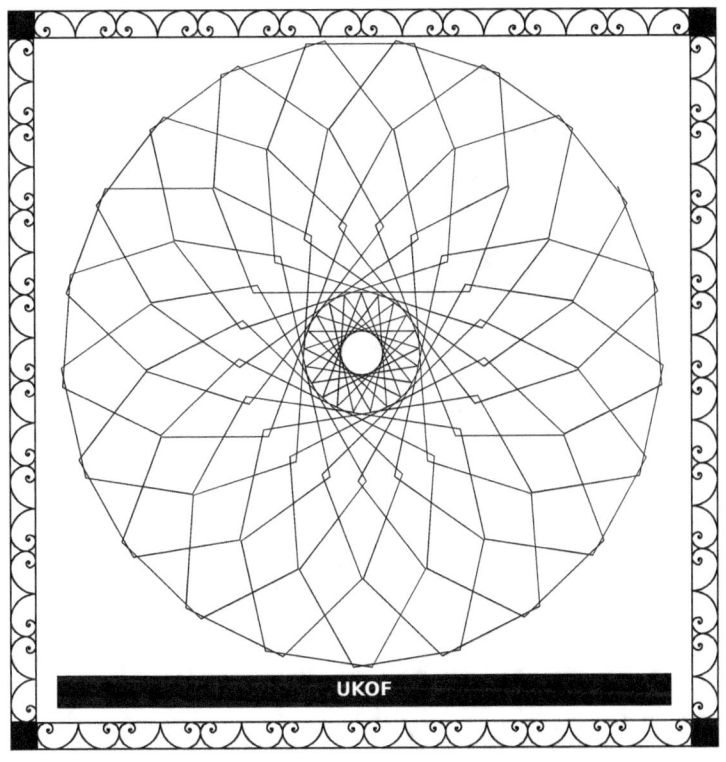

UKOF

The artist after all is a solitary being.
Virginia Woolf

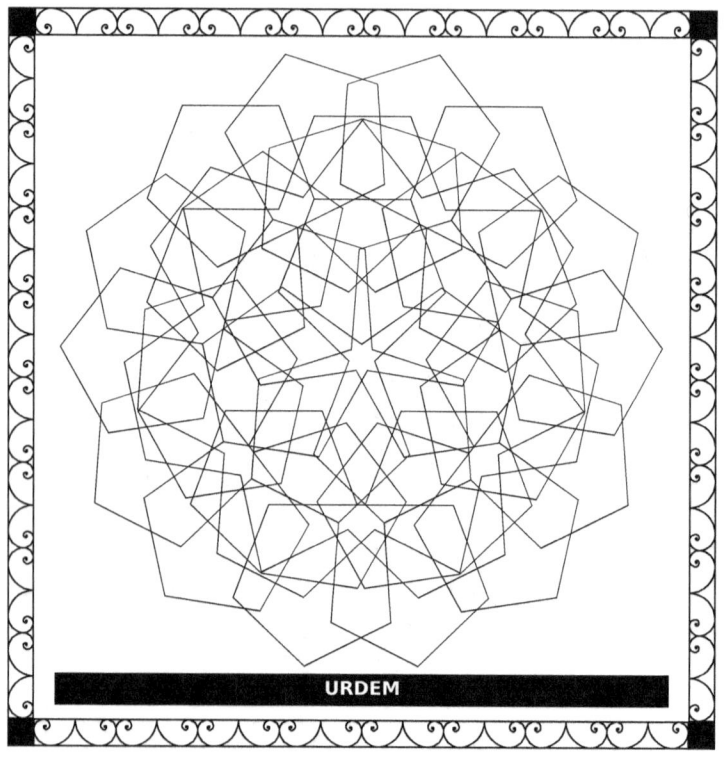

URDEM

Beauty is meaningless until it is shared.
George Orwell

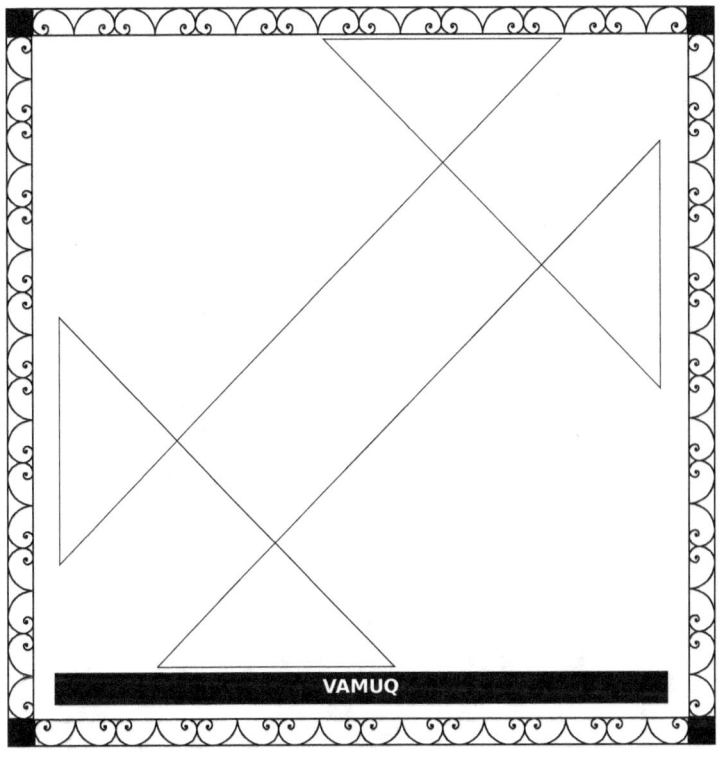

VAMUQ

Every work of art must retain something from the first days
of creation, something of the smell of earth, or one could
even say: something animate.
Wilhelm Lehmbruck

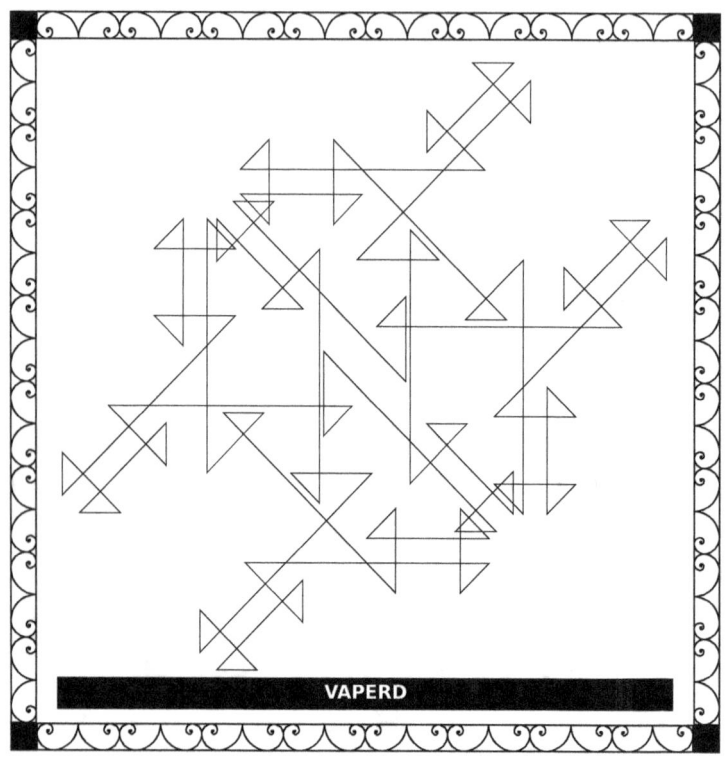

VAPERD

What strip-mining is to nature, the art market has become to culture.

Robert Hughes

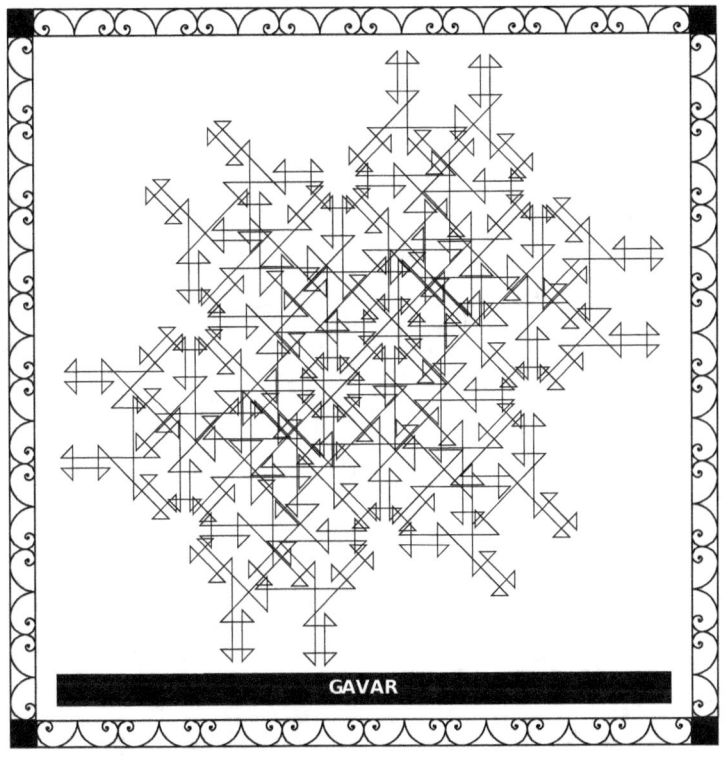

GAVAR

Chess for me is not a game, but an art. Yes, and I take upon myself all those responsibilities which an art imposes on its adherents.

Alexander Alekhine

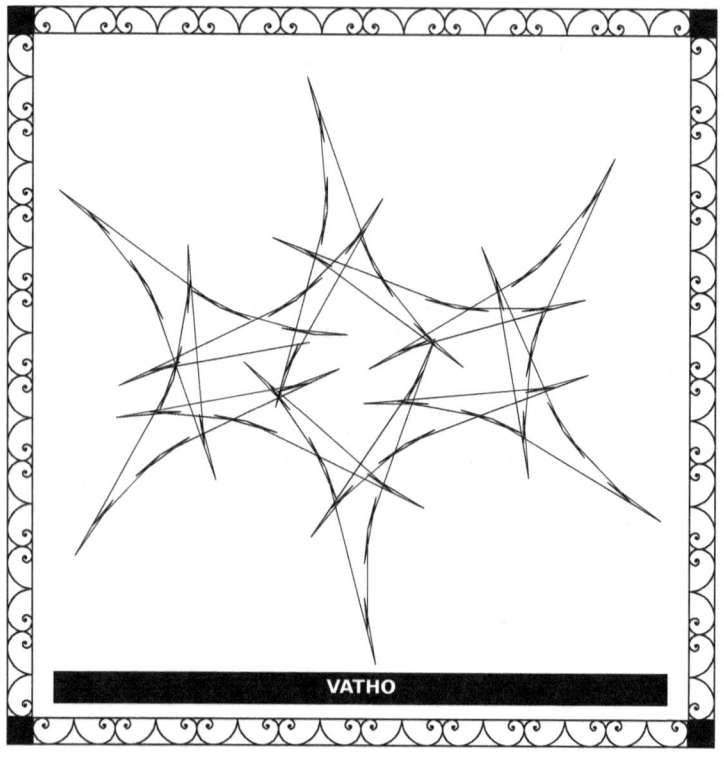

VATHO

Honest work is much better than a mansion.
Leo Tolstoy

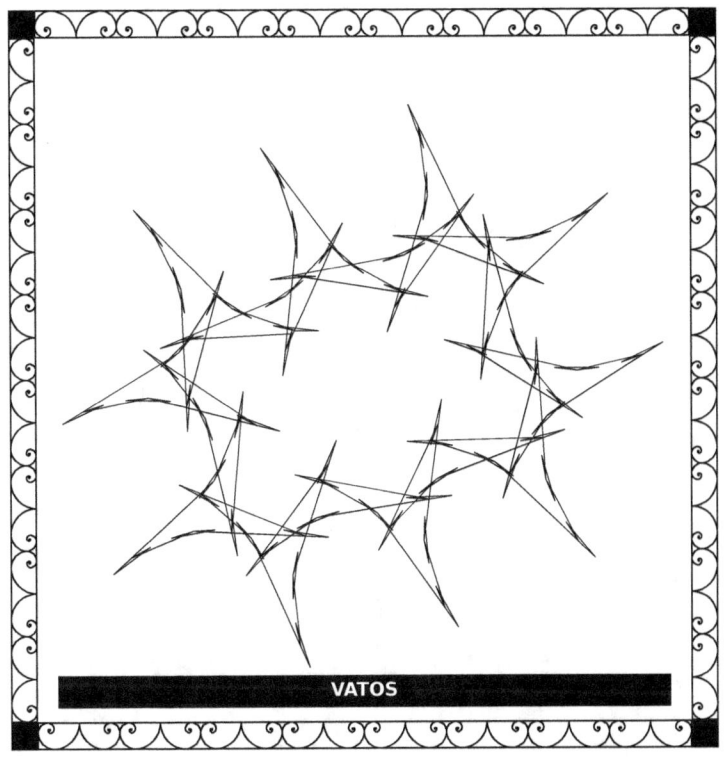

VATOS

I have always felt that one of the secrets of real beauty is simplicity.
Rita Hayworth

289

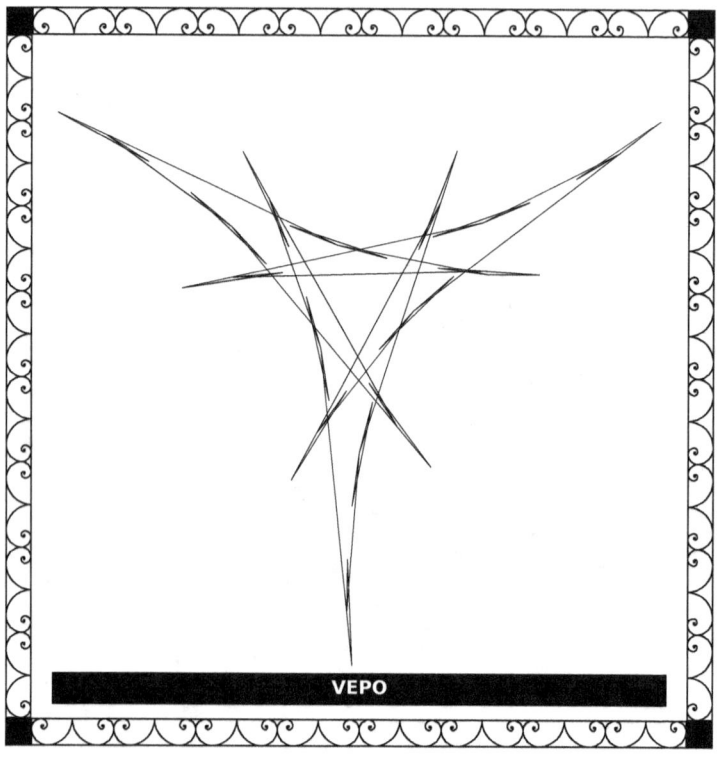

VEPO

Primitivism has become the vulgar cliche of much modern art and speculation.
Marshall McLuhan

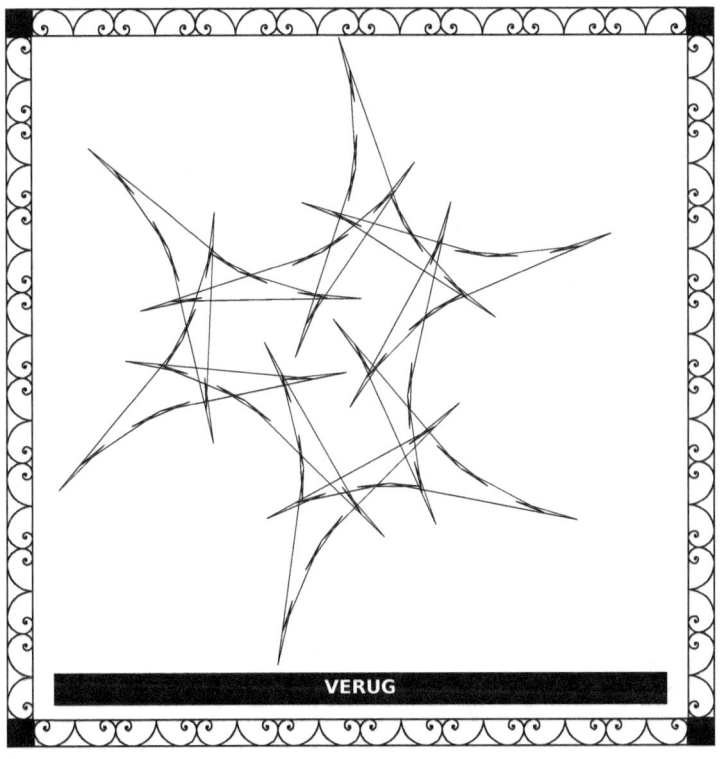

VERUG

You can't think, 'My life is more important than the work', and get the work. You have to think the work is paramount in your life. An artist's life is adventurous: one new thing after another.

Agnes Martin, Beauty Is the Mystery of Life

291

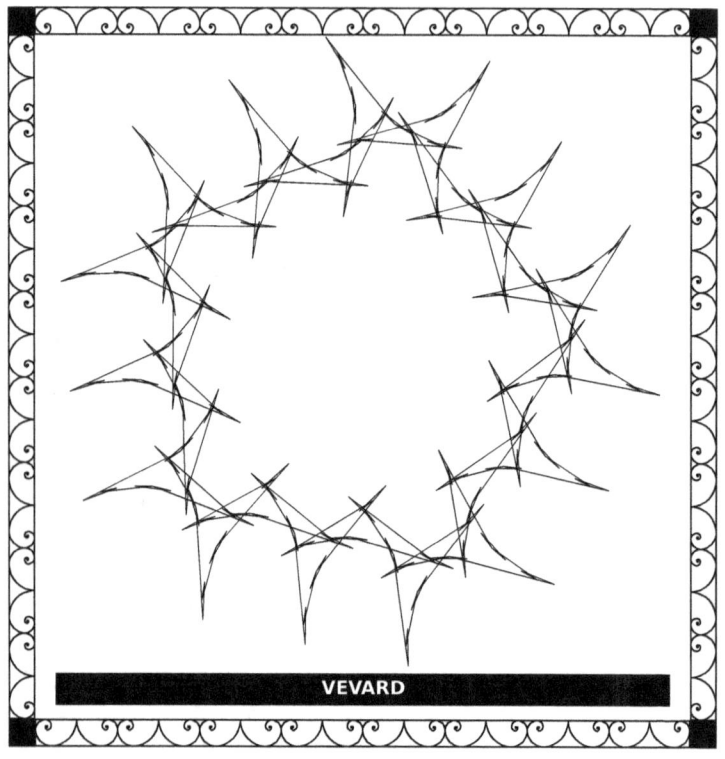

VEVARD

Fine art is that in which the hand, the head, and the heart of man go together.
John Ruskin

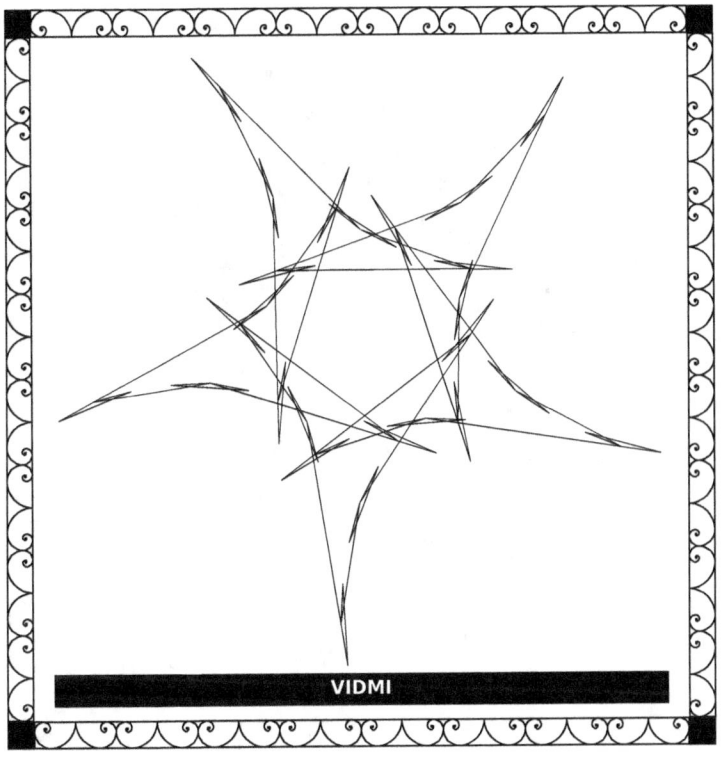

VIDMI

Art is a weapon and the weapons can change the world.
Good art is irreverent, excessive, controversial, incorrect,
irritating, ironic, bad behaving, playful and beautiful or
ugly.
Riiko Sakkinen

293

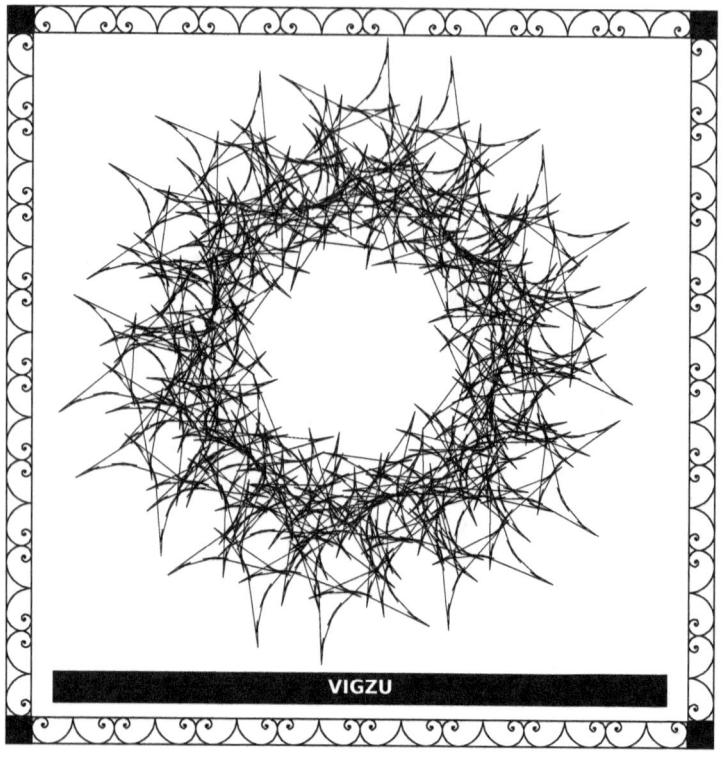

VIGZU

Until he extends the circle of his compassion to all living
things, man will not himself find peace.
Albert Schweitzer

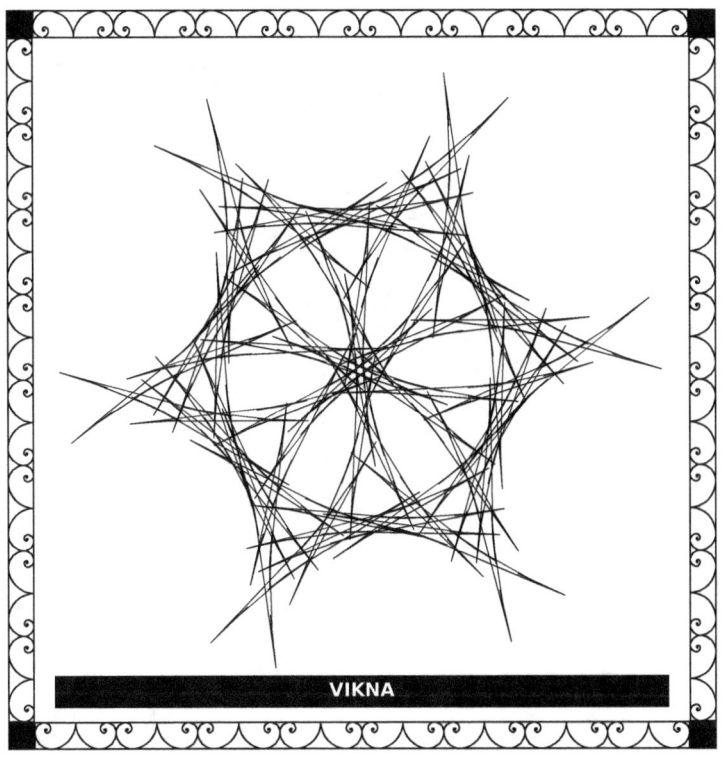

VIKNA

The purpose of art is to prepare us for death.
Andrei Tarkovsky

295

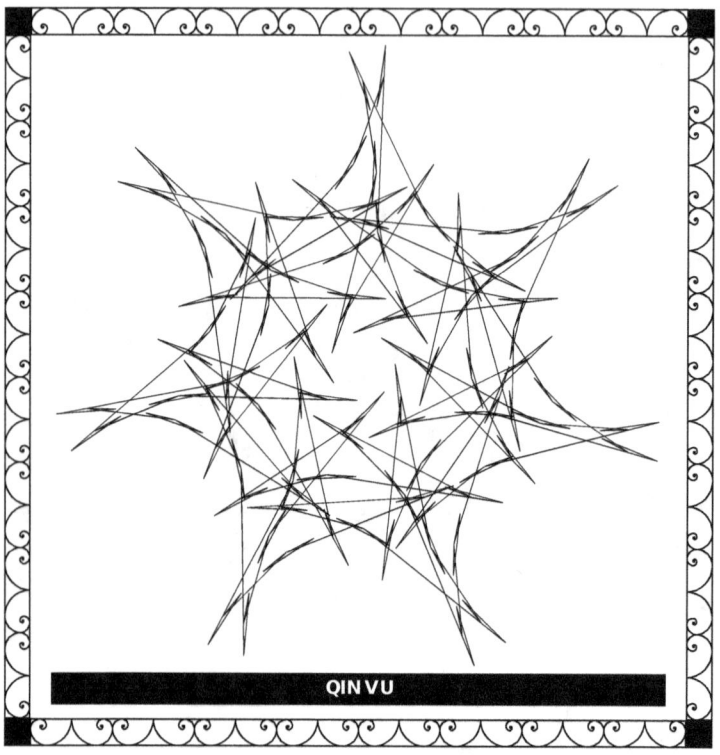

QIN VU

Art is the production of mental events in a concrete sensu-
ous form.
Susan Sontag

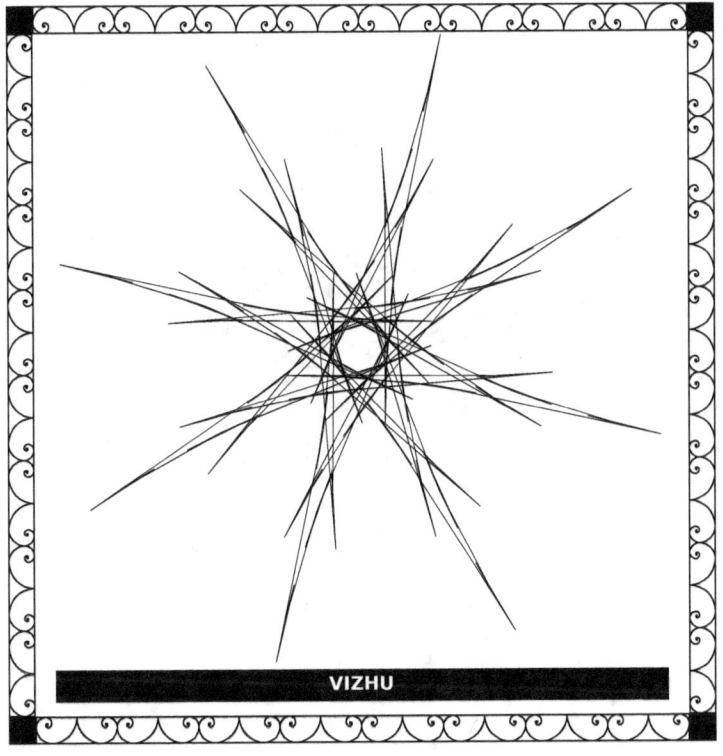

VIZHU

Every innovation scraps its immediate predecessor and re-
trieves still older figures — it causes floods of antiques or
nostalgic art forms and stimulates the search for museum
pieces.
Marshall McLuhan

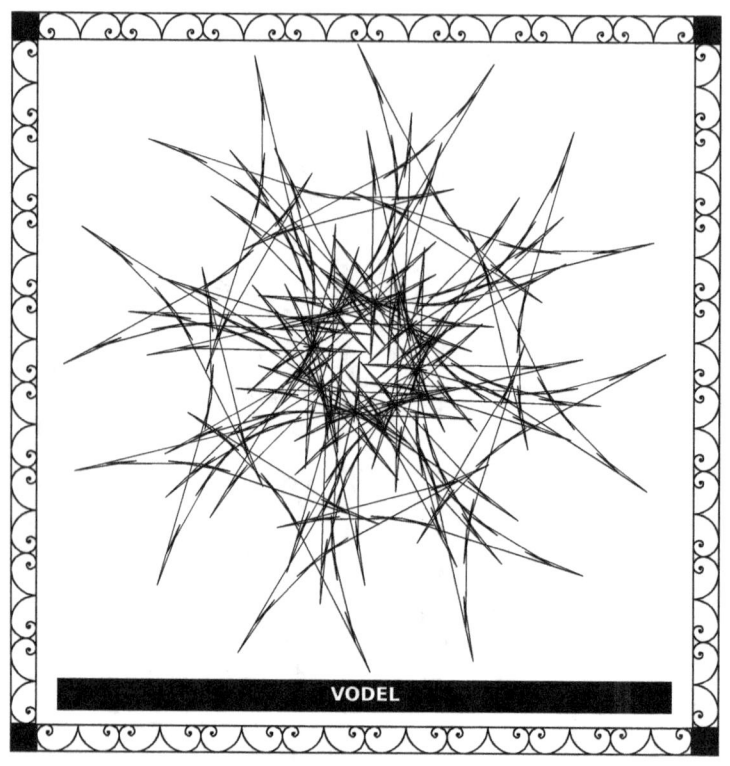

VODEL

Every art expression is rooted fundamentally in the personality and temperament of the artist.
Hans Hofmann

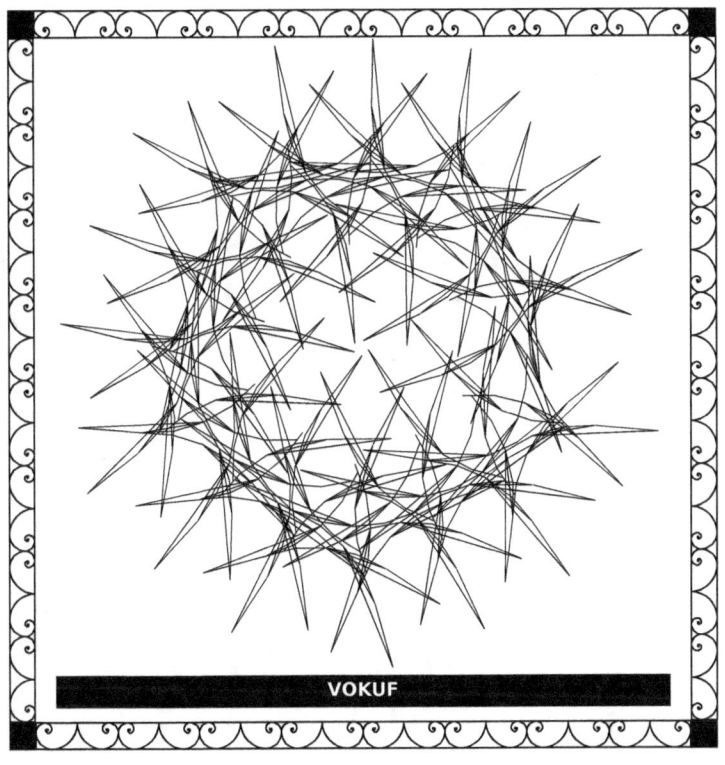

VOKUF

The world steals us from ourselves and solitude restores us. The world is composed of a herd, which are ever flying from themselves.

Anne-Therese de Marguenat de Courcelles, Marquise de Lambert

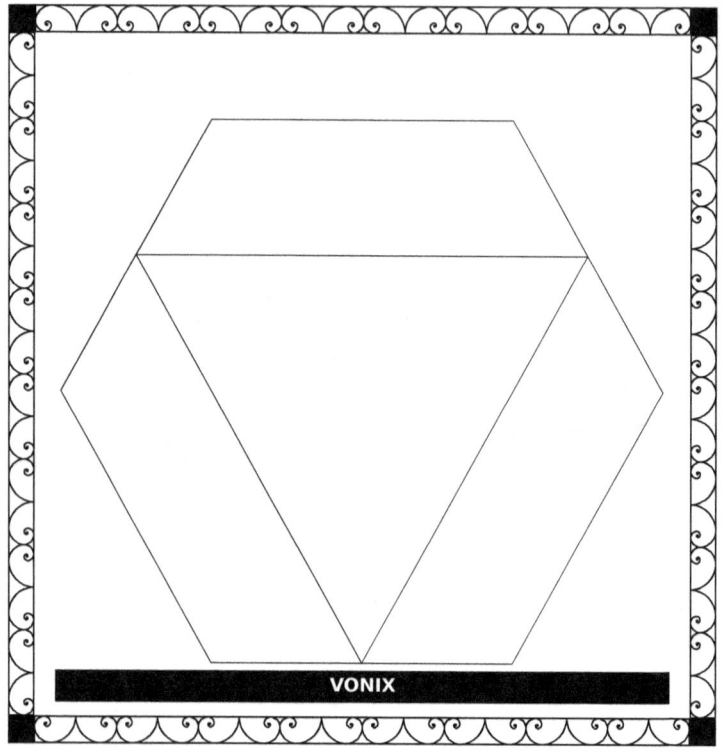

VONIX

Only utopian liberals could be surprised that the Nazis were art connoisseurs.
Camille Paglia

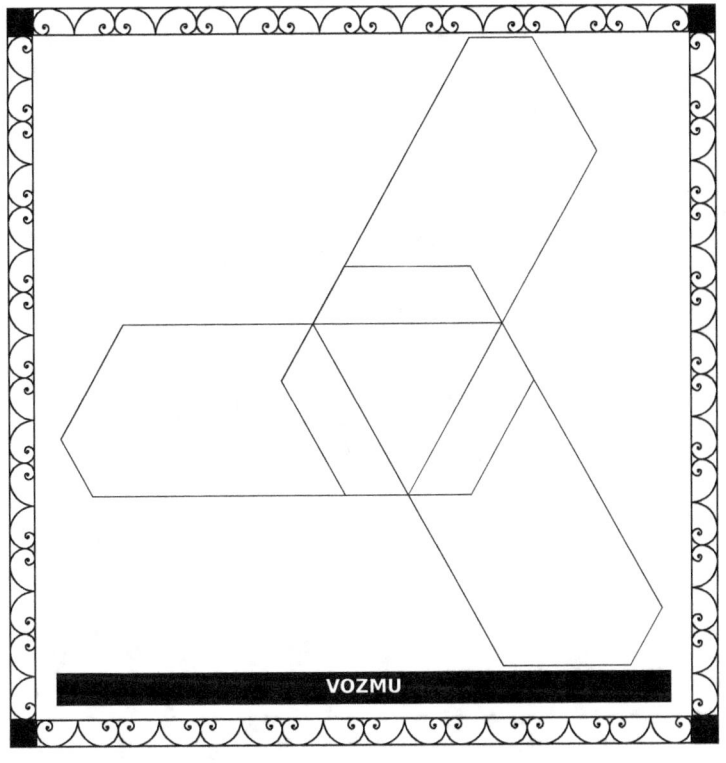

VOZMU

Life must not cease. That comes before everything. It is silly to say you do not care. You do care. It is that care that will prompt your imagination; inflame your desires; make your will irresistible; and create out of nothing.
George Bernard Shaw

301

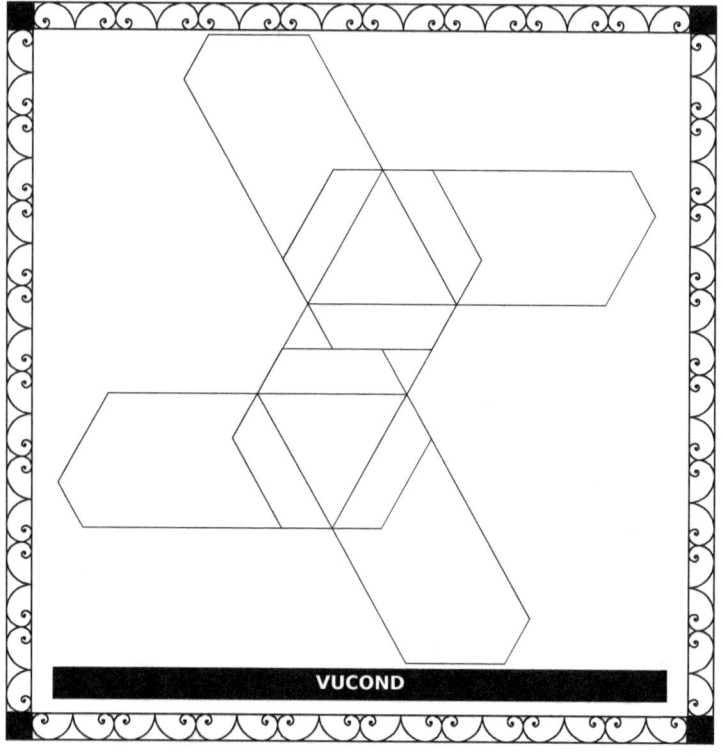

VUCOND

Profound statements must be drawn by the artist from
the most secret recesses of his being; there no murmuring
torrent, no birdsong, no rustle of leaves can distract him.
Giorgio de Chirico

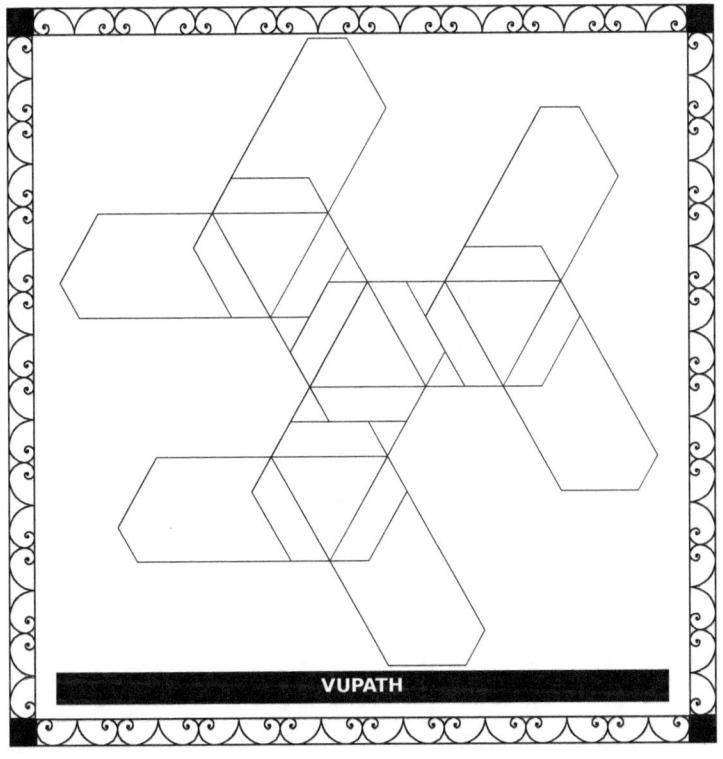

VUPATH

Basically there can be no categories such as religious art and secular art, because all true art is incarnational, and therefore religious.
Madeleine L'Engle

303

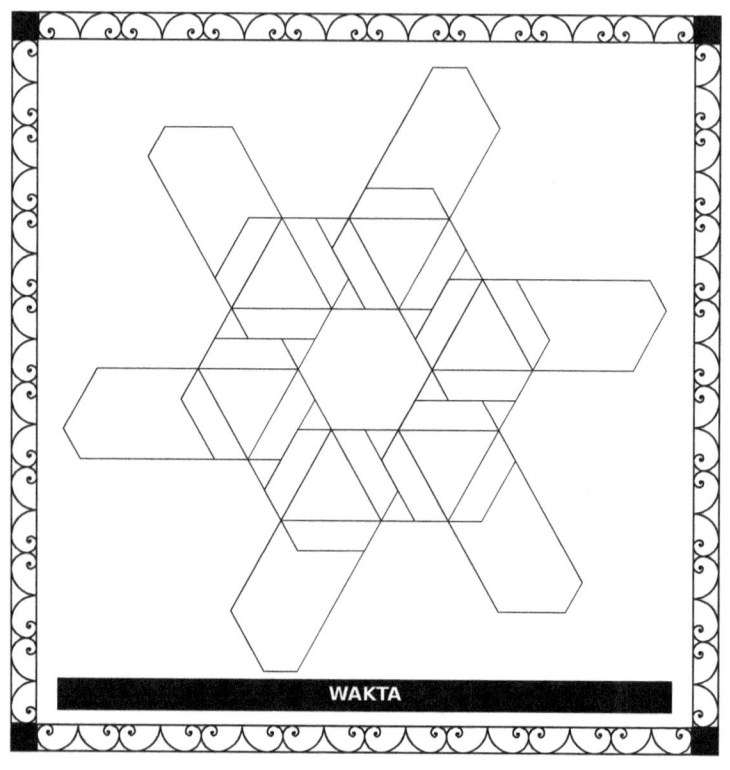

WAKTA

If I had to give you one piece of advice, it would be this: don't be intimidated by other people's opinions.
Paulo Coelho

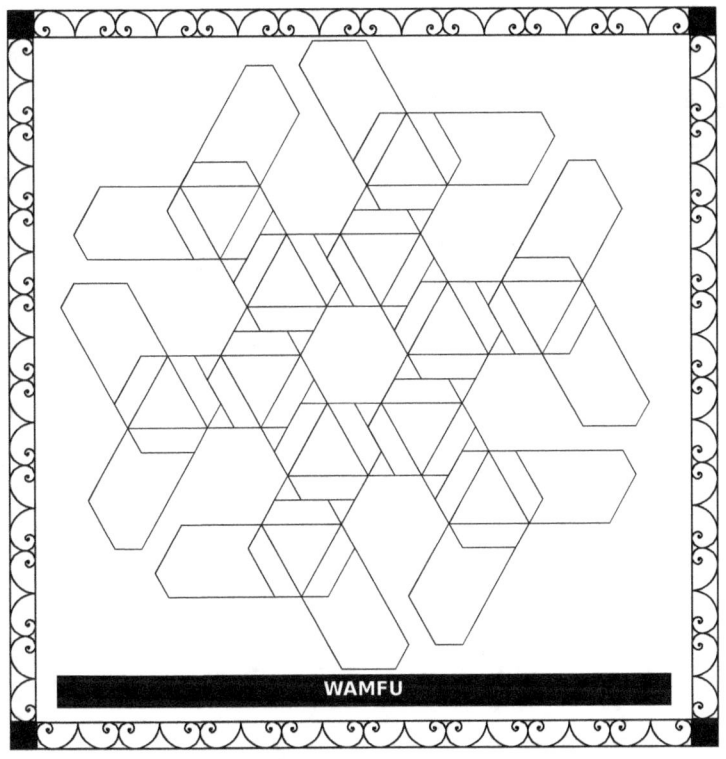

WAMFU

The greatest blessing that one can get from music is that it makes an artist immensely satisfied with life irrespective of the financial condition in which they may be.
Ram Narayan

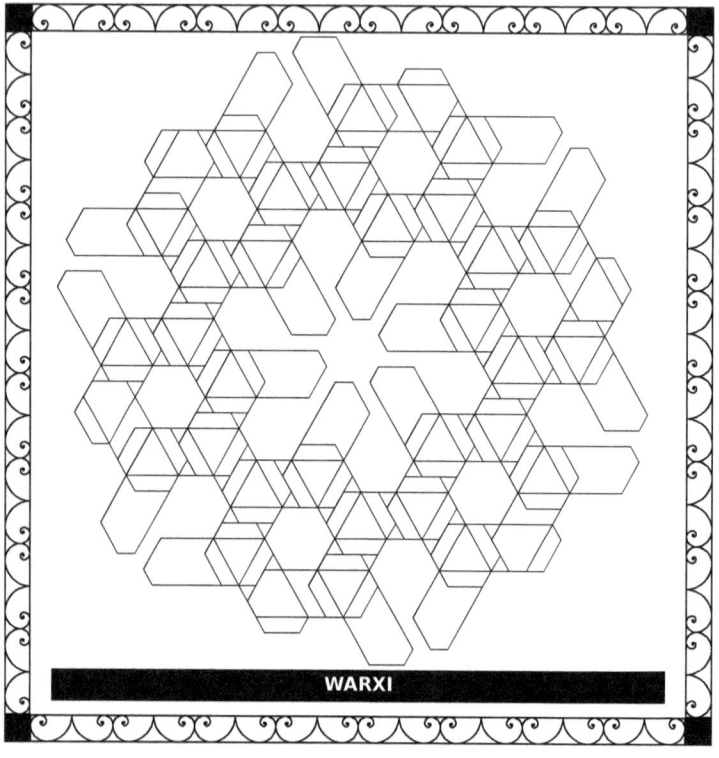

WARXI

All art is the struggle to be, in a particular sort of way, virtuous.
Iris Murdoch

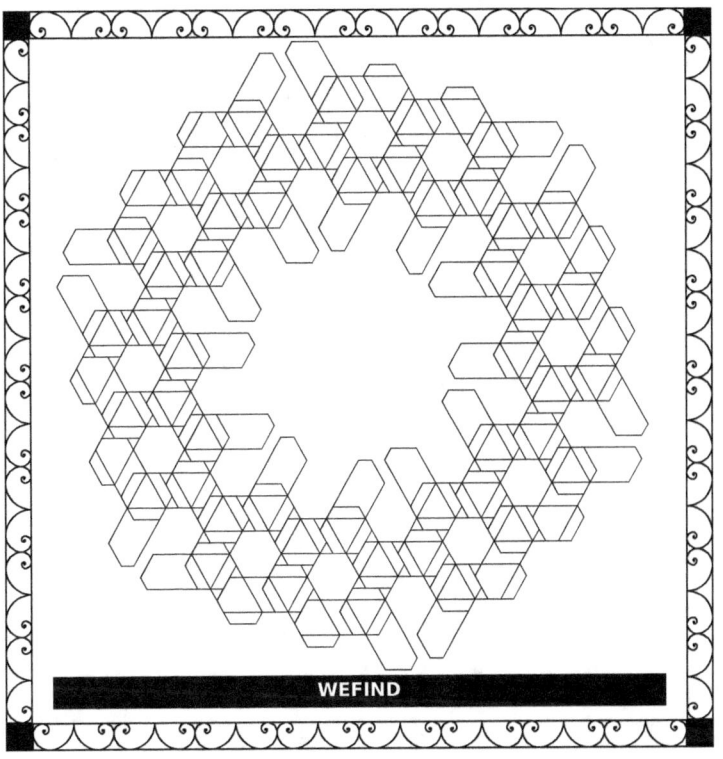

WEFIND

Both the physicist and the mystic want to communicate their knowledge, and when they do so with words their statements are paradoxical and full of logical contradictions.

Fritjof Capra

307

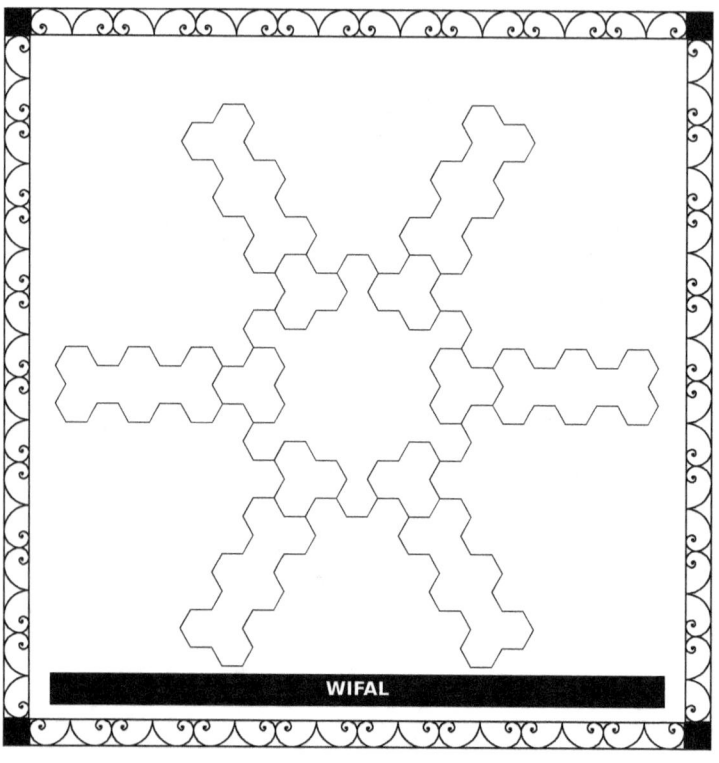

WIFAL

To look at something as though we had never seen it before
requires great courage.
Henri Matisse

308

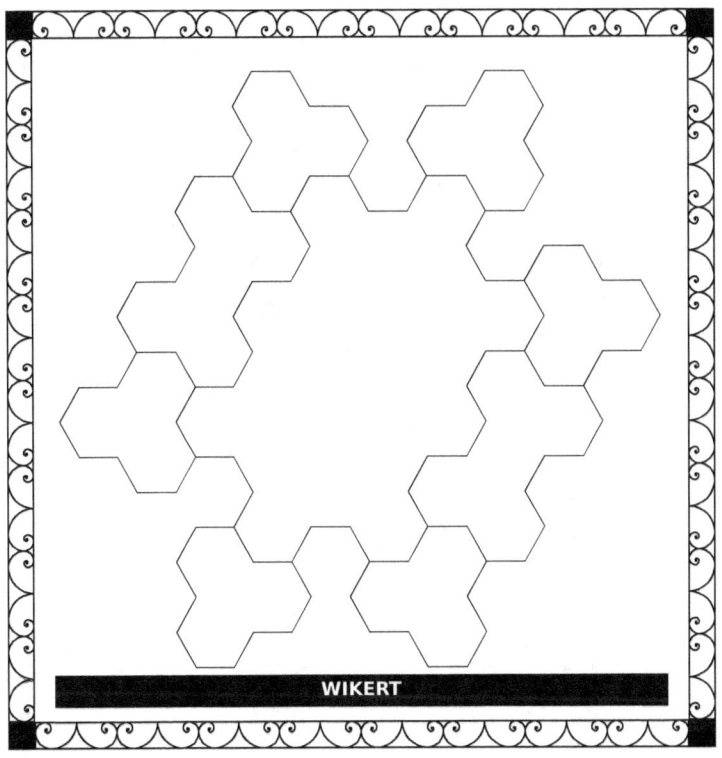

WIKERT

In art economy is always beauty.
Henry James

309

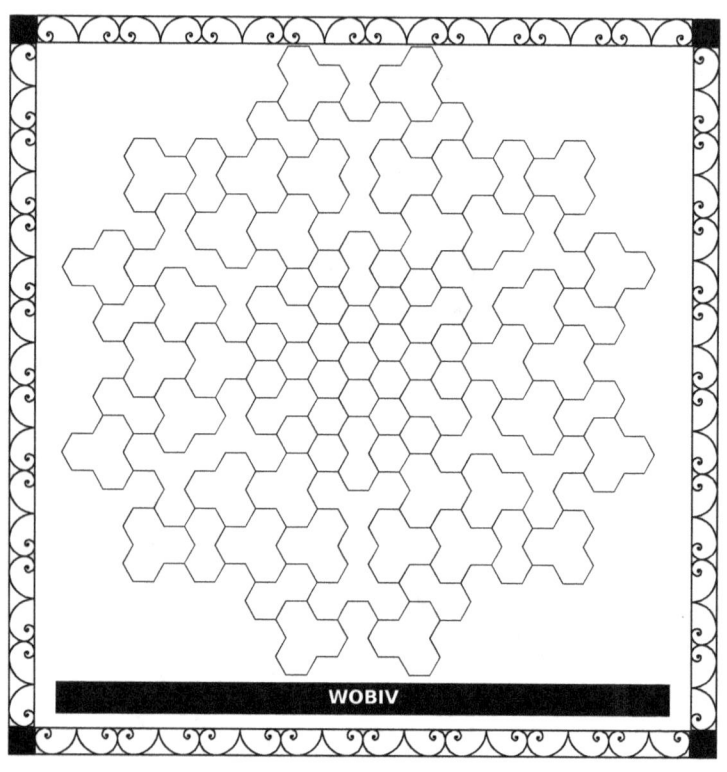

WOBIV

Character is like a tree and reputation like a shadow. The shadow is what we think of it; the tree is the real thing.
Abraham Lincoln

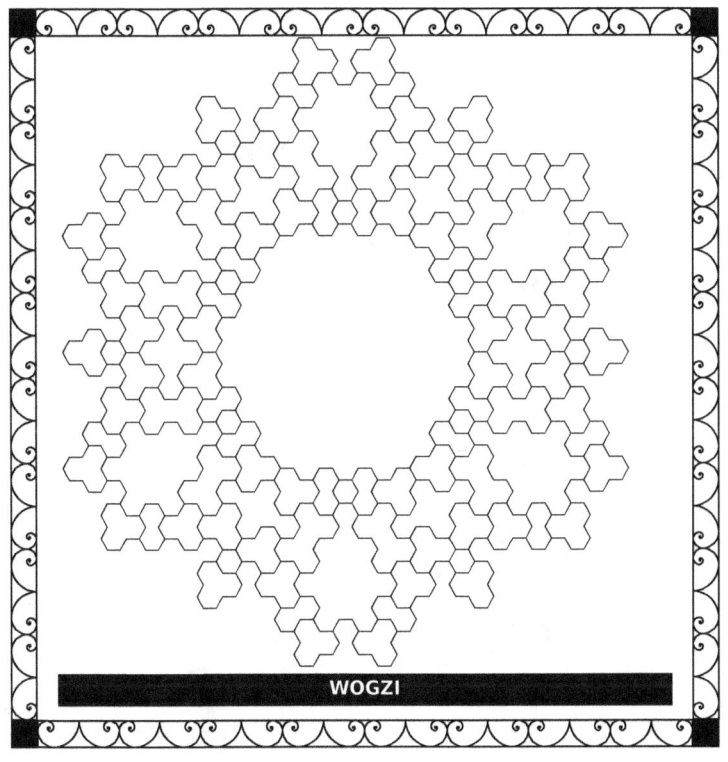

WOGZI

You must have something new in a landscape as well as something old, something that's dying and something that's being born.
Andy Goldsworthy

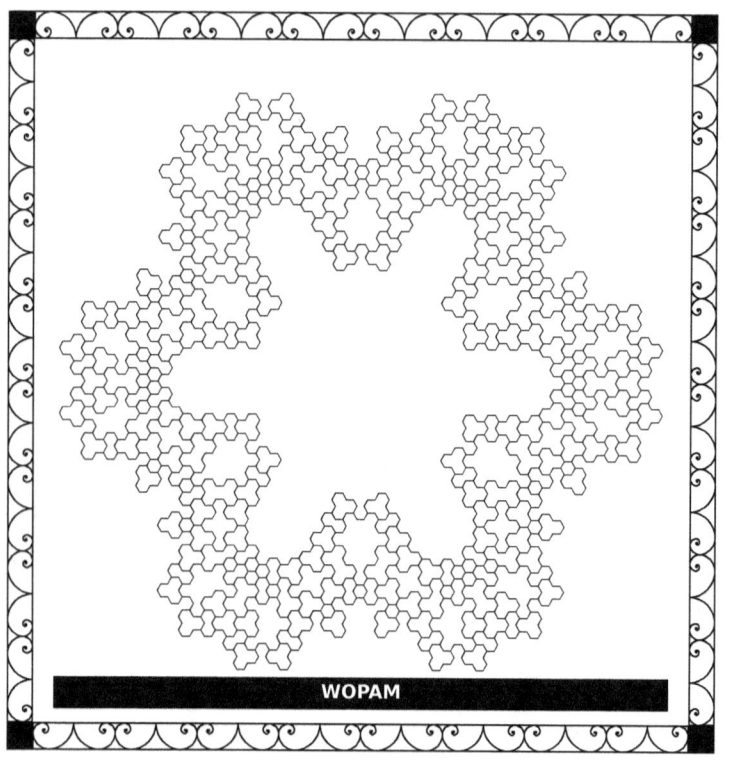

WOPAM

It became like a symbolic thing, to be an artist. After
Duchamp, I realized that being an artist is more about a
lifestyle and attitude than producing some product.
Ai Weiwei

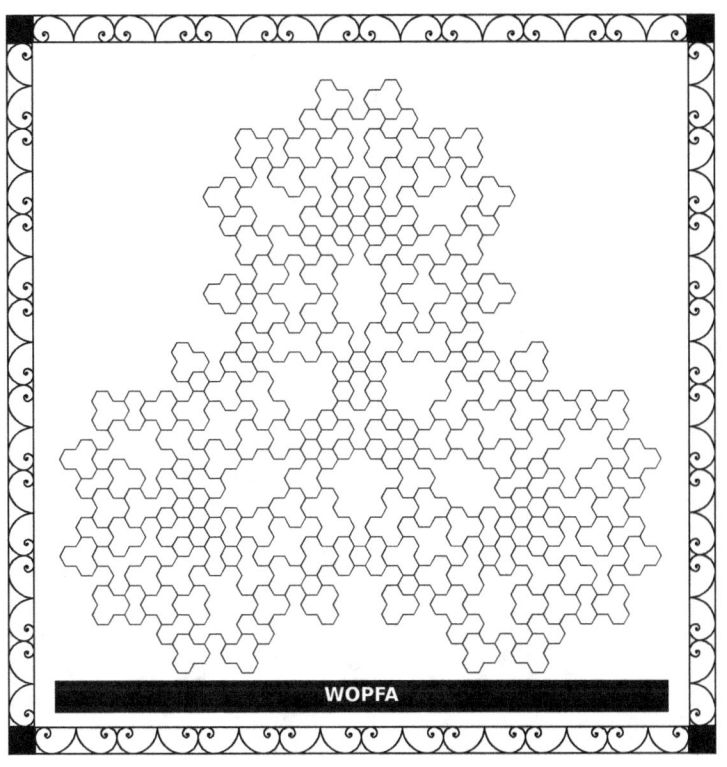

WOPFA

The only interesting ideas are heresies.
Susan Sontag

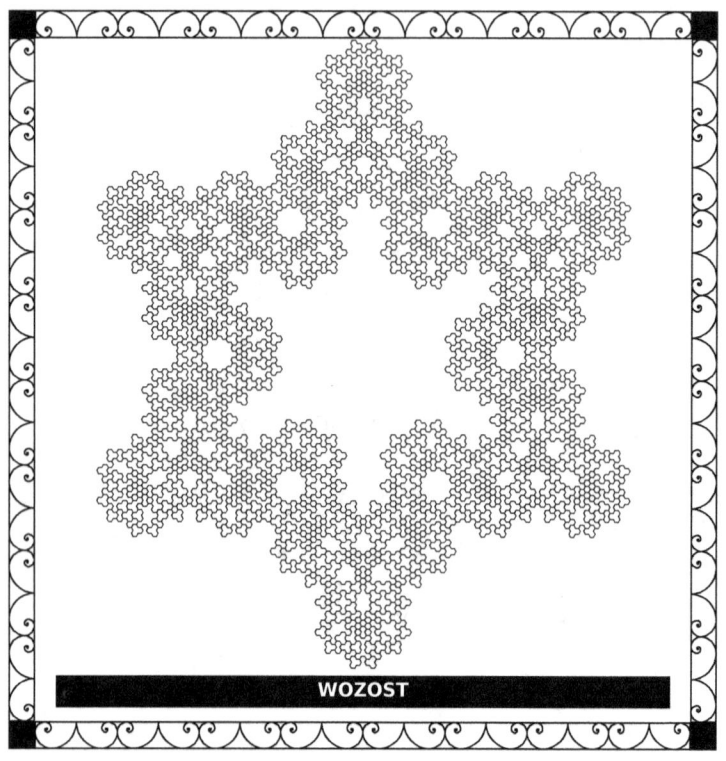

WOZOST

The function of the artist is to provide what life does not.
Tom Robbins

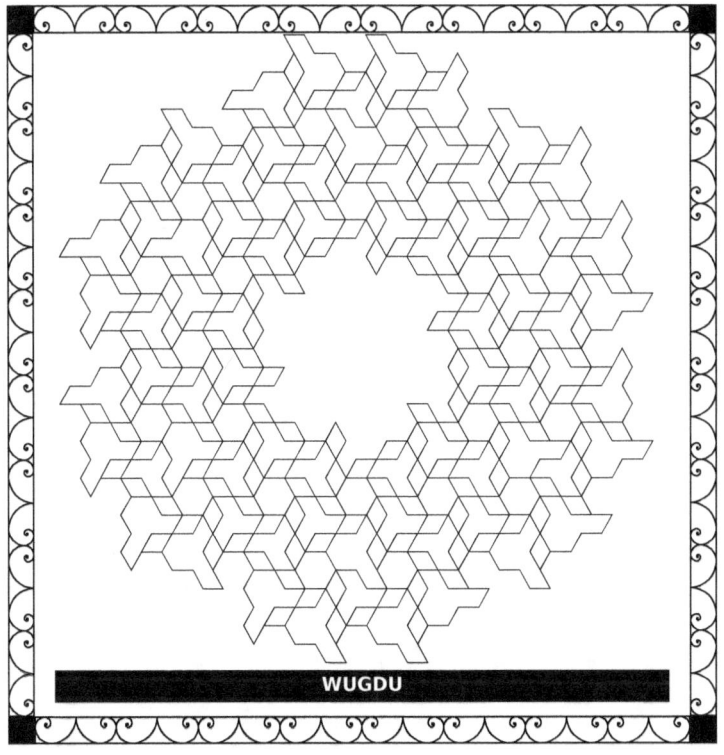

WUGDU

If you develop an ear for sounds that are musical it is like developing an ego. You begin to refuse sounds that are not musical and that way cut yourself off from a good deal of experience.

John Cage

315

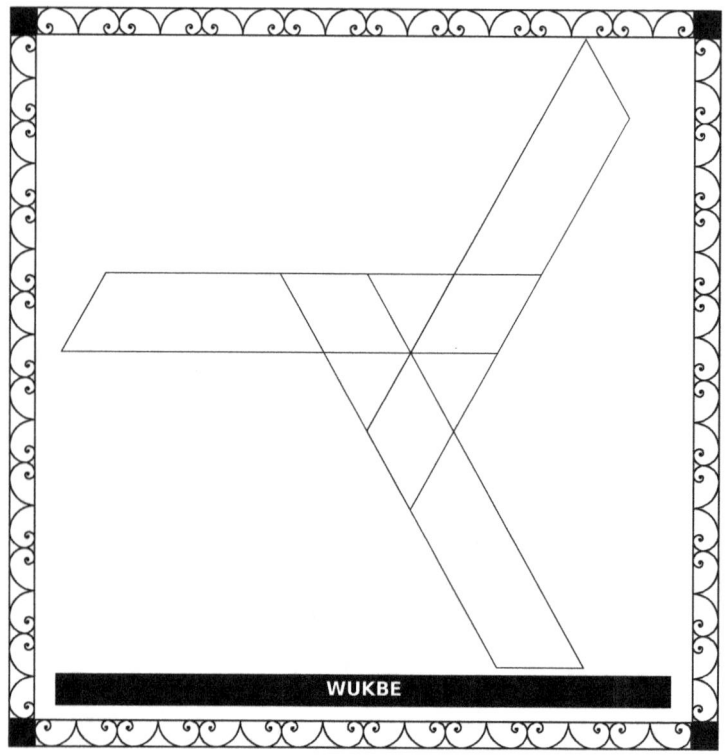

WUKBE

I like living. I have sometimes been wildly despairing, acutely miserable, racked with sorrow, but through it all I still know quite certainly that just to be alive is a grand thing.

Agatha Christie

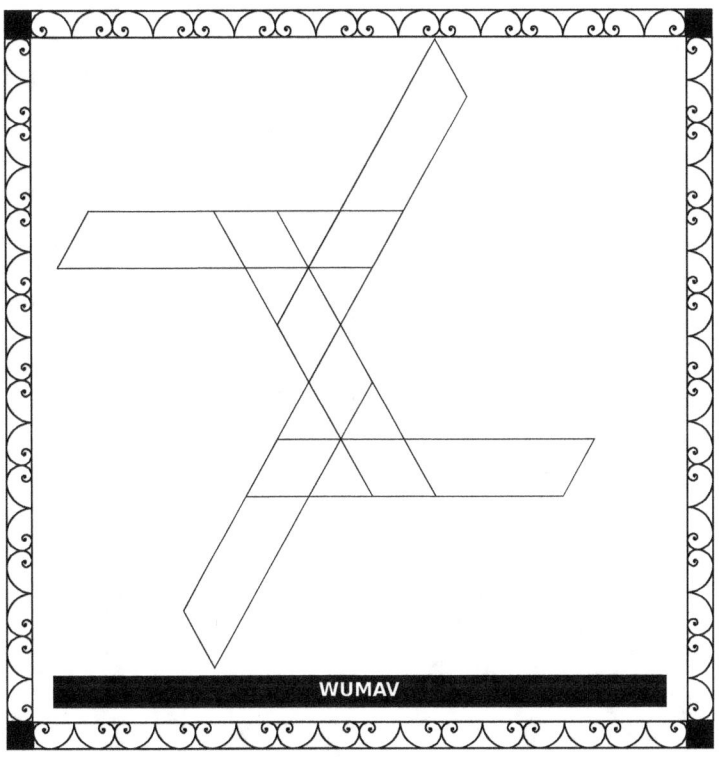

WUMAV

The line between art and life should be kept as fluid, and perhaps indistinct, as possible.

Allan Kaprow

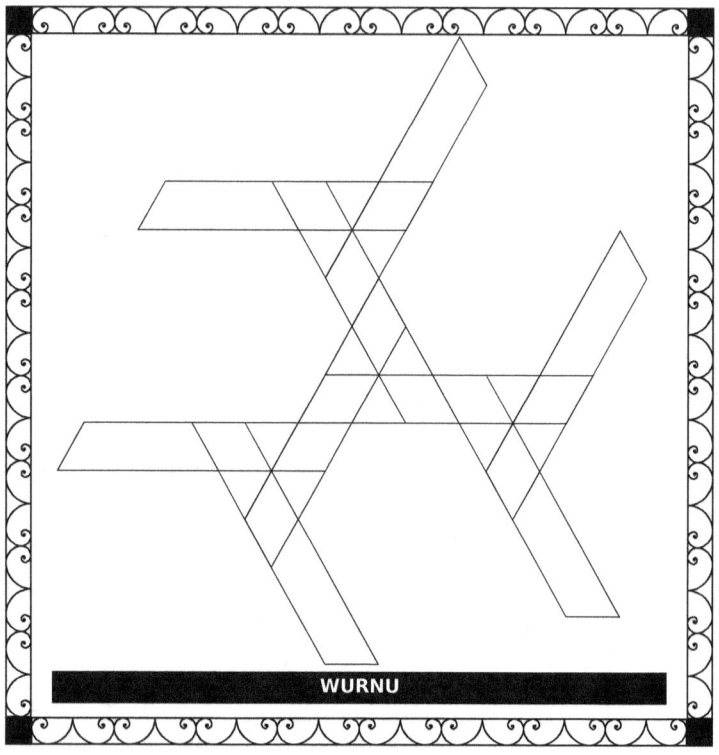

WURNU

Art is a form of nourishment (of consciousness, the spirit).
Susan Sontag

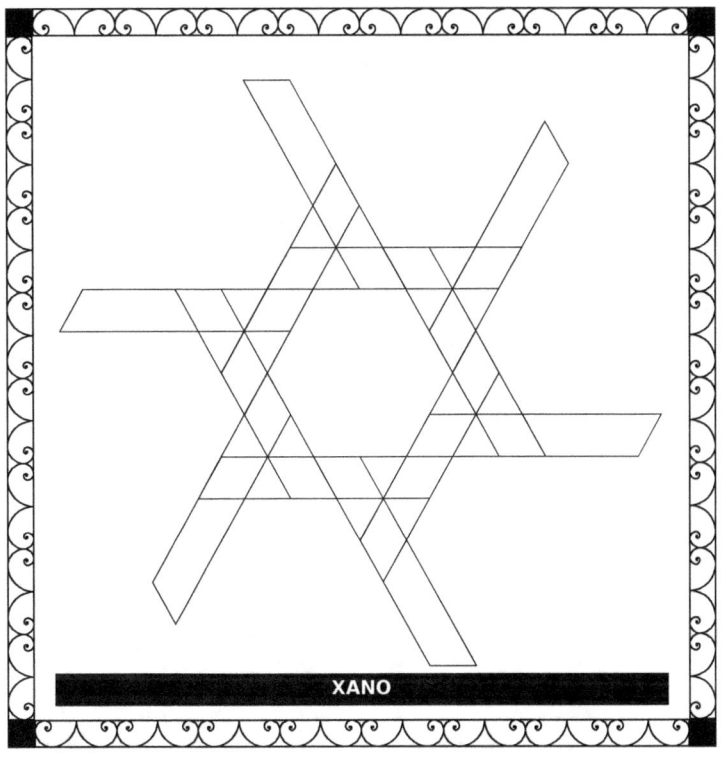

XANO

The reward of art is not fame or success but intoxication: that is why so many bad artists are unable to give it up.
Jean Cocteau

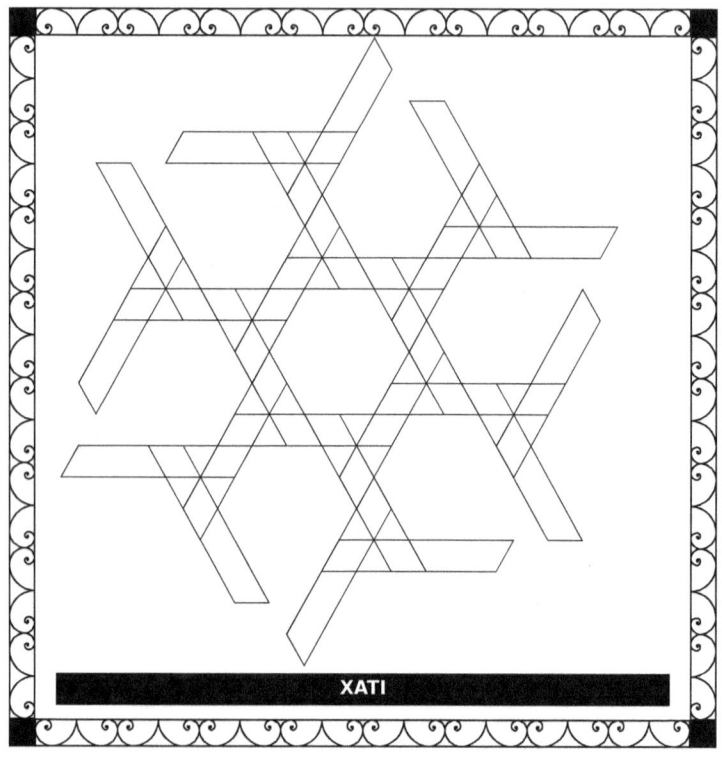

XATI

For astronomy is not only pleasant, but also very useful to be known: it cannot be denied that this art unfolds the admirable wisdom of God.
John Calvin

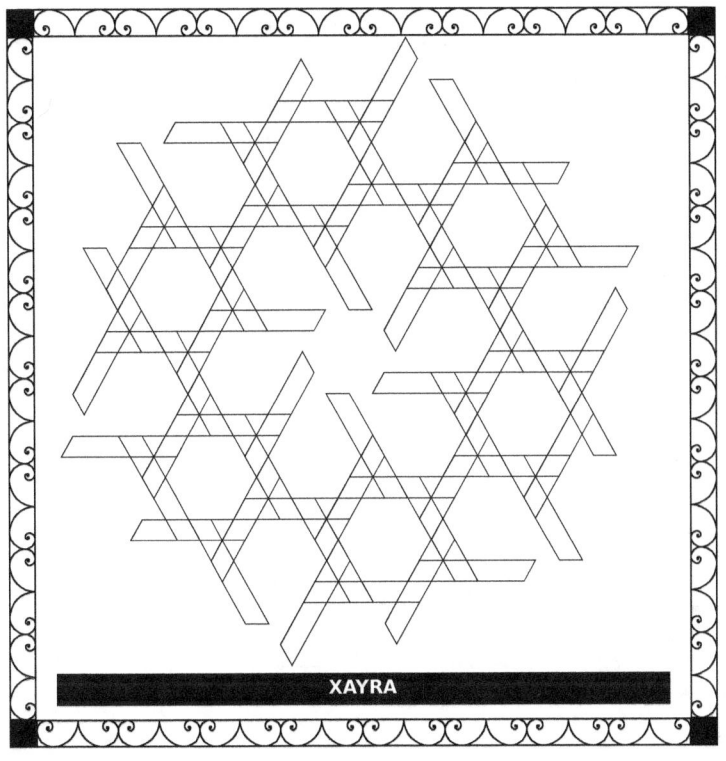

XAYRA

The beauty of mathematics often makes the subject matter much more attractive and easier to master.
Richard Hamming

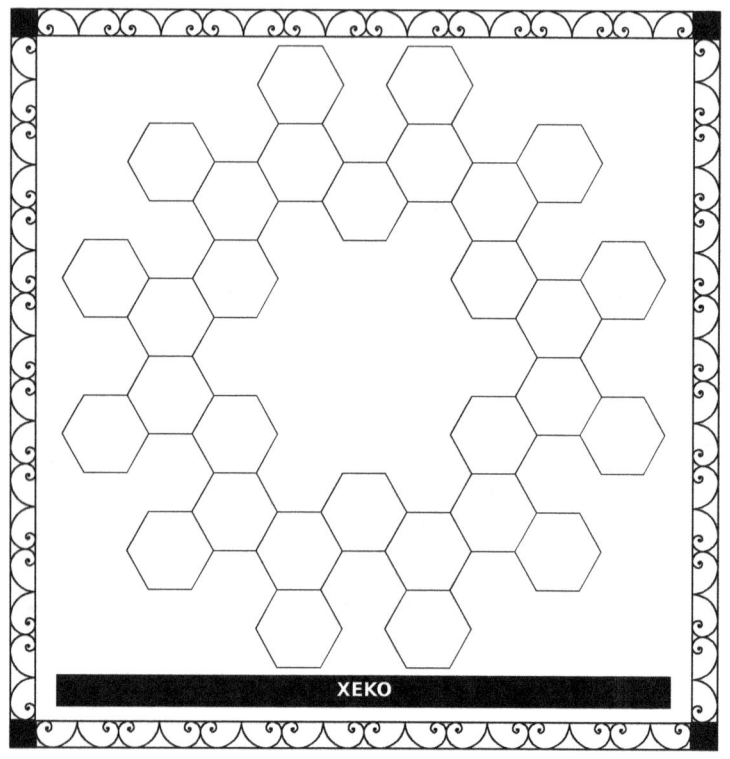

XEKO

There is a great deal of unmapped country within us which would have to be taken into account in an explanation of our gusts and storms.

George Eliot

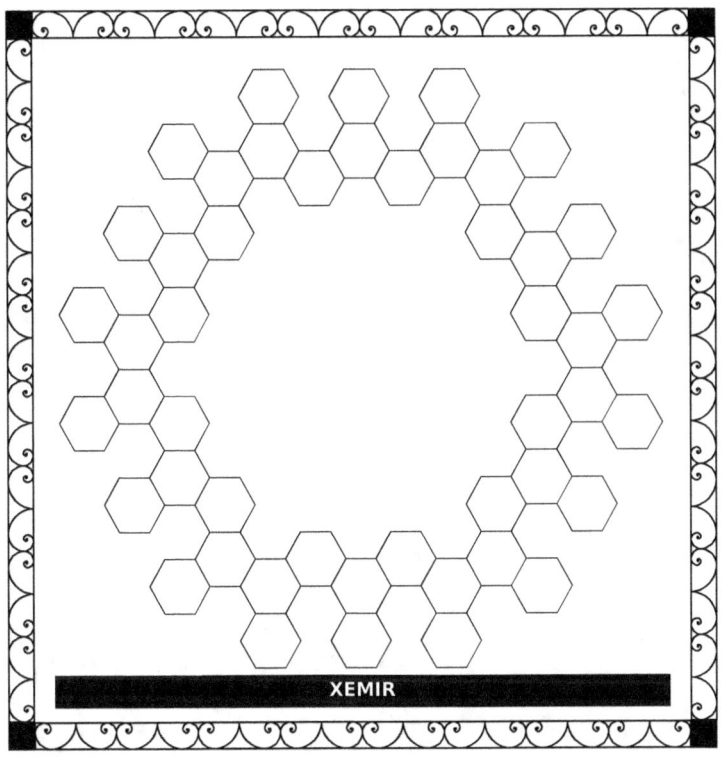

XEMIR

Every something is an echo of nothing.
John Cage

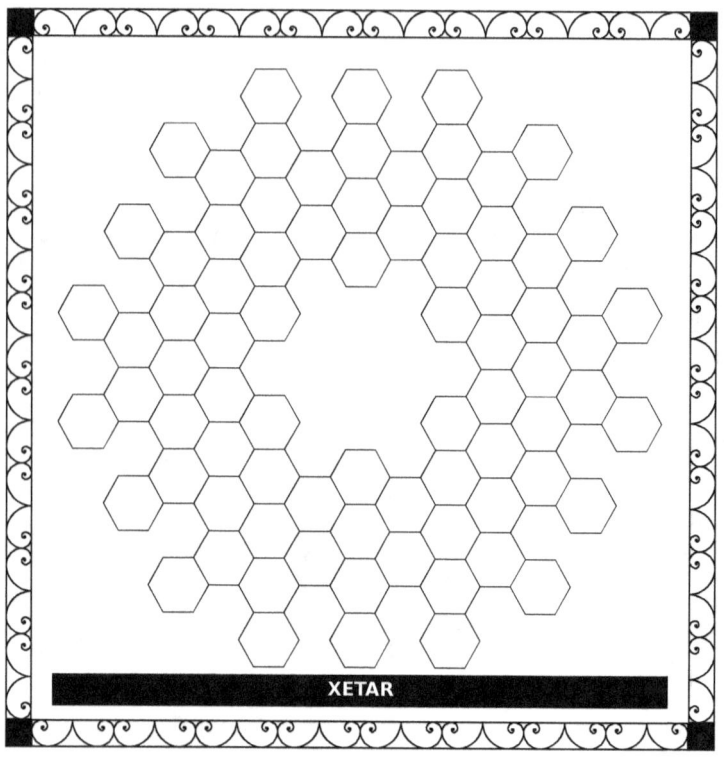

XETAR

You will be a beautiful person, as long as you see the beauty in others.
Bryant McGill

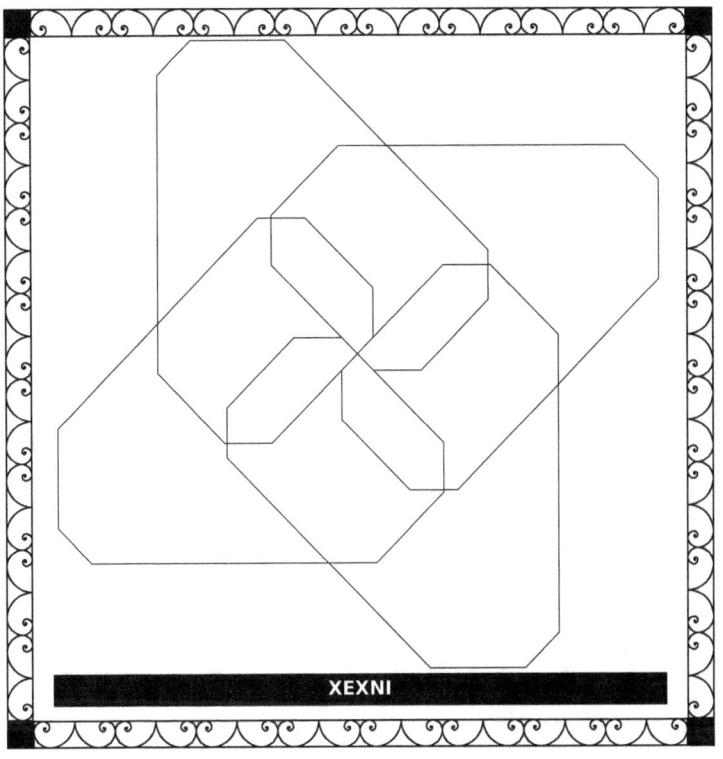

XEXNI

We thus see the artist performing a dual function: first, furthering the integrity of the process of self-expression in the language of art; and secondly, protecting the organic continuity of art in relation to its own laws. For like any organic substance, art must always be in a state of flux, the tempo being slow or fast. But it must move.

Mark Rothko

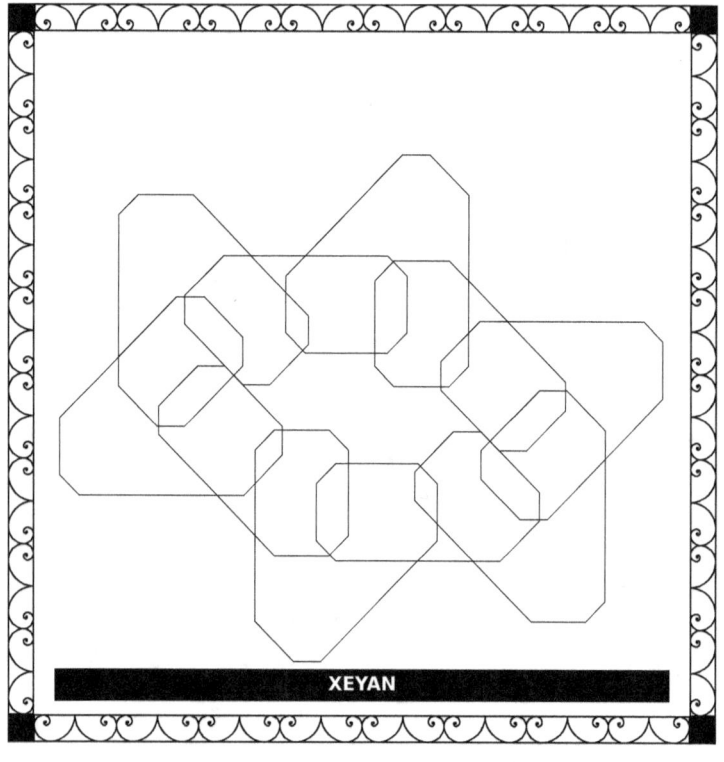

XEYAN

For myself, I refuse mentally to close the canon as if inspiration had run out! Why should we follow traditional thought more than modern thought?
Leslie Weatherhead

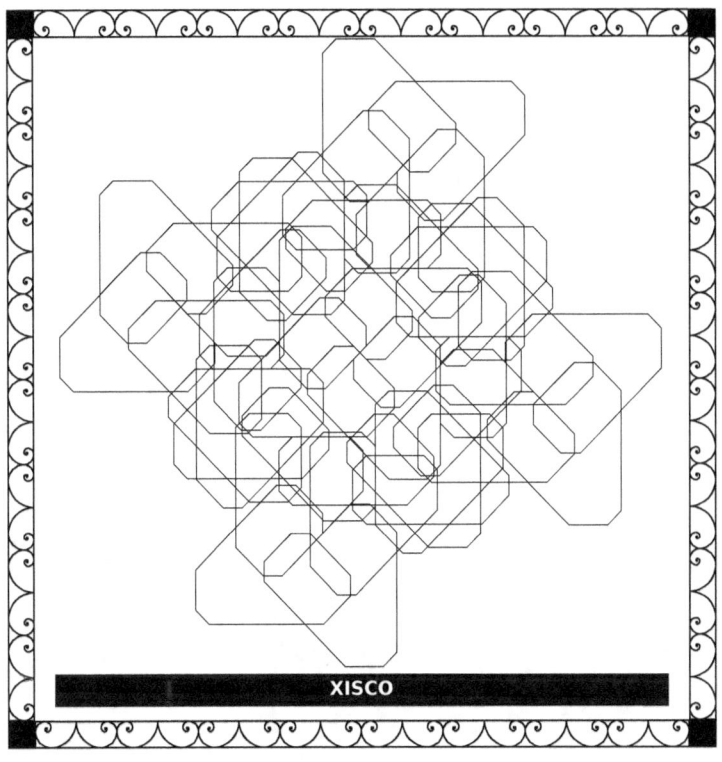

XISCO

To be an artist is to fail as no other dare fail...Try again. Fail again. Fail better.
Samuel Beckett

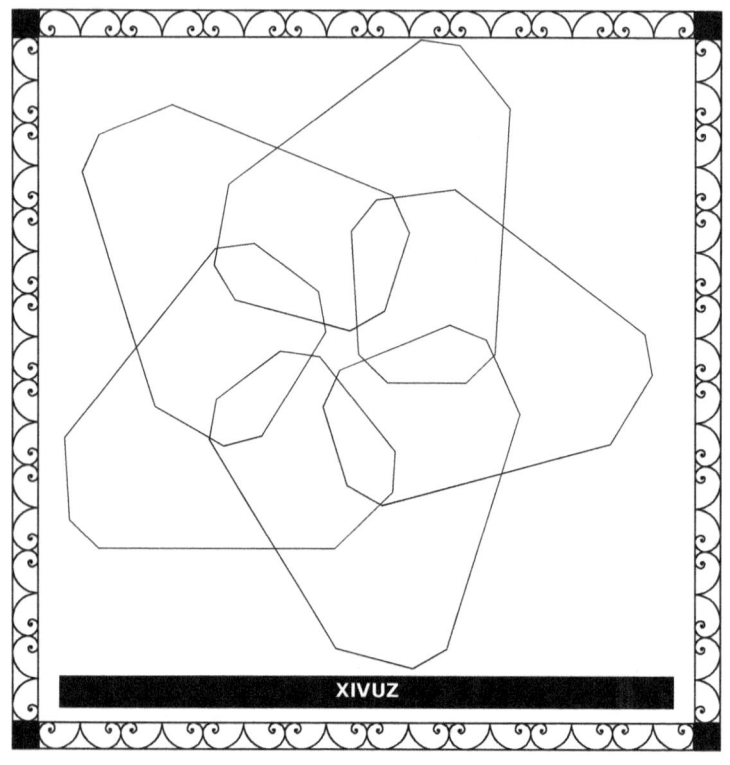

XIVUZ

Art is not life, but in a sense something contrary to life, since life is transient and changing, while art is permanent.
Daniel Bell

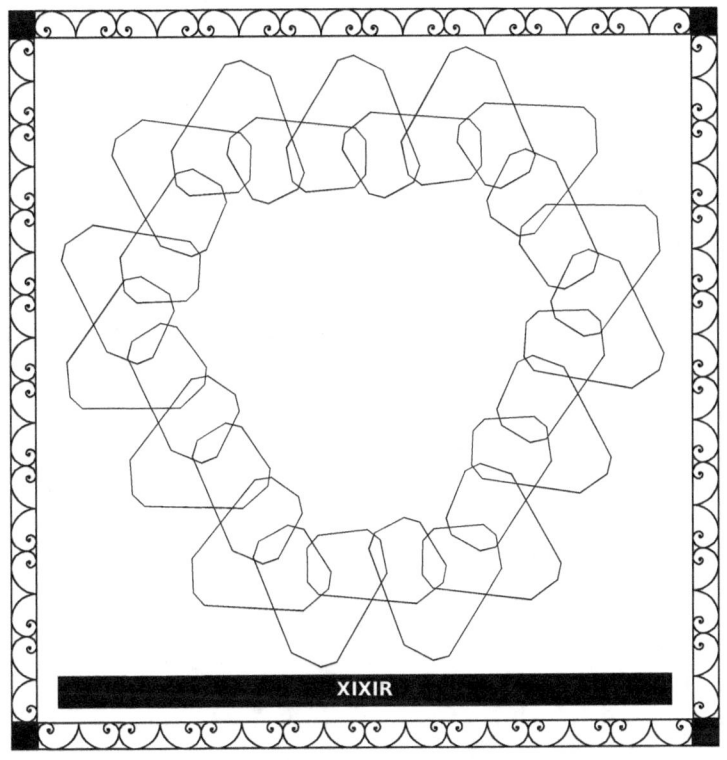

XIXIR

Conciseness in art is essential and a refinement. The concise man makes one think; the verbose bores. Always work towards conciseness.

Edouard Manet

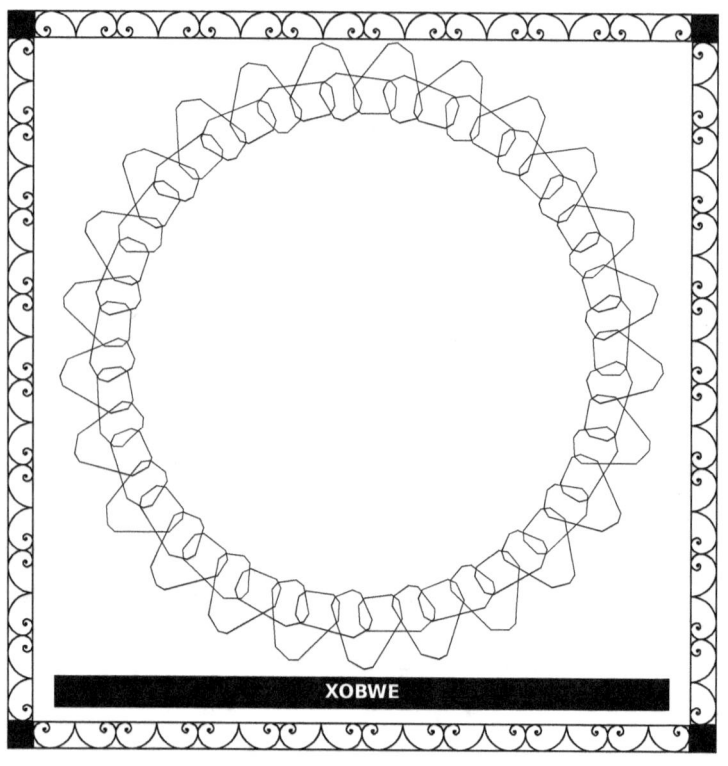

XOBWE

Great art is the contempt of a great man for small art.
F. Scott Fitzgerald

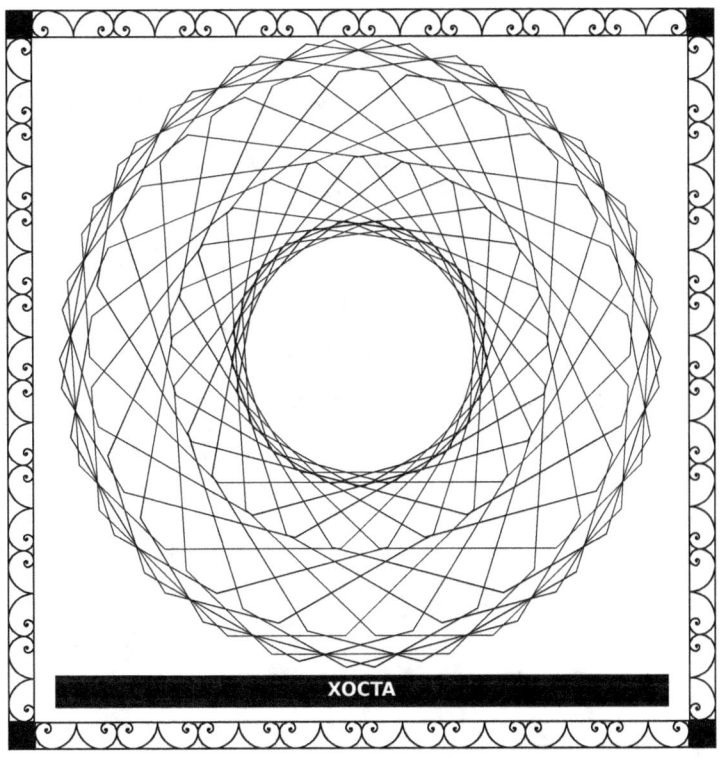

ХОСТА

The superior artist is the one who knows how to be influenced.

Clement Greenberg

331

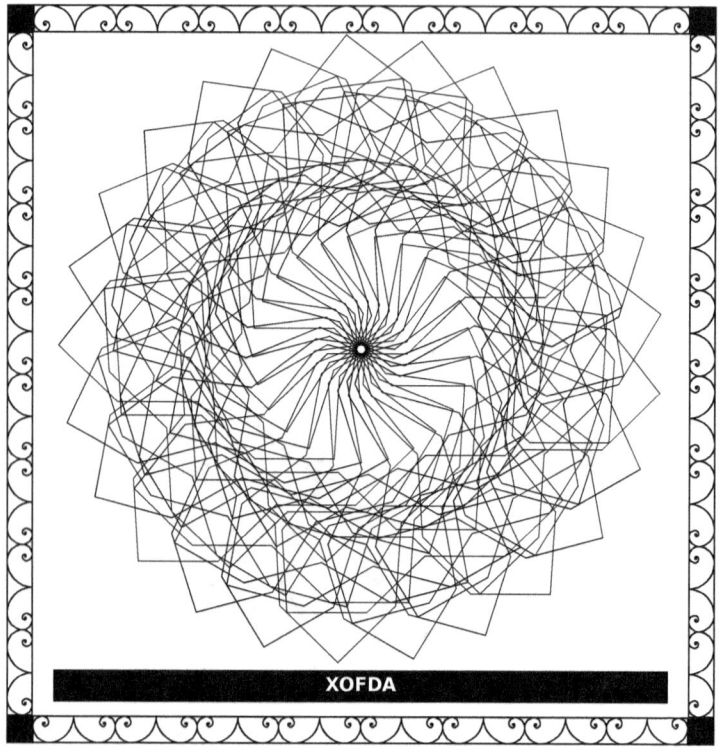

XOFDA

An original artist is unable to copy. So he has only to copy
in order to be original.
Jean Cocteau

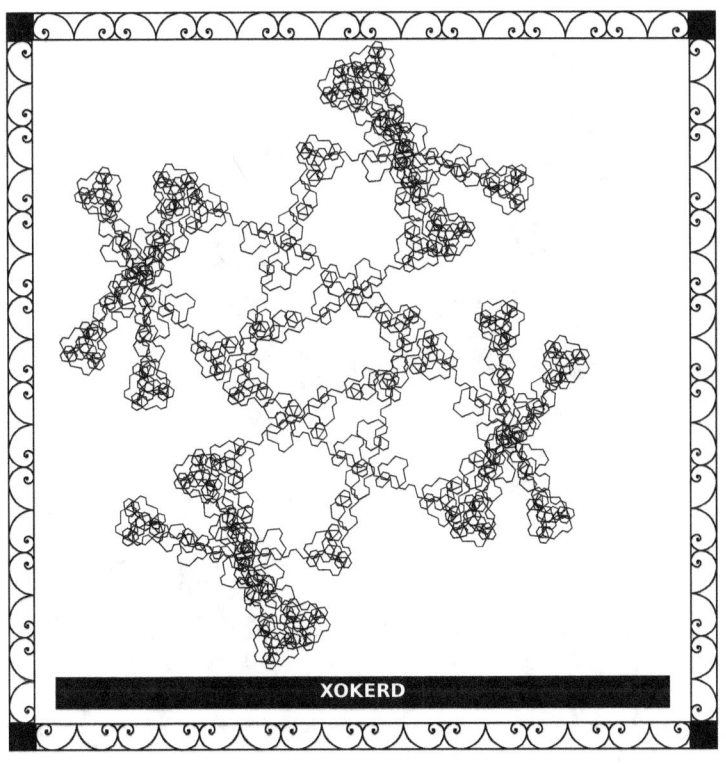

XOKERD

Every work of art is a transposition, a caricature,the passionate equivalent of a sensation received.
Maurice Denis

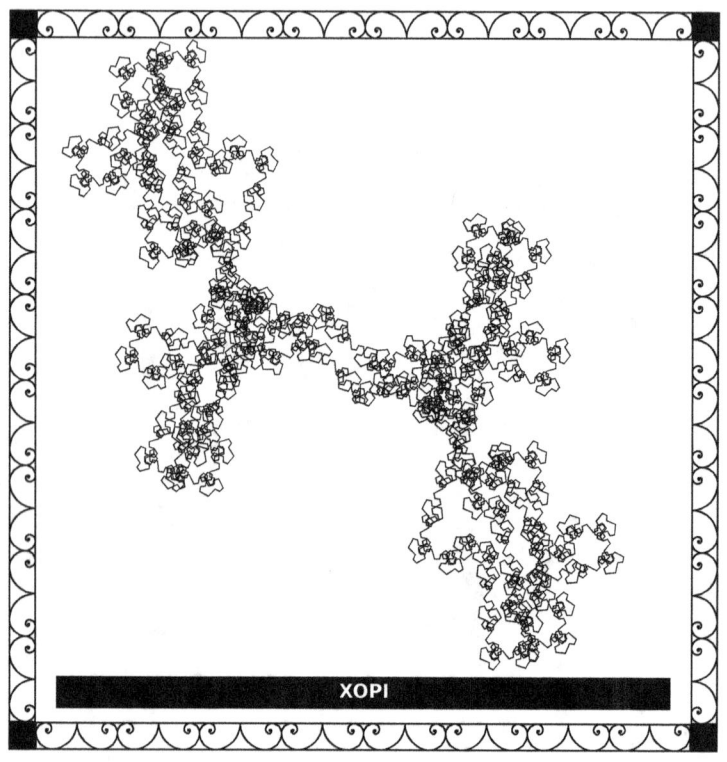

XOPI

In mathematics the art of asking questions is more valuable than solving problems.
Georg Cantor

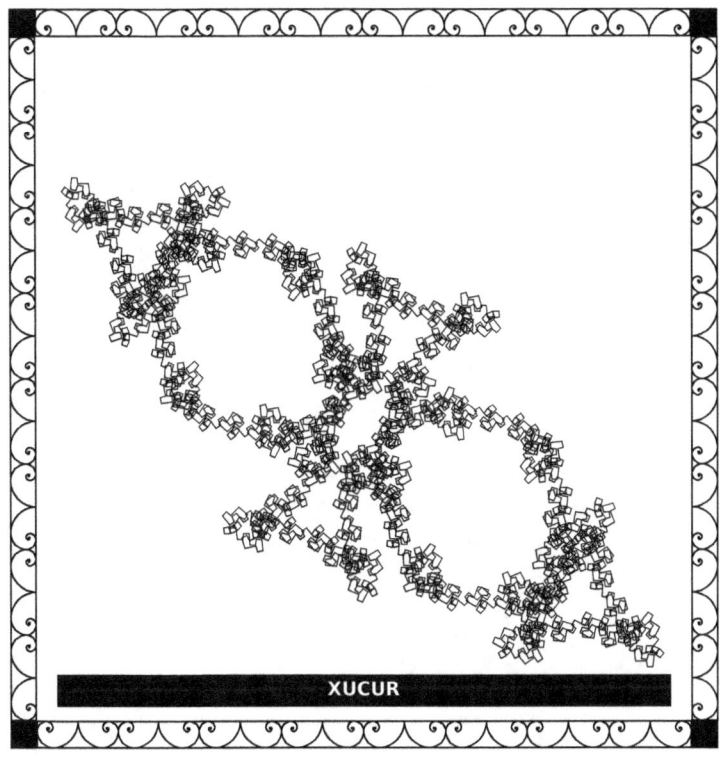

XUCUR

The arrogance of the artist is a very profound thing, and it fortifies you.
James A. Michener

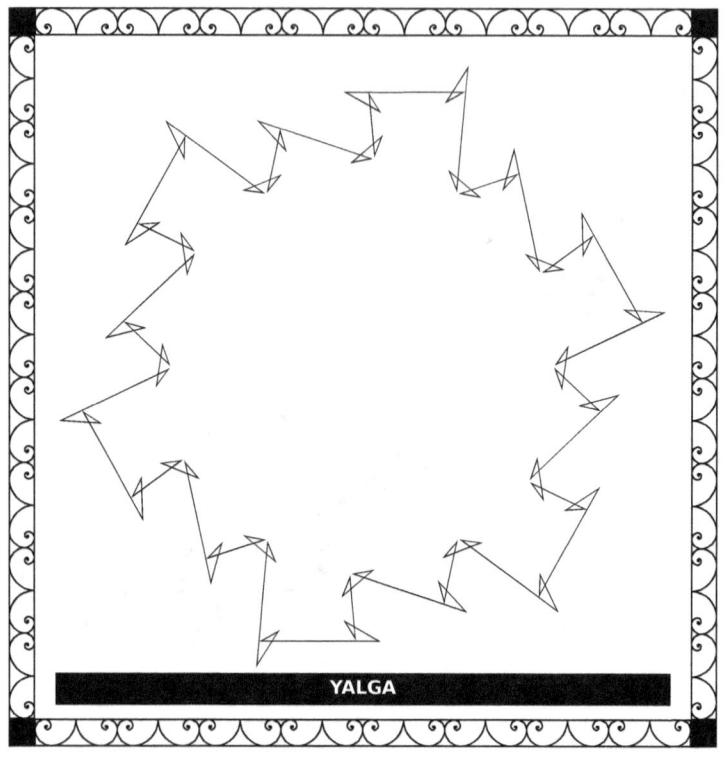

YALGA

One has a nose. The nose scents and it chooses. An artist
is simply a kind of pig snouting truffles.
Igor Stravinsky

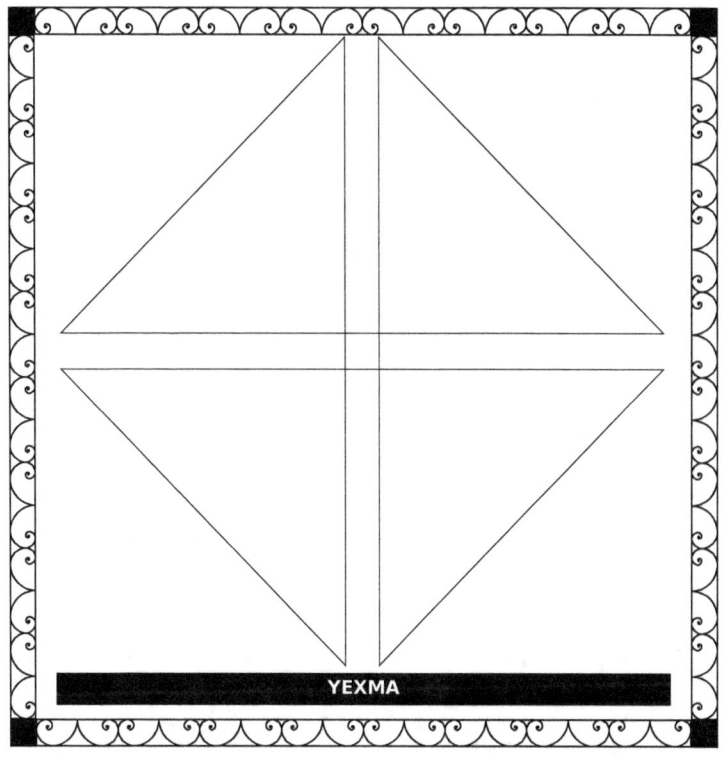

YEXMA

The artist produces for the liberation of his soul. It is his nature to create as it is the nature of water to run down the hill.

W. Somerset Maugham

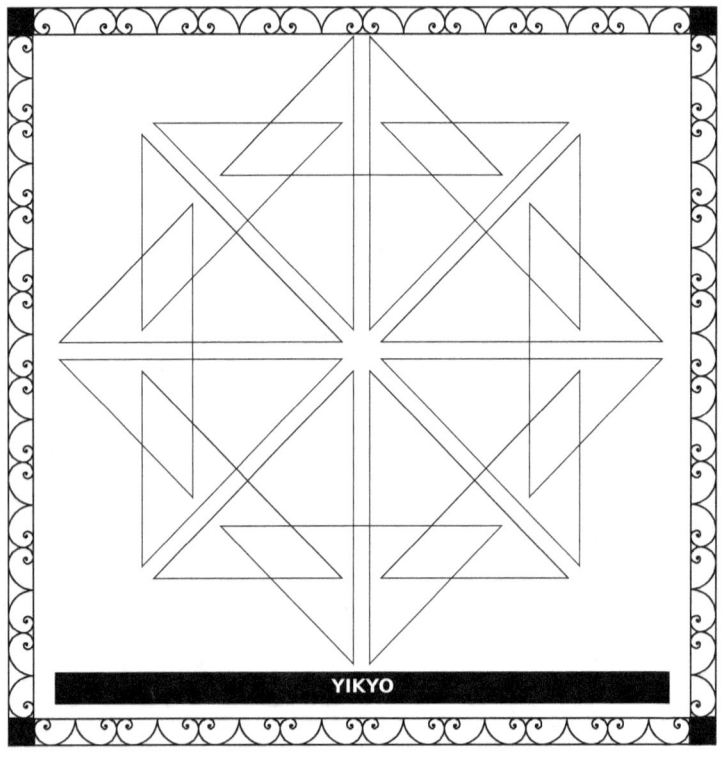

YIKYO

Art is the only serious thing in the world. And the artist
is the only person who is never serious.
Oscar Wilde

338

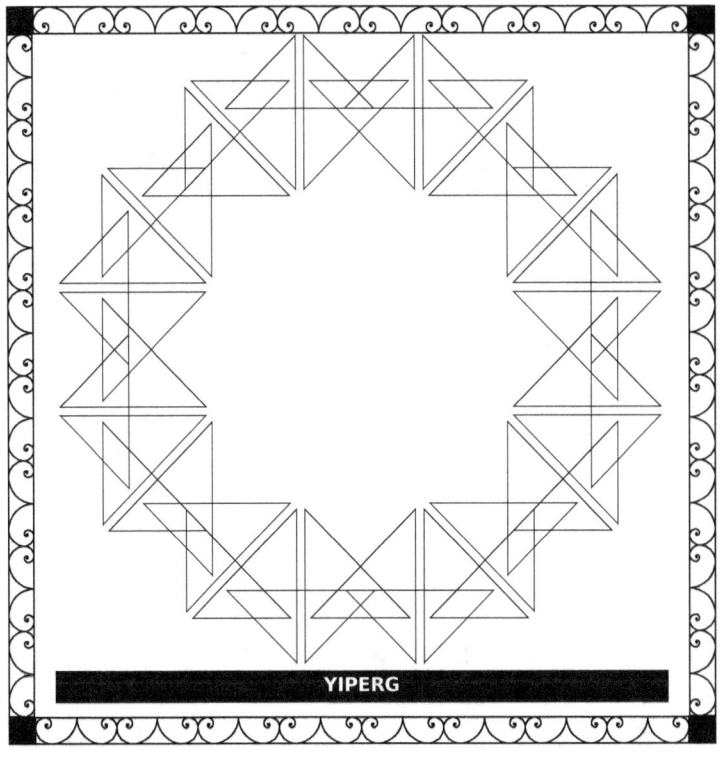

YIPERG

Life without industry is guilt, and industry without art is brutality.
John Ruskin

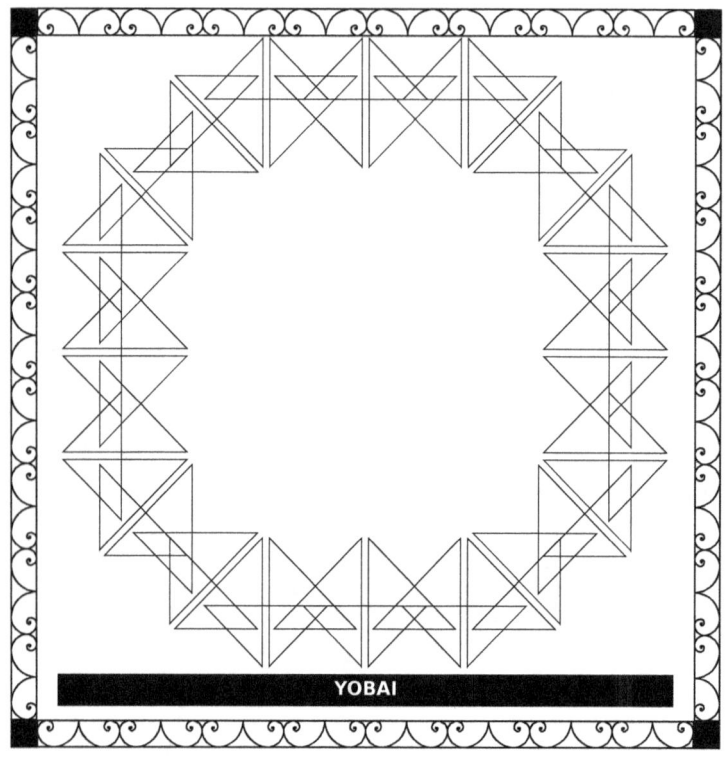

YOBAI

The function of art work is the stimulation of sensibilities,
the renewal of memories of moments of perfection.
Agnes Martin, On the Perfection Underlying Life

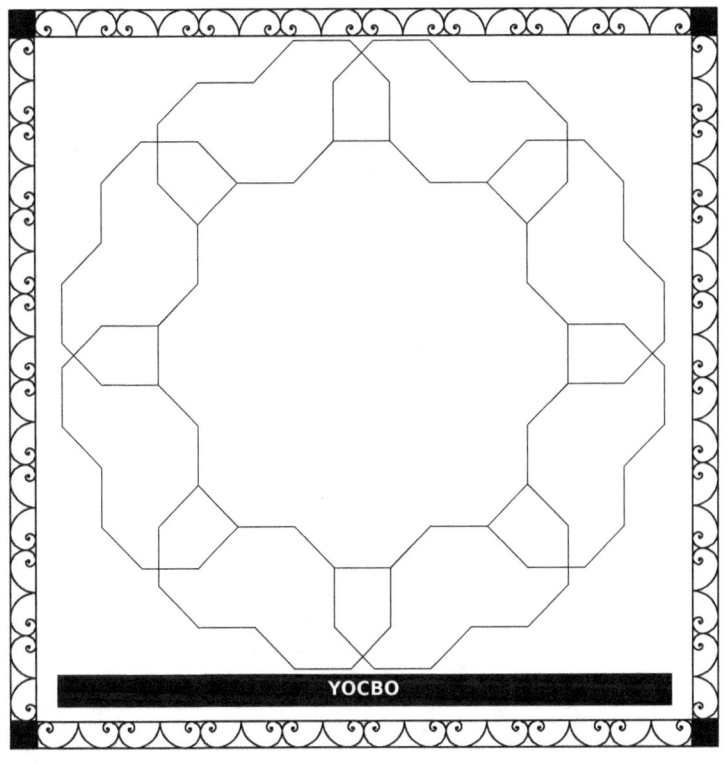

YOCBO

Acquire the art of detachment, the virtue of method, and the quality of thoroughness, but above all the grace of humility.

William Osler

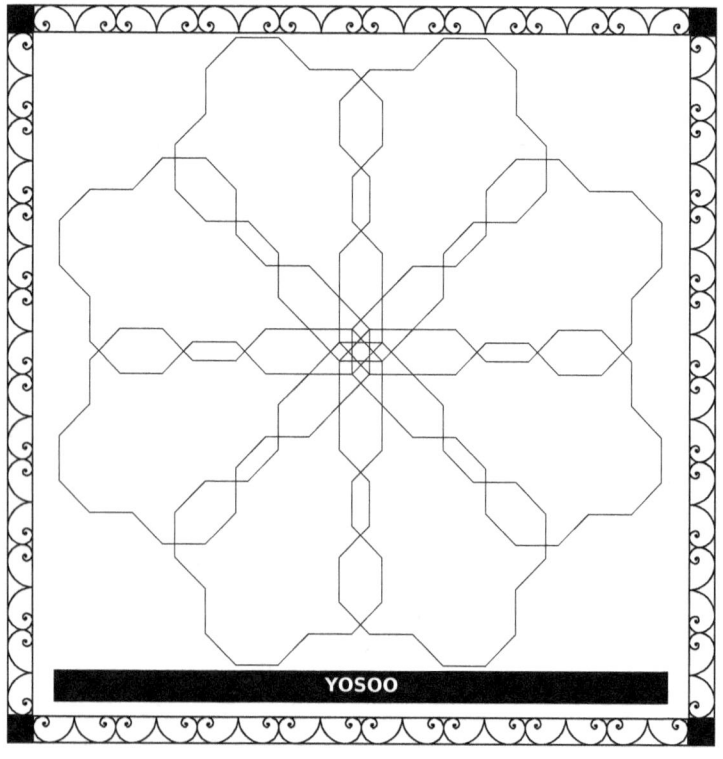

YOSOO

Every great work of art...is a celebration, an act of insubordination against the betrayals, horrors and infidelities of life.

Azar Nafisi

342

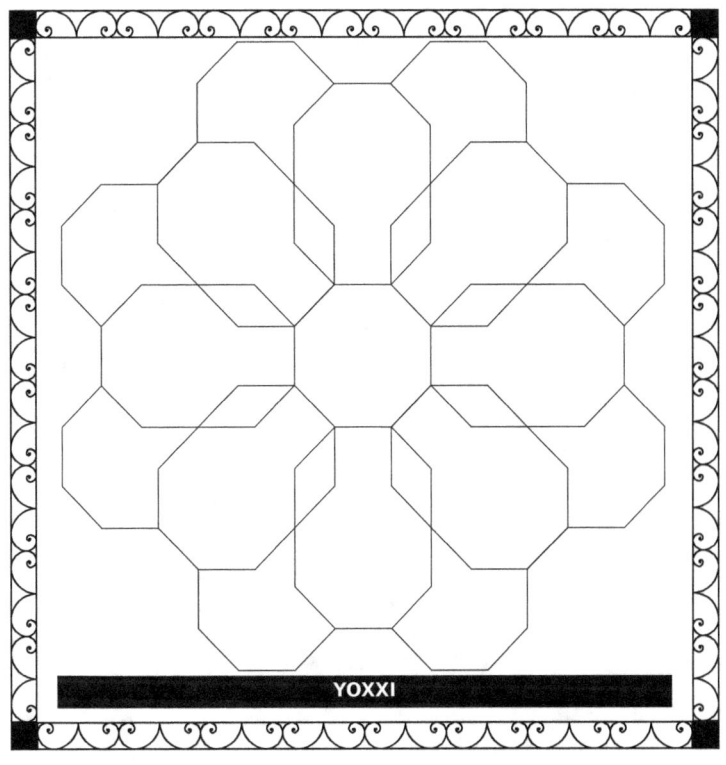

YOXXI

I would like to be a free artist and nothing else, and I regret
God has not given me the strength to be one.
Anton Chekhov

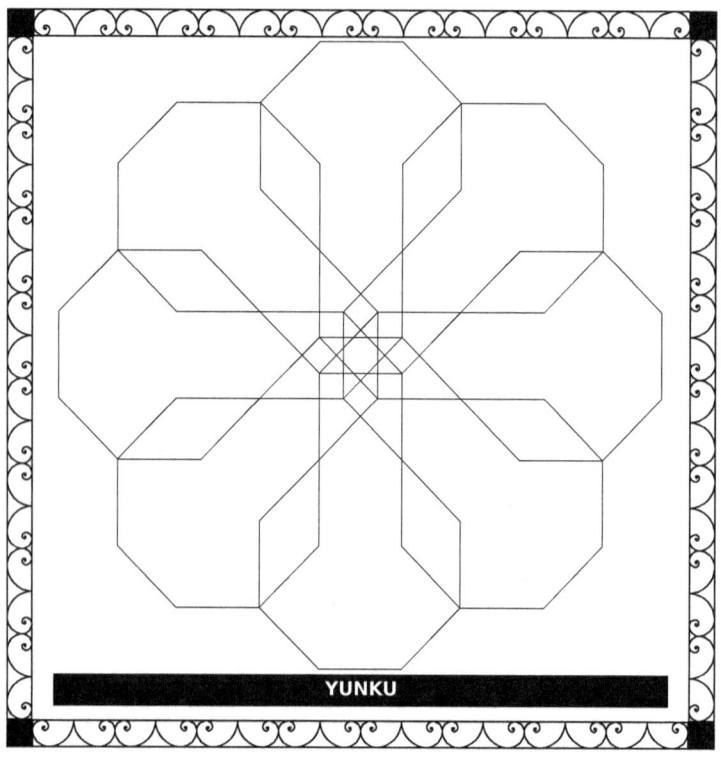

YUNKU

Complete honesty has nothing to do with purity or naivety. The full truth is unattainable to naivety, and the completely honest artist is not pure in heart.
Clement Greenberg

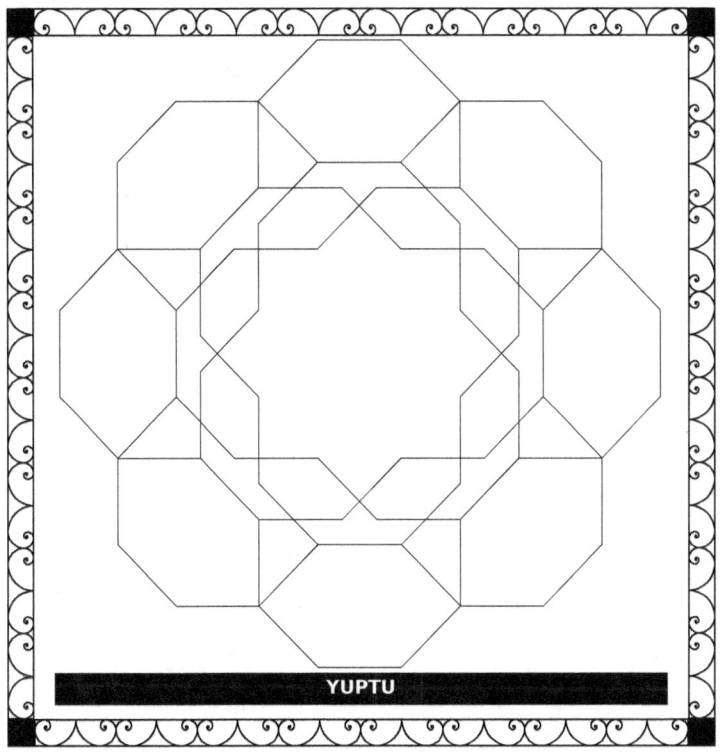

YUPTU

My art flatters nobody by imitation, it courts nobody by smoothness, nobody by petitelieness without either fal-de-lal or fiddle-de-dee; how then can I hope to be popular?
John Constable

345

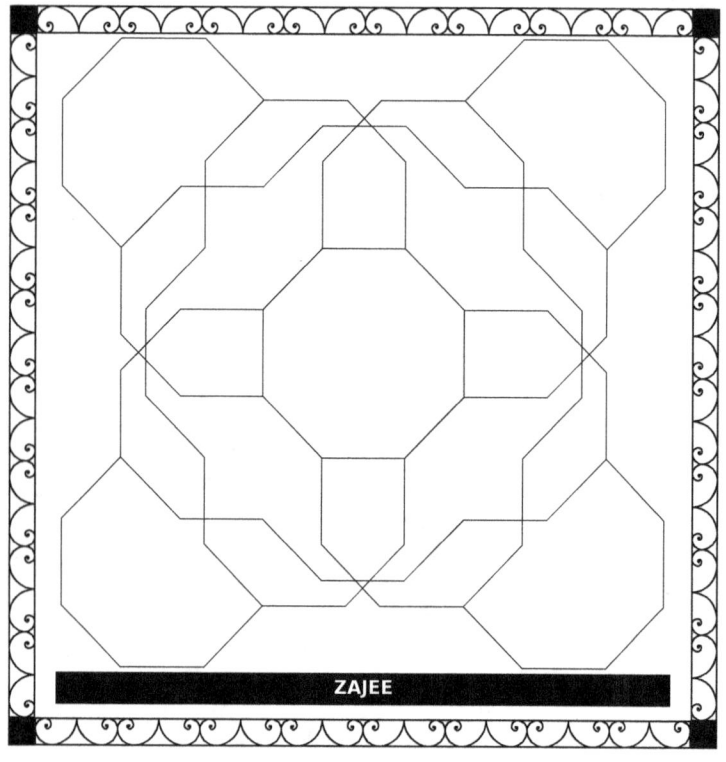

ZAJEE

Nonsense and beauty have close connections — closer connections than art will allow.

E. M. Forster

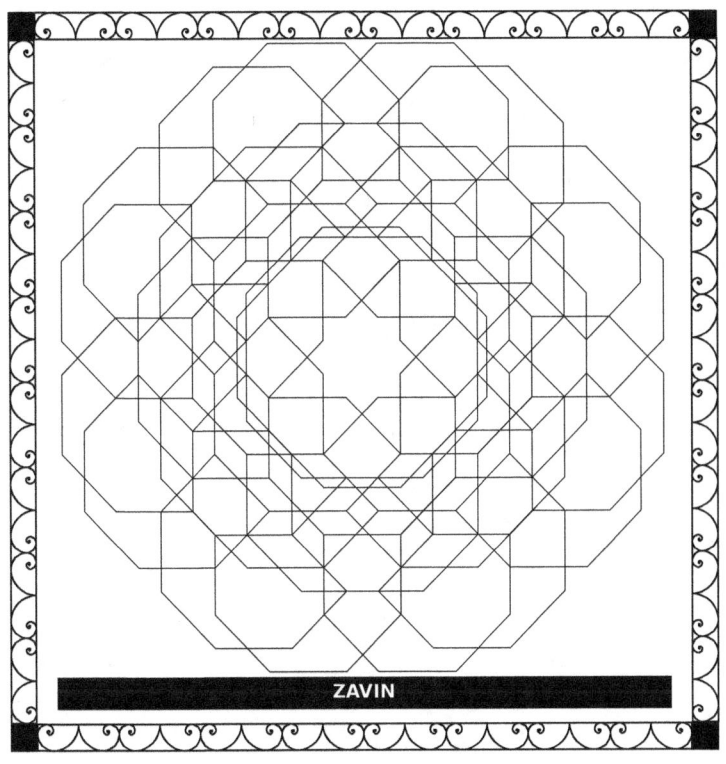

ZAVIN

It is in front of the the paper that the artist creates himself.
Stephane Mallarme

347

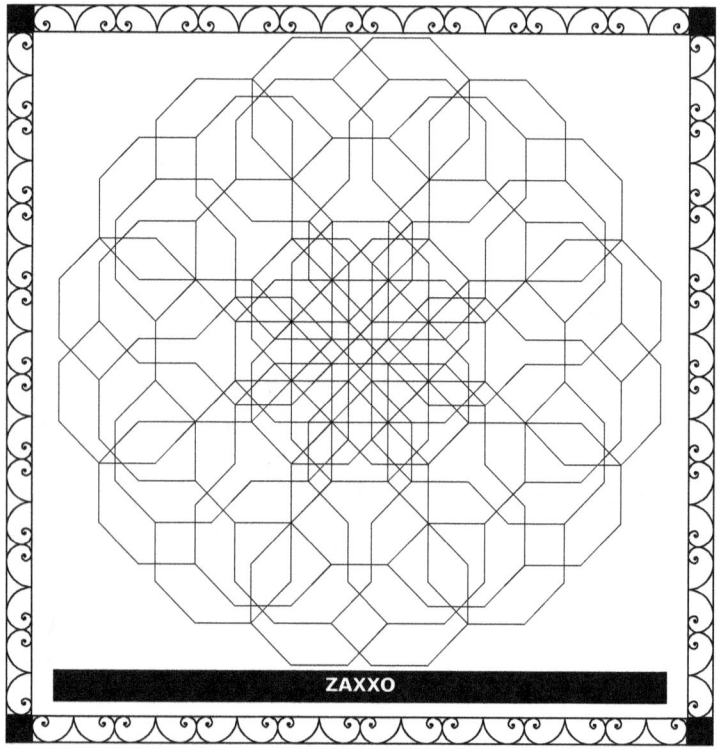

ZAXXO

An artist who theorizes about his work is no longer artist
but critic.
H. G. Wells

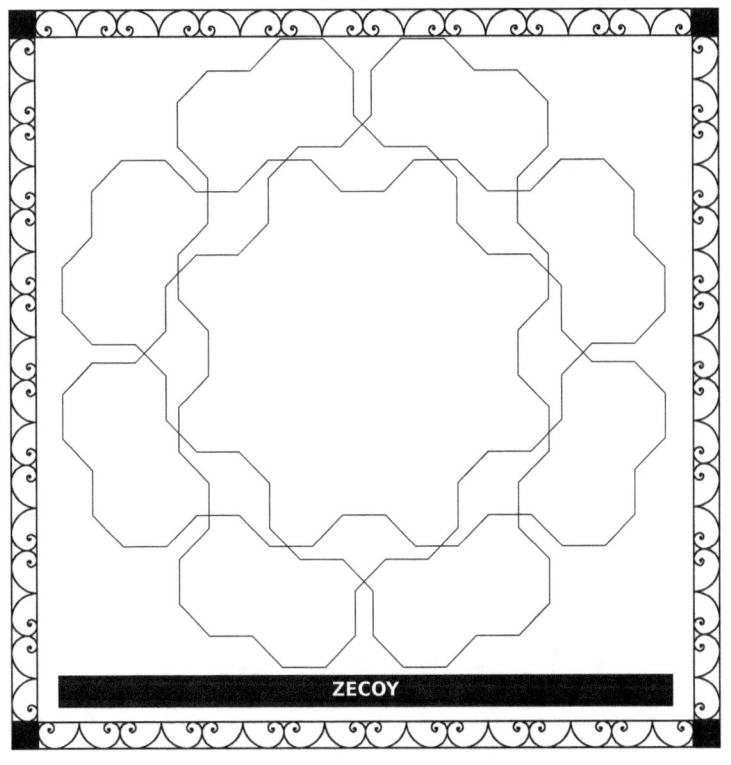

ZECOY

For Leonardo, painting is both an art and a science...
Fritjof Capra

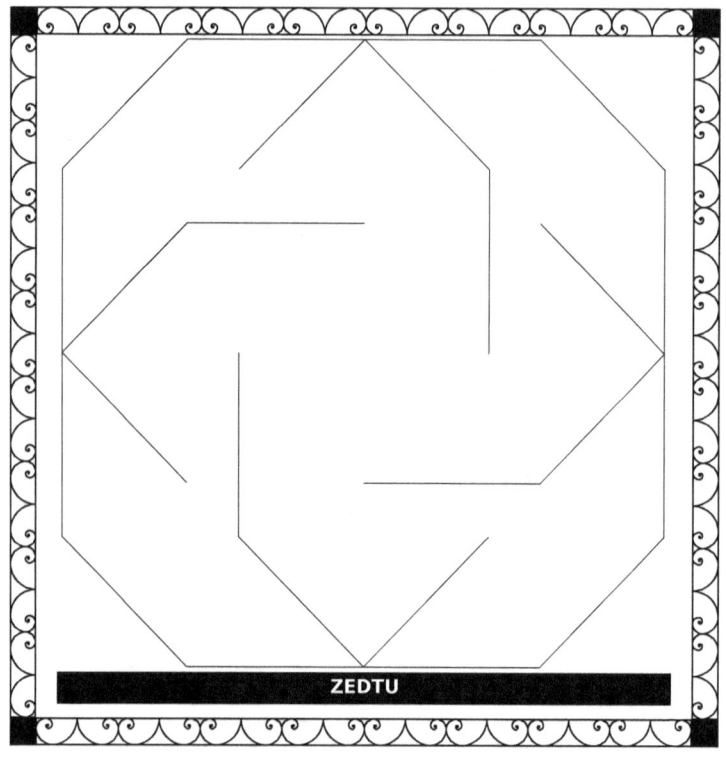

ZEDTU

Appearance should never attain reality, and if nature conquers, then must art retire.
Friedrich Schiller

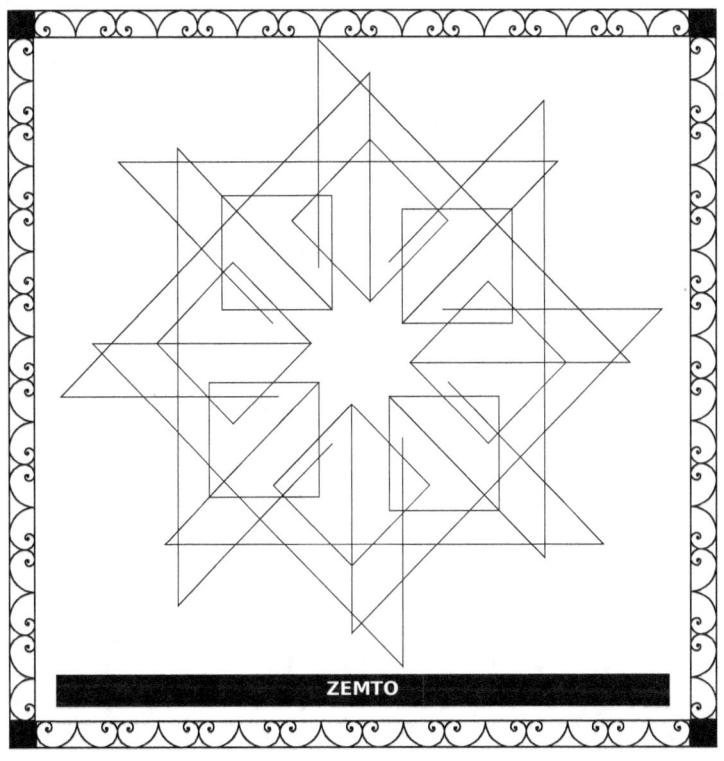

ZEMTO

Everything we do is music.
John Cage

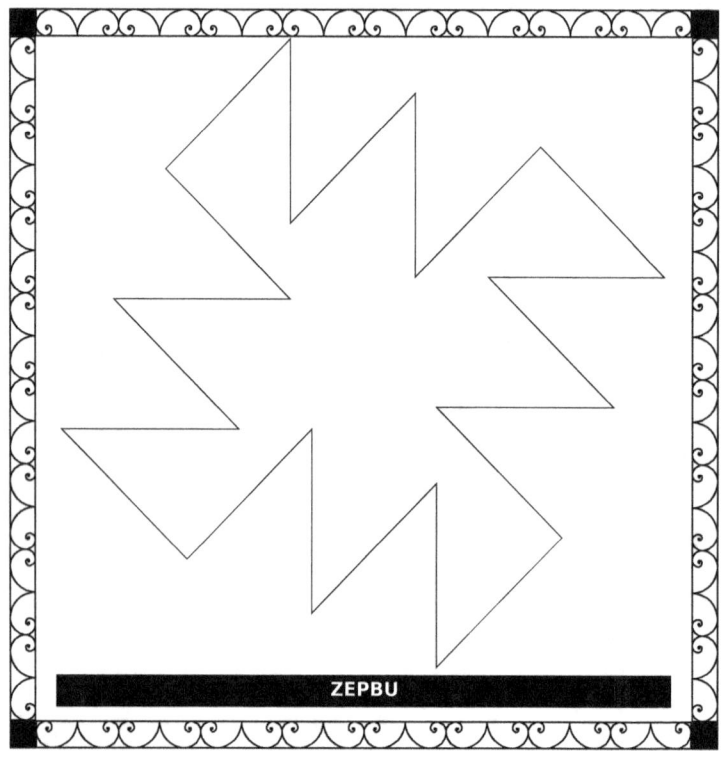

ZEPBU

Who knows where inspiration comes from. Perhaps it arises from desperation. Perhaps it comes from the flukes of the universe, the kindness of the muses.
Amy Tan

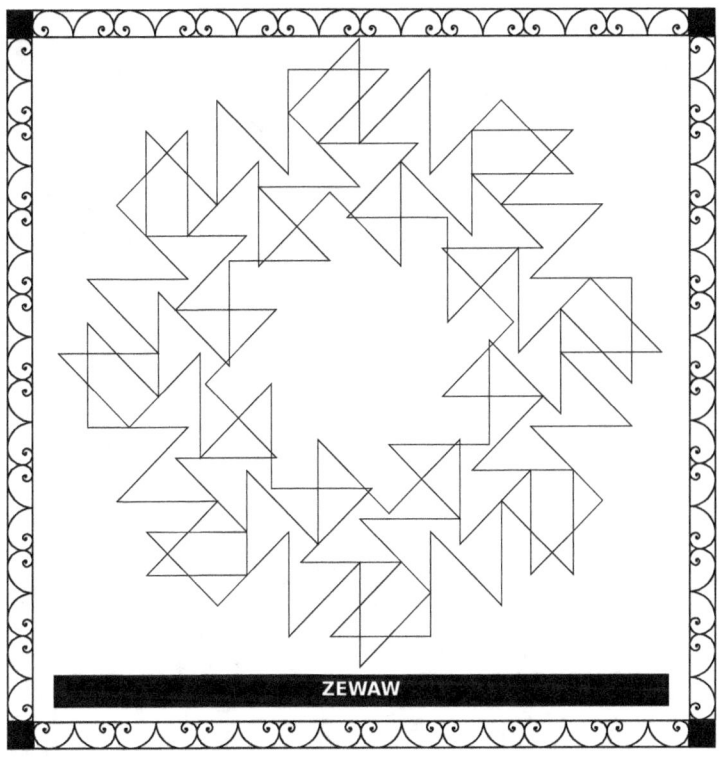

ZEWAW

The Greek "point of view" in both art and chronology has little in common with ours but was much like that of the Middle Ages.
Marshall McLuhan

353

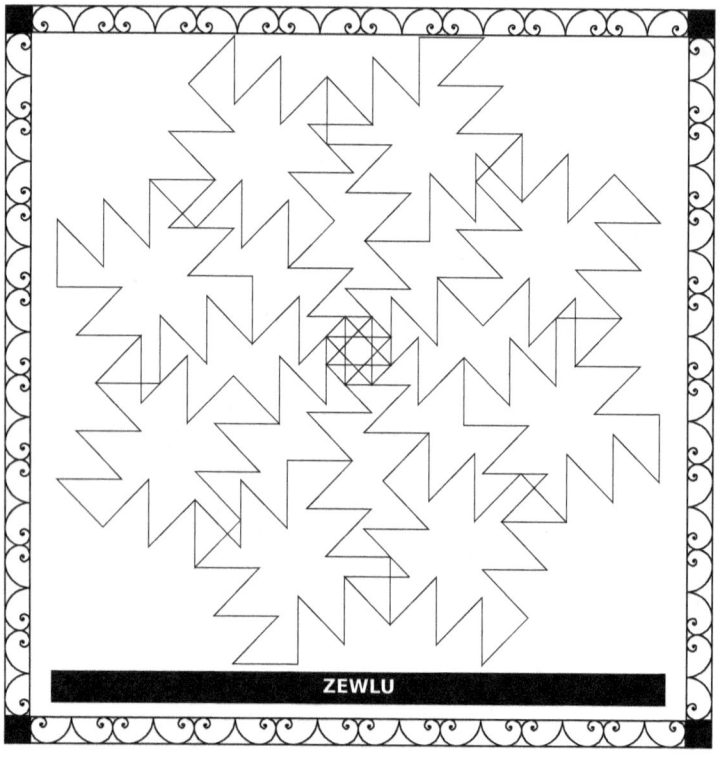

ZEWLU

Nature has mysterious infinities and imaginative power. It is always varying the productions it offers to us. The artist himself is one of nature's means.
Paul Gauguin

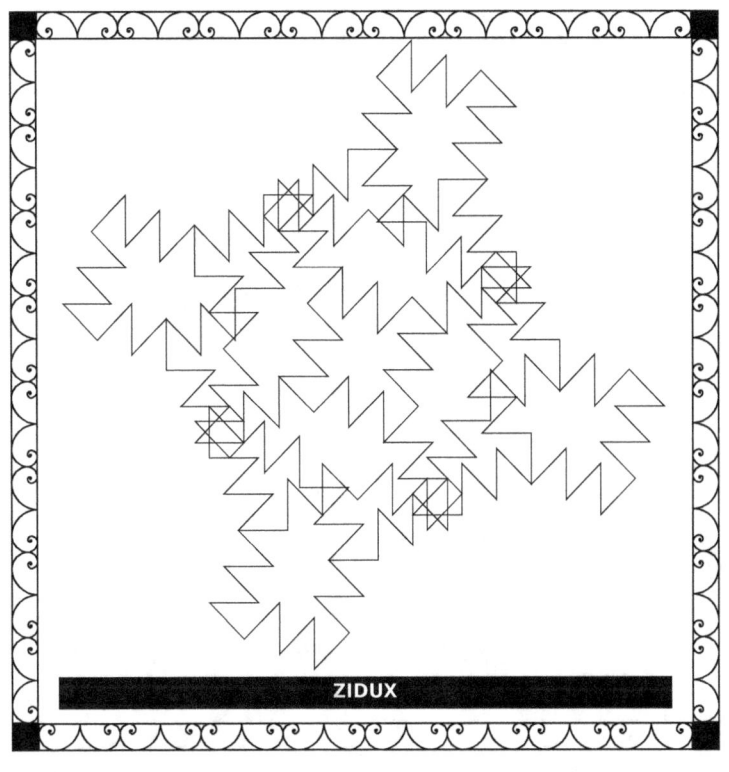

ZIDUX

All art preserves mysteries which aesthetic philosophers tackle in vain.
Anthony Burgess

355

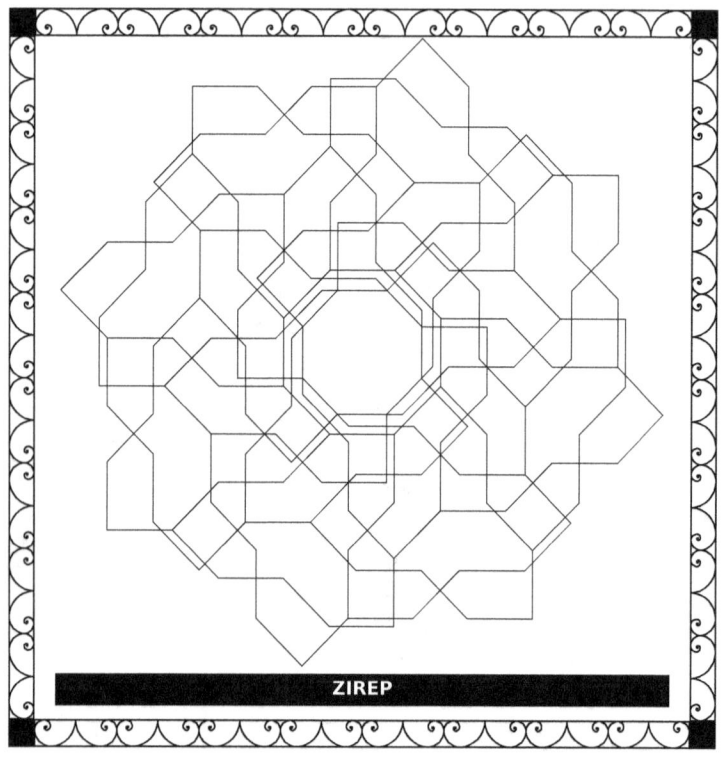

ZIREP

Experience is wine, and art is the brandy we distill from it.
Robertson Davies

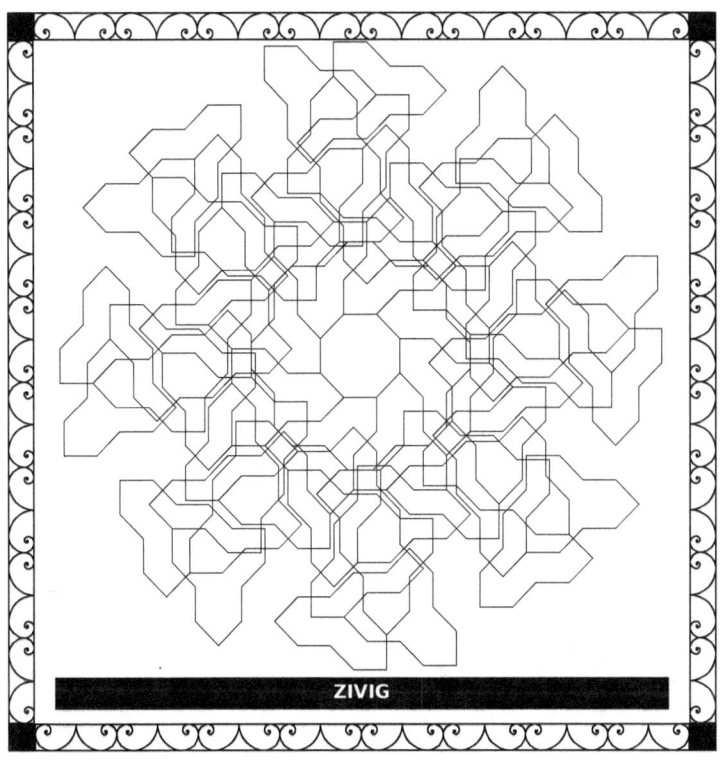

ZIVIG

It's the hardest thing in the world to give everything. Though it's usually the only way to get everything.
Alan Jay Lerner, Brigadoon

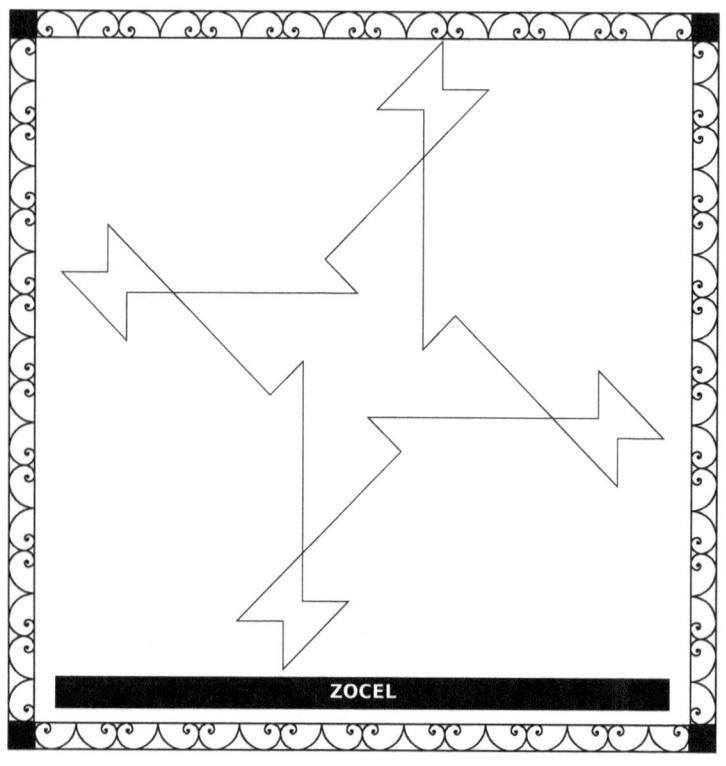

ZOCEL

To us art is an adventure into an unknown world, which can be explored only by those willing to take the risk.
Mark Rothko and Adolph Gottlieb

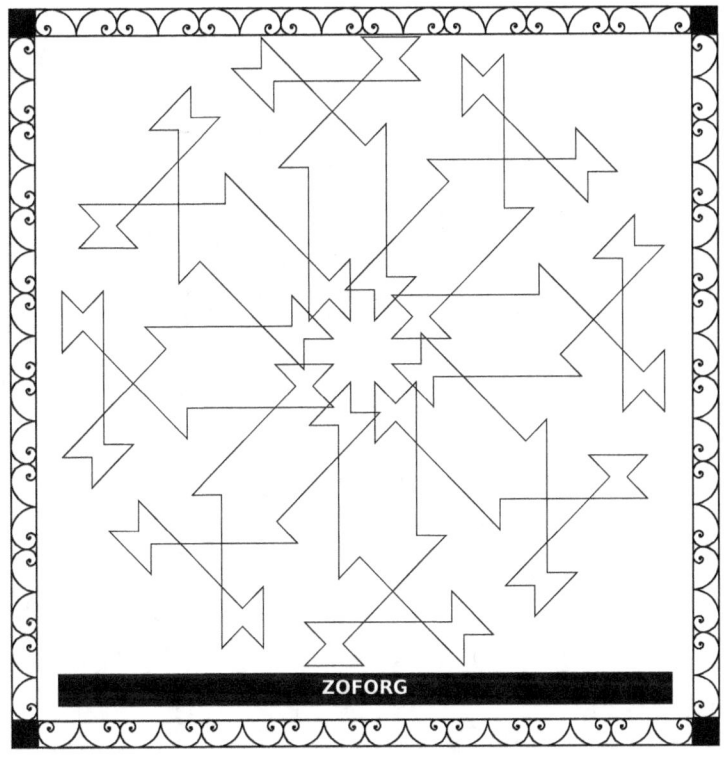

ZOFORG

Love stands opposed to death. It is love, not reason, that is stronger than death. Only love, not reason, gives kind thoughts.

Thomas Mann

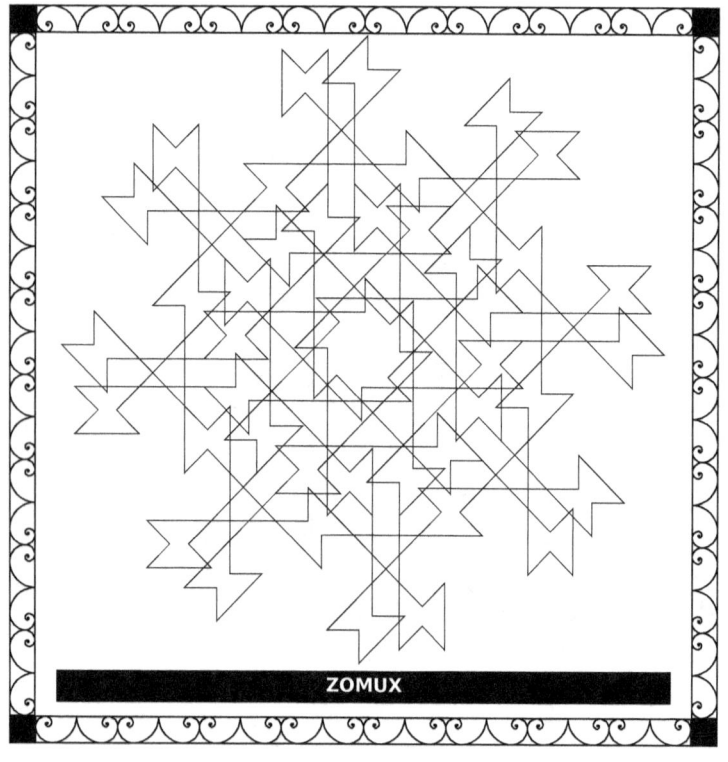

ZOMUX

No wine for me. Strange enough things happen when my head is clear. I want to know the difference.
Robert Jordan

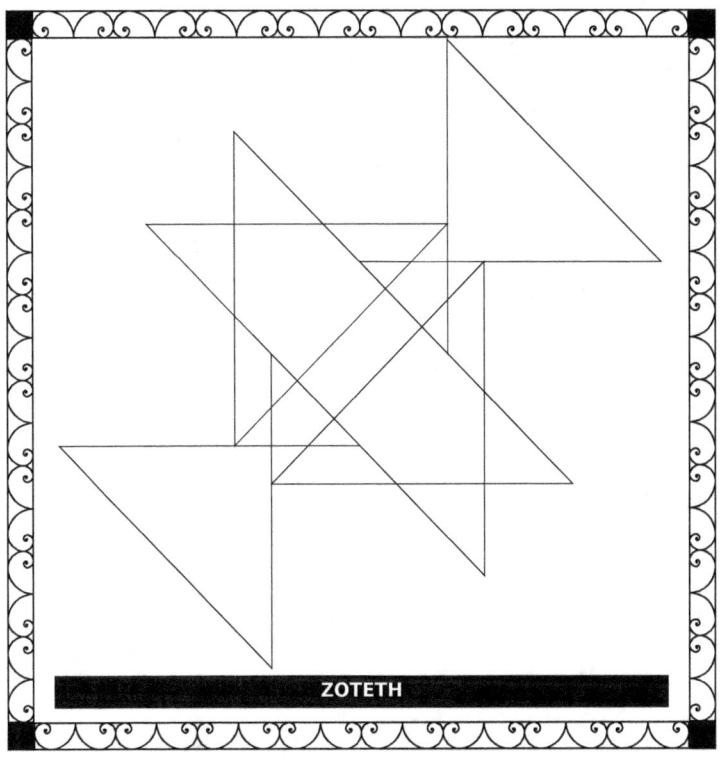

ZOTETH

Love is the extremely difficult realisation that something other than oneself is real. Love, and so art and morals, is the discovery of reality.
Iris Murdoch

361

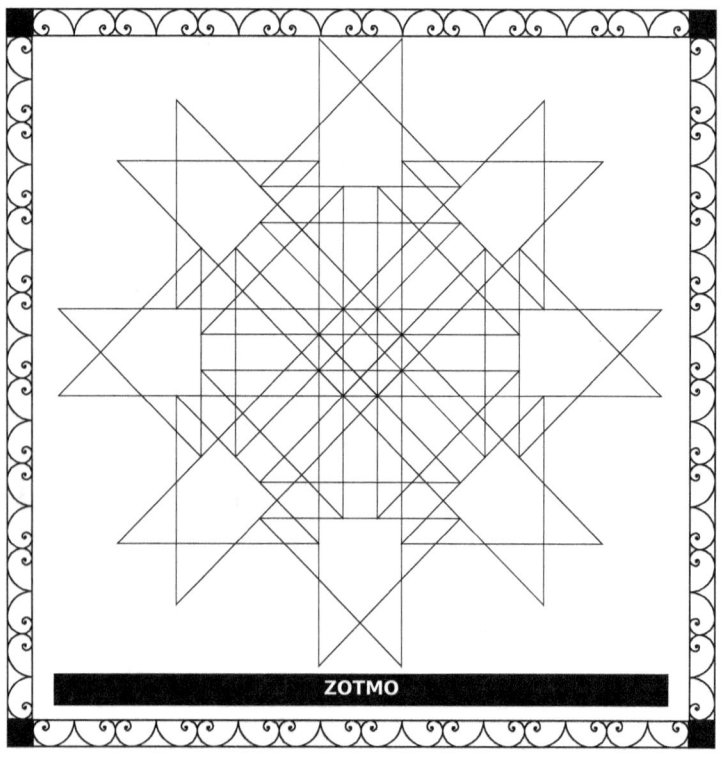

ZOTMO

Avant-garde art has become habitual, a dead letter with little spiritual consequence, however materially refined.
Donald Kuspit

362

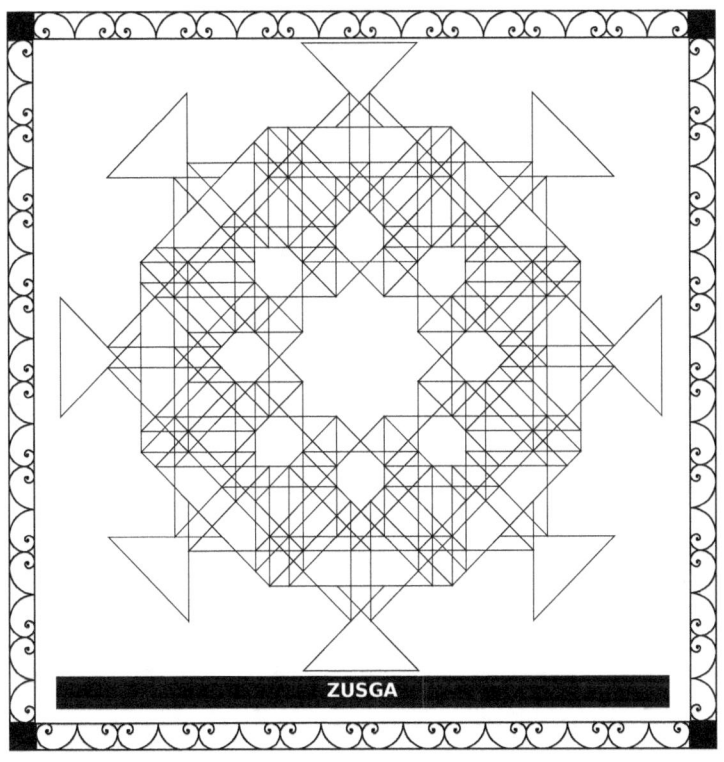

ZUSGA

This abdication of life demanded of the artist is to be achieved only relatively. Most artists have retired too absolutely; they grow rusty, inflexible to the flow of currents.
Anais Nin

363

APPENDIX A: GOLDEN RATIO

The golden ratio is an irrational number that is usually represented by the symbol ϕ. Its value is
$\phi = 1.618033988749895\ldots$
where the dots indicate that the numbers go on forever without repeating. There are many ways to describe and define ϕ (see list of references at the end for a more exhaustive list).

The simplest description of the golden ratio involves dividing a line into two segments. Call the length of the two segments a and b with $a > b > 0$. The lengths should be chosen so that

$$\frac{a}{b} = \frac{a+b}{a}$$

This equation says that the ratio of the longer to the shorter segment should equal the ratio of the line to the longer segment. Let $a/b = \phi$ then the above equation becomes

$$\phi = 1 + \frac{1}{\phi}$$

which simplifies to $\phi^2 - \phi - 1 = 0$. This quadratic equation for ϕ has two solutions:
$\phi_1 = (1 + \sqrt{5})/2 = 1.618033988749895$ and

$\phi_2 = (1 - \sqrt{5})/2 = -0.6180339887498949$. The first solution is the golden ratio ϕ and the second solution is $1 - \phi$.

If we recursively substitute for ϕ in the above equation we get

$$\phi = 1 + \cfrac{1}{1 + \frac{1}{\phi}}$$

Repeating this forever produces what is known as the continued fraction expression for ϕ.

$$\phi = 1 + \cfrac{1}{1 + \cfrac{1}{1 + \cfrac{1}{1 + \frac{1}{1 + \cdots}}}}$$

The continued fraction goes on forever but if you truncate it at some point what you get is the ratio of two Fibonacci numbers. For example

$$1 + \cfrac{1}{1 + \cfrac{1}{1 + \cfrac{1}{1 + \frac{1}{1}}}} = \frac{8}{5}$$

We will show below how the Fibonacci numbers can be used to approximate ϕ.

How does one create line segments that are in the golden ratio? You could just use a ruler and try to approximate a line segment of length ϕ but a better way to do it is as follows. Draw a square with sides of length 1 in any convenient unit as shown in figure 1. Next extend a compass from the middle of the bottom side of the square (marked AB in the figure) to the right corner of the opposite side as shown in the figure. Draw a circular arc from that corner down until it meets the extension line of the bottom side at point C. The points A, B, and C now define three line segments. Segment AB has length 1 and it is easy to show that segment AC has length ϕ and segment BC has length $1 - \phi = 1/\phi$. So segments AC to AB and AB to BC are in the golden ratio.

The golden ratio can also be defined in terms of dividing a rectangle into smaller rectangles. Take a rectangle of sides a and b with $a > b > 0$ and divide it into a square of side b and another rectangle with long side b and short side $a - b$. Do the same thing with the new smaller rectangle. Divide it into a square and another rectangle whose long side is equal to the short side of the containing rectangle. How many times can you do this division? If the ratio of the sides of the outer rectangle is the golden ratio, $a/b = \phi$ then you can keep on dividing forever. Such a rectangle is called a golden rectangle. Figure 2 shows an example along with the golden spiral which is inscribed in the golden rectangle.

Another way to define ϕ is in terms of a sequence of

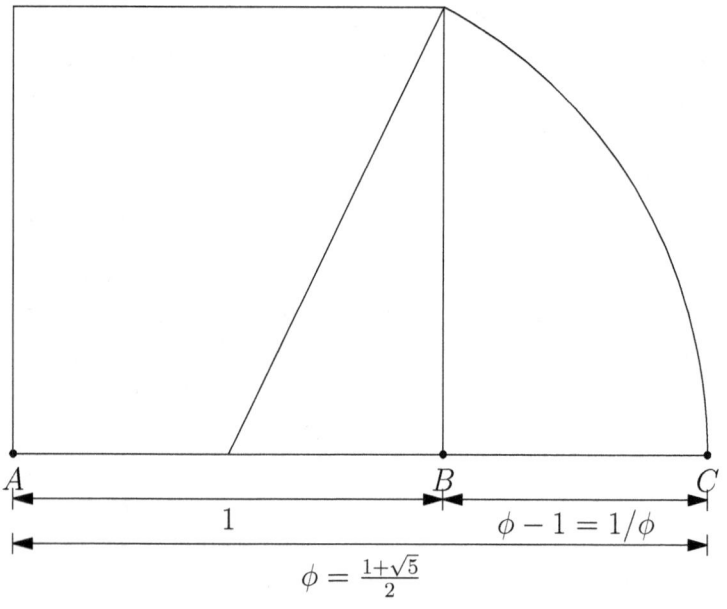

$$\phi = \frac{1+\sqrt{5}}{2}$$

Figure 1

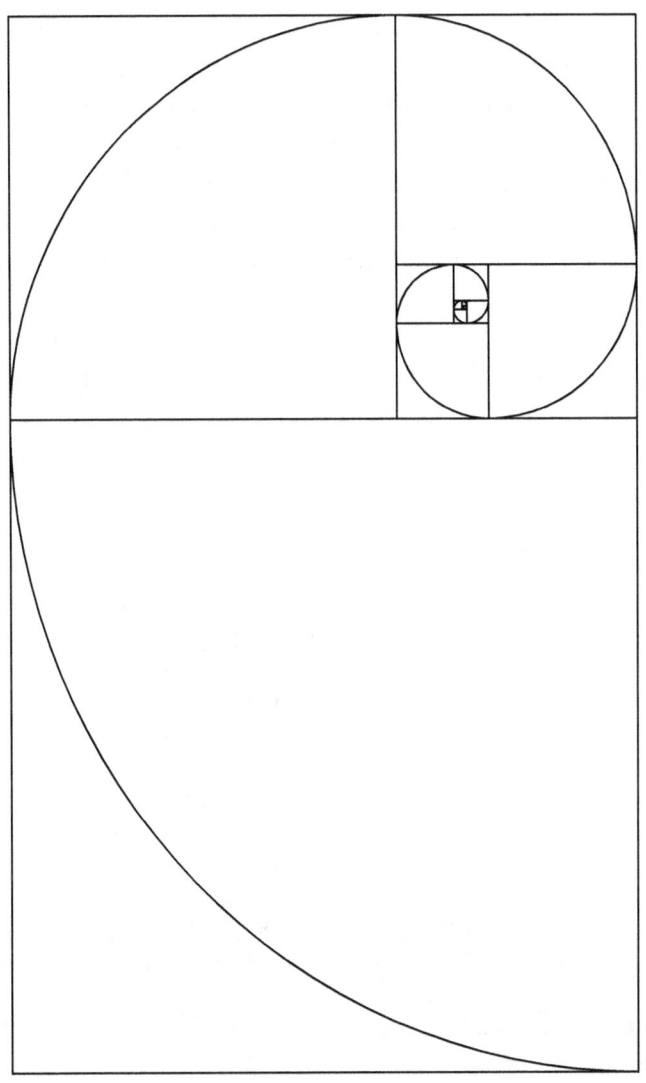

Figure 2

numbers called the Fibonacci sequence. There is a simple recipe for generating the Fibonacci sequence. Let the first two numbers be $F_1 = 1$ and $F_2 = 1$ then $F_3 = F_2 + F_1 = 2$, $F_4 = F_3 + F_2 = 3$, and in general $F_n = F_{n-1} + F_{n-2}$. The first 20 numbers are: [1, 1, 2, 3, 5, 8, 13, 21, 34, 55, 89, 144, 233, 377, 610, 987, 1597, 2584, 4181, 6765]. The properties of this sequence have fascinated mathematicians for centuries. The property we want to look at is the ratio of successive terms F_n/F_{n-1}. Table 1 shows fifteen of these ratios starting with 8/5.

n	F_n	F_{n-1}	F_n/F_{n-1}
6	8	5	1.6
7	13	8	1.625
8	21	13	1.615384615384615
9	34	21	1.619047619047619
10	55	34	1.617647058823529
11	89	55	1.618181818181818
12	144	89	1.617977528089888
13	233	144	1.618055555555556
14	377	233	1.618025751072961
15	610	377	1.618037135278515
16	987	610	1.618032786885246
17	1597	987	1.618034447821682
18	2584	1597	1.618033813400125
19	4181	2584	1.618034055727554
20	6765	4181	1.618033963166706

Table 1: Fibonacci sequence ratios F_n/F_{n-1} starting with 8/5 .

The ratios appear to be converging to the golden ratio

and this is indeed the case. If you continue calculating the ratio for larger and larger values of n you will get closer and closer to the value of ϕ. Only in the limit as n goes to infinity does the ratio become equal to ϕ. This makes ϕ an irrational number since it cannot be expressed as a ratio of two finite integers.

Suppose now that $F_n = \phi^n$. In that case each ratio F_n/F_{n-1} would be exactly equal to ϕ. This is obviously not true but let's suppose that it is and see what it implies for the value of ϕ. From the recurrence equation given above we get $\phi^n = \phi^{n-1} + \phi^{n-2}$ which simplifies to $\phi^2 - \phi - 1 = 0$. This is the same quadratic equation for ϕ that we found above with the two solutions: $\phi_1 = (1 + \sqrt{5})/2 = 1.618033988749895$ and $\phi_2 = (1 - \sqrt{5})/2 = -0.6180339887498949$. The Fibonacci numbers can expressed as a combination of the two solutions.

$$F_n = \frac{\phi_1^n - \phi_2^n}{\sqrt{5}}$$

Since ϕ_2 is less than 1, the term ϕ_2^n becomes very small for large values of n and F_n becomes approximately equal to $\phi^n/\sqrt{5}$. The ratio F_n/F_{n-1} then does converge to ϕ for large n.

The Fibonacci numbers are important because they can be used to approximate the irrational number ϕ with the ratio of two integers, F_n/F_{n-1}, to any desired degree of accuracy. When proportioning things according to the golden ratio you will not find a ruler that will let you measure exactly $\phi = 1.618033988749895\ldots$ but you can probably find a ruler that will let you measure the integers 377 and 233 to give you the approximation $377/233 = 1.618025751072961$ which is pretty close.

The Fibonacci numbers are also important with regard to the images in this book. Each image was generated using one of the golden ratio approximations F_n/F_{n-1}. The ratios are used as the slope of a line plotted on a cartesian plane. Starting at the origin, whenever the line crosses a horizontal grid line, mark it with a 1, and when it crosses a vertical grid line, mark it with a 0. In this way, each ratio F_n/F_{n-1} defines a binary sequence. The sequence is then converted into drawing instructions. This is how each of the images in this book was created. For more information on this process see our book *Pattern Generation for Computational Art*.

APPENDIX B: IMAGE GENERATION

Below is a list of commands for generating each image in this book. An explanation of their meaning can be found in our book *Pattern Generation for Computational Art*.

BAWHA chseq 5 3 24 | katrans t1.kat | turtledraw 0.0 120.0 f01m01.svg

BAZEX chseq 21 13 102 | katrans t1.kat | turtledraw 0.0 120.0 f01m02.svg

BEPAR chseq 89 55 432 | katrans t1.kat | turtledraw 0.0 120.0 f01m03.svg

BERRO chseq 377 233 1830 | katrans t1.kat | turtledraw 0.0 120.0 f01m04.svg

BIFUS chseq 1597 987 7752 | katrans t1.kat | turtledraw 0.0 120.0 f01m05.svg

BIRAZ chseq 89 55 432 | katrans t3.kat | turtledraw 0.0 120.0 f01m06.svg

BIRO chseq 377 233 1830 | katrans t3.kat | turtledraw 0.0 120.0 f01m07.svg

BODGE chseq 1597 987 7752 | katrans t3.kat | turtledraw 0.0 120.0 f01m08.svg

BOMZI chseq 21 13 102 | katrans t11.kat | turtledraw 0.0 120.0 f01m09.svg

BOSLA chseq 377 233 1830 | katrans t11.kat | turtledraw 0.0 120.0 f01m10.svg

BUPYA chseq 5 3 32 | katrans t1.kat | turtledraw 0.0 90.0 f02m01.svg

BUZAR chseq 21 13 136 | katrans t1.kat | turtledraw 0.0 90.0 f02m02.svg

CAFEX chseq 89 55 576 | katrans t1.kat | turtledraw 0.0 90.0 f02m03.svg

CALAF chseq 377 233 2440 | katrans t1.kat | turtledraw 0.0 90.0 f02m04.svg

CAWUS chseq 1597 987 10336 | katrans t1.kat | turtledraw 0.0 90.0 f02m05.svg

CAZFA chseq 89 55 576 | katrans t9.kat | turtledraw 0.0 90.0 f02m06.svg

CECFO chseq 377 233 2440 | katrans t9.kat | turtledraw 0.0 90.0 f02m07.svg

CEPUA chseq 1 1 10 | katrans t1.kat | turtledraw 0.0 144.0 f03m01.svg

CIJORT chseq 5 3 40 | katrans t1.kat | turtledraw 0.0 144.0 f03m02.svg

CIPNO chseq 21 13 170 | katrans t1.kat | turtledraw 0.0 144.0 f03m03.svg

COJOS chseq 89 55 720 | katrans t1.kat | turtledraw 0.0 144.0 f03m04.svg

COLOT chseq 377 233 3050 | katrans t1.kat | turtledraw 0.0 144.0 f03m05.svg

COLOU chseq 21 13 170 | katrans t0a.kat | turtledraw 0.0 144.0 f03m06.svg

COPEN chseq 1 1 10 | katrans t8.kat | turtledraw 0.0 144.0 f03m07.svg

COPEND chseq 5 3 40 | katrans t8.kat | turtledraw 0.0 144.0 f03m08.svg

COSIRT chseq 21 13 170 | katrans t8.kat | turtledraw 0.0 144.0 f03m09.svg

COZERT chseq 1 1 10 | katrans t9.kat | turtledraw 0.0 144.0 f03m10.svg

DAJMI chseq 5 3 40 | katrans t9.kat | turtledraw 0.0 144.0 f03m11.svg

DAMOJ chseq 21 13 170 | katrans t9.kat | turtledraw 0.0 144.0 f03m12.svg

DASORG chseq 1 1 10 | katrans t11.kat | turtledraw 0.0 144.0 f03m13.svg

DEHUN chseq 1 1 10 | katrans t12.kat | turtledraw 0.0 144.0 f03m14.svg

DERAND chseq 5 3 40 | katrans t12.kat | turtledraw 0.0 144.0 f03m15.svg

DERCO chseq 21 13 170 | katrans t12.kat | turtledraw 0.0 144.0 f03m16.svg

DESEV chseq 5 3 40 | katrans t15.kat | turtledraw 0.0 144.0 f03m17.svg

DEXAD chseq 21 13 170 | katrans t15.kat | turtledraw 0.0 144.0 f03m18.svg

DEXFU chseq 89 55 720 | katrans t15.kat | turtledraw 0.0 144.0 f03m19.svg

DISQA chseq 377 233 3050 | katrans t15.kat | turtledraw 0.0 144.0 f03m20.svg

DIZAG chseq 1 1 10 | katrans t1.kat | turtledraw 0.0 72.0 f04m01.svg

DOJMU chseq 5 3 40 | katrans t1.kat | turtledraw 0.0 72.0 f04m02.svg

DUBGO chseq 21 13 170 | katrans t1.kat | turtledraw 0.0 72.0 f04m03.svg

DUBIT chseq 89 55 720 | katrans t1.kat | turtledraw 0.0 72.0 f04m04.svg

DUFUA chseq 377 233 3050 | katrans t1.kat | turtledraw 0.0 72.0 f04m05.svg

DUGURD chseq 377 233 3050 | katrans t0a.kat | turtledraw 0.0 72.0 f04m06.svg

DUNEW chseq 21 13 170 | katrans t3.kat | turtledraw 0.0 72.0 f04m07.svg

ENDRET chseq 89 55 720 | katrans t3.kat | turtledraw 0.0 72.0 f04m08.svg

ETUN chseq 377 233 3050 | katrans t3.kat | turtledraw 0.0 72.0 f04m09.svg

FAZA chseq 5 3 40 | katrans t5.kat | turtledraw 0.0 72.0 f04m10.svg

FEKYA chseq 21 13 170 | katrans t5.kat | turtledraw 0.0 72.0 f04m11.svg

FELUB chseq 1 1 10 | katrans t9.kat | turtledraw 0.0 72.0 f04m12.svg

FENNO chseq 5 3 40 | katrans t9.kat | turtledraw 0.0 72.0 f04m13.svg

FERNI chseq 5 3 41 | katrans t13.kat | turtledraw 0.0 72.0 f04m14.svg

FIMEK chseq 21 13 171 | katrans t13.kat | turtledraw 0.0 72.0 f04m15.svg

FISEA chseq 89 55 721 | katrans t13.kat | turtledraw 0.0 72.0 f04m16.svg

FOMARD chseq 5 3 42 | katrans t15.kat | turtledraw 0.0 72.0 f04m17.svg

FOPOST chseq 21 13 172 | katrans t15.kat | turtledraw 0.0 72.0 f04m18.svg

FOZKI chseq 89 55 722 | katrans t15.kat | turtledraw 0.0 72.0 f04m19.svg

GAFGA chseq 1 1 14 | katrans t1.kat | turtledraw 0.0 102.857142857 f05m01.svg

GAFOD chseq 5 3 56 | katrans t1.kat | turtledraw 0.0 102.857142857 f05m02.svg

GAHARY chseq 21 13 238 | katrans t1.kat | turtledraw 0.0 102.857142857 f05m03.svg

GAVRA chseq 89 55 1008 | katrans t1.kat | turtledraw 0.0 102.857142857 f05m04.svg

GAVUZ chseq 377 233 4270 | katrans t1.kat | turtledraw 0.0 102.857142857 f05m05.svg

GETGE chseq 1597 987 18088 | katrans t1.kat | turtledraw 0.0 102.857142857 f05m06.svg

GINORY chseq 5 3 56 | katrans t0a.kat | turtledraw 0.0 102.857142857 f05m07.svg

GIRXI chseq 1 1 14 | katrans t8.kat | turtledraw 0.0 102.857142857 f05m08.svg

GISI chseq 5 3 56 | katrans t8.kat | turtledraw 0.0 102.857142857 f05m09.svg

GIZAH chseq 21 13 238 | katrans t8.kat | turtledraw 0.0 102.857142857 f05m10.svg

GODGI chseq 89 55 1008 | katrans t8.kat | turtledraw 0.0 102.857142857 f05m11.svg

GOFEX chseq 1 1 14 | katrans t9.kat | turtledraw 0.0 102.857142857 f05m12.svg

GOPEQ chseq 5 3 57 | katrans t13.kat | turtledraw 0.0 102.857142857 f05m13.svg

GOTAE chseq 5 3 58 | katrans t15.kat | turtledraw 0.0 102.857142857 f05m14.svg

GOXUG chseq 21 13 240 | katrans t15.kat | turtledraw 0.0 102.857142857 f05m15.svg

GOZAO chseq 1 1 14 | katrans t1.kat | turtledraw 0.0 154.285714285714 f06m01.svg

GUJARY chseq 5 3 56 | katrans t1.kat | turtledraw 0.0 154.285714285714 f06m02.svg

GUMKA chseq 21 13 238 | katrans t1.kat | turtledraw 0.0 154.285714285714 f06m03.svg

GUSEM chseq 89 55 1008 | katrans t1.kat | turtledraw 0.0 154.285714285714 f06m04.svg

HAGEX chseq 5 3 56 | katrans t0a.kat | turtledraw 0.0 154.285714285714 f06m05.svg

HAKFI chseq 1 1 14 | katrans t8.kat | turtledraw 0.0 154.285714285714 f06m06.svg

HEDOL chseq 5 3 56 | katrans t8.kat | turtledraw 0.0 154.285714285714 f06m07.svg

HEMORG chseq 21 13 238 | katrans t8.kat | turtledraw 0.0 154.285714285714 f06m08.svg

HEPZA chseq 1 1 14 | katrans t9.kat | turtledraw 0.0 154.285714285714 f06m09.svg

HEVOW chseq 21 13 238 | katrans t9.kat | turtledraw 0.0 154.285714285714 f06m10.svg

HEWAB chseq 89 55 1008 | katrans t9.kat | turtledraw 0.0 154.285714285714 f06m11.svg

HIFAR chseq 1 1 14 | katrans t11.kat | turtledraw 0.0 154.285714285714 f06m12.svg

HIFEY chseq 5 3 56 | katrans t11.kat | turtledraw 0.0 154.285714285714 f06m13.svg

HIJET chseq 21 13 238 | katrans t11.kat | turtledraw 0.0 154.285714285714 f06m14.svg

HOJEB chseq 1 1 16 | katrans t1.kat | turtledraw 0.0 135.0 f07m01.svg

HUHIND chseq 5 3 64 | katrans t1.kat | turtledraw 0.0 135.0 f07m02.svg

HUTIU chseq 21 13 272 | katrans t1.kat | turtledraw 0.0 135.0 f07m03.svg

IJAK chseq 89 55 1152 | katrans t1.kat | turtledraw 0.0 135.0 f07m04.svg

IPOW chseq 5 3 64 | katrans t5.kat | turtledraw 0.0 135.0 f07m05.svg

IWARD chseq 21 13 272 | katrans t5.kat | turtledraw 0.0 135.0 f07m06.svg

JAGEM chseq 89 55 1152 | katrans t5.kat | turtledraw 0.0 135.0 f07m07.svg

JAKA chseq 1 1 16 | katrans t9.kat | turtledraw 0.0 135.0 f07m08.svg

JASRO chseq 5 3 64 | katrans t9.kat | turtledraw 0.0 135.0 f07m09.svg

JAWNA chseq 21 13 272 | katrans t9.kat | turtledraw 0.0 135.0 f07m10.svg

JAZERG chseq 89 55 1152 | katrans t9.kat | turtledraw 0.0 135.0 f07m11.svg

JEKDO chseq 5 3 64 | katrans t13.kat | turtledraw 0.0 135.0 f07m12.svg

JEZOK chseq 21 13 272 | katrans t13.kat | turtledraw 0.0 135.0 f07m13.svg

JIJORY chseq 89 55 1152 | katrans t13.kat | turtledraw 0.0 135.0 f07m14.svg

JITARY chseq 1 1 18 | katrans t1.kat | turtledraw 0.0 80.0 f08m01.svg

JITOTH chseq 5 3 72 | katrans t1.kat | turtledraw 0.0 80.0 f08m02.svg

JIWAL chseq 21 13 306 | katrans t1.kat | turtledraw 0.0 80.0 f08m03.svg

JOFMI chseq 89 55 1296 | katrans t1.kat | turtledraw 0.0 80.0 f08m04.svg

JOJOZ chseq 377 233 5490 | katrans t1.kat | turtledraw 0.0 80.0 f08m05.svg

JOMOE chseq 5 3 72 | katrans t0a.kat | turtledraw 0.0 80.0 f08m06.svg

JONUO chseq 1 1 18 | katrans t8.kat | turtledraw 0.0 80.0 f08m07.svg

JOPOE chseq 5 3 72 | katrans t8.kat | turtledraw 0.0 80.0 f08m08.svg

JOTAC chseq 21 13 306 | katrans t8.kat | turtledraw 0.0 80.0 f08m09.svg

JUBI chseq 89 55 1276 | katrans t8.kat | turtledraw 0.0 80.0 f08m10.svg

JUWAL chseq 1 1 18 | katrans t9.kat | turtledraw 0.0 80.0 f08m11.svg

KAWAST chseq 5 3 72 | katrans t9.kat | turtledraw 0.0 80.0 f08m12.svg

KEBUM chseq 21 13 306 | katrans t9.kat | turtledraw 0.0 80.0 f08m13.svg

KEMHU chseq 89 55 1276 | katrans t9.kat | turtledraw 0.0 80.0 f08m14.svg

KEMUB chseq 1 1 20 | katrans t1.kat | turtledraw 0.0 108.0 f09m01.svg

KERNI chseq 5 3 80 | katrans t1.kat | turtledraw 0.0 108.0 f09m02.svg

KEXAC chseq 21 13 340 | katrans t1.kat | turtledraw 0.0 108.0 f09m03.svg

KISWO chseq 89 55 1440 | katrans t1.kat | turtledraw 0.0 108.0 f09m04.svg

KOFME chseq 377 233 6100 | katrans t1.kat | turtledraw 0.0 108.0 f09m05.svg

KOGNA chseq 5 3 80 | katrans t0a.kat | turtledraw 0.0 108.0 f09m06.svg

KOLKU chseq 5 3 80 | katrans t13.kat | turtledraw 0.0 108.0 f09m07.svg

KONLO chseq 21 13 340 | katrans t13.kat | turtledraw 0.0 108.0 f09m08.svg

KORLI chseq 5 3 80 | katrans t15.kat | turtledraw 0.0 108.0 f09m09.svg

KOWNO chseq 21 13 340 | katrans t15.kat | turtledraw 0.0 108.0 f09m10.svg

KOZBI chseq 89 55 1440 | katrans t15.kat | turtledraw 0.0 108.0 f09m11.svg

KUBUI chseq 1 1 22 | katrans t1.kat | turtledraw 0.0 65.454545454545 f10m01.svg

KUCUB chseq 5 3 88 | katrans t1.kat | turtledraw 0.0 65.454545454545 f10m02.svg

KURJI chseq 21 13 374 | katrans t1.kat | turtledraw 0.0 65.454545454545 f10m03.svg

LAGOB chseq 89 55 1584 | katrans t1.kat | turtledraw 0.0 65.454545454545 f10m04.svg

LALIC chseq 377 233 6710 | katrans t1.kat | turtledraw 0.0 65.454545454545 f10m05.svg

LANAC chseq 5 3 88 | katrans t0a.kat | turtledraw 0.0 65.454545454545 f10m06.svg

LASAK chseq 21 13 374 | katrans t3.kat | turtledraw 0.0 65.454545454545 f10m07.svg

LASUR chseq 89 55 1584 | katrans t3.kat | turtledraw 0.0 65.454545454545 f10m08.svg

LAXIS chseq 377 233 6710 | katrans t3.kat | turtledraw 0.0 65.454545454545 f10m09.svg

LEJEP chseq 5 3 88 | katrans t5.kat | turtledraw 0.0 65.454545454545 f10m10.svg

LENSA chseq 1 1 22 | katrans t8.kat | turtledraw 0.0 65.454545454545 f10m11.svg

LEPEL chseq 5 3 88 | katrans t8.kat | turtledraw 0.0 65.454545454545 f10m12.svg

LEPUJ chseq 21 13 374 | katrans t8.kat | turtledraw 0.0 65.454545454545 f10m13.svg

LETKA chseq 1 1 22 | katrans t9.kat | turtledraw 0.0 65.454545454545 f10m14.svg

LEXGE chseq 5 3 88 | katrans t9.kat | turtledraw 0.0 65.454545454545 f10m15.svg

LEXTO chseq 1 1 22 | katrans t12.kat | turtledraw 0.0 65.454545454545 f10m16.svg

LIGPO chseq 5 3 88 | katrans t12.kat | turtledraw 0.0 65.454545454545 f10m17.svg

LIGUTH chseq 5 3 89 | katrans t13.kat | turtledraw 0.0 65.454545454545 f10m18.svg

LITOQ chseq 21 13 375 | katrans t13.kat | turtledraw 0.0 65.454545454545 f10m19.svg

LOBUZ chseq 1 1 26 | katrans t1.kat | turtledraw 0.0 83.076923076923 f11m01.svg

LODIS chseq 5 3 104 | katrans t1.kat | turtledraw 0.0 83.076923076923 f11m02.svg

LOKURD chseq 21 13 442 | katrans t1.kat | turtledraw 0.0 83.076923076923 f11m03.svg

LOPIF chseq 89 55 1872 | katrans t1.kat | turtledraw 0.0 83.076923076923 f11m04.svg

LOVIRT chseq 377 233 7930 | katrans t1.kat | turtledraw 0.0 83.076923076923 f11m05.svg

LOXIX chseq 5 3 104 | katrans t0a.kat | turtledraw 0.0 83.076923076923 f11m06.svg

LOXNA chseq 21 13 442 | katrans t3.kat | turtledraw 0.0 83.076923076923 f11m07.svg

LUBIB chseq 89 55 1872 | katrans t3.kat | turtledraw 0.0 83.076923076923 f11m08.svg

LUFGU chseq 377 233 7930 | katrans t3.kat | turtledraw 0.0 83.076923076923 f11m09.svg

LUPDI chseq 5 3 104 | katrans t5.kat | turtledraw 0.0 83.076923076923 f11m10.svg

LUXCO chseq 1 1 26 | katrans t9.kat | turtledraw 0.0 83.076923076923 f11m11.svg

LUZRU chseq 5 3 104 | katrans t9.kat | turtledraw 0.0 83.076923076923 f11m12.svg

MABOB chseq 21 13 442 | katrans t9.kat | turtledraw 0.0 83.076923076923 f11m13.svg

MAXAST chseq 5 3 104 | katrans t15.kat | turtledraw 0.0 83.076923076923 f11m14.svg

MEGFU chseq 21 13 442 | katrans t15.kat | turtledraw 0.0 83.076923076923 f11m15.svg

MEKEY chseq 89 55 1872 | katrans t15.kat | turtledraw 0.0 83.076923076923 f11m16.svg

MELFO chseq 1 1 26 | katrans t1.kat | turtledraw 0.0 110.769230769230 f12m01.svg

MENUR chseq 5 3 104 | katrans t1.kat | turtledraw 0.0 110.769230769230 f12m02.svg

MEPOP chseq 21 13 442 | katrans t1.kat | turtledraw 0.0 110.769230769230 f12m03.svg

MEPUB chseq 89 55 1872 | katrans t1.kat | turtledraw 0.0 110.769230769230 f12m04.svg

MIMEST chseq 377 233 7930 | katrans t1.kat | turtledraw 0.0 110.769230769230 f12m05.svg

MODAO chseq 5 3 104 | katrans t0a.kat | turtledraw 0.0 110.769230769230 f12m06.svg

MONAC chseq 5 3 104 | katrans t5.kat | turtledraw 0.0 110.769230769230 f12m07.svg

MONPE chseq 1 1 26 | katrans t9.kat | turtledraw 0.0 110.769230769230 f12m08.svg

MOPOTH chseq 5 3 104 | katrans t9.kat | turtledraw 0.0 110.769230769230 f12m09.svg

MOSUN chseq 1 1 26 | katrans t1.kat | turtledraw 0.0 138.461538461538 f13m01.svg

MOWKA chseq 5 3 104 | katrans t1.kat | turtledraw 0.0 138.461538461538 f13m02.svg

MUWEJ chseq 21 13 442 | katrans t1.kat | turtledraw 0.0 138.461538461538 f13m03.svg

NACATH chseq 89 55 1872 | katrans t1.kat | turtledraw 0.0 138.461538461538 f13m04.svg

NAMAT chseq 5 3 104 | katrans t0a.kat | turtledraw 0.0 138.461538461538 f13m05.svg

NAMOR chseq 21 13 442 | katrans t0a.kat | turtledraw 0.0 138.461538461538 f13m06.svg

NEBIRY chseq 5 3 104 | katrans t5.kat | turtledraw 0.0 138.461538461538 f13m07.svg

NEFERT chseq 1 1 26 | katrans t9.kat | turtledraw 0.0 138.461538461538 f13m08.svg

NEJUI chseq 5 3 104 | katrans t9.kat | turtledraw 0.0 138.461538461538 f13m09.svg

NEKOU chseq 21 13 442 | katrans t9.kat | turtledraw 0.0 138.461538461538 f13m10.svg

NEZKE chseq 1 1 26 | katrans t11.kat | turtledraw 0.0 138.461538461538 f13m11.svg

NISNO chseq 5 3 104 | katrans t11.kat | turtledraw 0.0 138.461538461538 f13m12.svg

NOBFO chseq 1 1 26 | katrans t1.kat | turtledraw 0.0 166.153846153846 f14m01.svg

NOHUZ chseq 5 3 104 | katrans t1.kat | turtledraw 0.0 166.153846153846 f14m02.svg

NOLOST chseq 21 13 442 | katrans t1.kat | turtledraw 0.0 166.153846153846 f14m03.svg

NOTOX chseq 89 55 1872 | katrans t1.kat | turtledraw 0.0 166.153846153846 f14m04.svg

NOTUZ chseq 5 3 104 | katrans t0a.kat | turtledraw 0.0 166.153846153846 f14m05.svg

NOVUS chseq 21 13 442 | katrans t0a.kat | turtledraw 0.0 166.153846153846 f14m06.svg

NUPI chseq 1 1 26 | katrans t6.kat | turtledraw 0.0 166.153846153846 f14m07.svg

OGEST chseq 5 3 104 | katrans t6.kat | turtledraw 0.0 166.153846153846 f14m08.svg

OJAK chseq 1 1 26 | katrans t9.kat | turtledraw 0.0 166.153846153846 f14m09.svg

OMOV chseq 5 3 104 | katrans t9.kat | turtledraw 0.0 166.153846153846 f14m10.svg

ORCHOE chseq 21 13 442 | katrans t9.kat | turtledraw 0.0 166.153846153846 f14m11.svg

OSTAJ chseq 1 1 26 | katrans t11.kat | turtledraw 0.0 166.153846153846 f14m12.svg

PACWO chseq 5 3 104 | katrans t11.kat | turtledraw 0.0 166.153846153846 f14m13.svg

PAGURY chseq 21 13 442 | katrans t11.kat | turtledraw 0.0 166.153846153846 f14m14.svg

PAMAZ chseq 1 1 28 | katrans t1.kat | turtledraw 0.0 77.14285714285 f15m01.svg

PAPRA chseq 5 3 112 | katrans t1.kat | turtledraw 0.0 77.14285714285 f15m02.svg

PATUTH chseq 21 13 476 | katrans t1.kat | turtledraw 0.0 77.14285714285 f15m03.svg

PAZTO chseq 89 55 2016 | katrans t1.kat | turtledraw 0.0 77.14285714285 f15m04.svg

PEDUJ chseq 377 233 8540 | katrans t1.kat | turtledraw 0.0 77.14285714285 f15m05.svg

PEGOB chseq 5 3 112 | katrans t0a.kat | turtledraw 0.0 77.14285714285 f15m06.svg

PEJOR chseq 21 13 476 | katrans t0a.kat | turtledraw 0.0 77.14285714285 f15m07.svg

PENOM chseq 89 55 2016 | katrans t0a.kat | turtledraw 0.0 77.14285714285 f15m08.svg

PERUC chseq 3 5 112 | katrans t1.kat | turtledraw 0.0 77.14285714285 f15m09.svg

PIQTI chseq 13 21 476 | katrans t1.kat | turtledraw 0.0 77.14285714285 f15m10.svg

PITAQ chseq 55 89 2016 | katrans t1.kat | turtledraw 0.0 77.14285714285 f15m11.svg

PITIO chseq 233 377 8540 | katrans t1.kat | turtledraw 0.0 77.14285714285 f15m12.svg

POMUND chseq 21 13 476 | katrans t3.kat | turtledraw 0.0 77.14285714285 f15m13.svg

PORAP chseq 89 55 2016 | katrans t3.kat | turtledraw 0.0 77.14285714285 f15m14.svg

POTME chseq 377 233 8540 | katrans t3.kat | turtledraw 0.0 77.14285714285 f15m15.svg

PUGOZ chseq 3 5 112 | katrans t3.kat | turtledraw 0.0 77.14285714285 f15m16.svg

PUPCI chseq 13 21 476 | katrans t3.kat | turtledraw 0.0 77.14285714285 f15m17.svg

PUSDO chseq 55 89 2016 | katrans t3.kat | turtledraw 0.0 77.14285714285 f15m18.svg

QEQWO chseq 3 5 112 | katrans t5.kat | turtledraw 0.0 77.14285714285 f15m19.svg

QIFO chseq 13 21 476 | katrans t5.kat | turtledraw 0.0 77.14285714285 f15m20.svg

QIKUND chseq 55 89 2016 | katrans t5.kat | turtledraw 0.0 77.14285714285 f15m21.svg

QINVU chseq 3 5 112 | katrans t15.kat | turtledraw 0.0 77.14285714285 f15m22.svg

QOPOO chseq 13 21 476 | katrans t15.kat | turtledraw 0.0 77.14285714285 f15m23.svg

QOZUK chseq 55 89 2016 | katrans t15.kat | turtledraw 0.0 77.14285714285 f15m24.svg

QUDKA chseq 233 377 8540 | katrans t15.kat | turtledraw 0.0 77.14285714285 f15m25.svg

QUDORD chseq 1 1 42 | katrans t1.kat | turtledraw 0.0 171.428571428571 f16m01.svg

QULARG chseq 5 3 168 | katrans t1.kat | turtledraw 0.0 171.428571428571 f16m02.svg

RABOU chseq 21 13 714 | katrans t1.kat | turtledraw 0.0 171.428571428571 f16m03.svg

RADITH chseq 89 55 3024 | katrans t1.kat | turtledraw 0.0 171.428571428571 f16m04.svg

RASHA chseq 5 3 512 | katrans t4.kat | turtledraw 0.0 171.428571428571 f16m05.svg

RAVBU chseq 5 3 168 | katrans t0a.kat | turtledraw 0.0 171.428571428571 f16m06.svg

REBUQ chseq 5 3 500 | katrans t4.kat | turtledraw 0.0 171.428571428571 f16m07.svg

REFOP chseq 21 13 714 | katrans t6.kat | turtledraw 0.0 171.428571428571 f16m08.svg

REZUL chseq 21 13 714 | katrans t9.kat | turtledraw 0.0 171.428571428571 f16m09.svg

RIHIST chseq 1 1 42 | katrans t11.kat | turtledraw 0.0 171.428571428571 f16m10.svg

RINEJ chseq 5 3 168 | katrans t11.kat | turtledraw 0.0 171.428571428571 f16m11.svg

RINUG chseq 21 13 714 | katrans t11.kat | turtledraw 0.0 171.428571428571 f16m12.svg

RISEE chseq 89 55 3024 | katrans t11.kat | turtledraw 0.0 171.428571428571 f16m13.svg

RISSU chseq 1 1 42 | katrans t1.kat | turtledraw 0.0 137.142857142857 f17m01.svg

ROKOL chseq 5 3 168 | katrans t1.kat | turtledraw 0.0 137.142857142857 f17m02.svg

ROSBU chseq 21 13 714 | katrans t1.kat | turtledraw 0.0 137.142857142857 f17m03.svg

ROTHA chseq 5 3 168 | katrans t0a.kat | turtledraw 0.0 137.142857142857 f17m04.svg

ROZAJ chseq 1 1 42 | katrans t11.kat | turtledraw 0.0 137.142857142857 f17m05.svg

RUKON chseq 5 3 168 | katrans t11.kat | turtledraw 0.0 137.142857142857 f17m06.svg

RUNUK chseq 1 1 42 | katrans t1.kat | turtledraw 0.0 85.714285714285 f18m01.svg

RUPUZ chseq 5 3 168 | katrans t1.kat | turtledraw 0.0 85.714285714285 f18m02.svg

RUTIX chseq 21 13 714 | katrans t1.kat | turtledraw 0.0 85.714285714285 f18m03.svg

RUZOB chseq 89 55 3024 | katrans t1.kat | turtledraw 0.0 85.714285714285 f18m04.svg

SALAI chseq 377 233 12810 | katrans t1.kat | turtledraw 0.0 85.714285714285 f18m05.svg

SARES chseq 3 5 168 | katrans t1.kat | turtledraw 0.0 85.714285714285 f18m06.svg

SATES chseq 13 21 714 | katrans t1.kat | turtledraw 0.0 85.714285714285 f18m07.svg

SATIO chseq 55 89 3024 | katrans t1.kat | turtledraw 0.0 85.714285714285 f18m08.svg

SAZEND chseq 233 377 12810 | katrans t1.kat | turtledraw 0.0 85.714285714285 f18m09.svg

SEROE chseq 21 13 714 | katrans t3.kat | turtledraw 0.0 85.714285714285 f18m10.svg

SETOG chseq 89 55 3024 | katrans t3.kat | turtledraw 0.0 85.714285714285 f18m11.svg

SIROQ chseq 377 233 12810 | katrans t3.kat | turtledraw 0.0 85.714285714285 f18m12.svg

SIWURT chseq 3 5 168 | katrans t3.kat | turtledraw 0.0 85.714285714285 f18m13.svg

SIZYO chseq 55 89 3024 | katrans t4.kat | turtledraw 0.0 85.714285714285 f18m14.svg

381

SOMORD chseq 233 377 12810 | katrans t4.kat | turtledraw 0.0 85.714285714285 f18m15.svg

SOYAL chseq 3 5 168 | katrans t5.kat | turtledraw 0.0 85.714285714285 f18m16.svg

SUBLA chseq 13 21 714 | katrans t5.kat | turtledraw 0.0 85.714285714285 f18m17.svg

SUGAC chseq 55 89 3024 | katrans t5.kat | turtledraw 0.0 85.714285714285 f18m18.svg

SUJJO chseq 5 3 168 | katrans t8.kat | turtledraw 0.0 85.714285714285 f18m19.svg

SURQA chseq 21 13 714 | katrans t8.kat | turtledraw 0.0 85.714285714285 f18m20.svg

TACOY chseq 1 1 42 | katrans t9.kat | turtledraw 0.0 85.714285714285 f18m21.svg

TALED chseq 1 1 42 | katrans t11.kat | turtledraw 0.0 85.714285714285 f18m22.svg

TAPSI chseq 5 3 168 | katrans t11.kat | turtledraw 0.0 85.714285714285 f18m23.svg

TAQOO chseq 21 13 714 | katrans t11.kat | turtledraw 0.0 85.714285714285 f18m24.svg

TAROJ chseq 5 3 168 | katrans t15.kat | turtledraw 0.0 85.714285714285 f18m25.svg

TAVLO chseq 21 13 714 | katrans t15.kat | turtledraw 0.0 85.714285714285 f18m26.svg

TENO chseq 89 55 3024 | katrans t15.kat | turtledraw 0.0 85.714285714285 f18m27.svg

TEVIL chseq 1 1 42 | katrans t1.kat | turtledraw 0.0 68.571428571428 f19m01.svg

TIJGA chseq 5 3 168 | katrans t1.kat | turtledraw 0.0 68.571428571428 f19m02.svg

TIMZO chseq 21 13 714 | katrans t1.kat | turtledraw 0.0 68.571428571428 f19m03.svg

TOCKI chseq 89 55 3024 | katrans t1.kat | turtledraw 0.0 68.571428571428 f19m04.svg

TOHAS chseq 21 13 714 | katrans t3.kat | turtledraw 0.0 68.571428571428 f19m05.svg

TOJAN chseq 5 3 168 | katrans t8.kat | turtledraw 0.0 68.571428571428 f19m06.svg

TOKSI chseq 21 13 714 | katrans t8.kat | turtledraw 0.0 68.571428571428 f19m07.svg

TOZOS chseq 1 1 42 | katrans t9.kat | turtledraw 0.0 68.571428571428 f19m08.svg

TUGMU chseq 5 3 168 | katrans t9.kat | turtledraw 0.0 68.571428571428 f19m09.svg

TULOA chseq 21 13 714 | katrans t9.kat | turtledraw 0.0 68.571428571428 f19m10.svg

TUMLA chseq 1 1 42 | katrans t11.kat | turtledraw 0.0 68.571428571428 f19m11.svg

TUXEC chseq 5 3 168 | katrans t11.kat | turtledraw 0.0 68.571428571428 f19m12.svg

TUZATH chseq 1 1 42 | katrans t12.kat | turtledraw 0.0 68.571428571428 f19m13.svg

UFAO chseq 5 3 168 | katrans t12.kat | turtledraw 0.0 68.571428571428 f19m14.svg

UKOF chseq 5 3 168 | katrans t13.kat | turtledraw 0.0 68.571428571428 f19m15.svg

URDEM chseq 21 13 714 | katrans t13.kat | turtledraw 0.0 68.571428571428 f19m16.svg

VAMUQ chseq 1 1 4 | katrans t7.kat | turtledraw 0.0 135.0 f20m01.svg

VAPERD chseq 21 13 68 | katrans t7.kat | turtledraw 0.0 135.0 f20m02.svg

VARAG chseq 377 233 1220 | katrans t7.kat | turtledraw 0.0 135.0 f20m03.svg

VATHO chseq 34 21 110 | katrans t7.kat | turtledraw 0.0 175.0 f21m01.svg

VATOS chseq 55 34 178 | katrans t7.kat | turtledraw 0.0 173.75 f21m02.svg

VEPO chseq 8 5 39 | katrans t7.kat | turtledraw 0.0 176.5 f21m03.svg

VERUG chseq 21 13 102 | katrans t7.kat | turtledraw 0.0 174.551 f21m04.svg

VEVARD chseq 34 21 275 | katrans t7.kat | turtledraw 0.0 173.408 f21m05.svg

VIDMI chseq 8 5 65 | katrans t7.kat | turtledraw 0.0 173.65 f21m06.svg

VIGZU chseq 233 144 2262 | katrans t7.kat | turtledraw 0.0 173.101 f21m07.svg

VIKNA chseq 55 34 534 | katrans t7.kat | turtledraw 0.0 177.913 f21m08.svg

VIMGE chseq 21 13 238 | katrans t7.kat | turtledraw 0.0 174.155 f21m09.svg

VIZHU chseq 13 8 168 | katrans t7.kat | turtledraw 0.0 178.33 f21m10.svg

VODEL chseq 34 21 440 | katrans t7.kat | turtledraw 0.0 175.562 f21m11.svg

VOKUF chseq 34 21 275 | katrans t6.kat | turtledraw 0.0 173.408 f21m12.svg

VONIX chseq 1 1 6 | katrans t7.kat | turtledraw 0.0 60.0 f22m01.svg

VOZMU chseq 5 3 24 | katrans t7.kat | turtledraw 0.0 60.0 f22m02.svg

VUCOND chseq 13 8 63 | katrans t7.kat | turtledraw 0.0 60.0 f22m03.svg

VUPATH chseq 21 13 102 | katrans t7.kat | turtledraw 0.0 60.0 f22m04.svg

WAKTA chseq 34 21 330 | katrans t7.kat | turtledraw 0.0 60.0 f22m05.svg

WAMFU chseq 55 34 534 | katrans t7.kat | turtledraw 0.0 60.0 f22m06.svg

WARXI chseq 144 89 1398 | katrans t7.kat | turtledraw 0.0 60.0 f22m07.svg

WEFIND chseq 233 144 2262 | katrans t7.kat | turtledraw 0.0 60.0 f22m08.svg

WIFAL chseq 34 21 660 | katrans t3.kat | turtledraw 0.0 60.0 f22m09.svg

WIKERT chseq 55 34 534 | katrans t3.kat | turtledraw 0.0 60.0 f22m10.svg

WOBIV chseq 144 89 2796 | katrans t3.kat | turtledraw 0.0 60.0 f22m11.svg

WOGZI chseq 233 144 4524 | katrans t3.kat | turtledraw 0.0 60.0 f22m12.svg

WOPAM chseq 610 377 11844 | katrans t3.kat | turtledraw 0.0 60.0 f22m13.svg

WOPFA chseq 1597 987 7752 | katrans t3.kat | turtledraw 0.0 60.0 f22m14.svg

WOZOST chseq 6765 4181 65676 | katrans t3.kat | turtledraw 0.0 60.0 f22m15.svg

WUGDU chseq 233 144 2262 | katrans t9.kat | turtledraw 0.0 60.0 f22m16.svg

WUKBE chseq 5 3 24 | katrans t11.kat | turtledraw 0.0 60.0 f22m17.svg

WUMAV chseq 13 8 63 | katrans t11.kat | turtledraw 0.0 60.0 f22m18.svg

WURNU chseq 21 13 102 | katrans t11.kat | turtledraw 0.0 60.0 f22m19.svg

XANO chseq 34 21 330 | katrans t11.kat | turtledraw 0.0 60.0 f22m20.svg

XATI chseq 55 34 534 | katrans t11.kat | turtledraw 0.0 60.0 f22m21.svg

XAYRA chseq 144 89 1398 | katrans t11.kat | turtledraw 0.0 60.0 f22m22.svg

XEKO chseq 34 21 330 | katrans t13.kat | turtledraw 0.0 60.0 f22m23.svg

XEMIR chseq 55 34 534 | katrans t13.kat | turtledraw 0.0 60.0 f22m24.svg

XETAR chseq 233 144 2262 | katrans t13.kat | turtledraw 0.0 60.0 f22m25.svg

XEXNI chseq 5 3 32 | katrans t7.kat | turtledraw 0.0 45.0 f23m01.svg

XEYAN chseq 21 13 136 | katrans t7.kat | turtledraw 0.0 45.0 f23m02.svg

XISCO chseq 89 55 576 | katrans t7.kat | turtledraw 0.0 45.0 f23m03.svg

XIVUZ chseq 5 3 40 | katrans t7.kat | turtledraw 0.0 43.2 f23m04.svg

XIXIR chseq 34 21 165 | katrans t7.kat | turtledraw 0.0 42.2534 f23m05.svg

XOBWE chseq 8 5 325 | katrans t7.kat | turtledraw 0.0 43.2 f23m06.svg

XOCTA chseq 8 5 325 | katrans t0a.kat | turtledraw 0.0 43.2 f23m07.svg

XOFDA chseq 8 5 325 | katrans t9.kat | turtledraw 0.0 43.2 f23m08.svg

XOKERD chseq 377 233 3660 | katrans t4.kat | turtledraw 0.0 61.875 f24m01.svg

XOPI chseq 377 233 3660 | katrans t4.kat | turtledraw 0.0 73.125 f24m02.svg

XUCUR chseq 377 233 3660 | katrans t4.kat | turtledraw 0.0 84.375 f24m03.svg

YALGA chseq 8 5 78 | katrans t7.kat | turtledraw 0.0 151.765 f25m01.svg

YEXMA chseq 2 1 24 | katrans t0a.kat | turtledraw 0.0 135.0 f26m01.svg

YIKYO chseq 5 3 64 | katrans t0a.kat | turtledraw 0.0 135.0 f26m02.svg

YIPERG chseq 13 8 168 | katrans t0a.kat | turtledraw 0.0 135.0 f26m03.svg

YOBAI chseq 34 21 440 | katrans t0a.kat | turtledraw 0.0 135.0 f26m04.svg

YOCBO chseq 8 5 208 | katrans t2.kat | turtledraw 0.0 45.0 f26m05.svg

YOSOO chseq 13 8 336 | katrans t2.kat | turtledraw 0.0 45.0 f26m06.svg

YOXXI chseq 21 13 272 | katrans t2.kat | turtledraw 0.0 45.0 f26m07.svg

YUNKU chseq 8 5 117 | katrans t13.kat | turtledraw 0.0 45.0 f26m08.svg

YUPTU chseq 13 8 168 | katrans t13.kat | turtledraw 0.0 45.0 f26m09.svg

ZAJEE chseq 21 13 272 | katrans t13.kat | turtledraw 0.0 45.0 f26m10.svg

ZAVIN chseq 34 21 440 | katrans t13.kat | turtledraw 0.0 45.0 f26m11.svg

ZAXXO chseq 55 34 712 | katrans t13.kat | turtledraw 0.0 45.0 f26m12.svg

ZECOY chseq 21 13 272 | katrans t3.kat | turtledraw 0.0 45.0 f26m13.svg

ZEDTU chseq 8 5 117 | katrans t5.kat | turtledraw 0.0 45.0 f26m14.svg

ZEMTO chseq 2 1 24 | katrans t6.kat | turtledraw 0.0 135.0 f26m15.svg

ZEPBU chseq 2 1 24 | katrans t9.kat | turtledraw 0.0 135.0 f26m16.svg

ZEWAW chseq 5 3 64 | katrans t9.kat | turtledraw 0.0 135.0 f26m17.svg

ZEWLU chseq 13 8 168 | katrans t9.kat | turtledraw 0.0 135.0 f26m18.svg

ZIDUX chseq 34 21 440 | katrans t9.kat | turtledraw 0.0 135.0 f26m19.svg

ZIREP chseq 13 8 168 | katrans t9.kat | turtledraw 0.0 45.0 f26m20.svg

ZIVIG chseq 55 34 712 | katrans t9.kat | turtledraw 0.0 45.0 f26m21.svg

ZOCEL chseq 5 3 64 | katrans t11.kat | turtledraw 0.0 135.0 f26m22.svg

ZOFORG chseq 13 8 168 | katrans t11.kat | turtledraw 0.0 135.0 f26m23.svg

ZOMUX chseq 34 21 440 | katrans t11.kat | turtledraw 0.0 135.0 f26m24.svg

ZOTETH chseq 5 3 64 | katrans t13.kat | turtledraw 0.0 135.0 f26m25.svg

ZOTMO chseq 13 8 168 | katrans t13.kat | turtledraw 0.0 135.0 f26m26.svg

ZUSGA chseq 34 21 440 | katrans t13.kat | turtledraw 0.0 135.0 f26m27.svg

FURTHER READING

- *The Glorious Golden Ratio*,
  Posamentier and Lehmann, 2012

- *The Golden Ratio: The Story of Phi, the World's
  Most Astonishing Number*, Mario Livio, 2002

- *The Irrationals*, Julian Havil, 2012

- *Golden Ratio Wikipedia page*

ACKNOWLEDGMENTS

In ordinary life we hardly realize that we receive a great deal more than we give, and that it is only with gratitude that life becomes rich. It is very easy to overestimate the importance of our own achievements in comparison with what we owe to others.

Dietrich Bonhoeffer, letter to parents from prison, Sept. 13, 1943

We'd like to thank our parents, Istvan and Anna Hollos, for helping us in many ways.

We thank the makers and maintainers of all the software we've used in the production of this book, including: the Emacs text editor, the LaTex typesetting system, Inkscape, Evince and MuPDF document viewer, Maxima computer algebra system, gcc, Guile, awk, sed, bash shell, and the Linux operating system.

ABOUT THE AUTHORS

Stefan Hollos and **J. Richard Hollos** are physicists by training, and enjoy anything related to math, physics, and computing. They are the authors of

- **Information Theory: A Concise Introduction**

- **Recursive Digital Filters: A Concise Guide**

- **Creating Noise**

- **Creating Rhythms**

- **Art of Pi**

- **Pattern Generation for Computational Art**

- **Finite Automata and Regular Expressions: Problems and Solutions**

- **Probability Problems and Solutions**

- **Combinatorics Problems and Solutions**

- **The Coin Toss: Probabilities and Patterns**

- **Pairs Trading: A Bayesian Example**

- **Simple Trading Strategies That Work**

- **Bet Smart: The Kelly System for Gambling and Investing**

- **Signals from the Subatomic World: How to Build a Proton Precession Magnetometer**

They are brothers and business partners at Exstrom Laboratories LLC in Longmont, Colorado. Their website is exstrom.com

THANK YOU

Thank you for buying this book.

Sign up for the Abrazol Publishing Newsletter and receive news on updates, new books, and special offers. Just go to

http://www.abrazol.com/

and enter your email address.

www.ingramcontent.com/pod-product-compliance
Lightning Source LLC
Chambersburg PA
CBHW071248220526
45468CB00001B/34